73485

## Books by Duncan Emrich

*It's an Old Wild West Custom*
*Comstock Bonanza*
*The Cowboy's Own Brand Book*
*The Lucius Beebe Reader* (co-editor)
*The Folklore of Love and Courtship*
*The Folklore of Weddings and Marriage*
*The Nonsense Book*
*The Book of Wishes and Wishmaking*
*Folklore on the American Land*
*The Hodgepodge Book*

# Folklore on the American Land

# *Folklore on the American Land*

## *by Duncan Emrich*

*Little, Brown and Company – Boston ·Toronto*

LIBRARY OF CONGRESS CATALOG CARD NO. 72–161865

SECOND PRINTING

T 03/72


Acknowledgment of permission to reprint excerpted material
appears on pages 689-692

*Published simultaneously in Canada by Little, Brown & Company
(Canada) Limited*

PRINTED IN THE UNITED STATES OF AMERICA

*This Book Which I Have Enjoyed Putting Together*
*Is Dedicated First to My Wife*
*Sally Richardson Emrich*

*And Secondly to the Many Scholars, Folklorists, and*
*Collectors Whom It Has Been My Privilege to Know*
*in One Degree or Another*

*And Thirdly and Lastly and Thoroughly*
*to the People of America from Whom All This Material Comes*
*and to Whom It All Belongs as Long as We Remain a Free*
*People upon This Continent*

# *Preface*

This book has been undertaken with a straightaway didactic purpose: to give the general reader some idea of the breadth of the field of folklore in America, and to persuade him that it is much more than the current crop of "folksingers," than Paul Bunyan (stories about whom are not folktales), or Grandma Moses (whose work has been exploited out of all proportion to its real place in the field of folk art). This book is a general work and not intended primarily for the scholar or advanced student. It is an introduction to American folklore.

American folklore is so enormous that the hundreds of books already written about it have not covered the field, nor will the hundreds yet to be produced. An apology for the limits of this book is, therefore, not necessary. Some explanation of exclusions may, however, be in order. First, the great body of American folklore is carried on the mainstream of the English language, the *lingua franca* of the nation. I have arbitrarily, therefore, left out of consideration immigrant folklore in other languages (Greek, Italian, Russian, Polish, German) and even folklore in Spanish, although that has been on the land in the Southwest since before English was spoken there. If other folklore (German, for example) moves out of its limiting language (in a pocket of the American land) and moves into English and is transmitted in English, then it is included here — but not necessarily so stated, because it has become "American" and ceases to be "German." In the section on beliefs and superstitions (where I have borrowed heavily from Harry M. Hyatt's collecting in Adams County, Illinois) many of the beliefs are certainly German, Irish, or Negro in "origin," but I have not in this book made that sharp, scholarly distinction. In practice, the beliefs move back and forth in Adams County in American-English without reference to any other language or country in which they may have previously circulated. Second, with the exception of the "Buh Rabbit" tales told in Gullah, I have not included Negro material as Negro material. There may be a good bit of it here in the origin of songs ("Careless Love," "Frankie and Johnny"), or in proverbs and speech, in children's rhymes (from an inner-city school in Washington, D.C.), but I have not marked it as Negro. I was brought up in New England, and to me all these things were American. Times change, however, and I leave the search for identifying *negritude* to others. I confess to inadequacy: American folklore, it seems to me, should be a leveler, a freer, a common denominator, and not a divider or separator. (The double negative transcends race and so does the omen of a bird flying into a death-room.) We have Minnesota Fats, and we have Fats Waller: which is white and which is black, and what difference does it make? The important thing is that one is a top-notch pool-player and the other a top-notch musician. (Which reminds me of a conundrum-riddle that bears no relation at all to anything here, except that it is pure crazy, and I am glad to get it into the book somehow: What is it that is black and white and black and white and black and white? A nun falling downstairs. I apologize.) Where was I? Third, other than pointing up their existence and forms, I have excluded consideration of physical folklore (architecture, art, craft, cookery, cattle ranching, seafaring, fence construction, and all the others), since to include them — even assuming I were qualified to do so — would demand space at least the size again of this book with a quantity of illustrations to match. There are others more capable here than I, and their upcoming work will greatly increase our concept and appreciation of folklore in this area. Fourth and last, many exclusions have been made simply on the basis of space: cowboy songs and sea shanties have been included (in limited number and agonizingly selected!), while lumberjack songs and the songs of coal and hardrock miners left out. The choice here has been in some degree arbitrary, but also based on a desire to include the more representative materials of American folklore. I have justified on the latter basis the rather extensive inclusion of autograph album rhymes: they are more widespread and have touched more people, for example, than the songs of hardrock miners. In any event, inclusions and exclusions due to space are primarily a matter of personal taste. You would do it differently, I am sure.

Finally, I love my country and its traditions, and I happily and without apology wear my heart upon my sleeve for them. I have enjoyed putting this book together, and if even one-tenth of it (let us say, if even one single proverbial phrase in it) brings enjoyment to the reader or an added awareness of our greatness and goodness as a people, then all of it, to me, will have been worth that one bit.

DUNCAN EMRICH

*The American University*
*Washington, D.C.*

# *Author's Note*

Throughout the text and in the bibliographical notes, I have acknowledged publishers, scholars, field collectors of folklore, and informants (when known), and while not repeating their names here, do again express to them my appreciation for contributing selflessly and generously to the making of this book. I shall return their courtesies as it may be possible for me to do from time to time.

I wish here, however, to acknowledge especially the aid of the staff of the Library of Congress and, in particular, the assistance of Alan Jabbour, head of the Archive of Folksong, who transcribed the music here and who was otherwise most helpful with suggestions and comments; Joseph Hickerson, reference librarian in the Archive of Folksong, whose courtesy was unfailing and whose knowledgeable handling of requests served to make much of the bibliographic work the pleasanter; Virginia Daiker, Milton Kaplan, Jerry

## AUTHOR'S NOTE

Kearns, and particularly Leroy Bellamy of the Prints and Photographs Division, who assisted measurably in locating the photographs reproduced here; William Sartain, head of the Reader Service Section of the Stack and Reader Division, who simplified access to the collections of the Library; and to Legare Obear, chief of the Loan Division, who made possible the extended use of certain out-of-the-way materials. To them all and to the Library of Congress I am pleased to be indebted.

I am also grateful to Mrs. Joy Huston, who not only seemed to enjoy the various segments of this book as they were fed to her typewriter, but who also most intelligently and sympathetically turned a very messy manuscript into a thing of beauty for the printer.

D. E.

# Contents

# CONTENTS

# CONTENTS

# On the Pictures

Certain of these pictures — many of them great pictures by great photographers — directly reflect the words and songs of the text. Others seemingly do not at all: a family saying grace, lone farms on the endless land, lumberjacks happily smiling at you on a Saturday night, a homesteader playing dominos (with his daughter seriously watching his hand), small churches in the rural South. They are, however, as interwoven in the text as the writing of it — more so: they are the breath of the land: they breathe the land. They are the people of America. It is they whom you are looking at and whom you are reading. It is you, and your grandfather before you, and your sons and daughters after. You and they will live for a long time — much longer than the quick words and the loud voices and the pratings — much, much longer than those who would destroy you. The little men go, and the new and bitter dogmas. The land stays, and those of strong faith endure. These are their pictures.

# Illustrations

## ILLUSTRATIONS

# ILLUSTRATIONS

# *On the Music*

The music to the songs in this collection comes from both printed sources and field recordings. Examples from printed sources are transcribed as they appear in the source, with only minor adjustments to conform to the format of this book. Examples from field recordings are transcribed according to certain conventions to which it may be well to alert the reader. They are notated with a tonic (usually G) which avoids excessive sharps or flats and places the tune as much as possible within the compass of the staff. For those who crave a natural vocal range, transposition is an easy matter. Sharps or flats do not appear in the key signature unless they actually occur in the tune. Occasionally the meter of a tune varies so much that it is not indicated measure by measure. The old convention of adding initial and final part-measures to form a complete measure has been abandoned where it interferes with accurate transcription. Likewise, the convention of using flags for eighth or sixteenth notes with separate syllables — which makes vocal music harder to read — has been cheerfully abandoned in favor of beams. In short, the transcriptions follow conventions useful for folk music, not the standard musical conventions.

The transcriptions from field recordings aim for a happy medium between skeletal tunes and highly detailed notation of all the intricacies of folksong renditions. Enough detail has been included, it is hoped, to give a hint of the stylistic habits of American folksingers, but even the fullest transcription can never capture what can readily be had simply by listening to the documentary recordings themselves.

*Alan Jabbour, Head*
*Archive of Folk Song*
*The Library of Congress*

# Folklore on the American Land

# 1.

# *American Folklore*

## *One*

American folklore is as earthy as a Missourian's words for a fellow towns-man: "Him? He's so stingy he'd chase a mouse to hell for a punkin seed." It is as rough as a pair of canal-boatmen indulging in eye gouging, and as gentle as a lullaby from the Tennessee hills. It is as strong as a Conestoga wagon, and as cool as the slang of beboppers.

American folklore is the sailing ship (". . . before steam took to robbing us of our jobs") bound out from Boston, Savannah, Mobile — and the beat of the halyard shanty:

> *And what do you think we had for breakfast?*
> *Blow, boys, blow!*

*The starboard side of an old sou'wester,*
*Blow, boys, bonny boys, blow!*

It is the trail herd winding the long way north out of Texas to Montana, in dust, in heat and storm. It is the food of America — baked beans, chowder, maple syrup on johnnycake; smoked hams, hush puppies, Brunswick stew. It is the bindle stiff and gandy dancer, and the argot of the rails: gondola, reefer, shack, redball, high ball, ball the jack.

Folklore is the adobe house of New Mexico, the sod shanty of the Kansas and Nebraska frontier, the log-and-clay cabins of Virginia, the strung-together barns and houses of New England. It is the rhymes and games of children — duck on the rock, fox and geese, kick the can, mumblety-peg — and a tongue twister from Massachusetts:

How much wood would a woodchuck chuck if a woodchuck could chuck wood? A woodchuck would chuck as much wood as a woodchuck could, if a woodchuck could chuck wood.

And another from North Carolina:

*She sells sea shells,*
*Black bug's blood,*
*Shoat soup and sheep soup.*

Folklore is the hand-whittled lobster buoy of Maine and the branding iron of Wyoming, the hay lifts of Utah, and the rail fences of Kentucky. It is the bawdy story in the smoking room of a Pullman, and the jargon of crapshooters: eighter from Decatur, little Phoebe, snake eyes, box cars, the hard way. It is a juke joint jumping with improvised steps; and a banjo, guitar, and dulcimer on the front stoop.

It is the speech of Alabama and the Bronx, and the regional niceties of our land: "If there's anything that makes a Maine man sick to his stomach, it's northern Vermont." It is a sure statement: "Nobody ain't got no right to throw nothing in nobody's back yard." It is the names of America — Hell-fer-Sartin Creek, Jerked Beef Butte, the Stinking Water, Smith's Corners;

and the nicknames — Fourth-of-July Murphy, Slanting Annie, Bughouse McCabe, Rat-trap Perkins, and Four Day Jack.

Folklore is a farmer studying the clouds, and a hardrock miner in Arizona listening to the earth turning over on the graveyard shift. It is copper worn against rheumatism, a ghost, the howling of a dog at night, an entry in a family Bible, a four-leaf clover. American folklore is all the traditional knowledge and way of life of our people passed on informally from generation to generation.

The chief touchstone to folklore is the manner in which it is transmitted: One man tells another, one man shows another. Folklore circulates as easily as breathing, and as unselfconsciously. There are no fixed or formal controls, no classrooms and professors, no textbooks or printed pages, no sheet music or songbooks to serve as authority. The only authority is "Joe told me," or "That's the way Tex does it" — and even this much authority is rarely called in question.

Because of the way in which it is transmitted, the touch of the individual is upon every item of folklore. The material is traditional, yes, in the way that speech is traditional; but individual in the way that each man expresses himself. No two adobe houses of folk construction, no two Pennsylvania barns, no two Virginia smokehouses are exactly alike as dwellings are in the pea-pod "developments" of the mass-builder. The individual's mark is upon each.

Essentially, the character of folklore lies in the difference between the hand-made and the machine-made, the nonstandardized and the standardized, the individual and the mass. It is the difference between a pot of stew (meat, parsley, bay, veal knuckle, beef knuckle, celery, carrots, onions, red wine) simmering on the back of a stove and the standard contents of a tin can; the difference between home-made fudge and a Hotcha Bar of Kandy; between a static page of grammar and the language as she is spoke.

From the way in which folklore circulates, it is easier also to understand who the folk are in America. When the Library of Congress issued in its folksong series two songs sung by Judge Learned Hand, newspaper reporters were curious: "You don't consider him a member of the folk?" On the recording, Judge Hand himself answers: "That song ["The Iron

*Lincoln County, Oklahoma, 1939: lullaby*

*Merrimac*"] I learned about sixty years ago in Elizabethtown, which is a very small village in the Adirondack Mountains, Essex County, New York. It was sung by boys of my own age, and I know nothing more about it than that. I think possibly it was sung by my uncle's hired man, who had been in the Civil War, but of that I'm very uncertain. I don't know where we boys picked it up."

A hired man and a small village, however, are not essentials. Of the second song, "Phil Sheridan," Judge Hand says: "That song I first heard in the Harvard Law School — sometime about eighteen ninety-five or six. It was then sung by a man named George B. Eliot, who was afterward general counsel of the Atlantic Coast Line, and has since died. He was from North Carolina. I know no more of the song, never heard him sing any more of the song, nor have I any idea where it came from or where he got it."

To the extent that we acquire traditional knowledge and way of life in the hand-me-down manner in which folklore is transmitted, and also believe it, to that extent we are, like Judge Hand, members of the folk. Each of us has something, however little, of accepted folklore in our makeup — remembered rhymes from childhood, a family recipe, an off-color limerick, the jargon of an occupational group, or the fragment of a traditional song.

I have used the term "American folklore," but this needs some qualification. Actually, there is no folklore common to all the people living within a political boundary, and political boundaries cannot enclose or limit folklore. A song or way of speech does not stop at the confines of Ohio or Florida. Rather than political boundaries, the important background is the group. Local and regional differences, geography (desert, mountain, seacoast), language, race, trade and occupation, family and age, are the chief elements creating the myriad groups. The sum total folklore of all these groups constitutes American folklore, since they exist in America. The roots of much of this folklore, however, are worldwide.

The log cabin came to us from the Swedes (there has been some dispute about this) who landed in Delaware; the frame houses of New England were the contribution of the English; the branding irons of the Southwest came to us from Spain via Mexico; "The Streets of Laredo" was a song about a dying British soldier (what cowboy was buried to the sound of fifes and drums?); the customs of California tuna fishers came from Yugoslavs who sailed the Adriatic; Greek children played marbles with the knuckle-bones of sheep before "aggies" were known; the Christmas tree was inherited from Germany; the rhythms of a great segment of our music go back to Africa; and our speech borrows from the languages of the world. In the folk process of transmission, of course, these things take on the local and regional characteristics of our country and become our own: an English ballad sung with the accent and tempo of the Kentucky hills ceases to be English; a cowboy fashioning a "Quarter Circle U" in Montana is unaware of Spain; and a New York cab driver who beefs, "I'm the patsy," has no knowledge of the Italian word, *pazzi*, pronounced almost the same.

Folklore has, of course, taken a beating in our machine age. It began to take the beating with the advent of the Industrial Revolution in England, and the tempo has increased with the stepped-up commercial-industrial character of our society. We are, to put it baldly, the most past-destroying civilization the world has known; even our rear guard carries a banner proclaiming "the brand new." By and large, of course, this destruction has been for the good. Only a confirmed Minniver Cheevy would wish to replace a cold pill with asafetida and goose grease, or send housewives back to the butter churn. The folklorist has no desire to do so. His concern is with preserving a record of our past on the folk level, a record of our roots as a people, a complement to the bare facts of history.

The scholar and the museum preserve and study folklore in its own terms. A ship's figurehead in the Seaport Museum at Mystic, Connecticut, and a folksong in the Library of Congress have been moved out of their natural habitats, certainly, but they have not been altered. Similarly, studies of folklore at the Universities of Indiana, Pennsylvania, and California faithfully preserve the original materials. The scholars and the museums are the custodians of folklore, since the folk themselves cannot be.

On the non-academic level of our society, also, folklore has, in recent decades, become immensely popular. Collections of folktales hit the best-seller lists; "folksingers," so-called, are heard by millions; square-dance groups weekly attract thousands; and folk festivals are on the annual agenda of hundreds of communities from Asheville, North Carolina, to Reno, Nevada.

What is happening here, however, is neither a rebirth of folklore nor its preservation. It is a different kettle of fish. A singer of folksongs is not a folksinger. Nor is a story reshaped for print by a professional writer the same as a folktale told around a potbellied stove. A rodeo with chamber of commerce and Hollywood trappings is considerably removed from the roundup celebrations of working cowboys; and an Arthur Murray square-dance party, or a contrived folk festival, bears little relation to a Saturday night gathering in the Kentucky hills.

There is nothing wrong with this borrowing and use of folklore. It has gone on from time immemorial, and will continue. But the distinction between the real article and its borrowed counterpart should be kept in mind: folklore is one thing, the use of folklore is another. Once recognized, the confusion between what folklore is and what it is not — between the folk and the popular — disappears. Also it becomes clear that the present popularity of so-called "folklore" does not return the real folklore of the past to us, any more than an interest in the Crusades or the wild-and-woolly West returns those eras to us.

A similar, and equally natural, transfer of materials works in the opposite direction. The purest items of folklore originate on the folk level, but the folk also constantly borrow from the popular, or mass, segment of our society. As this material is altered through the folk manner of transmission, it loses its original character and becomes, in varying degrees, an item of folklore. To become *folk*lore, however, it must circulate and be subject to folk alteration.

A ready example of this alteration is the folksong "The Dying Cowboy," or "Bury Me Not on the Lone Prairie." Non-folk in origin, it had nothing to do with a cowboy. Its ultimate source is a poem, "The Ocean Burial," by the Reverend E. H. Chapin, who published it in *The Southern Literary Messenger* in 1839. The music for it was written by George N. Allen in 1850. The song dealt with a youth dying at sea:

> *O bury me not in the deep, deep sea,*
> *Where the billowy shroud will roll over me,*
> *Where no light will break through the dark, cold wave,*
> *And no sunbeam rest upon my grave.*

Transferred and adapted to the cowboy and the plains of Texas, it circulated orally and became a folksong. It exists today in a variety of textual and musical versions collected from old-timers throughout the country.

Because our own folklore is with us as naturally as spitting on bait, we are generally unaware of it. Consciousness of it usually comes when we notice customs and traditions at wide variance with our own.

A trip to Mexico is likely to teach a Kansan more about his own way of life than a decade of living at home. The sharp differences become clear. It is also of the nature of things that Easterners "discover" the West, and Westerners the East.

Consciousness of folklore, however, does not demand travel, nor does one have to leave one's own bailiwick to see it daily: the word folklore itself implies recognizable differences. Folk medicine, for example, implies the existence of the science of medicine; folk literature — oral and casual — implies the existence of a written literature; folk music an art music. Folklore is the lore of the folk existing as part of our society, yet set apart or distinguished from the more cultivated portion of it, while at the same time, paradoxically, rubbing shoulders with it.

Folklore is deep in us, immemorial. It is a child born with a caul, it is a pine coffin carried down a country road. It lies on the land, the roots and the greatness of a people. It walks with us on the sidewalks under the neon lights. . . . For some of us folklore is a memory of the American past, and our own past. For others it is a living heritage, as lively as a colt in the south pasture.

For both it is good, as grass roots are good.

## *Two*

Folklore itself and the study of folklore cover a vast field, and definitions limiting folklore, or attempting to limit it, narrowly to folk literature, to folk art, or folksong simply do not make sense. Marius Barbeau, the former great curator of folklore at the Canadian National Museum in Ottawa, recognizing also the vastness of the field, gave his definition of it somewhat more succinctly:

Whenever a lullaby is sung to a child; whenever a ditty, a riddle, a tongue-twister, or a counting-out rhyme is used in the nursery or at school;
Whenever sayings, proverbs, fables, noodle-stories, folktales, reminiscences of the fireside are retold;
Whenever, out of habit or inclination, the folk indulge in songs and dances, in ancient games, in merrymaking, to mark the passing of the year or the usual festivities;
Whenever a mother shows her daughter how to sew, knit, spin, weave, embroider, make a coverlet, braid a sash, bake an old-fashioned pie;
Whenever a farmer on the ancestral plot trains his son in the ways long familiar, or shows him how to read the moon and the winds to forecast the weather at sowing or harvest time;
Whenever a village craftsman — carpenter, carver, shoemaker, cooper, blacksmith, builder of wooden ships — trains his apprentice in the use of tools, shows him how to cut a mortise and peg in a tenon, how to raise a frame house or barn, how to string a snowshoe, how to carve a shovel, how to shoe a horse or shear a sheep;
Whenever in many callings the knowledge, experience, wisdom, skill, the habits and practices of the past are handed down by example or spoken word, by the older to the newer generations, without reference to book, print, or school-teacher:
Then we have folklore in its own perennial domain, at work as ever, alive and shifting. . . .

## Three

Harold Thompson was one of the great professors of English at Cornell and also teacher of folklore there in the early and middle part of this century. He loved his upstate York land and its people. In his introductory lecture to classes at the college, which stands high above Cayuga's waters, he always said: "The study of folklore is an opportunity to meet your grandfather."

That is about as succinct as you can get.

## Four

J. Frank Dobie, a man to swim the river with and a Texan, whose books on the mustangs, the longhorns, rattlesnakes, vaqueros, and cow people mirror the land he loved, stated his case for folklore very personally:

Here I am living on a soil that my people have been living and working and dying on for more than a hundred years — the soil, as it happens, of Texas. My roots go down into this soil as deep as mesquite roots go. This soil has nourished me as the banks of the lovely Guadalupe River nourished cypress trees, as the Brazos bottoms nourish the wild peach, as the gentle slopes of East Texas nourish the sweet-smelling pines, as the barren, rocky ridges along the Pecos nourish the daggered lechuguilla. I am at home here, and I want not only to know about my home land, I want to live intelligently on it. I want certain data that will enable me to accommodate myself to it.

I like folklore because it has color and flavor and represents humanity. . . .

And what, some people are asking, is to be done with all this collected folklore? For one thing, a number of intelligent people read it and enjoy it and are instructed by it as they read and enjoy and are instructed by history. This folklore is a part of our social history, as legitimate in its way as the best authenticated state papers.

J. Frank was one hundred percent right.

## *Five*

And so was Carl Sandburg, who summed it up in the title of a book: *The People, Yes.*

# 2.

# *Some Guideposts*

## *"Quaint"*

**B**ecause folklore is unsystematized and nonscientific, a notion occasionally and erroneously held about it is that it is "quaint." Certain items of folklore may, of course, become outmoded and curious to our present eyes, but there was nothing quaint about them when they were in use, nor is there anything quaint about them considered in terms of our history. There was nothing quaint about a sailing ship beating her way around the Horn, nothing quaint about cowboys driving a trail herd north from Texas to Montana. There was nothing quaint about General "Tooey" Spaatz picking his guitar, about Judge Learned W. Hand singing the song "The Iron *Merrimac*," nor about an Episcopal bishop retelling a clerical yarn. "Quaint" is a patronizing term. One would hesitate using it to describe the speech of a New York cab driver, or a magic charm fiercely held by a hill woman in the desperate moment of childbirth.

## The Values

Far from being quaint, the real values of folklore are many:

There is the per se value of any single item of folklore: the beauty of line of a hand-carved weather vane; the pleasure derived from a folksong; the enjoyment of boys shooting marbles; a May basket hanging on a New England doorknob.

There is the value of folklore operating in each of us as a balance to the standardized way of life in our society: the housewife who tires of packaged foods and reverts to family recipes; the father who teaches his son mumblety-peg rather than buying him the latest space suit; the college professor who steps down from the platform and relaxes with the current slang.

There is the group value of folklore which brings us closer to our fellow-men, the common traditional knowledge which informally binds us together more tightly than any formal organization: the knowledge of local legends, customs, and beliefs which cement a community, like Pioche or Eureka, Nevada; the customs and way of life of Maine lobstermen which set them apart from inland farmers; the hand-me-down traditions of Yale men, distinguishing them from their fellows at Harvard.

There is the value of folklore as a source of inspiration for artists in our country: for Thomas Hart Benton and Grant Wood in the field of painting; for Mark Twain and Erskine Caldwell in the novel; for Walt Whitman and Carl Sandburg in poetry; for Aaron Copland and Roy Harris in music. What these men have produced is not, of course, folklore, but they have gone to its roots for their material.

There is the value of folklore to our history, without which our history would be dry paper: the names themselves: Wounded Knee, the Alamo, Bull Run, La Ciudad Real de Nuestra Señora la Reina de Los Angeles (L.A. now!), Vicksburg, Powder River, the Stinking Water; and the men at Gettysburg (to take only a single example), the forty thousand who died in the one battle, who came down the long, dry roads from Wisconsin and Rhode Island, from Georgia and Alabama to meet forever in Pennsylvania, carrying with them not only their rifles and the fixed insignia of their regiments, but their beliefs and dreams and traditions which would be returned again to their homes and their nation with their deaths.

## "Popular"

Something which is merely popular is not necessarily folk. "Popular" is a quantitative term and does not describe the quality of the thing. The Ford automobile is popular, but it is not folk; the "Star-Spangled Banner," Stephen Foster, and the top tunes on the Hit Parade are popular, but they are not folk; a slick magazine is popular, but it is not folk. These things are not created, acquired, or transmitted in the folk manner, nor are they subject to the folk process of *re-creation*, the change wrought upon an item of folklore as it passes from person to person.

## "Communal Re-Creation"

The changes rung upon any single item of folklore, and the touch of the individual upon it as it passes from person to person within the group, have been admirably termed the process of "communal re-creation." Phillips Barry of Harvard, in the *Bulletin of the Folk-Song Society of the Northeast* (1933), coined the term to give more precise meaning to (and at the same time to displace) the vague, romantic, and now discredited theory of "communal creation." The latter envisaged an actual group force, and it was a theory, it has always seemed to me, propounded by the higher culture in an effort to explain away what must have seemed to it the puzzling anonymity of the folk literature which it considered worth studying. (How account, for example, for the anonymity of the great Scotch and English ballads?) Barry admitted the effect and the force of the group, but a force stemming from individuals within the group — which is quite a different thing. As a song moved from one person to another, it was constantly being re-created, for better or for worse, just as a pebble is polished to perfection or deteriorates within the movement of a stream. And anonymity was readily explained as the final and ultimate original source was lost in the mists of space and time. For the folk, no final and ultimate authority or original source is important.

The immediate transmittor and immediate source is the essential authority: "My grandmother sang this song," or "Joe Brown can show you how to make a whistle." Another general rule for folklore, then, is that it is constantly being re-created by individuals operating within the group, and that its origins are chiefly anonymous, both due, again, to the folk process of transmission.

Barry's theory of the process of re-creation implies also that at its point of origin the item of folklore was the creation of a single individual. Barry's chief interest was folksong, but we may consider the concept of individual authorship or creation to be generally true for the whole field of folklore, noting that exceptions to it are sufficiently rare to prove the rule, and that even where such exceptions occur, there is usually present a leader who dominates and guides the group, and who is, in effect, the creator, while the others present serve as assistants to the act of creation — as, in varying degrees, in the construction of a barn or the singing of a capstan shanty. Since we are dealing with the folk culture, it follows also that the purest (although not necessarily the aesthetically best or longest-lived) items of folklore are, at their point of origin, created by individuals belonging to the folk. Once created, they must circulate and be subject to the process of re-creation in order to become part of the folk culture. Without such circulation, they may still, of course, be considered isolated products of the folk culture, but not an active part of it, and, unless ferreted out by the collector, they exist in a greater vacuum than a yellowed, undergraduate poem in a family attic. On the one hand this may seem like fairly narrow hairsplitting, and on the other like too much insistence upon circulation and re-creation, but it is a valid and valuable approach to a culture where "publication" of a song or tale is oral, and where the "manufacture" of a lobster buoy, a hooked rug, or a branding iron is an individual matter (of re-creation) existing within a long-standing tradition.

## An Illustration of Re-Creation: Some Opening Stanzas of "Barbara Allen"

In the Archive of Folksong in the Library of Congress, there are well over two hundred different field recordings of the ballad "Barbara Allen." No two are alike, yet each one is "Barbara Allen," and each one is true and correct to the singer. None are false; each is a true folk ballad. But no one is *the* true and correct ballad, because all are true and correct. The ballad is "Barbara Allen," certainly; there can be no mistake about that whatever, but it has been re-created all along the line as it passed from individual to individual. Consider these few opening stanzas, leaving out of all consideration the variations occurring in the remaining text of each ballad and in the music:

> *In Scarlet Town where I was born,*
> *There was a fair maid dwellin'*
> *Made every youth cry "Wel-away,"*
> *Her name was Barbara Allen.*

> *In Lexington, where I was born,*
> *There was a young man dwellin';*
> *He was taken sick and very sick*
> *For the love of Barbara Allen.*

> *Away down low in Stony Town,*
> *There were three maids a-dwellin',*
> *But only one that I'd call my own,*
> *And her name was Barbara Allen.*

> *'Twas in the lovely month of May,*
> *The flowers all were blooming,*
> *Sweet William on his death bed lay*
> *For the love of Barbry Allen.*

> *'Twas early in the month of May,*
> *When all things they were swellin',*
> *Sweet William came from the Western States*
> *A-courting Barbry Allen.*

> *In the early fair days of May,*
> *When the green buds they were swelling,*
> *Sweet Willie on his death-bed lay*
> *For the love of Barbara Allen.*

*Mr. Sutterfield's Comment.* Mr. Berry Sutterfield of Marshall, Arkansas, stated to a collector of folksongs: " 'Barb'ry Allen' as I sing it has got seventeen verses, and if you hear somebody sing it with more or less than seventeen verses, it ain't right." For himself, Mr. Sutterfield is right as rain. But for himself only.

## Slippage, or Spillage

Perhaps the best single example of slippage of lines and stanzas from one song or songs to another is found in "Old Smoky," which, in spite of the firm base of the mountain, is nevertheless a mélange of "The Unconstant Lover," "The Cuckoo," "The Wagoner's Lad," "Courting Too Slow," "The Forsaken Girl," "Little Sparrow," and other similar love lyrics. Professor Kittredge of Harvard discussed this some time back — in 1917 — in the *Journal of American Folklore*. The mixup is a general one, and the lines and stanzas slip back and forth from any one of these songs to any one of the others. This slippage — and the word is a good one to describe this activity in folksong (and perhaps in other fields of folklore: children's rhymes) — is just that. It is not a conscious transfer of a stanza from one song to another. It is not entirely forgetfulness or absentmindedness, although some of that enters. It is slippage: where the subjects or "stories" of several song texts are so closely related in mood and content that a singer can move a line or whole stanza from one song to another without at the moment (or even later) being aware that he is doing so. He senses no outside intrusion whatever: the lines belong in his song.

It has happened to me with a different genre: I at one time knew and told rather well (in bastard French) four or five Marius and Olive stories fresh from their Marseilles tradition. On occasion I mixed them, and tagged the latter half of one to the beginning of another. In retrospect, the reason is obvious: the characters are the same in all stories, their roles are fixed, and their involvement in wild activity (even by French standards) is fairly predictable. Slippage was easy.

In a story, of course, this error or slippage becomes quickly evident. In song, it does not. And slippage in folksong — particularly in lyric song — is an integral part of folk transmission.

## The Folk Are Under No Obligation to Pass On Their Knowledge

In the sophisticated and popular segments of our society, we are under obligation to pass on to the next generation our knowledge of art, literature, music, science, printing techniques, machine repair, and all other aspects of knowledge essential to the continuity of society, to the well-being of our sons, and to the preservation of culture and industry. The folk are under no such obligation. There is no requirement upon them to do so. And the reason for this again is that all folk knowledge is casual, informal, and uncontrolled. It can be transmitted or it cannot; it may be or it may not. But there is no *must* about it. It is not taught or inculcated as knowledge is in the sophisticated and popular areas. Even a folksong is not taught within a family. It is heard by a daughter from her mother, and heard often enough to be acquired.

## The Touch of the Individual and the Life of an Item of Folklore

The touch of the individual is an important factor determining the life of any single item of folklore. Where a barber, a salesman, or a college student has an accomplished knack for storytelling, the story will grow and flourish under his touch, and be passed on for wider circulation by his listeners. ("I heard a good one today. . . .") Where the storyteller has no knack, the story withers and dies. Any item of folklore may, therefore, be polished to perfection as it circulates from one person to another, or it may, conversely, receive rough treatment, and ultimately disintegrate and vanish.

An item of folklore may also disappear for a variety of other reasons: it may, like a coonskin cap in the Panhandle, be unsuited to a changed environment; it may, like the slang of the Jazz Age, be worn threadbare and grow outmoded; it may be officially banned as street cries are banned, or Hallowe'en pranks; it may be replaced by a simpler, non-folk method of doing something, as the railroad eliminated the prairie schooner; or it may, as in the case of a folksong, simply be forgotten.

## The Bastardization of Folklore

Attempts to use and organize folklore for nationalistic ends (Nazi Germany) or for political purposes (Communist party) run counter to the very nature of folklore. These efforts merely serve to disseminate a bastardized folklore, and, if successful, to destroy real folklore by substituting mass (propaganda) concepts for it. Folklore is not of the mass; it is of the group and of the individual within the group.

## The Best Definition of Folk Art

Due to the enormous breadth of subject, the present book does not contain any particularized consideration of folk art and folk craft, or, for that matter, of any physical folklore such as folk architecture, folk industry, folk costume, folk cookery, and the like. There does belong here, however, the best definition of folk art that I have found. It comes from Dr. Robert Wildhaber, a great Swiss folklorist, who wrote it as an introduction to *Swiss Folk Art*, a catalogue descriptive of an exhibit held at the Smithsonian Institution in the Summer of 1969. The definition is a superb one for folk art and rids us once and for all of the nonsense words: "naïve," "primitive," "untutored," "simple," "Sunday painter," and other comparable vagaries which have cluttered the field. It is also more broadly useful as an added touchstone to characterize the essence of folklore: it belongs here because the definition, by extension, applies not only to folk art but to all of folklore:

This exhibition has been assembled by a folklorist, applying principles which for him are basic to his field. In his judgment, folk art has nothing to do with "art" in the accepted sense of the word. To state the case in somewhat exaggerated fashion: A work of art is a unique creation by an individual. Its only purpose is to express ideas and emotions in visual form, and thereby (hopefully) arouse equivalent ideas and emotions in the viewer. Folk art does not have to meet esthetic standards; being a part of folklore it has to be judged

*Amalia, New Mexico, 1943: wall painting*

by criteria that pertain to this branch of knowledge. Folklore deals with the traditional behavior of a group. By "group" we mean either an ethnic unit, the inhabitants of a geographically self-contained region, members of the same craft or professions, associations of people linked by age or other characteristics they hold in common. Whenever it becomes customary within such a group to decorate objects of any kind in a traditional manner, we speak of folk art in the true sense of the term. "Beautiful," as folklore interprets the word, only means that an object and its decoration follow the traditional formulae of a group. The decorations are not, therefore, "freely" invented forms of an individual artist, but are expressions of allegiance to the community. The decorations themselves may be traced to very different sources; they may merely reflect the desire to beautify an object; they may have an apotropaic intention, or have been derived from symbols of salvation, e.g., if they are Christian they may invoke the Divine blessing or the intercession and protection of the Saints.

An exhibition of folk art understood in this sense should not include precious objects of high esthetic worth, but the selection should reflect the traditional and typical objects typical of a group. There are admittedly gradations which are caused by the varying talent of the individual and his degree of esthetic sense. One object may be better made and more richly decorated than the next one. As a result, the inhabitants of a village or of a valley community will frequently go to the man who can do better and more attractive work than they themselves could. They will go to the village cabinetmaker, the mask carver or the painter of votive pictures; to the teacher who can produce a "correct" godfather's letter, or writes an appropriate wedding motto, and to the peasant or herdsman who can carve a love token more pleasingly. In all these cases we can speak of "folk artists," whether or not their names are known to us. We must not forget, however, that the quality of their work is not assessed by their ability to create something unique, but by their reaffirmation of traditional forms.

# 3.

# *Folk Language and Grammar*

It is good and necessary to know something of folk language and grammar, because they run like a defining thread through all of folklore. The thread is always colorful, and sometimes it is pure gold.

In honest prose: "*I nevver did keep no dairie as I should of did.  . . .*"

In proverb: " *'Tis as it is and it can't be any 'tiser.*"

In proverbial speech: "*There's no more peace here than for a cat in hell without claws.*"

In song:

> *Don't nevver place your eyes on beauty,*
> *For beauty is a thing that will decay,*

> *For the ripest rose in yonders garden —*
> *Oh, see now if it don't fade away.*

In the log books of whaling ships: *Captain William H. Raynard, ship* Abigail, *New Bedford, entry from a three-year voyage lasting from 1835 into 1838:* "Times are so dull, this dog's age. Off Cocos isle. Rain, dull musick. Saw nothin. That is the cry now days. The cooper is going ahead making tools for scrimsham. We had a fracas betwixt the cook and the stewart. . . ."

In beliefs and superstitions: "*One of us are going to hear of a death soon, because I am having goose-skin chills to run all up and down my arms.*"

In a weather account: "*The storm come and ramshackled the houses, but the cabins stood fast. . . .*"

In the marks of birth: "*My mother knew a woman that went one day to get some potatoes out of a sack, and as she put her hand in the sack a rat ran out. It scared her almost to death. She must of threw her hands behind her, for when her girl came she had a rat right on her behind.*"

And in the chants and cries of childhood:

> *Acka, backa, soda cracker,*
> *Acka, backa, boo,*
> *Acka, backa, soda cracker,*
> *Out goes you!*

One can say that folk language, grammar, speech, and vocabulary are an absolute touchstone to folklore. And almost: that where they are not found, there is no folklore.

Take a Vermont farmer's description of the construction of a barn as over against that by a professor of a school of architecture. A Georgia housewife's recipe for Brunswick stew as over against that found in either *Gourmet* or *The Ladies' Home Journal Cookbook* or *Betty Crocker* or *Fanny Farmer*. The language and way of speech is the touchstone. One is natural to the land, to the experience of the individual, to tradition; the other is removed and doctored.

Folk language and speech are by far the most active, widespread, and continuing elements in the field of folklore. They are in constant and daily use. They penetrate, in one degree or another, all levels of our society, and are created on all levels. They are transmitted on all levels in the folk manner. And they remain freer and more independent of the commercial-industrial trend toward fixed standardization than any other branch of folklore, partly because of the purely oral nature of their creation and transmission, and partly because there is no vast profit to be derived from "correct" standardization. There are, indeed, as Mencken points out in his *American Language*, only two forces, both ineffective, which attempt to carry the shibboleth of standardization (i.e., the King's English, textbook English, correct English) to the folk and to the greater part of the popular mass: the school-teacher, and the mail-order firms (I seem to remember a gentleman with a literary goatee) which advertise "correct speech." The two are ineffective because they are not selling a standard, tangible item like a can of soup or a pack of cigarettes, and no matter how they attempt to drill "I shall" and "I will" or "If I were you" into the heads of the folk, the folk will promptly forget all about it, and continue to say "I'll" (or "I'm going to," "I gotta") and "If I was you." As a matter of fact, the influence of the folk (with whom in this respect the bulk of the popular group is allied and from whom it is virtually indistinguishable) is far greater than any possible combination of radio, television, motion pictures, schools, colleges, "correct speech pamphlets to cure your social and business ills," and all other similar forces. The folk do not accord these importance, and since they do not, their language and speech remain folk, that of their own milieu — home, village, workshop — and do not take on characteristics alien to their way of life, to their normal conversation with family, friends, workers, or to the traditional language and speech, which they have picked up as naturally as rolling out of bed. Their language and speech, to put it briefly, has been transmitted to them orally in the folk manner, and has not been acquired formally. Any formal language, any King's English which has been foisted upon them has been sloughed faster than water from a duck's back; they leave a grade or high school classroom quite as innocent of the subjunctive as when they entered. And because the folk use their language continually, and the ha-

THERE HOT **5**¢ THERE GOOD

**POTATOE LOTKIZ**

MAKES A MEAL BY THEIR SELVES

*Central Ohio, 1938: food stand at a county fair*

rassed teachers can only reach them sporadically, all efforts to "civilize" them are about as effective as a barrel of sand to stop the Mississippi.

In any study of the folk language, there will be words which sound heinous and appalling to the cultivated ("between you and I," "you seen it"), as well as others which appeal for their color ("so stingy he'd skin a flea for its hide and tallow"). If the student of the subject cottons to the second group, and rares back in horror at the first, he will uncover for himself only that which is aesthetically interesting to him without arriving at a full understanding of folk speech. Without, in other words, placing those things which he does like in their proper relationship to the whole. To him, a repetitive word of admonition: there is nothing "wrong" about folk speech, any more than there is anything "wrong" with one of the variants of "Barbara Allen." We are studying the spoken language of the folk. It is rich, vigorous, changing, wholly intelligible, and, in the linguistic process, leagues ahead of the grammarian and the dictionary.

In this folk speech — Mencken's "American Vulgate" and what Professor C. C. Fries in his *American English Grammar* calls Vulgar English — certain grammatical patterns are fairly regular throughout the country. Professor Robert C. Pooley in an article, "The Levels of Language," in *Educational Method* (March, 1937) lists some of them as "inversions of the forms of irregular (or strong) verbs; the confusion of regular (weak) and irregular (strong) verb tense forms; a bland disregard of number agreement in subjects and verbs and pronoun relations; the confusion of adjectives and adverbs; and the employment of certain syntactical combinations like the double negative, the redundant subject, and the widely split infinitive." Mencken considers them in his *American Language* and its *Supplement* (*II*) under the chapter "The Common Speech," making the frequent point that these deviations from the accepted or standard speech are not, in fact, "errors" but, on the contrary, the living and growing language of the folk in their own milieus — correct where found. Standing alone on the printed page as verb forms ("I have saw") or as possessive pronouns ("yourn"), they seem to the educated to have no reason for being, and any study of them seems a complete waste of time. Listen, however, to the full, flowing speech as caught by the tape recorder, or, better still, as heard on the spot in some barroom or on some farm, and the isolated forms become wholly natural to

*Craigsville, Minnesota, 1937:*
*lumberjacks in a rural saloon on Saturday night*

the speaker and listener and an integral part of his intelligible discourse. As an example, the sentences of the accepted and standard speech — "I have never used a charge account" or "I have never purchased anything on a deferred payment plan" — become in the folk speech, "I never bought nothin' on time." The double-negative sentence is completely intelligible, and is, if anything, more effective in the communication of meaning than either of the preceding ones. It is also the natural form of expression for the particular speaker, and the two other sentences would seem as incongruous from his lips as the double negative from a Harvard professor. Thus, since the standard and accepted phrasing of American English is largely unfamiliar or unknown to the folk, it becomes necessary to take a look — however brief or superficial — at the grammar, syntax, and vocabulary of the folk language as a basic preliminary to the study of other aspects of folklore, not alone of folk literature (tales, riddles, proverbs, rhymes) but of all folklore, since language and speech form the chief means of communication and transmission.

# *Folk Grammar*

Professor Robert J. Menner of Yale in "The Verbs of the Vulgate" *American Speech* (January, 1926) points out that the spoken language of the linguistically uncultivated American is not a separate dialect (as, say, the Ozark or Gullah), but is rooted within the traditions of the English language, and that, in consequence, it is subject to certain long-operating traditional laws of the changing spoken language. This is true, just as it is also true that the uncultivated American — subject as he is to hearing standard English — will often vacillate between the use of alternative forms, correct and incorrect. The study of the speech of any given individual or group of individuals resolves itself, then, to a matter of degree of folk usage as over against standard usage, and the fact that here we limit our consideration to that which may be called purely folk does not imply that elements of the standard do not exist within the folk, for, of course, they do.

# *The Verb*

In a consideration of the verb, the following inflections and constructions depart from the accepted standard, and are found chiefly in the changing folk language.

TO BE.    In the past tense, the *were* form of the verb disappears, and the entire preterite is reduced, or leveled, to the single *was* form: we was, you was, they was. The subjunctive "If I *were* you" is lost, and becomes "If I *was* you." The past participle loses its auxiliary *have*, as in "Where you been?" and frequently is used as a distinct preterite with no present or past perfect sense, as "I *been* to town." In various sections of New England, *be* replaces *is*, *am*, and *are*, as in "How *be* you?" but this must be considered a regionalism. The common negative is *ain't*.

TO HAVE.    As an auxiliary, the verb *have* is daily heard as *a* in such phrases as "He couldn'*a* done it," and this *a* is corrupted to a distinct *of* in "He could *of* done it," and more markedly in "If he had *of* done it." As has been noted with *been*, the auxiliary *have* disappears before the verb, and "I've seen," "I've done," and "I've drunk" become "I seen," "I done," and "I drunk," acquiring at the same time a preterite rather than perfect sense. In "I seen him many times," the auxiliary *have* may be understood, but it certainly is not in "I seen him yesterday," which has become a pure preterite through loss of the auxiliary and transfer of the verb from the perfect. Losing its auxiliary role, *have* replaces *must* in "I have to (hafta) go," but this, in turn, is losing ground to "I gotta go."

THE CHANGING TENSE FORMS.    There are, in the language, so-called weak verbs which form their preterites and past participles by the regular addition of *ed* (race, *raced*, *raced;* drag, *dragged*, *dragged*), and strong verbs which form the same tenses by the internal change of a vowel (*begin, began, begun; write, wrote, written; see, saw, seen*). One may crudely say that the strong verbs are strong because they have independent guts of their own. Since the weak verbs, however, are by far the most dominant in the language, they have exerted great pressure on the strong verbs and pulled many into the regular *ed* pattern. Fries points out that "of the 195 old 'strong' verbs which still last in Modern English, 129, or about 65 percent have gone over to this regular pattern." Only sixty-six strong verbs remain which change the internal vowel instead of adding the dental suffix. He further points out that of these sixty-six, only forty-two have maintained a vowel change in the preterite, and past participle (*began, begun*); the other twenty-four have the same form in the preterite and past participle (*strike, struck, struck; swing, swung, swung*). These twenty-four, while maintaining a vowel change from the present to the preterite (*swing, swung*), have followed the example of the weak verbs by adopting identical forms in the preterite and past participle (*swung, swung*), although not adding a dental suffix.

The most notable activity, as far as the verb is concerned in folk speech, is the constant attack upon the forty-two verbs which still maintain a vowel change from preterite to past participle in Standard English. It is an attack that seems characterized by utter confusion, since the preterite shifts to the participle form; the participle, in turn, supplants the preterite; and the present also intrudes upon the preterite. On examination, however, certain traditional laws are seen to be operating. The pull of the regular weak verbs with the *ed* endings is apparent: I know him, I *knowed* him, I've *knowed* him; I throw it, I *throwed* it, I've *throwed* it; they grow, they *growed*, they've *growed;* I weave it, I *weaved* it, I've *weaved* it; I draw it, I *drawed* it, I've *drawed* it; and I steal it, I *stealed* it, I've *stealed* it. Where the strong past participle (as *taken*) remains and the auxiliary *have* is dropped, we have already seen that the past participle can supplant the preterite, thereby joining the twenty-four strong verbs which maintain identical forms in the preterite and past participle: I take it, I *taken* it, I *taken* it; I see, I *seen*, I *seen;* I drink, I *drunk*, I *drunk;* I sing, I *sung*, I *sung*.

At the same time, however, one will hear "I have saw it," "I have did it," and "I have sang it," the preterite moving to the past participle position in seeming opposition to the regular process described above. Mencken inclines to the view that this is self-conscious on the part of the folk, the result of the "schoolmarm's" warning her flock away from *I seen it* and *I done it* as preterites, and thereby driving them into the use of *saw* and *did* as past participles. I am inclined, however, to feel that the schools have very little to do with it, and that what is occurring is simply a confused upheaval prior to the final settling or leveling: first, the same speaker will vacillate between *I have*

*saw* and *I seen;* second, the regular pull to maintain the same vowel (*see,*
*seen, seen*) is stronger than the *I have saw* transfer; third, the transfer of
past participle to preterite is the more usual process (*drunk* for *drank,*
*growed* for *grew*); and fourth, extended examination of tape recordings will,
I think, verify that the *I have saw* and *I have drank* transfer occupies a distinctly minor position vis-à-vis the *I seen* and *I drunk.* The present existence
of *I have saw*, in other words, seems to me to be due to the fact that *I seen*
has not completed the process of driving *saw* entirely off the stage, and *saw*
is still remembered by the folk, and given an occasional part to play, albeit
an unusual one.

In addition to the foregoing, there can also be detected a shift from the
present tense form to the preterite, chiefly in instances suggesting a historical present: "I *give* him two bucks, and he *begin* his work, and then he *come*
at me for two more."

Other interesting deviations from Standard English which deserve brief
noting include the loss of the dental suffix *t* in the preterite of weak verbs
such as *sleep, slept* and *weep, wept:* "I *slep* all night; I *kep* a-goin'." In the
case of certain weak verbs, such as *ruin, earn, fear, kill*, and *scare*, the normal *ed* ending of the preterite becomes *t: ruint, earnt, feart, kilt*, and *scairt*.
A verb which already has its preterite ending will acquire an added one, as
*attacked* often becomes *attackted.* The verb *to use* has been virtually reduced
to an adverb with the meaning of *once upon a time, formerly*, or *there was a*
*time when* in such sentences as: "I use-to could quote the Bible, but I can't
no more," and "I use-to could sing, but now I lost my voice." In *use-to*, the *d*
of the preterite has been dropped entirely; the *s* is not heard as a *z*, and the
preposition *to* invariably accompanies *use* and is not associated with any following verb in the infinite. Last, the verb *done* frequently appears as an auxiliary: "He's done gone," and "I done went and sold it."

## The Adverb

The adverb in folk speech drops the distinguishing *ly* ending of Standard
English to become identical with the adjectival form: "He was *bad* hurt" or
"hurt *bad*," "That's *real* good," "He was *sure* quick," "He talks *loud*," "He's
working *regular* now," "I can beat him *easy*," "He's fighting *rough*." The *ly*

ending is similarly lost in such adverbs as *mightily* and *nastily:* "He treated me *nasty*," "He fights *dirty*." This loss of the *ly* is so universal in the folk speech that it has already affected Standard English: "he talks *loud*" would occasion no eyebrow raising. Similarly, the adjective form "I feel *good*" has supplanted "I feel *well*."

## The Adjective

The chief difference between the common speech and Standard English in the adjective is that the former has abandoned the comparative form for the superlative where only two items are under discussion: "Which is the tallest bottle [of these two]?" is always heard, never "Which is the taller?" Also "Which is the best?" and not, "Which is the better?"

*More* and *most* give way usually to the *er* and *est* endings of the compaartive and superlative, but when used are added to these forms, as, *more better*, *more sweeter*, *more easier*, *more nearer*, and *most hardest*, *most meanest*. The folk coin superlatives from the present participle used as adjective: *fightingest*, *lovingest*, *kissingest*, *drinkingest*, *talkingest*, all used without pronouncing the g. From their tradition also come *orneriest*, *onliest*, and *bestest*, *worstest*, *mostest*, the last developed on already existing superlatives.

## Relative Pronouns

The relative pronouns *whom* and *whose* are virtually non-existent in folk speech, supplanted by *who*, *what*, and *that*, standing either alone or in combination with prepositions. *Who* itself, as well as *which*, is frequently displaced also by *what* and *that*. "Whose book is that?" or "To whom does the book belong?" become "*Who* does that book belong *to*?" or, very often, "*Who* belongs *to* that book?" The examples are, of course, legion: "The guy *who* I saw," "Except the little ones *that* was too small to go," "I don't know *who* to go out with," "He's a guy *what* you can count on," "Who's beating *who*?" "Them *that* are left behind," "These cows *what* I own. . . ." Frequently the relative is omitted entirely: "There's a girl don't know what she's doing," or "That's a farm can't make no money." Here the introductory

"There's a girl" and "That's a farm" are felt to be subjects of the following verbs, and no need is felt for any relative.

Menner, in an article on "Troublesome Relatives," *American Speech* (June, 1951), cites also "That's the man *that* we couldn't think of *his* name," "It's the story of an Englishman *that his* father had lots of money," and, omitting the relative *that*, "That's the cat all the boys tried to shave *its* tail."

## Demonstrative Pronouns

In addition to the usual demonstratives (*this* and *that*, *these* and *those*) the folk have added the now widely used *them*, which can be heard in any part of the United States, as "In *them* days," "*Them* are no good," "*Them* kids are pretty wild," "I don't want none of *them* kind." To the usual demonstratives and to *them*, also, have been affixed *here* and *there* as adverbs to strengthen the distinction of distance implicit in *this* and *that* in Standard English, a distinction seemingly lost in folk speech without the *here* and *there* usage: "*This-here* boy and *that-there* girl ought to hit it off," "*Them-there* clocks won't work," "*These-here* boards are rough," "I wouldn't have one of *them-there* dogs on a bet." Also, *this one* and *that one* have elided to a distinct *thisn* and *thatn* in speech: "*Thisn*-here's no good," "*Thatn*-there don't belong to you," "I'll buy *thisn*," "What's wrong with *thatn?*"

## Personal Pronouns

The forms of the pronoun, standing alone, do not vary from Standard English in the folk speech except for the urban plural *yous* (*yous* guys, *yous* don't know what you're talking about) and the possessive *n* ending in *hisn*, *hern*, *ourn*, *yourn*, and, occasionally, *theirn*. In usage, however, the traditional nominative and objective forms shift positions, and the folk have no clear understanding of their Standard usage: "*Him* and *I* don't go together no more," "This is just between her and *I*," "*Us* and *them* ain't speaking."

The Southern *we-all*, *you-all*, *they-all*, and *we-uns*, *us-uns*, *you-uns* are widespread throughout the rural areas.

*The Glades area, south central Florida, 1941:*
*vegetable pickers playing a "skin game" in the back room*
*of a juke joint*

## The Noun

The noun in folk speech forms its plural and genitive as it does in Standard English with very few exceptions. There are occasional, rare double plurals, as *oxens* and *childrens*, which form the genitive plural with an additional *es*, as in *childrenses* and *folkses*. Lice is often *louses* (more universally than *mice* is *mouses*) in such phrases as "Those louses!" and "I wouldn't be seen with them louses." The folk speech also often retains the Middle English placing of the genitive *s* at the end of an attributive clause, as, "He's the man that lives in California's wife," "That's the woman that can't drink whiskey's husband," and "He's the man who's just had his teeth operated on's wife."

## The Articles

The Standard English use of the indefinite article *an* before a vowel or mute *h* is generally not observed in folk speech, and one often hears *a* apple, *a* insect, *a* oyster, *a* honor. Where the *n* is heard, it has moved to the noun, as in *a napple, a ninsect, a noyster, a nonor*. The indefinite article also appears before nouns denoting quantity, as *a plenty, a God's plenty, a many*.

The definite article *the* appears before nouns of sickness and disease where it is omitted in Standard English: "He's got *the* toothache, *the* fever, *the* rheumatism." It appears also before *both:* "I'll take *the* both of them."

## Numerals

The use of numerals accords with that of Standard English, except that one occasionally hears, when the dates of years are being given, *nineteen* and *one* for *nineteen hundred* and *one*, the *hundred* being omitted.

## The Redundant Subject

A subject-noun immediately or closely followed by a subject-pronoun, forming a double subject for the verb, is common in folk speech: "*The sailor boy he* was drunk, and *the mother she* went downtown"; "*Those grave robbers they* had"; "*The greatgrandmothers and the greatgrandfathers they* are all dead"; "Well, there was *a gentleman* one morning *he* looked out the window." In the third example, the redundancy may possibly be accounted for by the speaker's feeling that the double subject has gone beyond control and needs the brief and immediate *they* to summarize and restate it. In the last example, also, the subject *gentleman* is removed from its verb by *one morning*, and the redundant *he* may have seemed necessary. (It should be noted, however, that here the *he* is also in a position to act for the relative *who*.) In the first two cases no such explanations can be offered, and I am inclined to think that as a general rule the redundant subject exists merely for the sake of euphony. I am drawn to this conclusion as the result of listening to many tape recordings and noting that in the overwhelming number of cases no pause occurs between the subject and the redundant pronoun. The pronoun does not, in other words, exist for the purpose of emphasis. To write the words with a comma is, therefore, inaccurate: "*The sailor boy*, *he* was drunk." They should more properly be written: "*The sailor boy-he . . . the mother-she* went downtown." Their appearance, of course, serves no useful purpose except to maintain a steady sentence flow, equivalent, on the shop girl's level, to the constant repetition of "He says to me he says that I've been going out too much, and then he says if I keep on. . . ." The steady flow of the sentence, plus, on occasion, the folk need for a tightly joined subject-verb relation where the sentence seems to be running wild will, I believe, account for the redundancy in virtually all cases. "Me, I'm going to town" or "Him, he ought to have his head examined" are emphatic and bear no relation to the foregoing, since they are at the same time contractions of "As for me," and "As for him."

## The Double Negative

The double negative is so common that it scarcely needs comment. Where the negative is called for, the double usage occurs almost invariably among the folk, and can be heard within any five minutes of conversation. The erudite may attempt to point out that "I don't need no shoes" grammatically means "I need shoes," but they will be talking nonsense as far as the spoken language goes. The double negative does not create a positive for the folk; it creates a reinforced negative, precisely as we say "No, no." (If every double negative used in the United States tomorrow were to be literally understood and enforced as a positive, the country would be in a state of utter chaos by eleven A.M.) Its prevalent usage, however, is due not so much to the reaffirmation of the negative as it is to the euphony of the *n* sounds and to imitative laziness. It is easier to say "They never wore no shoes" than "They never wore any shoes." It is easier to stay in the negative, in other words, than to shift out of it. Run-of-the-mill examples from four minutes of tape recording in the Library of Congress include: I don't owe nobody five cents; I ain't got no clothes; they can't get no more; I never had no shoes until I was thirteen; we didn't know nothin'; he didn't have no home. Triple negatives are not uncommon: I don't know nothin' neither; I didn't never send him to be no soldier. If there were any reason for employing six or eight in a row, the folk, once in the negative, would use them. And they would have valid historical and linguistic justification, extending back to Shakespere and Chaucer, for doing so. The usage is forceful and colorful, wholly intelligible, and a living part of the language process. Who would wish to change, for example, a Vance Randolph quintuplet from the Ozarks: "I ain't never done no dirt of no kind to nobody."?

# *Folk Etymology*

Kenneth and Mary Clarke in their informative *Introducing Folklore* (New York, 1963) succinctly define folk etymology as "that process by which the folk change a loan word so that it makes sense within the limits of their own vocabulary and understanding." This is simple and clear, and there are no problems. A few examples suffice to illustrate, and my favorite one of all is "Picketwire":

When Spanish explorers moved north out of Mexico into our Southwest, a small band of perhaps thirty reached the southern edges of what is now Colorado. God did not give them peace. They were slain to the last man by

Indians on the bank of a river running then, and running now, across lower Colorado. None survived. Their bodies were left — to become bones under that relentless sun. There was no priest with them. They died without absolution.

Later, a following group of explorers moved north and came upon the same river at the same point, and the skeleton bodies. One names the land for events upon the land: always when there has been no name, and particularly where there has been a great or terrible event to commemorate.

The second band of Spaniards did so. They named the river with a great and sonorous Spanish name: El Río de las Animas Perdidas en Purgatorio. The River of the Souls Lost in Purgatory.

In time, French trappers moved across the land. They heard the Spanish name, but they were not about to use it. They shortened it to a reasonable Purgatoire, and that is the way the name rides on the maps today: the Purgatoire River.

But now the folk etymology: Kentuckians and men from Texas and elsewhere came to the river and heard its name, but knowing no French, they heard the name "within the limits of their own vocabulary and understanding" as Picketwire. So to them and to generations of Coloradoans after them — men who read no maps, but who knew their way around the land — the river became the Picketwire. I have heard old-timers so name it. (Just as I have heard the same old-timers call the Colorado River the Grand.) Purgatoire — Pugatoire — Pigatoire — Pigitoire — Pickitoire — Picketwire. Folk etymology.

Another name in the same French-Kentucky-frontier tradition is a town (hamlet rather, or bend in the road) in Indiana near Bloomington called Gnaw Bone. Kentuckians moving west had never run across the French and had never, in consequence, heard of the French town Narbonne. They clearly heard Gnaw Bone, and so it is on the highway marker today. Narbonne: Gnaw Bone. "Within the limits of their own vocabulary . . ." Folk etymology.

There are numerous such borrowings and misunderstandings, and one can hear them every day if one cocks an ear for them, or lies in wait to trap them. On a David Susskind TV show (April 1970) I heard and he heard one of his participants clearly say that "those men are flustrated." This is not quite as clear as "sparrow grass" for "asparagus," but it is, nevertheless, solid indication that the woman speaking knew the word "flustered" and had herself (hearing someone use "frustrated" and having no knowledge of it other than possibly related to "flustered") come up with "flustrated." Definitely and positively, with no hesitation. She used the word twice with complete conviction of its correctness and existence. Susskind will remember, because he was sufficiently taken aback to repeat the use of it.

On another TV show (or was it the same?) a woman also positively said that someone "had to take the blunt end of it." This was quite interesting, because here "the brunt of it," making no sense to the woman, required her to substitute or to hear "blunt" for "brunt" and, consequently, demanded the use by her of the added word "end" to make full folk sense. "The brunt of it" becomes "the blunt end of it"!

In a folklore class at American University, I had a charming young student (Susan Feldman, and charming because she almost fell out of her chair laughing at herself and her own etymology), who gave me a relatively short term paper on "Folklore in the Short Stories of Erskine Caldwell." Whipping to her twelfth-page climax, she deprecatingly informed me that the preceding matter of her paper was only enough, but certainly enough, "to wet the appetite."

Now Miss Feldman, from New York City, had no knowledge and no reason whatsoever in 1970 to have knowledge of a *whetstone* or of *whet* as a verb meaning to sharpen. Without knowing anything about whetstone or whet, she nevertheless knew precisely what the phrase "to whet one's appetite" meant, except that she had heard it and used it clearly and distinctly as "to wet one's appetite." I am not certain of this, but I have the feeling that she may have related the phrase to the crystal purity of the dry martini. In any event, folk etymology. And operating on the college level at that. Susan Feldman was not downgraded for this lapse from Standard English, but given a plus for inadvertently providing a superb example of folk etymology.

A half dozen added examples:

"Bois Brule" in Michigan becomes "Bob Ruly," and "L'Eau Frais" (a river in Arkansas) becomes "Low Freight." "Cole slaw" very readily becomes "cold slaw," and the French "écrevisse" through sound alone is easily turned to "crayfish." In England the pleasant "Route de Roi" becomes "Rotten Row," and off the coast of Spain the Arabic "Djebal el-Tarik" (the mountain of Tarik, who invaded in 711) has become "Gibraltar," and all knowledge of him forgotten. Similarly, the Turks who drove the Greeks from their land in the 1920's changed Constantinople (Constantine-polis: the city of Constantine) to Istanbul, thus ridding themselves forever of the hated Greek name. Except that: "Istanbul" is a pure development of folk etymology, and is purely Greek: travelers and merchants from the north going to the city of Constantine simply said, as we do when questioned, "I'm going to town" or "I'm going to the city." Sto polis. Sto polis — sto bolis — sto boulis — stom boulis — Stamboul — Istanbul. The Greek name is there forever: "to the city."

# The Vocabulary of the Folk

Mencken and others have pointed out that the vocabulary of folk speech is not limited to a few hundred words, as was once incredibly believed, but that it contains, on the contrary, virtually as many words as those employed by a person using Standard English. The basic vocabulary has to be the same: everything tangible and visible must have a name, and the names of folk speech and Standard English for these things are essentially one and the same. If, however, in the hills of Kentucky or the backwoods of Michigan, there are no skyscrapers, why should the people use the word? Why not simply "tall buildings"? I remember when I was in Constantine, Algeria, and had been absent from the States for some time, two touring American architects dropping in on me and in the course of conversation asking about the unfinished "high-rise" buildings at the edge of the city. I had no idea what they were talking about. "High rise." It still seems to me a ridiculous made-up word.

The folk would not use such a word. Neither do they employ the fine language of theoretical and scientific studies, nor the delicate linguistic nuances of the professor, philosopher, or literary and art critic. They are unaware of these vocabularies because, like many of us, they have no need for them. However, by the same token (a deadly phrase), the professor, philosopher, and urban sophisticate would not understand the specialized vocabulary of a farmer, carpenter, or cowboy. Yet apart from the differences stemming from disparate training, occupation, and milieu, a member of any or all of these groups is wholly intelligible to a member of another. We are Americans: the language (the *lingua franca* of New Mexico and Maine) is American-English: we can speak to each other from one end of the continent to the other without barrier.

A chief difference between folk and Standard English lies not in the words themselves, the vocabulary, but in the arrangement of the words and their usage. The words *boy* and *days*, for example, are common to both groups, but the arrangement of them in a phrase "*In my boy days*, I use-to go swimming" would not be the manner of their arrangement in Standard English. *In my boy days* may even be an uncommon arrangement of the words in folk speech, yet any member of the folk and of the Standard English group readily understands what is meant — even though it may sound momentarily odd or curious. Similarly, any member of the folk would also understand the Standard English counterpart, "When I was a youngster" or "When I was young."

Vance Randolph's *Down in the Holler: A Gallery of Ozark Folk Speech* contains many examples of such non-Standard arrangements and usages. Randolph tells of a lawyer in southwest Missouri who needed the exact date of a woman's death to enter in some legal papers. When the lawyer queried surviving relatives, he was told, "Aunt Suly died *just past the peak of watermelon time*." The dead woman's most intimate friend said, "She took sick *when we was just about knee-deep in August*." Another neighbor thought that Aunt Suly had passed away right "*at the start of kitchen-settin' weather*," which means the first chilly period of early fall, when people sit around the wood range in the kitchen.

I think I prefer any and all of these to, let us say, "August 11."

# 4.

# A Manuscript
## of the Folk Language:
## Samuel M. Van Swearengen

In the period immediately preceding the last World War, I met, in the Windsor Hotel on Denver's Larimer Street, a gentleman by the name of Samuel M. Van Swearengen. The Windsor, as anyone who lived in Denver at the time knows, was the most elegant hostelry on the skid row. To it flocked old prospectors who no longer looked to the Sangre de Cristo, cowboys who remembered the days of the long trails north from Texas, one-time gamblers who spoke of dust and of thousands, and old age pensioners who qualified for the munificent largesse of the state of Colorado. Sam Van Swearengen was one of these last. He lived in a small room at the Burlington Hotel, just down the street, but preferred to sun himself in the expansive air of the great Windsor lobby. He had been born in Chariton County, Missouri, in 1869, and was seventy-two years old in the Denver of 1941.

At the time, I was teaching at the University of Denver, and collecting folksongs on the side. I was hell bent for folksongs, and am afraid I contributed my small share to the madness now sweeping the land. So I pestered the old gentleman for his contribution, which was, except for a "Jesse James" variant, a virtual zero. Since there was more to life, however, than folksongs, and because the bar was handy and he liked his whiskey straight, we talked of other things and saw much of each other. He was lonely, and my wife and I gradually became his "children" (he so addressed us in letters), and he, in turn, gravitated into the orbit of our Christmas doings, motor rides in the country, and similar goings on.

Not too long after we first met him, he diffidently handed me a manuscript "pertaining to my life." It had been started several years before, and, for lack of encouragement, consisted of some twenty pages, no more. It was typewritten, but unlike anything I, or anyone else, had ever seen. The type was single-spaced and ran tightly from one side of the paper to the other, with no margins. There was no paragraphing, and no punctuation except for an occasional and uncertain comma, found only in the first few pages, and rare periods, appearing only after numerals. And every word was capitalized. I give the forthright and plunging opening of the manuscript, *verbatim, literatim, et punctatim.*

In Writing This Book I Have Carictorized It In The Best Manner Posible For Me To Remember As I Am A Man of 66. Years Of Age And Did Nevver Keep No Dairie Of The Dayley Happinings As I Should Of Did But Nevver Thinking Of Writing This Book, I Just Have To Go Back In Memory As Fare As Posible And Give The Facts As Best I Can Remember I Whas Borne In Chariton County Misouri On January 19Th 1869. And Whas About 18 Mounths Old When My Mother Died She Died Leaving My Self And My Little Baby Brother Ho Whas About Two Mounths Old At Her Death, And My Father Not Beeing Very Well Fixed With The Necesary Things Of Life My Grand Parrents Taken Me And My Brother To Raise And Everything Went Good Tell About Four Years Later My Grand Mother Died Leaving Us To The Murcy And Care Of Aunts And Uncles For Whitch Had No Experience In Raising Of Children And Some Of Them Whas Onley Children Them Selves

Quite apart from the spelling, which reflects with remarkable accuracy the pronunciation of rural Missouri, here was Mencken's "common speech" in full flower: the preterite *did* becomes a past participle. The past participle *taken* becomes a preterite. The double negative is happily at home. The auxiliary *have* becomes a complete and unequivocal *of*. The personal relative pronoun of the plural walks boldly forth as *for whitch*. *Good* becomes an adverb. *My self* is in the objective case, and *self* and *selves* are entities set apart from *my* and *them*.

I forgot about folksongs and encouraged Van Swearengen to go ahead and beat out some more of his life on his old turret-revolving Oliver typewriter, a relic salvaged from earlier, dining-car days on the railroad. Even with the problem of capitals, to which he clung, and an aged hunt-and-peck system, the work progressed more rapidly for him than if he had attempted writing in a slow, longhand scrawl. Writing with pen and pencil was labor. His schooling had been small:

And As Far As A Edication Whas Concirned My Grand Father Awlways Had A Plow Handle Ore A Chopping Ax For Us In Stead Of A School Book So Our Edication Whas Very Mutch Limited. . . . But At That She [a stepgrandmother] Did Make My Grandfather Start Us To School And We Got To Go About Two Mounths And I Lurnt More In That Time Than I Evver Had Lurnt Before In My Life [age eleven at this time] That Two Mounths In School Give Me A Start And I Became Interested in Books From Then On And Studyed At Home With The Help Of My Younger Uncle I Got Right Along Fine And All Of The Edication I Evver Got Whas By My Own Efforts And As I Grew Older Nature And Horse Sence Tought Me A Great Deail And Not Bragging At All I Had A Good Fore Sight On Things And I Worked Out Lots Of Them By Self Expearence And By Whatching Others Do Things.

Within the two passages quoted, there occur differences of spelling for the same word — *experience, expearence; far, fare; grandfather, grand father* — and this holds true throughout the whole manuscript. It is wholly natural and easily accounted for by the fact that Van Swearengen's limited "edication" gave him no fixed standard of correctness. His vacillation indicates uncertainty and unfamiliarity with his medium. Van Swearengen vacillates as well in his use of verbs, interchanging *did* and *done*, *took* and *taken*, and other forms, thus reproducing with a high degree of fidelity the folk lan-

*McHenry County,*
*North Dakota, 1942:*
*farms on the vast plains*

guage. But the problem of selection or choice (*if* it arose in his mind) seems not to have bothered him any more than punctuation, particularly when the story or facts move rapidly. It is the account itself which is important to him, and he gets it across in spite of hell and high water, and in spite of occasional wild entanglements with complicated sentences.

I furnished him with paper and a loose-leaf notebook, the combination proving a slight stumbling block, since Van Swearengen either began on the reverse of the page or inserted the page upside down without regard for the punched holes. Whenever he or I read the manuscript, it was, consequently, whirling like a top. I gave him no instructions other than to "write what you feel like writing." Above all, I refrained from any comment whatever on spelling, punctuation, capitalization, grammar, syntax, and word order. I received all of that absolutely deadpan. The story was the thing.

After he had typed a hundred or more pages, however, I did finally feel sorry for the old man punching out capitals for every word, and I told him there was no need to capitalize them all. As a result, he capitalized nothing, and the last pages of the manuscript, which ends with the Lord's Prayer, look like something out of Stein and e. e. Cummings.

In all, Van Swearengen typed 272 single-spaced pages, quite apart from peripheral odds and ends which he did not consider part of the main manuscript. In them he covers his life on the farm in Missouri, his brief schooling, his boyhood pleasures trapping and duck hunting, and the hardships of his early days. He reviews his various jobs as a young man: making barrel hoops, work on the railroad, a job at the Armour plant in Kansas City, his "corear" as a butcher and grocer, a job as a news "butch" on the Denver run, work as a dining-car steward. He tackles his marital troubles with candor: "How The Holy Roolers Stole My Wife." He describes visits to Kentucky, to New Orleans, and Pike's Peak with graphic detail. And he closes the manuscript with some fine, wild haymakers directed at hypocritical church people, and the government of Colorado, with which he was embroiled over the matter of old-age pensions.

There is not, of course, too much order to the manuscript. It rambles as people do when talking, and the chronological sequence is only occasionally observed. As a piece of writing, however, it is as unselfconscious a work as I have seen. It reads from the life, and, within definite sequences, moves rapidly and colorfully. It has the smell and feel of America, with no apologies. It is, in short, a unique document, not alone for the insight it gives to our language "as she is frequently spoke," but also because it is a full-bodied autobiographical work from a person belonging to a cultural group which is usually inarticulate in this respect.

As proof of the pudding, I give here two excerpts. I have punctuated, sentenced (sometimes with difficulty), and paragraphed. I have also reduced the capitals for easier reading. I have not touched the spelling, grammar, or syntax. All words within brackets are my own. Words in parentheses occur in the original, but are better omitted for clearer understanding. Mr. Van Swearengen, gentle reader:

## My Revenge on Old Schoolmates for Thire Cruell Treatments in School

Well, I guess it did look a bit auquard to some of the school chlidren to see sutch great big schoolers in school and couldent say thire A.B.C., but it whas, as I thought, nothing to pick on us for, just because we, as menney others, wear neglected to that capasity. But it looked as tho the hold school had it in for me and my brother because we had bin so neglected, and thay looked up on us as just two fools. But at that we had a surprise for them just every naw and then, and the surprise we usley had for them whas one that thay did not forget eathor just ovver night. For thay would just humiliate the very lives out of us tell we would get mad, and then if we should lick one of them, then the hold school would pile on us and just beet the hell out of us. And we got to whire we would not even go out on the play grounds to play at all, for we did not whant to be fighting all the time.

And one day the teachor asked us why we dident go out and play ball with the rest of the boys, and we told him the hold story, and he sed, "Well, you come out, and if one of them ses a word to you that he should not say, I will take him in custody." And we went out with him and stayed close to him, for we whanted him to se if eneything did start. And we hadent bin playing long tell a great big boy that whas older and lots larger than our selves sed, "Well, let's chuse up and get our balls teams and have a ball game." And he sed, "Well, I will take one of the fools, and you can have the other." And at that very juncture the school mastter sed to him, "You come in the house with me." And he took him in, and he had a dam good big stick, and he wore it out on that guy and made him go to the dore and tell the hold school that it whas him that whas the fool. But, at that, he then had it in for us then and after, and for years after we quit school.

And we had a big old fashioned saw mill in our neighbor hood, and thay had a set of corn burs, and every Saturday thay would do custom grinding for the people in the neighbor hood. And we would most every Saturday would take a sack of white corn to the mill and get it grownd, for we used in them days just lots of corn bread. And on one Saturday we had [gone], me and my brother bouth, at the mill, as we took a sack with about one bushell and a half to the sack. And this boy that got the licken at school came to the mill the same day, and he came up to me, and sed, "Naw, by God, you have forgot the time you caused the school teacher to lick hell out of me, have you not?" And I told him to shut up, that I did not whant no more trouble with him. And he sed, "Well, it is not what you whant that you are going to get the most of," and he begain pulling of his gloves, and I knew just what whas comming right then.

And we wear standing right before the fore [fire] box of the boiler, and the fireman had a great big poking stick standing right up thire by the side of the fire box, and I just grabed it, and I just had time to hit him with it, and he fell as dead as log. And he fell in the fire besides, but you bet your bottom dollar that I did not help to drag him out. But the fireman drug him out, and sed, "By God, you have killed him." And they worked with him for a while, and he begain breathing again so I whas all right, as I knew that then I hadent killed him, but if I had, I would have nevver have shed one tear. And, at that, I shure thought I whas in for it with them all in after years.

But it went for about two years before I even saw one of the bunch again, and at all times after that I carried my pistol everytime I went out from home, as I well knew that if I evver saw him again, that if he thought that he had eney chance, he would try it out again. And it went on tell one day the folks had a old time picnic in the neaghbor hood, and we met at the picnic, and I said right thire — "Hear is whire I am going to have to use my gun." And when I would be near him I awlways had my hand on that gun, for I did not know just when he might light on me. And my uncle whas thire at the picnic, and him self and my uncle whas just about the same size and about the same in streangth, and I guess he thought it best to not start eneything, for if he did, it might be more than he could stop. And he given it up as a bad job, and I nevver saw him for about another year.

And when I did se him, as it happend, I did not have my gun, and I just made shure we would have a little bit of hell. But he came right up to me, and sed, "Helo, Sam." And I spoke to him. And he sed, "Han't it about time we wear grown up and forgetting our boyhood difucultys?"

And I sed, "Well I guess it would be about the best thing we could do."

And he sed, "Yess, let's be friends" — that he realized that it whaim [whas him] that whas the cause of it all, and sed he whas sorry for it all.

So I sed, "Well, gone buys is gone buys." And all after that he whas as good a friend as I evver had.

## The Wild Irish Minister at the Country School House

Well I remember, in pioneer days in old Mo, when thire whas a church in about every hundred squire miles, and in them days the school houses whas used extencivley for religious services. And the people all knew automaticly the church days for certain ministers, and thay all would hitch up thayer ox teaims and some times start before day light on Sundays to church, as thay had to do this to even think of getting to church in time to hear the sermons. And in them days when the people reialy had hearts, some of them would start the day before, as that they lived so far, if they trusted to getting up and going the same morning, thay nevver would arive at all. And as we lived about three miles from the nearest school house in our neighbor hood, my grandfather would make us all get out and walk, as we could beet the oxen at that, and him self and his wife and a minister that whas whidely known as the Wild Irishman. And as my grandfathers home whas as near as eneybodys to the school house, the Wild Irishman had a apointment every fourth Sunday in eatch mounth, as in them days thay wear called circit riders, and that whas his date in his circut. His name reialy wear Charley Davis, but he whas known greater by his alias name as the Wild Irishman. And as I sed, he used to come to my grandfather's house on Saturday night before every fourth Sunday.

And in them days, I guess he whas what whas thought to be the top minister, for it seemed as that every body that whas church inclined would try to hear him, and would pour in for miles around. For you could start to church Sunday morning, and you could se people for four ore five miles away comming creeping over the prearie in a ox wagon. And as the school house whas in the woods, but you would have to go out to the edge of the prearie before you could get thire, and then you had a full view of what might be seen on the pririe. And at times church would be half ovver before some of the people that you might se comming would arrive.

And as my grandfather whas a old Kentuckyen, and had bin used to in Kentucky of moon shine whiskey, he hardley evver whas without sompthing of a intoxicating nature in his house to drink. And, of corse, this old Irish minister whas a full fledged Irishman, and thire is no use to, ore for me to try to, tell you what he whas most fond of, as if you know the Irish, you know that [what] thay reaily do like. And it has accurred to me that if thay will not pertake of the forbidden fruit, that he is not a full fledged Irishman. And that this specual time my grand father had just finished making sorgum molases, as in them days we [made] our own sorgum. We raised our own cane that we made them of, and thay wear reaily home made sorgum. But as I whas going to say, my grandfather had a fashon of when he wear finishing his sorgum, he would make a fifty gallon barrell of what he called mathiglum, and it whas boiled down out of cane juce just the same as sorgum. And he would run it of just as soon as the green scum quit forming on top of the juce, and then he would spike it with a gallion of the best whiskey he could find. And in them days good whiskey whas not hard to find, for if he couldend find the kind that might suit him, he awlways had plenty of corn in his crib, and he knew just how it whas done, and he generly had a barrel of stuff that would knock you cokoo faster than whiskey. And that old Irishman reaily did like that in prefurences to whiskey, and he would come to grandad's on Saturday night, and some times when he whas not due on that part of his circut.

And I nevver will forget a old German man that used to go to hear the

Wild Irishman preach. And at this special time the old German happened to be thire, and sed when that Wild Irishman got started that day on his serman, "he schust could show you Jesus Christ and the angells chust flooting in the air." And you your self could se them, as the Wild Irishman's serman whas so natural that that minister that day "schust" showed that hold congregation the in sides of haven. And thire whas the throne of God as plain as if it whas. And he showed him his dead wife sitting on the right of Christ, and holding thayer little dead gorl in her arms, but the child whas not dead thire. And he showed them all the conveniences that a man had what whas a church member, and shoed them all the difurent departments that thire wear in haven. He showed the departments whire the people whas kept that had nevver sined, and whire the people whas held that had sined just a little, and whire the people whas kept that had bin sinners tell thay foundout that thay wear going to die. And that preacher told them that thay whas punished according to his deeds, and told them that the less a man sined, the less he whas punished. And he then, in return, showed them hell, and showed them what a terible place hell wear. And he [the old German] sed, "Vell, I shust could se hell and de devell shust as plain as if I wear reaily in hell." And I will admit my self he could show you a picture of things tell thire would be sompthing funney about it. But he nevver could nor he nevver would undertake this untell he whas just three sheets in the wind.

And he had a influence over the weak minded people that thay thought he whas a second Christ. And we had a man in our neighbor hood that had more common sence them days than the averidge, and he sed that old Irish preacher whas awlways drunk, and could blow his breath in to the faces of his congretion tell thay all becam cookoo two, and then thay all could se things. But, at that, this old preacher held his conregations so well that he begain to get pretty well fixed financily. And if he had of just stayed with my grandfathers old mathiglum barrell, he would have held his [own until] years later. But as he had gotten far enough of of [off of] the donations of his brothers and sisters of the four stops a mounth, that his little farm whas payed for, and he had money to keep a hired man to run it besides.

And as when my grandfather whas married the third turm, it whas this old Wild Irish minister that aplyed the past[e] that seailed the tie. But it whas not long after my grandfather['s] third turm whas started, tell by

*Williamson County, Illinois, 1939:*
*couple dancing in the Oke-Doke dance hall,*
*patronized by miners and farmers*

some means he begain to get away from that old minister. And I nevver did lurn for shure what had happened, but I reaily think he barrowed some cash from my grandfather and forgot to return it, as I hurd my grandfather say in years after that the Wild Irishman whas not the man that people took him to be. For I reaily do belive he had away to hyponitize the weaker parts of his congregation tell thay did amagine that thay had bin seeing things that he whas showing them. But in time thire whas quite a few people lost confidences in him, as I think that his colections did not at all times just suit him, and he would barrow five ore ten at a time from some of them; as I well know that his congregations fell of as soon as him and my grand father desolved as partners, and he quit getting his mothiglum regolar. For I have hurd him say him self that he had to have a little machine oil ore the old machine would not cut.

Well, about the time that I got married that old preacher went to ocupy one of them compartments that he used to show his congregations, but I nevver knew just what department he inhearieted. But I guess it whas one of the best that thire wear whating when he arived, as he ought to have had a good one, for he would tell the people not to do as he did, but to do as he told them that thay should do. For this old gent could be full to the brim and set down at the table, and deliver the finest blessing you evver hurd. And I sometimes think it whas just his gift of speach that made his surmons so inticing, and that it whas not what he sed that whas [what] the people fell so hard for, but it whas just the way he might express him self while saying of it.

Naw I well know on one occasion when he came to the old country log school house to fill his apoint ment, that at this one time thire wear another old Irish gent went to hear him. But I have awlways thought that this last old man must have bin a Catholic, for he did not seem to take eney great intrest in our old Irish preacher. And if eneything hit the old Irish preacher two hard, he could not do a bit of good that hold meeting. It seemed as tho it would un nurve him in someway. And I well remember that at that special time the Irish preacher got up to adress his congregation, and sed, "Well, we whant to se how meney thire is hear that would like to go to Heaven, and let them all be known by rizing to your feet." And every body in the church stood up, and as thay stud up, the minister set down. And as he did this, the other Irishman sit down also. And at that he rizen at once, and sed, "Well, my brother, I supose you whant to go to Hell, do you?" And he [the other Irishman] sed, "Well, I don't know that I reaily do, but I hated to se you go by your self." And don't you know that unstrung the old Irish preacher tell he couldent preach at all, because it greated sutch a laugh that I guess thire whas not a man in the house that did not just squall out as loud as [he] could, as I well know if I had to quit laughing, it would have busted me wide open. And the minister seemed to have lost his charm right thire, for he could not talk after that. So it whas quite a while before he came back, and lots of the people had begain to think he had deserted us. But not so easy as all of that!

For well I remember that in the spring of 1881, whan that big blazing star apeard in the east of evenings, and it whas sompthing that no one had evver saw at no time before, and that whas food for his religious propiganda. And he begain telling the people that it whas the same blaze that God apeard to Moses in when God apeard to Moses in a burning bush, and told him to go fourth and deliver the children of Iserill from under bondige. And meney of a time have I saw him lead the congregations out in the church yards of a night to whatch for God to apear as He did to Moses, and told them it whas shure to come, as thire whas a comandment that God wished to give him as just how to proceed in his religious frenzy. And the fools, if I should venture to call them that, would sneek right by his side, and especily some old fashiond lady that whas short in the top story, and some of the men also, and he would have them scared in a inch of thayer lives. And thay would give to him when thire own familys whas reaily in need badley. But that blazing star whas a kind of a mystery. Some people, after a while when they got used to it, sed, "O, it whas Haley's commit." But it run up from the size of a big star to the far end it would be four ore five foot across, and its length whas from ten to fifteen feet long. And it whas in the elements the hold summer through. It would apear as the sun went down, and disipear when the sun would raise. It would be in the west of a morning. Naw you don't have to believe me regarding this story, for it does seem to me naw days like a fairy story, but eneyold person that whas hear in 1881 can tell you the same story. But at that that star whas a harvest for that old Wild Irish minister, as thay all thought if he whas with them, that thay wear saved without a doubt, that he could keep them from eney harm what so evver.

Then in the spring of 1882, the Faroah locusis like to have eaten the crops up in Mo, and he then renewed his attact with the locust propiganda, and he told the people that whas the same locusts that whas sent up on Pharoah. Them and the frogs whas plegs that God had sent up on Pharoah for his treatment of God's people. And told them that God whas going to apear to him as he did to Moses, and apoint him meditator to make a settlement with the people for some great sin that they had comitted, and that he had to have that star whatched every night tell it disipeared. And the poore, well, I shouldent say fools, but that whas reaily what some of them whas, they would give that old Irish minister, if thay did not have but two sides of bacon hanging in thayer smoke houses and thay had twelve in [the] family, thay would cut down one and send it to him to have him pray for them. And he told them all about when Moses whas found in the baskett of the bull-rushess, and whas raised by Pharoah's doughter and made one of the rullers ovver the land of Egept. And that God had chozen Moses to betray Pharoah and lead the children of Iserill from under bondge, as thay wear made slaves buy Pharoah. And he showed them how Moses smit the watter of the Red Sea, and led the children of Iserill saftly through that open chanell, and how the Egyptians started to falow, and as Moses and the children of his own burth passed through, the watter closed and cought Pharoah's army that he had sent in persuit of Moses and the children of Iserill.

And he told them as to Moses having led the children of Iserill in to the wilderness, whire thire wear thousands of reptiles ore, in other words as we call them, snakes. And that the reptiles wear so sevear that when a man whas bitten, if he dident do sompthing at once, it ment sertin death to him. And Mosees whas informed by God to prepair him self with a brazen imige of them reptiles, and when a man whas bitten, just hold it up and demand the man that whas bitten to look up at the brazen serpent, and he would be healed Omeditly. And that Moses did so, and saved the children of Israiell from that pleg. And he told them that he whas as Moses, and if thire whas one of them that would evver be bitten by eneykind of a serpent, all thay had to do whas to call up on God in his name, and that thay would suffer no more.

And that summer as we wear harvesting, one of his desiples got bitten by a spread headed vipor. And he started to bind by hand some wheat that had been cradled over night, and this serpent had crawled under it to take refuge from the hot sun that day. And this poore old simp would do nothing but pray to God in this old minister's name, so the next night he quiled over in the bed and died. And some of them thought of sending for Brother Davis to come and reserect him as Christ did Lauseris, but when thay sent for Brother Davis he whas out on his circut, and thay could not get him at all. And thay kept him tell he swelled so big that thay had to just squeeze him in his coffin to get the lid on it. And after he begain to smell, thay lost hopes then, and buried him.

And this old hypocrite of a minister told his people, ore his folowers, about Moses smitting the rock so his people could have fresh whatter to drink, and told them that thay need not fear no droughts, as he had them all masterd from naw on. But at this turn in the tide, as the mathiglum barrell had bin taken from the old minister's reach, it seemed as tho that he had lost his grip to a great extent. But how he did build a heaven right hear on earth and demonstrated it to his folowers as long as the sacrements lasted! And thay lasted for four ore five years before eneyone could begain to se that this great man whas slipping just a bit. For he had built him self so high in the estimations of the people that thay ore his desiples thought it whas Christ the second time. And some one told them in a fun making way that if it whas Christ, He had changed His nationality, for when He first came He whas a Jew, and if this whas Him naw, He whas a old flanell mouth Irishman.

This whas one of his favorite hyms:

> *Up to that bountifull givver of life,*
> *Gethering home, geathering home. Up*
> *To that city that commeth no strife,*
> *God's children air gethering home.*
>
> *Gethering home, gethering home,*
> *Nevver to sarrow, nor nevver to rome,*
> *Geathering home, geathering home,*
> *God's children air geathering home.*

*Up to that bountifull mansions on high,*
*Geathering home, geathering home,*
*Up to that mansion beyond the skyes,*
*God's children air gethering home.*

[As an orthographic *lagniappe*, I give Van Swearengen's final words exactly as they appear in the manuscript, and, in doing so, call attention to the simplicity and honesty of his search for the eternal truth — the search of an American from Missouri, unbound and unstraitjacketed by age-old laws. Here is humility, but no fear:]

and naw as we proceed to close our subjects we will offer up our heart felt thanks with a prayer as we know that a prayer will not hurt you if evven it dose you no good and as we air just to whire we don't know whitch way to stepp we feel that the good god will hold us responsible for not just knowing whither we might be right ore rong for its the right way we would like to follow if we just had the knowledge as to whitch way whas the right way naw we will proceed in prayer

*Our Father in haven hallowd by thy name*
*thy kingdom it will be done in earth as it is*
*in haven*
*and give us this day our daily bread and*
*forgive us our debts as we forgive our*
*debtors and leed us not in to condemnation*
*but bear us from all evil thine is the*
*glory and the power forevver*
    *A,Men*

# 5.

# *Proverbs*
# *and Proverbial Speech*

Proverbs are not for the very young. This was most happily proven on a "Candid Camera" (CBS network TV) program on January 30, 1966, which was caught by an alert folklorist, George Monteiro, and more permanently preserved by him in a contributory note to *Western Folklore* (1968) "Proverbs in the Remaking."

It would seem that Candid Camera had moved in on small, innocent, and unsuspecting youngsters of the Brookside School, Baldwin, Long Island, to "test the idea that young children are not familiar with proverbs." The children were asked to complete proverbs fed to them by a member of the Candid Camera staff. They did so, and the proverbs were thoroughly re-made. In those that follow, the words before the slash are the fed words of traditional proverbs, and the words after are the completions of the youngsters. Read them aloud with a moment's pause at the slash:

*The pen is mightier than | the pencil.*

*Two heads are | enough.*

*A rolling stone | plays a guitar.*

*A fool and his money are | very attached.*

*To be or not to be is | bad.*

*Early to bed and early to rise makes a man | tired.*

*Spare the rod and | throw in the reel.*

*Half a loaf is better than | vegetables.*

*Man does not live by | getting married.*

*You can't get blood out of a | sick duck.*

*Fools rush in where | people are crowded.*

*Ask me no questions and I'll tell you | the answers.*

*A bird in the hand is | warm.*

*Early to bed and early to rise makes a man | not watch TV.*

The Brookside School proverbs are amusing because you are aware of the true proverb and recognize the "zany" or "incorrect" departure from it.

Which brings us to a contradiction. Throughout this book I have emphasized and insisted upon the individual's touch in folklore, that is, that no two items are alike, and that as an item of folklore moves from one person to another it is subject to change and re-creation. Proverbs are an exception. They become fixed with usage. There is no departure (the Brookside School excepted) from the wording of the true proverb. It is as fixed as a phrase in the Bible, from which, in fact, many of them come.

A proverb is difficult to define. So difficult, in fact, that the two great American authorities (Archer Taylor of the University of California and Bartlett Jere Whiting of Harvard) virtually give up the attempt in various of their books and articles on the subject.

WHITING: To offer a brief yet workable definition of a proverb, especially with the proverbial phrase included, is well nigh impossible.

TAYLOR: The definition of a proverb is too difficult to repay the undertaking. . . .

WHITING: Happily, no definition is really necessary, since all of us know what a proverb is.

TAYLOR: Let us be content with recognizing that a proverb is a saying current among the folk. At least so much of a definition is indisputable. . . .

TAYLOR AND WHITING TOGETHER: [A proverb is a saying] which summarizes a situation and in its own inimitable way passes some sort of judgement on it or characterizes its essence.

TAYLOR AND WHITING TOGETHER: The old description of proverbs as "short, plain, common, figurative, ancient, and true" is "as good as any formal definition."

Lord John Russell said that "a proverb is the wisdom of many and the wit of one." Professor Whiting points out that that is a nice phrase, but it is not a definition. Nevertheless, it contributes something. One hundred thousand persons can save pennies, and continue to save them, and continue to save them, and it means little except the saved pennies until along comes a Benjamin Franklin with an apt truth concentrated into: "A penny saved is a penny earned," or "Take care of the pennies and the dollars will take care of themselves." The wisdom of the thousands has been there over the years in the saving process, and the wit of one has crowned and honored their work with a proverb.

Proverbs are, in effect, the capsuled wisdom, the distilled knowledge of the people. They are based on observation, experience, or, without either of these being firsthand, accepted as useful truisms on a hand-me-down basis from the past. They circulate, as all folklore does, both in time and space, and tend to have the authority of generations on their side. Their ultimate origin may be literary: from the Bible, Shakespere, *Poor Richard*, *The Way to Wealth*, McGuffey's *Readers*, and the Farmers' Almanacs, or they may spring directly from the folk, in New Mexico, Tennessee, wherever. They may be used to leaven conversation, to make a succinct observation directly applicable to the subject of the moment, to enforce an argument, to invoke authority, to admonish or instruct. They tend to lean toward law and legality, and one does not readily dismiss them out of hand: the ancestral past is, after all, being invoked, and if not that, at least the strength of observed custom and the community.

Harold Thompson quotes a Yorker who sums all this up rather well: "Those sayings are a hundred percent true. Bring the kids up on them."

The true proverb consists of a complete sentence ("Haste makes waste") or, in some instances, a sentence with the verb omitted but understood ("Penny-wise and pound-foolish"). There are two groups of true proverbs: those which are simply a statement of fact, usually based on experience ("Set a thief to catch a thief"; "Few words are best"; "Rain before seven, stop before eleven"; "Silence gives consent"), and those which are metaphors that one applies to the situation at hand ("Don't change horses in the middle of the stream"; "There is small choice in rotten apples"; "In a calm sea every man's a pilot"; "A rolling stone gathers no moss").

Some proverbs would seem to give contradictory advice, and Nicholas Breton noted this in the Elizabethan period with *A Crossing of Proverbs:* "Look before you leap," as opposed, to, for example, "He who hesitates is lost." Standing alone there is, of course, contradiction between the two proverbs, but there is actually no contradiction since the two would never be used at the same time to describe or characterize a given situation: only one would apply. And proverbs, in many cases, are stated after an event has taken place, so that "Look before you leap" could literally apply to a man who has already fallen in the water, and "He who hesitates is lost" to a hunter who has allowed the rabbit to go over the hill before firing his gun; or each might, metaphorically, apply to two stock market transactions where the individual involved has lost his shirt for different reasons.

There are numerous stylistic devices in the proverbs, and none are accidental. *Alliteration:* Live and learn; Live and let live. *Rhyme:* Man proposes, God disposes; There's many a slip betwixt the cup and the lip. *Repetition:* There's no fool like an old fool; Love me, love my dog. *Contrast:* Enough is as good as a feast; Better late than never; A good beginning makes a good ending. *Contrast reinforced by parallelism:* Young saint, old devil; Out of sight, out of mind; Like master, like man; Like father, like son. *Assonance:* A rolling stone gathers no moss. *Paradox:* No news is good news. *Meter:* Early to bed and early to rise, Makes a man healthy, wealthy, and wise. In their own way, proverbs are as strictly disciplined in structure as a sonnet. Their chief greatness lies in the jewel-like precision of their few words. Try improving on: Honesty is the best policy; All's well that ends well; Still water runs deep; It's a long lane that has no turning; April showers bring May flowers. To change a single word ruins all.

There is a sharp distinction between the literary proverb and the folk proverbs. The touchstone again is transmission. The literary proverb — because of its length and vocabulary — does not circulate among the folk. The following are from eighteenth-century almanacs.

*He who exalts himself and backbites his neighbor does an essential injury to both.*

*He who seeks after his own virtues and others' vices will find himself engaged in business which affords little satisfaction.*

*A head, like a house, when crammed too full and no regular order observed, is only littered instead of being furnished.*

*It would be well for the business of the world if young men would stay longer before they went into it, and old men not so long before they went out of it.*

Those were in almanacs which circulated widely. None have survived in anything resembling folk tradition, and they appear here only because they were rescued "by way of example" by Ruth B. Tolman in an article in *Western Folklore.*

A few that she found may well have had some sort of folk circulation, or at least deserved to have had:

*Death keeps no calendar.*

*Fools make feasts and wise men eat them.*

*Time past can never be recovered.* (That goes back to Chaucer.)

*The sleeping fox catches no poultry, and there will be sleeping enough in the grave.*

Those are worth keeping in memory, and principally because it is possible to keep them in memory. With the more "literary" ones, that is not the case. They are not to be remembered and said, but read.

After the true proverb there come the proverbial comparisons and pro-

*Raceland, Louisiana, 1938:*
*back bar and proverbial advice*

verbial phrases. These are not as tightly controlled or fixed by any means as the true proverb, and they take several forms, ranging from the simple adjectival "dead as a duck," "green as grass," "ugly as sin," "easy as pie," and the adverbial "kick like blazes," "bleed like a stuck pig," "run like mad," "watch like a hawk," to the more advanced "so . . . that" or "more . . . than" patterns. Here American folk speech thoroughly takes over: "He's so stingy he'd chase a mouse to hell for a punkin seed," "He's got more brass than a burglar."

In order to control their materials, folklorists have catalogued proverbs and proverbial phrases alphabetically, as, for example, Frances Barbour has done in her *Proverbs and Proverbial Phrases of Illinois*, selecting the chief noun of the proverb by way of index:

> A — *Never say A without B.*
> (Never begin something you do not intend to proceed with.)
>
> ABC — *Simple as ABC.*
>
> ABE — *Honest as Abe.*
>
> ABSENCE — *Absence makes the heart grow fonder.*
> *Conspicuous by its absence.*
>
> ACCIDENT — *Accidents will happen.*
> *He looked like an accident going somewhere to happen.*
>
> ACE — *An ace in the hole.*
> *Ace of trumps.*
> *Black as the ace of spades.*
>
> ACORN — *Great oaks from little acorns grow.*
> *Like stealing acorns from a blind pig.*

Other students have sorted proverbs by subject: death, women, war, medicine, weather, food, work, industry, folly, stupidity, marriage, and so on. By way of example, these on women from around the world:

*Woman is a calamity, but no house ought to be without this evil.* (Persia)

*Taking an eel by its tail and a woman at her word leaves little in the hand.* (Sweden)

*The tongue of a woman is a sword which never rusts.* (Japan)

*Beware of beautiful women as you would of red pepper.* (Japan)

*It is better to have a disorderly wife than to remain a bachelor.* (Sudan)

*The wiles of women which are known to men are ninety and nine, and not even Satan has discovered the hundredth.* (Nigeria)

*It is better to put out to sea in a leaking boat than to entrust a secret to a woman.* (Russia)

*Beat your wife with the butt end of an axe. If she falls down, sniffs and gasps, she is deceiving; give her some more.* (Russia)

*A beautiful woman smiling means a pocketbook weeping.* (Italy)

*When buying horses or taking a wife, shut your eyes tight and commend yourself to God.* (Italy)

*It is much easier to take care of a sackful of fleas than a woman.* (Hungary)

*Adam ate the apple, and our teeth ache from it.* (Hungary)

*A woman has seventy-seven thoughts at once.* (Czechoslovakia)

*When a woman whistles, seven churches tremble.* (Czechoslovakia)

*When three women agree, the stars will come out in broad daylight.* (India)

*Where women are honored, there the gods are pleased.* (Arabia)

*For sweetness, honey; for love, a wife.* (India)

None of the above are from the United States, but we do have our own:

*All women look the same after the sun goes down.*

*Every woman is wrong until she cries, and then she is right instantly.*

*You can't marry a widow because the widow marries you.*

*Matrimony is an insane idea on the part of a man to pay some woman's board.*

*All that is required in the enjoyment of love or sausages is confidence.*

Women's Lib may scream about these, but they are there and cannot be erased. I do not think there is much hurt in them. I think as many women are amused by them as men. It is possibly only the insecure who tremble.

A third approach to the proverb and the related proverbial phrases is the collection and study of them geographically, that is, by country, state, county, and town. This makes good sense. It gives us some idea of what makes a particular region or community tick.

I give here selected proverbs and proverbial phrases collected in half a dozen or more States. Many of them are general and found all over the lot. Some, however, are purely local. Check them for yourself. They are quite wonderful. They are America:

## *Maine*

From the WPA files in the Library of Congress:

*He's as awkward as a cow with a musket.*

*So mean he'd steal a fly from a blind spider.*

*It's raining pitchforks and barn shovels.*

*He hasn't the brains God gave geese.*

*We don't want cats here that can't catch mice.*
(No lazy persons wanted on this job.)

*He doesn't know how many beans make five.*

*You'd better quit before you begin.*

*You can't teach your grandmother to suck eggs.*
(This is universal and constantly baffles me: why the phrase?)

*He flies around like a parched pea in a hot skillet.*
(Many, many of these phrases are incredibly descriptive, earthy. Would you not give a day's wages to meet the man who created that one? And the next?)

*Hottern'n love in haying time.*

*Strong as a horse.*

*Blind as a bat.*

*Slick as an eel.*

*Hungry as a bear.*

*Busy as a bee.*

*Slick as a whistle.* (Remember making one out of small elm?)

*Crazy as a loon.*

*Flatter than a flounder.*

*Sly as a fox.*

*Mad as a hatter.*

*Slow as cold molasses.* (January in Maine.)

*Stubborn as a mule.*

*Slick as a weasel.*

*Mad as a wet hen.*

*Thin as a rail.*

*Warm as toast.*

*Snug as a bug in a rug.*
(Nowhere else in the English language will you find "ug" reaching such classic heights.)

*Fog as thick as pea soup.*
(Anywhere off the coast of Maine. That could not come from Iowa or Nebraska or the Dakotas. It is a sea simile.)

*Keep your chin up.*

*Apple pie order; neat as apple pie.*
(In New England still, pies are placed in a cool pie cupboard in the cellar, neatly ordered in rows. A line of ships going into battle has been described as moving "in apple pie order.")

*You never can tell by the looks of a cat how far he can jump.*

*He's too slow to catch a cold.*

*Never trouble trouble till trouble troubles you.*

*Make hay while the sun shines.*
(That goes back to fifteenth-century England.)

*It's an ill wind that blows no good.*
(Every wind must blow some good: at the outer edge of a hurricane the wind will be gentle and send ships on their way.)

*If you don't do any more than you are paid for,*
*You won't get paid for any more than you do.* (Pure Yankee.)

*If you believe all you hear,*
*You can eat all you see.*

*You can't teach an old dog new tricks.*
(That comes out of England, of course, and so do many others from Maine.)

*A stitch in time saves nine.*

*A new broom sweeps clean, but an old broom gets in the corners.*
("A new broom sweeps clean": I wonder how many men have lost jobs simply because others have followed the proverb.)

*Better late than never,*
*But better never late.*

*You can catch more flies with molasses than you can with vinegar.*
(The normal proverb has "honey," but this is New England and the ships coming up from the West Indies.)

*One swallow doesn't make a summer.*

*Helpless as spilled beans on a dresser.*

*The early bird catches the worm.*

*You can lead a horse to water, but you can't make him drink.*

*You can't have your cake and eat it.*

And this is certainly Maine:

*Don't wait for your ship to come in. Row out and get it!*

And still another:

*Don't worry about why a black hen lays a white egg. Get the egg!*

## Tennessee

Gathered by Herbert Halpert:

*So tight she screaks.* (Screaks: a great word.)

*Hotter than firecrackers on the Fourth of July.*

*Like two shoats in a churn.* (Insanely busy.)

*Looks like something the cat dragged in.*

*Looks like death warmed over.*

*Looks like death eating crackers.*

*Running around like a chicken with its head cut off.*

*Bright as a new penny.*

*"Independent as a hog on ice"*

*Independent as a hog on ice.*
(The saying has moved to Tennessee, but it belongs in New England.)

*As clean as a hound's tooth.*

*Drunk as a fiddler's bitch.*

*Crooked as a barrel of snakes.*

*As hot as a June bride in a featherbed.*

*Playful as a kitten.*

*Close [tight] as the bark on a tree.*

*Doesn't know beans when the sack is open.*

## *Texas*

Collected by George D. Hendricks, who must know and love his land:

*The past is a bucket of ashes.*

*You can't get dollars by pinching nickels.*

*So drunk he couldn't find his ass with both hands.*

*Mouth tastes like a brown Airedale.*

*So dumb he couldn't tell beans from buzzard tails.*

*Sure as God made little apples.*

*Pretty as bluebonnets on a hill.* (How beautiful that is!)

*Cute as a bug's ear.*

*Surprised as a calf looking at a new gate.* (Picture that.)

*Sweet as cherry pie.*

*Happy as a pig in a peanut patch.*

*As far as Hell and back.*

*Easy as pie.*

*Crazy as a professor with nine degrees.*

*Right as rain.*

*So lazy he wouldn't holler "sooey" if the hogs were eating his toes.*

*So drunk he couldn't hit the floor with his hat.*

*So stupid he couldn't tell his ass from page eight.*
(I like that. Not page three or seven, but eight.)

*So sick he was afraid he wouldn't die.*

*Happy as if he had good sense.*

*Busy as a tumblebug in a cow track.*

*So slow he couldn't herd turtles.*

*I feel like I've been s——t at and hit.*

*God made Texas when he was a small boy wanting a sandbox.*
(Oh Texas, Texas!)

*An empty wagon rattles the most.*

*The noblest sight on earth is a man talking reason and his wife listening to him.*

*Stay away from the proud man who is ashamed to weep.*

*There's no such thing as the fastest gun.*

*Less than the self-righteous man is the deadly but honest rattlesnake to be feared.* (The phrasing is non-folk; the sentiment is.)

*Misfortune, like the rattler, does not always give warning before striking.*

*Crooked as a barrel of fishhooks.*

*Rain like a cow pissing from a forty-foot ledge on solid flat flintrock.*

And more Texas (collected by Mary Jourdan Atkinson):

*He might as well be singing psalms over a dead horse as trying to make a doctor out of that boy.*

*I've seen wilder heifers than you milked in a gourd, ma'am.*
(I like that genteel "ma'am"; it softens all.)

*He amounts to about as much as a notch on a stick and the stick thrown away.*

*When he says "frog," she jumps.*

*He has about as much use for that as a hog does for a sidesaddle.*

*He couldn't sell ice water in hell.*

*His feathers fell off when I told him that.*

*It's raining bullfrogs and heifer yearlings.*

*That rain was a gully-washer and fence-lifter.*

*It made a noise like pourin' peas on a dried cowhide.*

And the next few, also from Texas (collected by A. W. Eddins):

*Cut your peaches, gals; thunder ain't rain.*

*Short visits make long friends.*

*Talk is cheap but it takes money to buy whiskey.*

*She'll soon wish she was back under her mammy's bed playing with the cats.* (Don't ever tell me the folk have no feeling for language.)

## New York State

These are chiefly from Harold W. Thompson and his good book *Body, Boots, and Britches*:

*Never speak loudly to one another unless the house is on fire.*

*They'll never comb gray hair together.*
(Of a quarrelsome couple. How more succinctly, gently, and aptly could you phrase the situation?)

*The world is your cow, but you have to do the milking.*

*God sends every bird its food, but He does not throw it into the nest.*

*Dirty hands make clean money.*

*A young man idle and an old man needy.*

*Woman's work: Well, I must wash, iron, bake, and make a shirt for Will.*

*Reach for the high apples first; you can get the lower ones any time.*

*He doesn't know twice around a broomstick.*

*He doesn't know enough to suck alum and drool.*

*He doesn't know enough to pull his head in when he shuts the window.*

*A drunk man will sober up, but damn a fool.*

*Sicker cats than that have been cured.*

*It's all down hill after the Equator.* (From the Navy.)

*Feels like being nibbled to death by ducks.*

*Pity is a poor plaster.* (Can you phrase that in any way better?)

*There's no help for misfortune but to marry again.*

*A liar needs a good memory.*

*Sue a beggar and catch a louse.*

*An apple never falls far from the tree.*

*Hope is a good breakfast but a bad supper.*

*When drums speak out, laws hold their tongues.*
(Compare Herman Melville: "When a ship of any nation is running into action, it is no time for argument, small time for justice, and not much time for humanity.")

*Give a pig when it grunts and a child when it cries, and you will have a fine pig and a bad child.*

*Big as life and twice as natural.*

*Handy as a hog with a fiddle.*

*Happy as a skunk in a hen roost.*

*So thin you have to shake the sheets to find her.*

*Tight as a blonde's belt.* (Why that?)

*Fits like a saddle on a sow.*

*Makes more noise than a boatload of calves.*

*Face long enough to eat oats out of a churn.*

*He's scared skinny.* (You will not forget that.)

*There's no disgrace in poverty, but it's damned inconvenient.*

*Say something plunk and plain.*

## New Mexico

Collected and reported by folklorist T. M. Pearce:

*A quick nickel is better than a slow dollar.*

*He can count to 20 if he takes his shoes off.*

*This gal wasn't no bigger than a pound of soap after an all-day washin'.*

*Give some people everything you have, and they still want the moon for a cow pasture.*

*Down to chili and beans.* (Down to his last cent.)

*He's all gurgle and no gut.*

*It sure is hell when it's this way, and it's this way now.*

*If you marry an Englishman, your children will never blow pipes.*
(Pure Scotch, that.)

*She can shovel it out the back door faster than her husband can bring it in the front.*

*As crooked as a crock of guts.*

*If you gave some people a free beer, they would want an egg in it.*

*So drunk he didn't know whether he was riding or flying a kite.*

*It scared me pea-green and purple.*

*She's as pretty as a red heifer in a flower bed.*

*He was the big bug under the cow chip.*
(A person who considered himself important.)

*He's the whole team — the little dog under the wagon.* (The same.)

## Mississippi

Collected by Ernest Cox:

*I'm not fit to drive a hen from the door.* (Fairly sick.)

*So green that when it rains, he'll sprout.*

*As smart as forty crickets.*

*Grinning like a jackass eating briars.*

*Poor as a lizard-eating cat.*

*He looks like the tail end of bad luck.*

## Nebraska

Noted by Ruth Odell:

*She's all painted up like a new saloon.*

*I knew him when he used to be able to get his hat on.*

*Stick around a while, we're going to open a keg of nails.*
(Hardly an invitation.)

## North Carolina

Gathered by Joseph D. Clark, George P. Wilson, and Leonidas Betts:

*As sorry as a worn-out shoe.*
(I like the Southern use of "sorry." You do not find it in New England.)

*Tall as a Georgia pine.*

*Long as a country mile.*

*He wouldn't give you air if you were in a jug.*

*Empty barrels make the loudest noise.*

*Beauty won't make the pot boil.*

*Beauty is only skin deep.*

*All over hell and half of Georgia.*

*Believe half you see and nothing you hear.*
(Or also: One see is worth twenty hears.)

*The blacker the berry, the sweeter the juice.*

*Your mother wears combat boots.*

*More fun than pushing little biddies into the creek.*

*Sounds like a dying calf in a hailstorm.*

*I wouldn't know him from Adam's housecat.*

*Worse than a suck-egg hound.*

*Don't die on third.*

*Naked as a jaybird.*

*He's going to hell as straight as a blue-wing hawk.*
(The beauty of that, as with many of these, lies in the specific "blue-wing." It is "page eight" again.)

*Don't measure my bushel by your peck.*

*Never dance with the mate if you can dance with the captain.*

*To fling a Joe Blizzard fit.*
(Joe Blizzard lived in Kipling, North Carolina, and was known for his violent temper. The saying, until collected by Betts, had been a purely local one. It deserves national adoption.)

*No bigger than a gnat's ass.*

*Bless the bridge that carries you over.* (A toast? Advice?)

*Little boats must keep to the shore.*

*An idle brain is the devil's workshop.*
(Which is why captains encouraged scrimshaw on the long whaling voyages.)

*If you want a thing done, go; if not, send.*

*Gone back to get another armful.* (Said of intermittent weather.)


# Massachusetts

These were collected at the turn of the century:

*Don't stay till the last dog's hung.*

*The still pig eats the swill.*

*No man dies without an heir.*

*There's as much odds in folks as there is in anybody.*

*A short horse is soon curried.*

*Dung hills rise and castles fall.*

*Doesn't know enough to be assistant janitor to a corn crib.*

*Don't need it any more than a cow does two tails.*

*To feel like a stewed witch.* (The morning after.)

*There's no more peace here than for a cat in hell without claws.*

*Let them skin their own skunks.*

*God Almighty's overcoat wouldn't make him a vest.*

*As Irish as Biddy Murphy's pig.*

*Strong enough to float an egg.* (Tea, soup, coffee. . . .)

## The Ozarks

Out of the Ozarks (which comes from the French "Aux Arks" — *Arks:* the shortened form for the Indian Arkansas), Vance Randolph has collected a prodigious number of proverbial phrases and ways of speech. A few of them:

A fat little man with a square head and no neck worth mentioning was under discussion: "*He looks like a young jug with a cork in it.*"

Of an untidy chap: "*He looks like he's been chawin' terbacker, and spittin' ag'in the wind.*"

*He walks like he was belly-deep in cold water.*

*Empty as a dead man's eye.*

Of a man who had just been stung by yellow jackets: "*He was actin' like a windmill gone to the bad.*"

A backwoods dandy commented complacently: "*Them Bear Holler gals is a-chasin' me like pigs after a punkin!*"

In Boone County, Arkansas, a barefoot young farmer said to his sweetheart: "*The days when I don't git to see you are plumb squandered away and lost, like beads off'n a string.*" (Beautiful!)

When a country boy wanted to marry the banker's daughter, he encountered considerable opposition. "*By God, I'll wade knee-deep in blood, an' nobody cain't stop me!*" he shouted. "*I'll get that gal if I have to tear the stars out of heaven!*"

Of difficult and hazardous enterprises:

"*It's as easy as puttin' butter up a wildcat's ass with a hot awl!*"

"*I'd just as soon shin up a thorn tree with a armload of eels!*"

"*It's a good deal like climbin' a greased pole with two baskets of eggs.*"

A fellow in Baxter County, Arkansas, professed an enormous dislike for the Robinson family. *"Hell is so full of Robinsons,"* said he, *"that you can see their feet stickin' out of the winders."*

*"That man is so contrary that if you throwed him in the river, he'd float upstream."*

*"Why, there ain't room enough to cuss a cat without gettin' ha'r in your mouth."*

Discussing a young woman's occupation: *"A waitress!"* he cried. *"Why, she ain't got manners enough to carry guts to a bear."*

*"My man's kinfolks don't amount to a poot in a whirlwind!"*

*"This world is a goose, and them that do not pick will get no feathers."*

On a very hot day, an old woman said: *"Ain't it awful? I feel like hell ain't a mile away and the fences all down!"*

When a neighbor's wife kept pestering him for an automobile, the husband cried out, *"Car! Where in hell would I get a car? You think I can run it out of a hole with a ferret?"*

*"To listen at Jim Henson talk,"* said a quiet little man, *"you'd think he could put out hell with one bucket of water."*

Commenting on the demoralizing effect of alcohol, a farmer in Benton County, Arkansas, remarked: *"Everybody's lappin' up this here moonshine nowadays. Some of these young gals from town get to drinkin' it, an' layin' out nights, an' the first thing you know they're a-givin' milk!"*

A farmer, listening to a foul-mouthed politician: *"That feller reminds me of the time the skunks littered under our barn."*

An old man, expecting to die soon: *"It won't be long till they'll be puttin' the green quilt over me."*

A hillman took a drink out of a jug, and sighed happily. *"That stuff is so good a feller cain't hardly bite it off."* Another expert agreed: *"That's the pure quill, you can smell the feet of the boys that plowed the corn!"*

*"Her tongue was always a-waggin' like the south end of a goose."*

*"You look like a sick dog with a thorn in his foot."*

*"He looked like the hindquarters of bad luck."*

Of a restless, amorous young hillman: *"Tom he just goes a-roamin' 'round like a bug on a hot night."*

A country boy so frightened *"his teeth was a-rattlin' like a hog eatin' charcoal."*

*"My son-in-law's so lazy that he stops plowin' to poot!"*

*"My brother is so unlucky, it would be money in his pocket if he'd never been born!"*

Tantalized by a provocative but recalcitrant young woman, a hillman suddenly burst out: *"I cain't stand no more of this. It's like smellin' whiskey through a jail-house winder!"*

One of our young men grabbed a pretty schoolteacher and tried to "wrastle her down," but she kicked him in the stomach and knocked the wind plumb out of him. *"That schoolmarm like to ruined me,"* he complained. *"I just stood there with my mouth open like a widder-woman's pig!"*

## Oregon

These were collected by Helen M. Pearce and reported in "Folk Sayings in a Pioneer Family of Western Oregon." The pioneer family in question came overland in the 1850's and had roots in England, Ireland, Maryland, and Illinois:

*That looks like last year's bird's nest.*
(And some have it "with the bottom punched out.")

*He's coming head 'n' tail up.* (Really hurrying.)

*She's got a hen on.* (Hatching up some scheme.)

*He thinks he's some punkins.*

*He's pretty small potatoes.*

*It's as handy as a pocket in a shirt.* (Any convenient gadget.)

*He got cut off at the pockets.* (Cool reception, or fired.)

*She's got eight acres of Hell in her.*
(A determined and pugnacious woman. Again, the specifics and the feeling for words: "eight acres.")

*He didn't know straight up when he saw it.*

*He knew everybody and why they left Missouri.* (The early West.)

*He's struck pay dirt.* (Mining country.)

*The wheel that squeaks the loudest gets the grease.* (Freighting country.)

*He's on the skids.* (Lumber country.)

## *Kentucky*

From separate collections by Gordon Wilson, George Boswell, and Herbert Halpert:

*That animal ought to have his tail cut off right behind his ears.*

*He was raised in a barn with the north door open.*

*He doesn't know beans from bird eggs.* (Beans pop up all over the place.)

*If you can't talk, shake a bush.*

*Nobody knows the come-out of a lousy calf.*

*She throws chicken fits.*

*If his brains were in a bird's head, the bird would fly backwards.*

*The more you see some people, the better you like dogs.*

*A man who kicks his dog will beat his wife.* (Quite probably true.)

*She drove her ducks to a poor pond.*
(Did not marry as well as she might have.)

*Fine words butter no parsnips.*

*Nothing but money is sweeter than honey.*
(Nice rhythm, nice rhyme, and clear thinking.)

*Drunk as a covey of boiled owls.* (It would be amusing to see that covey.)

*He's small potatoes and few to the hill.* (Virtually nothing.)

*He's all vine and no 'taters.* (Even less.)

*The sweeter the rose, the sharper the thorns.*

*Cute as a speckled pup under a red wagon.* (Nice?)

*I'm so hungry I could eat a sow and six pigs.*

*He may look citified, but he's still got a tick in his navel.*
(That will cut you back.)

*Dark as seven black cats in a sack.*
(The balanced choice of words again: "dark" not "black.")

*Thicker'n fiddlers in hell.*

*You wouldn't know beans if you had your head in the pot.*

*He lives so far back in the hills, they have to wipe the owl s—t off the clock to see what time it is.*
(Wonderful words. Wonderful. It would be nice to know the individual who created them, and those who must certainly have enjoyed them on the spot. We must forever be indebted to Halpert for finding and preserving this gem.)

From eastern Kentucky, collected by Leonard Roberts:

*So drunk he looked like he was walking on eggs.*
(Very, very precise in his motion.)

*So foolish if you put his brains in a cricket's head, it would run back'ards.*

*So forgetful he'd leave his hind end if it was loose.*

*Runs so gentle it sounds like a lamb a-sucking.*

*Times are so hard a quarter looks like a wagon wheel.*

*So grumpy he don't do a thing but set in the chimley corner, rock his shoe toe, and whistle hard times.*

*Farm so steep he can look down the chimley and see what his old woman is fixing for supper.*

## Louisiana

From Congressman T. A. Thompson at Julie Hall's Restaurant in Washington, D.C.:

*It takes a carpenter to build a barn, but any jackass can kick one down.*

*If you get in a fight with a skunk, you're bound to come out smelling a little.*

## Illinois

From Frances M. Barbour's work:

*Doesn't know beans from buckshot.*

*So drunk he couldn't hit his ass with a handful of sand.*

*Better go supperless to bed than rise in debt.*

*Beware of him who has nothing to lose.*

*You can take the boy out of the country, but you can't take the country out of the boy.* (I seem to have heard something like that around somewhere.)

*He's walking in high cotton.* (Doing very well.)

*Drunker than seven hundred dollars.*

*So hoarse he talked like a duck with a dumpling in its mouth.*

*She pounced on it like a duck on a June bug.*

*Creep and creep beats hop and sleep.*
(The tortoise as over against the hare.)

*She acts as if she were Mrs. Jesus Christ.*

*Good, better, best!*
*Never let it rest*
*Until your good is better*
*And your better, best.*

*Let him stew in his own juice.*
(Chaucer; Wife of Bath's Prologue: "That in his owen grece I made hym frye. . . .")

*Chatters like a chipmunk.*

*Between the devil and the deep blue sea.*

*It will be a cold day in hell before. . . .*

*Like a bat out of hell.*

*Half past cornbread and going on biscuits.* (I'm hungry, mother.)

*When in doubt, don't.*

*Drunk as a fiddler's bitch.*
(Them crazy fiddlers and their dogs! Again and again and again.)

*Raining cats and dogs.*

*As much chance as a snowball in hell.*

## California

Collected by Owen S. Adams:

*Back up and grease!* (Prepare for a job before starting work on it.)

*The men and dogs for the barn, the women and cats for the kitchen.*

*He was biggest when he was hatched.* (Hasn't measured up to his promise.)

*He doesn't know if he's going, coming, or standing still.*

*It's impossible to make a two-year-old-calf in a minute.*

(In spite of what some of our students may believe, there is no such thing as instant Utopia.)

*One is afraid, and the other dassn't.*

*Make haste slowly.*

*There is a Jack for every Jill.*

## Idaho

Collected by Herbert Halpert, who happily for us moved around the country a bit:

*Poor people have poor ways, but rich ones have damn mean ones.*

*Well, there goes a ten-dollar Stetson on a five-cent head.*

## Pennsylvania

Collected by Mac E. Barrick:

*All mixed up worse than a dog's breakfast.*

*No bigger than a minute.*

*As easy as one-two-three.*

*You look like the running gears of hard times.*

*Like a wart on a pickle.*

*Arms going like windmills.*

*Girls with fat cheeks have hearts like flint.*

*The quickest way to do many things is to do one thing at a time.*

*It's a poor road that doesn't have an inn at the end of it. (From Ireland?)*

*Dead, and too dumb to fall over.*

*Even a blind pig finds an acorn sometime.*

Rabelais made a full chapter out of proverbs in his *Gargantua*. François Villon wrote a *ballade* composed of them. Without the earthy proverbs of Sancho Panza, the *Don Quixote* of Cervantes could not be. Pieter Breughel has a painting in which, in the single scene, there are more than one hundred proverbs of his time alive in his great color. Herman Melville, James Fenimore Cooper, William Faulkner, Thomas Wolfe, Mark Twain, Erskine Caldwell . . . name them.

Francis Bacon said that "the genius, wit, and spirit of a nation are discovered in its proverbs."

I think we can believe him. As it applies to Texas and Massachusetts and Idaho and Maine . . . and America.

# American Names

Place Names
Names of Western Mining Camps and Mines
Cattle Brands
Quilt Names
Names of Ozark Fiddle Tunes
Names of Racehorses
Hound Dog Names
Nicknames

# 6.

# *Place Names*

All of our writers with any roots in the land have loved American names: Faulkner, Wolfe, Whitman ("*Mississippi!* the word winds with chutes — it rolls a stream three thousand miles long . . . *Monongahela!* it rolls with venison richness upon the palate"), Sandburg, Benét ("I have fallen in love with American names . . ."), MacLeish ("The Cinquecento is nothing at all like Nome/or Natchez or Wounded Knee or the Shenandoah"). Robert Louis Stevenson stated it clearly in *Across the Plains* in 1892:

There is no part of the world where nomenclature is so rich, poetical, humorous, and picturesque as the United States of America. All times, races and languages have brought their contribution. Pekin is in the same State with Euclid, with Bellfontaine, and with Sandusky. The names of the States them-

*Boundary County, Idaho, 1939:*
*the crossroads names are West*

selves form a chorus of sweet and most romantic vocables: Delaware, Ohio, Indiana, Florida, Dakota, Iowa, Wyoming, Minnesota, and the Carolinas: there are few poems with a nobler music for the ear: a songful, tuneful land.

The history of the land is in the names, and remembered in the names without the need of books or teachers. The word-of-mouth names: Chickamauga, Concord, Manassas, Sumter, Valley Forge, Gettysburg, Abilene, Dodge, Mount Vernon, Appomattox, Antietam, Philadelphia, Salem, Richmond, Mobile. We take them for granted, but we know them. And we are here because of them.

As with Robert Louis Stevenson, but more so because we are Americans, it is difficult not to be moved (put it positively: it is our privilege to be moved) by the roll call of the States as we listen to them called forth with the power of democracy at the National Conventions:

> Alabama!
> Alabama casts ten ballots . . .
>
> Arkansas!
> Arkansas votes . . .
>
> Idaho!
> Idaho casts all its votes for . . .
>
> Iowa!
> Iowa casts twenty ballots . . .
>
> Utah!
> Utah passes . . .
>
> Wyoming!
> Wyoming votes . . .

It is utterly fantastic and incredible that we should be so lucky. Not lucky, really. It came to us the hard way: from Lexington to Normandy, from the Wilderness to Kasserine. Not lucky, really: the power of democracy: we are the only nation in the history of the world where peoples have asked by vote to join another, to be part of us: Alaska, Hawaii. They had the opportunity to vote either way. They voted to be with us. (Czechoslovakia? Hungary? Romania?) When Patton's troops moved through Sicily from Africa to Europe, the Sicilian people for a brief moment thought happily and madly and with love that they could become a part of the United States. They would at that time have voted that way with a wild and ecstatic frenzy. (Lithuania? Latvia? Esthonia? Do they even exist?)

I make no apology for "editorializing" in the preceding paragraph or two. It is part of our treasure of names — powerful and lovely.

> New Hampshire!
> New Hampshire votes . . .
>
> New Mexico!
> New Mexico casts all its ballots . . .
>
> North Dakota!
> North Dakota votes . . .

Places need names first. The associations and connotations come later. They need names simply, to begin with, for identification purposes. "I'll meet you at . . ." The fork in the road? Smith's Corners? Georgetown? Fifth and Fifty-seventh? They come into being very casually or quite consciously. Casually: "You know where that gravelly ford is near Brown's place . . ." Gravelly Ford. Consciously: "We shall name it New Bedford . . . New Haven . . . New York . . ."

By way of broad generalization, the names casually and informally given and accepted lean more to the folk side than those formally and consciously stamped upon the land.

Place names are created in a variety of ways:

*Surnames* given to the land are among the commonest, and they can be divided into two broad groups. The one contains the names of *founders and settlers*, knowledge of whom is almost purely local and who may actually be all but forgotten except for the place name itself: Hyattsville, Hagerstown, Spencer, Jackson Corners, Hogansville, Butler, Dawson, Millidgeville, Barnwell, Russellville, Felton, Malone, Woodward, Hammon, McKinney, Smithtown Center, Brentwood, Selden, and so on indefinitely. These names are to be found by the thousands in every state and every county in the United States.

The second group of *surnames* found on the maps are those honoring *historical or otherwise important personages*, many of them quite naturally associated with patriotic events in the United States: Washington, Franklin, Lincoln, Leesburg, Monroe, Madison, Lafayette, Baltimore (Lord Baltimore), Calvert County (Lord Calvert), Raleigh (Sir Walter), Delaware (Lord de la Ware), Georgetown (George II), Annapolis (Queen Anne), Virginia (named by and for Queen Elizabeth, the Virgin Queen), Ouray and Winnemucca (Indian chiefs in, respectively, Utah and Nevada), Carson City (Kit Carson), Denver, Reno. These and others like them, out of a belief in the continuity of the nation and its history, are to be found in every state and in the majority of counties.

A second grouping — and these are chiefly along the eastern seaboard — are the *English place names of the Old World* brought by the first settlers to the New. One can understand their reasoning: the use of the names of the towns of their origins was a strong link and comfort in a strange land (the umbilical cord was not yet cut), and they also carried the pride of their past and heritage with them. "Let us name these places for the places of our birth and our growing up, so that our children . . ." They are many, and many of the names also had constant rebirth when later pioneers moved out of the eastern towns and carried the names west. But in the East they were: Portland, Portsmouth, Boston, Plymouth, *New* Bedford, Middlesex, Worcester, *New* Hampshire, *New* Haven, Hartford, *New* London, *New* York, Southampton, Westchester, Bath, Yarmouth, Dover, Gloucester, Exeter, Epping, Richmond, Marlborough, Greenwich, Milford, Cambridge, Dartmouth, and so on. There were Dutch town names (Haarlem and Niew Amsterdam) and French (New Orleans) brought over, but they were not nearly as numerous as those of the English. Like the Spanish names, their names were, by and large, not the names of Old World places but names freshly given here.

A third division are the *"foreign"* names, *chiefly Spanish* and *French*. Very few of these recall towns or cities in Spain or France, and the reason is twofold: first, the names were given by explorers (not settlers) who described the land for purposes of remembering it and for the recognition of those who might come after: Sierra Nevada (snowy mountain range), El

Río Grande (the big river), Las Vegas (the plains), Detroit (the narrows), Boise (the woods), Mount Desert (the bald or unwooded hills of the Maine island); and second, the Spanish and French explorers were accompanied by priests who saw to it that the great names of the Faith were implanted on the land: Santa Barbara, San Diego, San Francisco, Santa Cruz, San Juan Bautista, St. Lawrence, St. Croix. These names preempted those of the towns and cities of the Old World.

Considering these names, it is instructive to look at a map of the United States and — without reference to the history books — to see there the imprint and extent of (for example) Spanish penetration, conquest, and settlement. In the East it is Florída, Cape Canaveral,* and St. Augustine, but in the West it is more evident. From Las Cruces, New Mexico, the tide of Spanish conquest and exploration moved north into central Colorado, where the Spanish names begin to peter out at La Junta and Pueblo and where the line ends at Buena Vista, Salida, and the northern reaches of the Sangre de Cristo Mountains. The names are rich in legend and history: Socorro, Belén, Las Animas, Albuquerque, Santa Fe, Santa Rosa, Alamogordo, Trinidad.

In Arizona, the Spanish names move north by way of the San Pedro and Gila Rivers, north from Nogales, Casa Grande, Mesa, and by way of the San Francisco Peaks into southern Utah. Here the line ends abruptly save for the memory of Escalante's expedition in 1776 — a town is named for him — and for the American name of Spanish Forks, south of Salt Lake, which the Spaniards never saw. The land was barren and dry, poorer than the land to the south. And so was Nevada, and the Spanish names there are few — Las Vegas, Alamo, Caliente, the Amargosa Desert (the bitter desert) — all in the south. But the great rivers that rise in the Rockies and flow through the dry states to the sea, one to the Pacific and one to the Atlantic, were named by them — the Rio Grande and the Colorado. So also were the mountains to the west, from which Nevada takes its name.

As for California, one need only follow the coastline north from Mexico: every other name is Spanish from Coronado to San Francisco. And in the San Francisco Bay area alone: San Rafael, San Pedro, San Pablo, El Cer-

---

* Cape Canaveral: reduced now to Kennedy. I think the late President, with his sense of history, would himself have opposed the change of name, one of the very earliest map-given names, closely following The Tortugas and Florída, named by De Soto in 1513.

rito, San Leandro, San Bruno, San Mateo, Palo Alto, Vallejo, Santa Clara, San Jose — to name only the well known. The Spanish names on the Western coast are, in effect, a balance to those of the English in the East.

A fourth name-group (and these are quite non-folk in their bestowal) are those drawn from *classical and ancient world sources*. The prize here, of course, goes to upper York State: Ithaca, Utica, Syracuse, Rome, Troy, Corinth, Athens, Ovid, Homer, Brutus, Cato, Cicero, Pompey, Ulysses, Virgil, Egypt, Carthage, Babylon, Tyre, Phoenicia — to list perhaps a tenth of them. They are concentrated here, but they appear elsewhere in the land: Athens (Georgia), Memphis (Tennessee), Alexandria (Virginia), Cairo (Illinois). Harold Thompson in his *Body, Boots, and Britches* — a most readable and informative book on upstate York life and folklife — has pleasant things to say about the New York naming. The names are, of course, part of the total American scene, but when one lines them up one after the other — without bothering to separate them by York hills and miles — they read like a Saratoga racing form or the jottings of a doodling classicist. Of interest, but not stemming from the land. And yet they belong to the land, now.

Almost entirely folk are the following ways of naming the land:

First is the *naming based on the physical geography of the country, frequently descriptive*: Camelback Mountain, Rabbit Ears Pass, Painted Desert, Six-Mile Canyon, Midnight Mesa, Powder River (from its gunpowder-like sand), Crater Lake, Flowing Wells, Hat Mountain, Lone Butte, Great Salt Lake, Grand Junction (where the Gunnison and Colorado rivers join), Chimney Rock, Black Canyon, Rocky Ford, White River, Pyramid Lake (with its perfect rock pyramid rising out of the water), Thimble Mountain, Hardscrabble Hill (very poor land), Blue River. The Spaniards and the Indians (and all men, for that matter) named the land in this fashion. Horace Beck in his *Folklore of Maine* gives a number of examples from that coast:

A light-colored island is White Island, while one that is black-ribbed becomes Iron Bound, and one that looks like the stern of a frigate, Shipstern. Two round islets close together are the Double Shots, while a low, grassy isle is Green Island. A small island with a couple of trees is Two Bush or, if one tree, One Bush. A limestone island that looks like a horse's head is White

Horse and its mate of granite, Black Horse, while a rock in between becomes Colt Island. A spoon-shaped island is Spoon Island.

Off Portland are the Hue and Cry ledges. These are

two groups of twin ledges. The first ledge in each case breaks the sea's back, and it goes roaring on to break again with lessened violence on the next ledge. These are the East and West Hue and Cry ledges.

Those are exceptional names. One more from the New England coast:

At the entrance to Buzzard's Bay, on the starboard hand, is a reef with a number of rocks showing above high water with a large rock at the extremity. In a northeaster these rocks look like a family of pigs rooting in the surf and, because of the bottom, the breakers sometimes make a squealing sound as they pile in. This is the Sow and Pigs Reef. And because sailors had a superstition that if they tattooed a pig on their right foot and a rooster on their left they would, by the nature of the animals, not only be preserved from drowning but be assured of food, a pile of rocks on the port hand entering the bay became Hen and Chickens, and the large boulder at the end became the Old Cock.

The second way of folk-naming, closely related to the preceding, comes from the *flora and fauna on the land:* Coyote Wells, Lone Pine, Cedar Springs, Cottonwood Wash, Sycamore Creek, Bear Valley, Beaver Creek, Aspen, Yucca, Antelope Peak, Grasshopper Flat ("there were a million grasshoppers there . . ."), Eagle Point ("a favorite nesting place for eagles"), Gooseberry Creek, Alder Gulch, Wildcat Hollow, Moosehead Lake, Maple Springs, Blueberry Hill, Chestnut Grove, Wild Horse Canyon. Those were the things that men saw upon the land, and the names followed naturally and readily. There are scores of thousands of these.

A third way of folk-naming was to record *unusual or noteworthy events, activities, and happenings:* Massacre Lake, Deadman Gap, Murderer's Grave, Skull Valley, Skeleton Canyon, Burnt Ranch, Bloody Basin. They are by and large self-explanatory, records of violent death. But it was not necessary that the events be that sensational to be recorded forever on maps. There is Coffeepot Creek in Oregon, named in pioneer days: "A coffeepot fell out of an immigrant's wagon and was run over by a wheel and ruined."

There is Kettle Creek in the same State: "A packhorse belonging to Enoch G. Vaughan and David M. Dennis bucked his pack off and jammed the kettle beyond use. The kettle lay in the water for many years." Wagon Tire Flat in Arizona: "An old wagon tire was for years leaning against a tree on this flat." Patty Houston of Cameron, West Virginia, wrote me: "My mother who is now 86 years old was born about 10 miles south of Washington, Pennsylvania, in a little village then known as Plumsock. The present name of the village is Conger, but I liked the old one which was so named because an old lady's cow set her foot 'plumb sock' in the middle of the pail at milking time." The account is in the folk tradition.

In the WPA manuscript material on Maine in the Library of Congress:

There is a hill in the northwestern part of Gray called Pumpkin Hill. It was given this name by a man named Colley, because Jabez Benson, who lived there, always raised a lot of pumpkins, and a local verse about him went:

> *Jabez raised the pumpkins,*
> *Hannah baked the pie,*
> *Jabez ate so many*
> *He thought to God he'd die.*

And there is still another Pumpkin Hill in Maine on the road from Bowdoin to Bowdoinham:

It was so named because a farmer was hauling a load of pumpkins along the road. He reached the crest of the hill, when the wagon became unhitched from the horses, the wagon upset, and the pumpkins bounced and rolled down the hill, across the field, and into the woods. Ever since, the place has been known as Pumpkin Hill.

There is coastal humor. Beck reports:

South and a little east of Matinicus lies a miserable, cucumber-shaped rock pile with only a few trees and a tiny, exposed, foul harbor, Criehaven, that now bears the name of Ragged Island. We need no story to tell us that some poor fisherman was marooned there during a cold winter's night in the eighteenth century. We know how he thrashed up and down in a vain attempt to keep warm. We know the dark thoughts he had for company in his arduous vigil, and we know, too, that he was rescued safe, sound, and unrepentant. How do we know all this? On a chart issued in 1790 the island appears, not as Ragged Island, but simply Cold Arse.

Before touching upon Indian names (I have left these to the last), there is always the ubiquitous *"miscellaneous"* category. Everything that is left over from all other groupings belongs here. Among the names are those Mencken calls the "purely fanciful": Hot Coffee (Mississippi), Shin Pond (Maine), Shy Beaver (Pennsylvania), Gizzard (Tennessee), and Noodle (Texas). There are also Truth and Consequences (New Mexico) and Santa Claus (Arizona). Some of these are explicable, but I would generally place here all inexplicable names, such as some of Beck's from Maine: Miss Underhill's Chair, Bunker's Whore, the Lecherous Priest, the Tar Pooch, Junk of Pork. There are such curious names in and around every community, and they belong to "miscellaneous" until otherwise stashed away and sorted to satisfaction. Some of them will never be. They pleasure us with conjecture.

Our heritage of *Indian names* is an extraordinary one, and deserves to be more consciously recognized and popularly known. We use the names daily (Mississippi, Allegheny, Monongahela, Susquehanna, Penobscot, Omaha, Cayuga), forgetting the Indian past, with no knowledge of their source or meaning, and little understanding of why they happen to have been preserved. The names are everywhere in the country, and there is no state without them. They are purely folk in creation, and their preservation has also largely been folk — even to malpronunciations and misspellings through folk transmission. The fact that they have been preserved by the hundred thousand testifies clearly to the very close relation and friendly contact between the explorers, pioneers, first settlers and the Indians.

To begin with, the Indian names are "micro-names," in the sense that the Indians (anywhere on the continent) never named full mountains or rivers, but only parts of them. The entire length of the Mississippi, for example, had no meaning whatsoever for tribes living in short sections along its banks: those in the north had no inkling of the length of the river or its mouth at the Gulf, and those to the south knew nothing of the length to the north and its source. There was no large sense of geography. The Indians named what they saw, and they named what was to their use and purpose.

Almost one with philosopher Berkeley: "If it is not visible, it does not exist." A full mountain was not visible; a full river was not visible. Where the Indian stood and what he saw was, of course, visible, and that he named. Then how do the full rivers (Mississippi, Penobscot) take their names? Quite simply. The European explorer, accustomed to the single name for an entire river (the Thames, the Seine), met the first Indians who could give him any name at all at the mouth of a river (Penobscot) or at its source (Mississippi) and, with his European background, assumed that the "micro-name" given him was actually the name for the whole river, whereas in actuality it was simply a local tribal name for a very small segment of the river. Luckily for us these micro-names, enlarged to our greatest rivers, have a pleasing sound; they might have been dreadful had the explorers in each instance started at the other end where a different tribe had a different name.

With the micro-names it is obvious, of course, that the Indians named the land for what they saw on the land and for the identification any one of them needed to inform another. They also named places for events and occurrences. A few samplings will suffice: Meduncook ("the sandy place"), Monhegan ("the faraway island"), Pemaquid ("long point"), Waluga ("wild swan" lake), Schoharie ("driftwood"), Oneonta ("stony place"), Keuka ("boats drawn out" for a portage), Yavapai ("the sun people," an Indian tribe), Vamori ("swamp"), Chilchinbito ("water in the sumacs"), Hassayampa ("place of water and big rocks"), Wyoming ("great plains," originally from Pennsylvania and transferred by act of Congress to the State), Oklahoma ("red people"), Mississippi ("big river"), Arizona (from the Papago *aleh-zon*, "little spring"), Penobscot ("at the sloping rock"), Omaha ("upstream people"), Michigan (from *michi-guma*, "big water"), and Chicago ("place of wild onions").

Consider for a moment the roll call of Indian names in New York State, which, for Harold Thompson, have "the thrill of a Homeric catalogue." The counties: Allegany, Cattaraugus, Cayuga, Chautauqua, Chemung, Chenango, Erie, Genesee, Niagara, Oneida, Onondaga, Ontario, Oswego, Otsego, Saratoga, Schenectady, Schoharie, Seneca, Tioga, Wyoming. The cities: Poughkeepsie, Lackawanna, Cohoes, Ossining, Tonawanda, Oneonta, Mamaroneck, Mineola, Saranac Lake, Canandaigua, Patchogue, Tuckahoe, Cheektowaga, Nyack, Mount Kisco, Hoosick Falls. The Long Island tribes:

the Canarsies, Setaukets, Patchogues, Shinnecocks, Montauks, Manhassetts, Cutchogues, and Rockaways. And Manhattan itself meaning "hilly island."

Such a roll call can be duplicated in every state of the Union. I think it might be good that they be so gathered together for grade school students in each state — to give them some concept of history, of early settlement, of the meanings of the names of their communities and places, and of the white and red man's first relations with each other. It is difficult, now for example, to think that the total Indian population of the State of Maine, according to the 1970 census, is 2,195. There are probably more of their names than that left on the land.

By way of summing up this section, I telephoned Donald J. Orth, who is Chief of the Geographic Names Section of the Department of the Interior, to query him on two points: one, the number of place names (of natural features and populated places) in the United States, and, two, the percentage of those which he estimated to be folk in origin.

To the first question, the number of names, he gave me careful estimates. Based on a thorough across-the-board nationwide sampling of the names on the quadrangle maps of the United States Geological Survey (scale 1:24,000), he conservatively arrived at a figure of two and one-half million names. However, taking into consideration the innumerable creeks and hollows and washes, valleys and hills and one thing and another that never "made it" onto the maps (and also places which have come into being since the maps), he upped his overall total to three and one-half million names. I think this is a good, solid, conservative figure. I would even be willing to raise it by another million, but let us accept the three and a half figure, coming as it does from an authority in the matter.

To the second question, the percentage of those names he considered to be folk in origin, he responded by asking me what I meant by "folk" in this instance. "Those names which have come into being casually and informally, as over against those consciously and formally given to a place — Smith's Corners and Badger Creek, as over against Ithaca and New York." His response was unhesitating and astonishing: "Ninety-five percent."

# 7.

# Names
# of Western Mining Camps
# and Mines

Men's activity on the land is perhaps nowhere more clearly reflected than in the names given to mining camps and to the mines themselves. The names begin with the standard and hopeful "Gold" and "Silver" and are found in all the Western mining states: Gold Hill, Gold Flat, Goldfield, Gold Run, Gold Point, and Gold Springs; Silver City, Silver Creek, Silver Glance, Silver Hill, and Silverton. Tin Cup in Colorado was christened by the prospector who panned the first gold from a drinking cup, the town name setting a modest standard for the later adjoining settlements of Iron Cup, Silver Cup, and Gold Cup. Other towns were not as modestly named: Ophir, Golconda, Eureka, Bonanza.

Virginia City, Nevada, site of the great Comstock Lode, was named by James Fennimore or Finney, one of its early prospectors. Filled to the ears with local whiskey, he fell down and broke the bottle he was carrying.

Drunk, ragged, filthy, and flea-ridden, he, nevertheless, as a Virginian rose with Southern dignity and humor to make good use of the liquid: "I christen this town Virginia!" Ed Schieffelin in Arizona was told that he would find his tombstone if he went prospecting in Apache country. Schieffelin struck it rich, and the town was, of course, Tombstone.

The men staked their claims and named their mines with humor, imagination, sentiment, patriotism, and wishful thinking. They boasted: the Plutocrat, the Gold King, the Ton a Minute, Copper Queen, Bullion, Champion, Mammoth, the undisputed Matchless, High Ore, Hidden Treasure, the Little Giant, the Tip Top, the Millionaire Mine, and, in Nevada, the cocky Jumbo Gold — in the Awakening Mining District of the Slumbering Hills. Other miners were cautious, with no desire to tempt the fates: the Humbug, the Midget, Poorman, Speculator, Last Dollar, and Last Chance. One miner on Canyon Creek in the Coeur d'Alene district of Idaho bluntly named his claim the Ore-Or-No-Go, a put-up or shut-up exhortation to himself and Mother Earth.

Of the men who named their mines patriotically, Winfield Scott Stratton deserves the crown. Stratton had followed Cowboy Bob Womack's discovery of gold into Cripple Creek, Colorado, in 1891 and located rich mines throughout the district. Beginning with the Independence, he named them the Washington, Abe Lincoln, Madison, White House, American Eagle, Yankee Girl, and Plymouth Rock. A lone Southerner raised the Blue Flag there in isolated protest, and received strong support to the north, where the famous Robert E. Lee helped to make Leadville a boom camp. At Telluride there was the Liberty Bell, and in Utah there were the Yankee and Uncle Sam at Eureka. The Coeur d'Alene had its Bunker Hill, and White Oaks, New Mexico, its Old Abe.

They named them for the places from which they had come: the Drumlummon Mine, the Portland, the Shannon, Liverpool, Penobscot, Alabama, Atlanta, Pennsylvania, Georgia. For their wives, sweethearts, and local loves: in Butte alone, the Emma, Nettie, Cora, Alice, Minnie Jane, Minnie Healy; in Cripple Creek, Ada Bell, Theresa, Mary Nevin, Mollie Kathleen, Little Ida, Orpha May, Mary McKinney, and Rose Nicol. Anna J. was serious enough as a name, but Fanny B. Mine was christened with evident humor. And was the May B, a woman, or a question mark, or both? Mines were named for animals, hornets, and birds: in Idaho and Montana, the Badger, Moose, Wild Horse, and Buffalo; on the Comstock Lode, the Yellow Jacket; in Colorado, the Chicken Hawk and Bluebird. But the great Tiger Mine in the Coeur d'Alene took its name not from any Bengal beast but from the traditional nickname for the gambling game of faro.

Mines were solidly named for their owners — the Hale and Norcross, Gould and Currey, the S. Burns, and the Gleason — but the more entertaining are those named by accident, or with imagination and curious reasoning. When N. C. Creede located his first rich mine in Colorado, his partners shouted happy profanities. But Creede himself was not a cussing character. The best he could do, seeing the ore, was to exclaim, "Holy Moses!" — and Holy Moses the mine became. Again, in Montana, two partners had agreed not to name their claim until they struck pay dirt. One of them, weary, left his work to nap, but the other continued puttering around in the prospect hole. Digging away, he came on a body of glistening ore. Scrambling out of the hole and up the hillside, he shouted excitedly to his partner, "Wake up, Jim, we've struck it!" And the mine took its name, Wake Up Jim. The Neversweat in Butte was named by the miners themselves because the workings were cooled by an unusual current of air. The Anaconda was so called by Michael Hickey, who had read Horace Greeley's account of "Grant's army encircling Lee's forces like a giant anaconda." Two tenderfoot druggists named the rich Pharmacist. In Montana and Idaho there are the Orphan Boy and the Orphan Girl, claims sadly remote from all others in the neighborhood.

For the majority of the names there are explanations, but there are many whose origins have been lost as the camps were deserted, and their knowledgeable residents drifted on or died. How account, for example, for the Butterfly Terrible, the Bopeep, Wobbly Legs, and Old Lout? The Asteroid stood out like a star from all other claims, and the St. Lawrence was named for the patron saint of two Irishmen. But what of the Gin Shot, the Sun and Moon, the City of Paris, and the You Like?

I have given a little space to these names of mines (there are thousands and thousands of them) simply to point up that place-naming is not limited to towns and geographical features, but includes men's activities on the land

— for which there must be identifying names. Cattle brands, for example, can be place names, since each brand is an identifying name not only for the cattle but for the ranch as well. The names of railroads (with their nick-names) are also place names: it does not matter that they run on for hundreds of miles and pass many towns and settlements: so does the Mississippi. The names of buildings are place names: the Empire State, the Chrysler, the Waldorf, the Drake; and so are the names of restaurants and stores. And the names of ships, in their way, are place names also, individually set apart and identified — the *Flying Cloud*, the *Cumberland*, the *Ranger*, the *North Star*. It does not matter that they move over the oceans, any more than it matters that a named train — *The Twentieth Century*, *The Wolverine*, *The Overland*, *The Zephyr* — moves over its rails. Wherever and whenever they are, they are places. I'll see you on board the *America* — I'll see you on *The Chief*. Places.

Many of these names are, of course, quite ephemeral: cattle brands die out, railroads change names, ships last only for their lifetime, and buildings are torn down and replaced. Let us consider them, then, as belonging to a second rank, with the first rank continuing to be reserved for the more permanent natural features and populated places. But let us not exclude them either: for their lifetimes they are place names.

# 8.

# *Cattle Brands*

Cattle brands are symbols of ownership, and are at the same time names and, more frequently than not, place names.
The S—S of Nevada is a symbol of ownership.
But it is also pronounced and written out as a name: S Bar S.
And it is a place: the S Bar S Ranch, some forty miles east of Reno.

$$S-S \quad \text{S Bar S}$$

A few other examples:

, the symbol; Hat Creek, the name; the Hat Creek Ranch, a place.

*Quarter Circle U Ranch, near Birney, Montana, 1939:*
*branding irons*

Ⓧ , the symbol; Circle X, the name; the Circle X outfit or ranch, in Rio Hondo, Texas, the place.

P⤐ , the symbol; P Lazy Y, the name; the P Lazy Y Ranch in the Baboquivari Mountains south of Tucson in Arizona, the place.

Apart from their use on cattle, the best illustration of brands as names (and as names related to places) are the wooden-top desks of schoolchildren in the cattle country of the Southwest, where, instead of carving their initials or names, the children carved with jackknives the brands of their families or ranches. These stood as strongly and firmly for their names as the initials of youngsters did in the schoolrooms of the North. Also, no two brands were the same, whereas in the North the initials of two children might well be. (Formica-top desks, by the way, are eliminating all this folklore.) The caskets of cowboys and cattlemen are another example, where, on the casket itself, the brand of the ranch was burned deep before the box was lowered into the grave. A wooden headmarker might give the man's name, but deeper in mother earth the brand — the name and the place — would for a much longer time than the weatherbeaten headboard identify him as once belonging to the Pitchfork L ranch or the Bar Slash J.

Ψ  Pitchfork L Ranch         ⁻/J  Bar Slash J

Brands are read in one of three ways, depending upon the way they are designed: from left to right, from top to bottom, or from the outside to the inside.

*From left to right:*

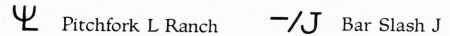

S–E                    P⤐                   ⁻A
S Bar E              P Lazy Y               Bar A

*From top to bottom:*

S Bar E             P Lazy Y             Bar A

*From the outside to the inside:*

Circle X            Box M               Diamond C

There is precision and imagination in the creation of the single letters which form the base of most brands. To begin with, there is no such thing as a small, or lower-case, letter. (Some are in script, but not lower case.) All are capitals. But these capitals have great variety and go to create a range alphabet of of unusual color. Take the letter R, by way of example:

R, or Block R       Tumbling R          Lazy R

Crazy R             Reverse R           Flying R

Walking R

Drag R

Running R

Circle R

Box R

Diamond R

Half Circle R

Quarter Circle R

R Quarter
Circle

Swinging R

Rocking R

Cross R

Half Diamond R

Rafter R

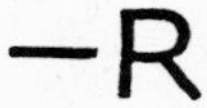

Bar R

R̄

Bar R

R—

R Bar

R̲

R Bar

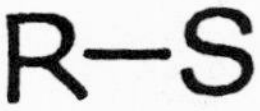

R—S

R Bar S

R—S

R Bar S Connected

R̠

R Bench

‾R‾

Half Box R

R̸

Barbed R

R/

R Slash

The problem of locating a particular brand out of thousands — in order to find the owner and the range — seems at first glance impossible to the uninitiated. Actually, it is relatively simple, and the cowboy who uses a brand book can turn to the proper page and entry as easily as a college student to a given word in his dictionary. All brands beginning with a letter are arranged alphabetically, so that anyone looking for the A Lazy Y brand or A Quarter Circle will find it under the letter A in an ordered sequence. (A Lazy Y will, of course, come towards the end of the A entries, preceded by AA — Double A, A Running B, ACD, ALF, A Tumbling R, AY, and finally, in order, A Lazy Y.) The same holds true for all brands beginning with a numeral, and the Two Bar X or Three Slash L are located under the numerals 2 and 3. Following the letters and numerals, the commonest characters with which brands begin are listed in sequence, normally in the order given for the *Wyoming Brand Book:* Bar, Slash, Quarter Circle, Cross, Heart,

*Highway 10, Miles City, Montana, 1939:*
*cattle brand sign for tourists*

Diamond, Box, Half-Box, and Triangle. After these come the picture brands, which are also alphabetized as much as possible, the *Anchor* brand preceding the *Anvil*, and the Lazy *Ladder* following the Pocket *Knife*.

Consider these relatively simple and well-known brands, not only as brands and symbols, but as names and place names as well. They are the West, just as the names of the mines and mining camps are the West, just as the names of the mountains and valleys, just as the names of the men who first knew the West.

Lazy Ladder          Flying Six          Seventy-Six

Bar Nothing

Tumbling Anchor

Pitchfork L

Lazy Fiddleback

Buckle J

W Slash
Running M

U Bar U
Connected

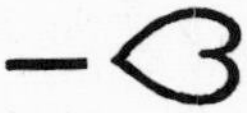

Bar Lazy Heart

Bible

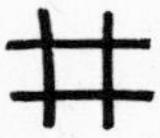

Pigpen

Diamond Bar
Lazy S

Bar
Wineglass

Diamond Dot
J Connected

Diamond
and a Half

Half Diamond
S

A Up A Down

A Open A

Diamond A
Connected

A Bench

A Bar B

Triangle
X

A Running M

Circle Bar

Goose Egg

Diamond Dot

Sun Bar

Quarter Moon

Horse Track
or Piece of Pie

KER

Barker

Spur

Ox Yoke     Bridle Bit     H Crazy Y Connected

Fifty-Two     Forty-Four     Sixty-Three

With these letters, figures, and characters, the possible brand combinations are limitless. With them, the rancher of the West — using his fertile imagination and a hot iron — turned the hides of his cattle into walking statements reflecting his humor and romance, his belief in private property and his individualism. The so-called heraldry of the range, handed down in practice from Spain and Mexico, came into being on the Western plains.

Many ranchers were content simply to brand their initials or, where their names were short, to burn them fully on the hide. Charles S. Wilson of Meeteetse, in Park County, Wyoming, adopted the S C W brand, and Orville A Sturgis of Glendo used a slight variant of his initials with the O Open A S, O ∧ S . W. B. Coy of Torrington used his full surname, C O Y, varying it also with C O Lazy Y and Reverse C O Lazy Y, ꓛO≺ . A. J. Olsen of Shoshoni branded his nickname, O L E, upon his stock. Lum Richards of Hope, New Mexico, registered the L U M brand; Mrs. Lura Yates of White Oaks also used her first name, L U R A; while L. W. Neatherlin of Roswell adopted the last syllable of his name, L I N.

Where men had names which lent themselves to graphic presentation, the brands acquired a double reading, interpreted either in terms of the symbols or, more likely within the immediate region, as the cattleman's real name. F. S. Harter of Wheatland, Wyoming, adopted the Heart R brand, ♡R , and Joseph Hartle of Fort Bridger the Heart L (Inverted Heart L Connected), ⚲. B. J. Keys of Worland took the Key S, ♂S ; the Barkey brothers of Buffalo the Bar Key, ⊣♂ ; and C. D. Bell of Rimrock, Arizona, the obvious Bell, 🔔 .

Unabashed proclamations of love for wife or sweetheart wandered the range, four-legged, peripatetic Valentines. Where a woman's name was short, the rancher branded it in full: L I Z, L I L, A N N, F A Y, J O Y, and R A E. Where the name was too long to make an easy brand, ranchers used the Heart, which often encircled the single initial of her first name or more boldly preceded both initials. The Hearts were frequently pierced with arrows, and in the West, as elsewhere, there were Broken and Bleeding Hearts.

Men who had a penchant for gambling created the Seven UP brand, which is found in every state, ⊃P , and the KENO brand, which varies from Frank Stout's in Sheridan, Wyoming, ⨧NO , to Joe Kincaid's in La Veta, Colorado, ⨀NO . The aces of diamonds, clubs, and hearts were popular, but the ace of spades is conspicuous by its absence. The lucky Seven Eleven brand, 7// , appears frequently.

Brands lived impermanently, for the lifetime of the cattle, upon hides. Where stock flourished and increased, the brands grew and were passed from generation to generation. Where cattle sickened and died, when drought or storm came to the land, when ranches failed, the brands died also.

Yet even where the brands have disappeared from the range, a very solid record of them has been kept in registers and brand books. This was done haphazardly at first, locally, and voluntarily, in scrapbooks and notebooks, simply for mutual protection and information. Then under the pressure of local custom and the settling of disputes, the registering of brands became a matter of law, administered by each county. And finally, as the brands overlapped and gross and conscious similarities were found in the brands of bordering counties, an even broader and more centralized authority became necessary. Today all brands are registered under the authority of each state with the various state boards of livestock commissioners, and the brands themselves published periodically in book form with supplements as needed.

The brand books, now rare and collectors' items except for those of recent issue, were the stockmen's and cowboy's bibles. They read the seemingly meaningless hieroglyphics with the attention of scholars and, trained as they were, could trace from them the history of the cattle industry, range by range, county by county, state by state. Early and local brand books — such as the *La Junta Tribune Brand Book* of 1886, which listed brands in Las Animas and parts of Pueblo, Huerfano, and Bent Counties in Colorado, and Colfax County in New Mexico — were usually published with descriptive cuts, two to a page, of steers with brands imprinted on shoulder or side, and accompanied by a large fold-in map of the region upon which were superimposed all the brands of the region, indicating the range area of the owner's cattle. The more recent brand books, however, have dispensed with maps and engravings, and picture the brands only in small and crude line drawings, listing them, with the ranch addresses of their owners, in double columns, forty-six brands to a single page. The books are durably bound in either leather or heavy board, printed on thin Bible paper, and issued in narrow, notebook format, consciously intended for the working use of cattlemen. They slip easily into a shirt pocket or the hip pocket of Levi's.

The number of brands runs into the tens of thousands. At one time it interested me to make a rough survey of the number of brands in eight Western states: Nevada, New Mexico, Arizona, Utah, Wyoming, Colorado, Idaho, and Montana. Taking at random the official brand books of Wyoming, Colorado, Arizona, and New Mexico for different years, these astonishing figures appear: for the year 1907, the *Brand Book of the Territory of New Mexico* listed more than 24,380 brands. Wyoming, for the year 1916, recorded approximately 14,400. Colorado claimed 23,250 in 1906. And for 1933, Arizona listed more than 7,360. For the eight states in question there have certainly been no fewer than one hundred thousand *registered* brands. And when one considers the brands which were never recorded and those which have been lost or destroyed, it is no exaggeration to estimate a total of at least three hundred thousand for the area. Add Texas, Oklahoma, Kansas,

Nebraska, the Dakotas, Oregon, and California, and a figure of half a million different cattle brands for the West becomes an unquestioned figure — and an unquestionably low one, at that.

# 9.

# *Quilt Names*

The names are as spectacular as the quilts themselves: Tennessee Star, Swallows-in-the-Window, Rose of Sharon, Johnny-Around-the-Corner, Trail of the Covered Wagon, Toad-in-the-Puddle, Philadelphia Pavement, Circuit Rider, Blazing Sun, Hand of Friendship, Job's Tears, Rocky Road to Kansas, Cat Track, Princess Feather, Country Husband, Drunkard's Path, Shoo Fly, and Tail of Benjamin's Kite.

Standing alone they are lovely. Placed with the quilts themselves they make descriptive sense. This is difficult to believe, but it is so: the poetic name moves with and is tied to the pattern (modified and changing perhaps, in the manner of folklore) from grandmother to granddaughter, family to family, community to community, quilting bee to quilting bee.

Most museums around the country with any representative collection of Americana — Sturbridge, Winterthur, Cooperstown, Williamsburg, Shelburne — have examples of American quilts, and they are to be found also in the collections of local historical societies. The best single collection, however — and not of the quilts themselves, but portraits of their patterns — is in the Index of American Design, housed in the National Gallery of Art in Washington. The Index came into being during the Depression, when unemployed artists were given work by the Government in an imaginative program to record — with sketchbook and paintbox — surviving examples of the traditional arts and crafts of America. In consequence, there are some thousands of drawings and watercolors of branding irons, spurs, weathervanes, homemade toys, kitchen utensils, farm implements, costumes, and other folk art and craft items — including quilts. The names of the quilts are there with the patterns; and some (some only!) of the names in broad groupings, are these:

*Flowers.* Black-Eyed-Susan, Bleeding Hearts, Bluebells, Bouncing Betsy, Canada Lily, Lazy Daisy, Daisy Chain, Dancing Daffodils, Dogwood Blooms, Old Fashioned Flower Garden, Golden Poppies, Jack-in-the-Pulpit, North Carolina Lily, Tiger Lily, Kentucky Peony, Prairie Queen, Ragged Robin, Dixie Rose, Rose of 1840, Texas Rose, Rose of Tennessee, Rose of the Carolinas, Topeka Rose, Wild Rose, Scotch Thistle, Kansas Sunflower, Sweet Pea, Tulip Blocks, Tulip Tree, Texas Tulip, Windblown Tulip, Rare Old Tulip.

*Birds.* Brown Goose, Dove of Peace, Dove-in-the-Window, Four Little Birds, Goose-in-the-Pond, Square and Swallow, Turkey Tracks, Fox and Geese, Duck and Ducklings, Duck's Foot-in-the-Mud, Goose Tracks, Hovering Hawks, Peacocks and Flowers, Swallow's Flight, Birds-in-the-Air, Duck Puddle, Wild Goose Chase.

*Stars.* Tremendously popular, they made beautiful designs: Blazing Star, Christmas Star, Columbia Star, Big Dipper, California Star, Crazy Quilt Star, Cowboy's Star, Dolly Madison Star, Free Trade Star, Log Cabin Star, Leavenworth Star, Ozark Star, Missouri Star, Polaris Star, Savannah Beautiful Star, Shining Star, Shooting Star, Star Bright, Star and Crescent, Star and Plume, Star of the Four Winds, Star of the Sea, Star Spangled Banner, Star of North Carolina, Star and Planets, Star Lanes, Union Star.

*Coffee County, Alabama, 1939: spring housecleaning—*
*quilts and bedding hanging in the sun*

*The Sun.* Harvest Sun, Rising Sun, Summer Sun, Sunburst, Sun Dial, Sunbeam, Sunshine and Shadow.

(One begins to believe — does one not — that grandmother had better names for these things than anything Madison Avenue might dream up?)

*Trees.* Charter Oak, Cherry Tree and Birds, Dogwood, Falling Timber, Christmas Tree, Forest Pattern, Little Beech Tree, Pride of the Forest, Temperance Tree, Tree Everlasting, Tree of Life, Lone Oak Tree, Pine Tree.

*Religion.* The great cementing force of an earlier America poured its symbols into the quilts: Children of Israel, Cross and Crown, Cross Upon

*Alvin, Wisconsin, 1937:*
*quilting*

Cross, Crowned Cross, Crown of Thorns, David and Goliath, Adam and Eve, Garden of Eden, Golden Gates, Golgotha, Heavenly Steps, Hosanna, Jacob's Ladder, Job's Tears, King David's Crown, Many Mansions, Path of Thorns, Pilgrim's Pride, Scripture Quilt, Solomon's Crown, Star of Bethlehem, Tree of Paradise, Weeping Willow and Dove of Peace, World Without End.

What would one not give to see a great national exhibit of the best of all these quilts! The quilts framed or draped, and the story of each told for the visitor. *There* would be art and history rising out of the land! It would be pleasant to ask the "pop" and "modern" artists to move over for a time, and to let the meek who contributed so much to the making of this American earth inherit it for a moment.

*Proper Names.* Aunt Dinah's Delight, Barbara Frietchie Star, Aunt Sukey's Patch, Burgoyne's Quilt, Aunt Martha's Wild Rose, Joseph's Coat, Joseph's Necktie, Martha Washington's Wreath, Mrs. Cleveland's Choice, Peeny Pen's Cottage, Hobson's Kiss, Queen Charlotte's Crown.

*Animals*, of course. Bear's Paw, Bear's Foot, Cats and Mice, Four Frogs Quilt, Hens and Chickens, Snake's Trail, Turkey Tracks, Flying Bats, Cat Track, Snail's Trail, Bull's Eye.

*Games and Puzzles.* They must have absorbed the entire family, since boys as well as girls stitched the quilt patches in winter evenings before the fire (President Coolidge did so at the age of ten): Boston Puzzle, Bachelor's Puzzle, Catch-Me-If-You-Can, Crosses and Losses, Eight Hands 'Round, Farmer's Puzzle, Fool's Puzzle, Jack-in-the-Box, Follow the Leader, Leap Frog, Jigsaw Puzzle, Puss-in-the-Corner, Star Puzzle, Tic-Tac-Toe, Steeple Chase, Swing-in-the-corner, Whirligig.

*Geometric figures.* These very naturally evolved, both out of the pieced patches and the appliqued designs: Broken Circle, Box Quilt (very, very popular), Chained Five Patch, Cube Work, Double Pyramid, Hexagonal Star, Honeycomb Patch, Octagon, Octagon Star, Roman Square, Sawtooth, Square and Circle, Squares and Stripes, Thousand Pyramids, Tumbling Blocks, Windblown Square.

And last, of course, is the ubiquitous *Miscellaneous.* The names of these patterns cut across everything that made us a nation: Little Red School House, Horseshoe, Mariner's Compass, Kansas Dugout, Country Cross Road, Wagon Tracks, Old Homestead, Railroad Crossing, Forest Path, Buggy Wheel, Cabin-in-the-Cotton.

We will not really know these quilts again. Listen to their names, and admit that you are in some measure moved by their genuineness, their simplicity, their honesty, and their unconscious poetry: American Bride's Quilt, Broken Dish, Churn Dash, Cincinnati Cog-Wheel, Country Farm, Courthouse Square, Homespun, Ice Cream Bowl, Hero's Crown, Old Town Pump, Pincushion and Burr, Ship of Dreams, Prairie Queen, True Lovers' Knot, Weather Vane, Spring Beauty, Stepping Stones, Widow's Troubles,

Old Town Pump, Old Maid's Ramble, Hit and Miss, Friendship, Flower Pot, Flying Dutchman, Arrowheads, Children's Delight, Circular Saw, Brick Wall, Crib Quilt, Grandmother's Dream, Improved Nine Patch, Lost Ship, Oddfellow's Cross, Rolling Pin Wheel, Sugar Bowl, Compass, Primrose Path, Wheel of Chance, Young Man's Fancy, Bow Knot, Trail of the Covered Wagon, Stone Wall, Rail Fence, Flutter Wheel, Friendship Knot, Country Lanes, Cross Stitch Garden, Carpenter Square, American Log Patch, Bridal Stairway. . . .

# 10.

# Names of Ozark Fiddle Tunes

In an article in *Midwest Folklore*, Vance Randolph tells us that for a matter of thirty years, between 1920 and 1950, "I was accustomed to disport myself at dances in the Ozark country, and heard many of the traditional fiddle tunes." During that time he never had enough money to buy a recording machine of his own, and the foundations and learned societies refused to finance a study of backwoods fiddle tunes. So he reluctantly abandoned any collecting project — except that, happily, in the 1940's he made about one hundred disc recordings of tunes at hand for the Library of Congress, with a machine loaned to him by that institution. These are, of course, in the Archives.

To further depress him at the time, he was told by "a college professor" that even the titles of the fiddle tunes had "no folkloristic value" because they

"were floating and impermanent, and subject to so many local variations. . . ." Dear God!

Anyhow, Randolph, not knowing one note of music from another and "not
competent to write down the tunes," nevertheless, like the extraordinary
pack-rat jaybird collector that he is, collected the names of the tunes. And
these names are an incredible lot! They take us right into the hills of Arkansas, Missouri, Tennessee, Kentucky, the Carolinas (this is all Southern and
mountain stuff), into their Saturday nights, and into the cabins and punch-
eon-floor "social halls" of the dances and parties.

Some of the names have Scotch and English antecedents, but the majority
are indelibly indigenous and American. Some are a little rough, and some
carry over occasional racial slurs, but as a whole all reflect the life of the hill
country.

Read them slowly, against the backdrop of the cabins, the oil lamps and
lanterns, the swift feet and stamp of the dancers, the swirl of gingham, the
rhythmic shouts of the callers, occasional drunken responses from the floor,
and — above and through all — the harsh rasp of the fiddle. Outside it is
black night with the pines pushing up to the stars. Inside it is Broken-
Legged Chicken, Drunkard's Hiccoughs, Goose in the Millpond, Pouring
Soapsuds Over the Fence, Hell and Scissors, Sixteen Days in Georgia, and
Took Her Out Behind the Barn. Saturday night in an America that was:

All Around the House, All Around the Water Hole, All I've Got is Done
and Gone, All Little Indians Don't Get Drunk, All of Them's Done Gone,
All the Way from Pike, Annie Dickson, Annie Poke, Andy Over the Weaving Shed, Arkansas Pumpkins, *Arkansas Traveler,** *Aunt Katy*, Aunt Lucy
Deal.

*Babes in the Woods*, Backbone and Spareribs, *Baker Number Two*,
Baldy Holler, *Bear Creek Sally Goodin*, Beau of Oak Hill, Belly to Belly,
Been in the Pen So Long, Big Bottom Rag, *Big Indian*, Big Limber, Big-
gerlo, Biggest Prick in the Neighborhood, *Big Sweet 'Taters in Sandy
Land*, Big Time at Our House, Bile Them Cabbage Down, Bill Mathes
Wagoner, *Billy in the Low Ground*, Black Betty, *Black-eyed Susan*, Black

---

* All of the titles set in italics are those of recordings which Vance Randolph deposited
in the Library of Congress. The Archive of Folksong has additional recordings of fiddle
tunes in its collections, and a long-playing record (L62) of twenty-nine of them has recently been issued.

*Greene County, Georgia, 1941: convict camp*

Mountain Rag, Blueberry Blossom, *Bluebird Waltz*, *Blue Mule*, Bonaparte's March, *Bonaparte's Retreat*, Brakes of Little Sandy, Buckskin Billy, Buck Creek Girl, *Buck Snort*, Buddy Layden, Buggeroo, *Bugs in the 'Taters*, Build Up the New Ground, *Buffalo Gals*, *Bully of the Town*, Bunch of Blackberries.

Cackling Hen, Callahan's Reel, *Campbells Are Coming*, Captain With His Whiskers, Careless Love, *Carolina Rattlesnake*, Charming Betsey, Chase the Squirrel, Chicken Pie, *Chicken Reel*, Chilly Wind, Chilly Withers, *Chinese Breakdown*, Chopping Wood in Kansas, Cincinnati Hornpipe, Cindy, Clabber Cod Stomp, Clark's Hornpipe, Clucking Hen, Come Get Your Nubbin, Come to the Milk, Coming into Little Rock, Coming Round the Mountain, *Coming Through The Rye*, *Coming Up the Turnpike*, Cornstalk Fiddle, Cottage Hornpipe, Cotton Eye Joe, Cows in the Corn, Cricket on the Hearth, *Cripple Creek*, Cuckoo's Nest, Cumberland Gap.

Damon's Window, Dancing Juber, Devil Amongst the Tailors, Devil Caught a Nigger, Devil Down Hill, *Devil's Dream*, *Devil's Reel*, Devil in the Kitchen, Devil Take a Yaller Gal, Devil Wants a Woodchuck, Devil Was a Whittler, Dill Pickle Rag, Dorine Hornpipe, Down in Rockingham, *Downfall of Paris*, *Dry and Dusty*, Duck in the Kitchen, Durad's Hornpipe, *Durang's Hornpipe*, Durene Hornpipe, Dutchman's Hop.

Early in the Morning, Eating Goober Peas, *Eighth of January*, Eight More Miles to Louisville, Eliza Green, Evening Shade Waltz, Everybody Knows What Maggie Done.

Farmer's Stomp, Fence Corner Peaches, Fiddler's Reel, *Fever River*, Fire Down Below, *Fire in the Mountain*, *Fisher's Hornpipe*, *Flop-Eared Mule*, Flower of Edinborough, Fly Around Nancy, Foot Loose and Fanny Free, *Forked Deer*, Forked Deer Hornpipe, Forked-Horn Deer, *Fort Worth*, Four Patter Down, *Fourth of July*, Four Thumbs and Two Left Feet, *Fox and Hounds*, *Frankie and Johnny*, Frankie's Rag, Frenchman's Hornpipe, Fry a Little Meat.

*George Booker*, *George Washington*, Getting Upstairs, Gilderoy, *Girl I Left Behind Me*, Girl on a Log, Give the Fiddler a Dram, Go 'Way from My Window, *Going Up the Mountain*, Good Boy Johnny, *Goodnight Waltz*, Go See the Widow, Go Sheep Go, Granny-Rag Blues, *Granny Will Your Dog Bite*, *Gray Eagle*, Grease That Wooden Leg Sally Ann, Greasy Kate,

Great Big 'Taters in Sandy Land, Greenback Dollar Bill, *Green Corn*, Green Mountain, Green River Waltz, *Guitar Fandango*.

Hangtown Gals, Ham Fat Smoking in the Pan, Happy Jack, *Haste to the Wedding*, Heel-and-Toe Polka, Heights of Alabama, Heights of Alma, *Hell Among the Yearlings*, Hell Broke Loose in Georgia, Hell to Pay in Tulsa, Hickory Hornpipe, Highland Fling, *Highway Nigger*, Hit or Miss, Hockey Mountain Reel, Hog-Eye Sally, Hold It Steady, Holler Lulie, Holler Poplar Hi-de-O, Homemade Sugar, Hop High Lady, Hopping on the Green, Hop Light Ladies, Horses on the Bridge, Hot Springs Holler, Hull's Victory, *Hung My Jawbone on the Fence*.

*Ida Red*, *I Don't Love Nobody*, I'll Go No More A-Roving, Indian Eat the Woodchuck, Indian Hoecake Done, Indian Hoedown, *Indian Whoop*, Irish Jig, *Irish Washerwoman*, It's Good for Your Knockers, It Don't Make No Difference, I Wish We Was On Some Foggy Mountain Top.

Jack of Diamonds, Jackie on the Green, Jackson's Victory, *Jackson Walking to the White House*, Jaybird Setting on a Limb, *Jeff Davis Blues*, Jenny Jenkins, Jenny Lind Polka, Jenny Nettles, Jenny Put the Kettle On, Jim Bee Wagoner, Joe Bowers, Johnson Boys, Johnson Girls, *Josh Fine Waltz*, Josie Shuck Her Pants Down, Jump and Buck, Jumping Buck, Jump Jim Crow, Jumping Judy, Jump Up Trouble.

*Kansas City Blues*, Keep Away from the Federals, Kick High Toody, Kicking Mule, Kiowa Stomp, Kitty Cline, Knock Along John, Knocking At the Door, Ku Klux Over the Hill.

Lady's Fancy, Lady in the Lake, Lardner's Reel, Last of the Callahans, Lazy Kate, *Leather Breeches*, Life on the Ocean Wave, Like It or Lump It, Limping Sally Waters, Little Betsey Brown, Little Black Bull, *Little Brown Jug*, Little Foot Up and Big Foot Down, Little Girl Dressed in Blue, Little Johnny Bryan, Little Liza Jane, *Little Old Schottische*, Little Sally Waters, Liverpool Hornpipe, Lonesome Oak, Long-Eared Mule, Long John, Lost and Gone, Lost Girl, Lost Indian, *Lover's Waltz*.

MacLeod's Reel, *Make Me a Pallet on the Floor*, Mamie's Favorite, Marmaduke, Marmaduke's Hornpipe, Midnight Breakdown, *Mike and Charley*, Miller's Frolic, *Mississippi Sawyer*, *Mistress McCloud's Jig*, Missouri Quickstep, Mole in the Ground, Money Musk, *Monkey on a Dog Cart*, Monkey on a Stick, More Holler Than Wool, Muddy River, Muddy Waters,

Murphy's Brew, My Girl's Gone Crazy, My Last Gold Dollar, My Last Old Dollar Is Gone.

Name It and Take It, Nancy Rollin, Nancy Rowland, *Natchez Under the Hill*, Nelly Gray, Newton's Dream, New Ring on My Horn, Nigger in the Pea Patch, Nigger On the Hillside, Nigger Stole a Pumpkin, Nightingale Waltz, No Pitch Hot.

Old Aunt Sally, *Old Banjo Jig*, Old Bill Cheetum, Old Blue Sow, Old Dan Tucker, Old Fort Smith, Old General Price, Old Granny Rattletrap, Old Gray Mare, *Old Hen Cackles*, Old Jaw Bone, Old Jim Lane, *Old Joe Clark*, Old Joe Shelby, Old Man Muller, *Old March*, Old Miller, *Old Molly Hare*, Old Mother Finnegan, Old Quickstep, Old Sally Goodin, *Old-Time Schottische*, *Old-Time Wagoner*, Old Wooden Bucket, On My Way to Georgia, *On the Banks of the Old Tennessee*, Out Behind the Smokehouse, *Over the Waves*.

Paddy on the Turnpike, Paddy Won't You Drink Some, Pass the Bottle Boys, Peekaboo Waltz, Pick the Devil's Eye Out, Piedmont, Plains of Abraham, Pollywog Hornpipe, Poor Johnny, *Pop Goes the Weasel*, Pop It With Your Thumb, Pop the Question, Possum and Sweet 'Taters, Possum Sop, Possum Up a Gum Stump, Pouring Soapsuds Over the Fence, *Pretty Little Girl I Left Behind*, Pretty Little Miss, Pretty Little Pink, Pretty Little Thing, *Pretty Little Widow*, *Pretty Polly Ann*, Puncheon Floor, Put Sugar On It, Put Your Little Foot Down, *Put Your Little Foot Right There*.

*Rabbit in the Briar Patch*, Rabbit in the Pea Patch, *Radell Clog*, Raggedy Ann, Ragged-Ass Bill, *Ragtime Annie*, Rattlesnake Shake, Red River Rising, *Rickett's Hornpipe*, Rippling Water, Rippling Waves, Rippy Toe Rag, Roaring Lion, Roaring River, Rocky Road to Dublin, *Rocky Road to Texas*, Rocky Run, Rolling in the Grass, Rolling on the Ground, Rosin the Bow, Rosie Roller, Roxie Ann, *Rubber Dolly*, Run Boys Run, Run Johnny Run, *Run Nigger Run*, *Rye Straw*, *Rye Whiskey*.

Saddle Old Kate, *Saddle Old Spike*, Sailor's Hornpipe, *Sal's Got a Wooden Leg Laid Away*, Sally Ann, Sally Get Your Hoecake Done, *Sally Goodin*, *Sally Johnson*, Sally Put the Kettle On, Sandy Bottom, *Scot Number Two*, Shake 'Em Up Early, Shake It Up Julie, Sheepie Shell Corn, Shelving Rock, Shifting Sands, Shirt Tail West, Shoo Fly, Shoot Her With a Leather Gun, *Shortening Bread*, Short Sweetening, Shucky Beans, Sifting

Sand, Sigel's Retreat, Silver Hill, Sixteen Days in Georgia, Skip the Willer, Snider's Jig, Snowbird in the Ash Bank, Soapsuds Over the Fence, *Soldier's Joy*, Sourwood Mountain, Spanish Fandango, Spanish Leather, Spanish Two-Step, Speed the Plow, Spotted Pony, Spotted Tail, Squaw in the Canebrake, Squirrel in the Tree, Stagolee, Sticks and Stones, Stick It in the Middle, Stinking Bear, Stonewall Jackson's Ride, Stop Shaking My Tree, Strap Buckner's Fancy, *Sugar Betsey Ann*, *Stony Point*, Sugar Hill, Sugar in My Coffee, Sugar in the Gourd, Sugarfoot Rag, Sweet Evalina.

Talking to the Devil, *Take Me Back to Texas*, Take Me Back to Tulsa, Take Out for the Kitchen, *Take Your Foot Out of the Mud*, 'Taters On the Table, Ten Little Indians, Tennessee Breakdown, *Tennessee Wagoner*, Ten Steps Forward, Texas Cow Thief, Texas Dixie, That's What Mamma Said, Thunderbolt Hornpipe, Ticklish Reuben, Tie Your Scabbard Down, Tishamingo, *Tom and Jerry*, Too Many Chinches, Took Her Out Behind the Barn, Trouble on the Way, *Tulsa Waltz*, Turkey Buzzard, Tucker's Old Place, *Turkey in the Straw*, *Turn Down the Kivver*, *Twin Brothers*, Two Big Pumpkins, Two Little Girls.

Uncle Bud, *Uncle Joe*, Under the Peach Tree, Up and Down the Broomstick, Up Jumps the Devil, Up Jumps Trouble, Valley Doree, Valley Sweet Green.

*Wagoner*, *Wagoner in B-Flat*, Wake Snakes, *Wake Up Jacob*, *Walls of Jericho*, *Walk Along John*, Walk in the Parlor, Walking to the Pasture, *Way Down Yonder*, Weavering Way, Weaving Way, *Wednesday Night Waltz*, What Makes a Nigger Love 'Taters So, Wheel Buzzard Wheel, Where Is My Pants At, Whipples' Hornpipe, Whistling Reuben, Whistling Rufus, *White River*, White River Charley, White River Shore, Who's Keeping Tally, Wiggle-Ass Jig, Wild and Woolly, Wild Goose A-Flying, Wild Hair Frolic, *Will Your Mule Carry Double*, Wilson's Clog, Wind On the Wabash, Woolsey Creek.

Yankee Run Fast, Yellow Gal, Yellow Jacket, Yellow-Leg Chicken, Young Man's Fancy, You Never Can Tell, You Told Me a Lie, Zack from Tackus, Zig-Zag Hornpipe, Zip Coon Stomp.

I have put all these wonderful names here to further preserve them and make them more widely known. They should never be lost.

Go back over them every so often: Sal's Got a Wooden Leg Laid Away,

Wiggle-Ass Jig, Sheepie Shell Corn, Old Granny Rattletrap, Josie Shuck
Her Pants Down, Chopping Wood in Kansas, Big Sweet 'Taters in Sandy
Land, Cows in the Corn, George Washington. . . .

   Listen to your people and your country.

# 11.

# *Names of Racehorses*

Ernst Pulgram in his exceptional monograph, "Theory of Names," published by the American Name Society (1954), defines a proper name (which is what we have been looking at in "Place Names," "Quilt Names," and "Names of Fiddle Tunes"): "A proper name is a noun used . . . in a non-universal function . . . which is attached as a label to one animate being or one inanimate object . . . for the purpose of specific distinction from among a number of like or in some respects similar beings or objects that are either in no manner distinguished from one another or, for our interest, not sufficiently distinguished." The key is the "*one* animate being [Suzie] or *one* inanimate object [Rose of Sharon]" whose distinctive names set them apart and distinguish them from *dogs* or *poodles* generally, or from *quilts* or *patchwork quilts* generally, as well as specifically from *Towser* next door or from *The Drunkard's Path* pattern. It is the difference between *boy* and *Tom*, *railroad* and *D & R G W*, *baseball player* and *Stan Musial*, *horse* and *Man o' War*. The former are common nouns, the latter proper names. The former are generally written minuscule or lower-case, and the latter majuscule or upper-case: girl — Mary.

Pulgram speaks of the names we give to animals that have become the pets or associates of man:

I should like to call attention briefly to those animals which, on account of their intimate association with man for so many centuries, even millennia, have become domesticated. . . . They are all given names by their human owners and friends, as a rule human names, or at least names which, under certain circumstances, could equally well serve humans. The only difference is that in many cases imagination is given free rein with animals, and the discretion which one feels obliged to employ when naming humans, for the sake of local custom, good taste, or tradition, may be discarded. Among the most-named, so to speak, indeed much over-named, animals are racehorses. A racing form provides a study in exuberance unmatched in other realms of onomastics.* But the owners of stables are really in a very difficult position: the name must be unique for every single horse, but it is also desirable that it be lucky, "beautiful," sonorous, flamboyant, and memorable, and that it indicate, if at all possible, the horse's genealogy. The names are, of course, all declarative, even though the meaning . . . may remain somewhat obscure, if not altogether incomprehensible, to the ordinary habitué of the track.

There are fixed rules laid down by the Jockey Club of New York for the naming of thoroughbred and standardbred horses, the chief of which is that a name may not consist of more than fourteen letters, nor more than three words. Louise M. Ackerman in an article, "Naming the Nags," in *Names* (1953), further says that "the name may not be that of a living person, nor a famous or notorious person. It may not be a trade name, an advertising slogan, nor a copyrighted name, such as the title of a song, a play, a movie, a book, or a magazine. Nor may it be a name the spelling or pronunciation of which is similar to a name already in use." An applicant for a name must submit three names to the Registrar of the Jockey Club, who may approve the first, second, or third choice if any one of these meets all requirements. If none do, the applicant must apply again and submit an additional three.

* Naming, the study of names; from the Greek word *onoma*, name.

These restrictions apart and the regulations accepted, the field is wide open for the "onomastic exuberance" that one finds daily in *The Morning Telegraph* and *The Daily Racing Form*, two or three issues of which should be in the library of any individual aspiring to broad knowledge of the American scene.

At the time of writing her article, Louise Ackerman had a colt named Chesty Sweeper.

To a person not familiar with the blood lines of thoroughbred horses, that name has no particular significance, but the name is a combination of parts of the dam's name, Chestacola, and the sire's, Sweeper's Son, both officially registered with the Jockey Club. Combining names to indicate the breeding is a common way to name foals. Star Blen was sired by the stallion Blenheim II and out of the dam Starweed. Star Blen's half brother, Bull Weed, is by Bull Lea and out of the same dam, Starweed. Spotted Bull . . . is a stallion sired by Bull Dog and out of Spotted Beauty. Other examples which come to mind are: Battle Dust by Battledore and out of Cloud O' Dust, Grand Admiral by War Admiral and out of Grand Flame, and Teddy's Comet by Teddy and out of Flying Comet. . . .

She continues:

Man O' War's sire was Fair Play whose blood line is considered one of the three great American lines. Breeders always hope for another Man O' War. The names of many of Fair Play's descendants are combinations of words with either Fair or Play included: Fair Rochester, Fairday, Fair Avis, and Fair Star; Chance Play, My Play, Display, and Head Play. These names all indicate the famous forbear. . . .

She points up considerable wit in the choice of some names:

Sometimes a foal is named by inference rather than by actual repetition of parts of names. The recent sensation, Native Dancer, is by Polynesian and out of Geisha Girl. The parents of Eiffel Tower were Beau Pere and La France. Pretty Paws is by Gallant Fox. Guillotine's dam is Blade of Time, who was sired by Sickle. Greek Ship is by Heliopolis out of Boat. . . .

And sees rather obvious humor in others:

Of course, not all foals are named in serious vein. I suspect facetious intent when I see such registered names as Little Sip (sired by High Ball), Wee Nip (out of Bourbonette), Dustaway (by Whisk Broom II), Fizza (by Bubbling Over), Big Pebble (out of Beach Talk), Quickly (by Haste), The Cad (by Lovely Night out of Kissantell), Get Off (out of On Her Toes), and Slap and Tickle (by Greek Bachelor). Whoever named these thoroughbreds was having fun!

Not only do some owners "have fun," but all owners, members of their family, trainers, and whoever else may be involved contribute to the traditions of the sport and the folklore of the tracks and stables whenever time for name choosing comes around. Some of the names announce genealogy to those conversant with such matters; others brag of swiftness, pluck, determination; some are hopeful and call on Lady Luck, while others urge the horses on; some describe the horse in terms of color and spirit; some are frankly sentimental for good old Ireland or Barbara, or whatever; some are sassy and slangy with the language of Damon Runyon, of the track, bar, and nightclub; some have meaning only for the owner, while others seem altogether meaningless. Consider these beetles (as my friend Johnny Kelly called them) running during the last year at Shenandoah Downs, Belmont Park, Aqueduct, Lincoln Downs, Monmouth Park, Scarborough Downs, Saratoga, Delaware Park, Pimlico, Bowie, and other tracks around the country:

Go Go King, Go Dunce Go, I'm Adorable, Slippery Skipper, Flight King, Irish Jon, County Monaghan, Greek Mommy, Northern Rebel, Karen Baby, Off Her Tree, Cut the Comedy, Miss Switch, Sea Queen, Spit and Polish, Swiss Cheese, True North, Ta Wee, Do Drop In, Target Hitter, Missile Belle, Spot Check, Snow Cub, Dusky Evening, Sing Man Sing, Our Hope's Caper, Money Calls, No Back Talk, Straphanger, Stuffed Shirt, Native Heath, Boom Me In, Jet Whisper, Mark To Win, Raspberry Sherbert, Winter Folly, Northeast Gal, Julie Blue Shoes, Lady Dot, Bold I Am, Where's David, Bid Spades, Curry Sauce, Fast Attack, Feel Free, Roman Sonnet, Greek Glass, Brave Flyer, Rare Luck, Gay Blush, Form Fit, Sing Prince Sing, Pass The Drink, Stolen Base, Va Bene, Bold Grecian, Class Is Out, Imahit, Soundasadollar, Needlewoman, Eggy, Hot Gravy, Dear Barbara, Corn Off The Cob (a four-word exception to the Jockey Club rules),

Cathy Honey, Baffle, Poppa Grande, Beep Bop, Am A Lark, Line of Battle, Tropic Dancer, Mydottie, Mamagogo, I Found Gold, Pete's Chick, Marpoise, Glitch, Bubbly Dame, Dancer's Lad, Brandy Snap, Whiskey Mountain, Betty Bird, Gentle Broom, Sea Chant, Sempre Diritto, Spin A Wheel, Cabaret Doll, Sorry Baby, Easy Squeeze, Careful Now, Brandy Lady, Queens Sugar, Tinker Your Tune, Bold Nell, Miss Sable, Eltobepoor, Ol' Fee Fee, Native Comet, Beguiling Miss, Salmon River, Hurry Back Jack, Cut The Kidding, Nifty Lass, Bronze Mama, Konk, Foxy Jay, Red Dancer, Native Motion, Hunk, Helio's Tune, Lady Quickstep, Beer Chaser, Sly Polly, Gold Boy, Frosty Pink, Tropic Beach, Dusky Duchess, Black Mink, Suave Host . . .

And one could go on indefinitely: Nevada Sally, Knock On Wood, Tyrolean Dancer, Broken Song, She Is Gorgeous, War Horn, Moose Magic, Pass The Brandy, Flirtation, Leadville Johnny, Helen's Restless, Fleet Huntress, Helio Bull, Send Me Roses, Soft Excuse, Glen Nymph, Better Bee Hip, Amber Flash, Family Planning, Peppermint Doll, Bonnie and Gay . . .

One *could* go on indefinitely: the Jockey Club Register now has close to a million and a half names.

# 12.

# Hound Dog Names

These are not the fancy names of the AKC dogs, such as that of the small, gray (silver, the kennel calls him) poodle given to us by a lady going somewhere. His ancestry includes Champion Hollycourt Plume Argente, Ch. Smilestone's Silvern, Hollycourt Toujours Gai, Ch. Blakeen Joe Silver, Ch. Hollycourt Blue Ice, and comparable others through four generations. He came to us (from the lady) as Crestwoods Pierre. But even in northwest Washington I could not see myself walking him and calling him Pierre, let alone Crestwoods Pierre, so for no reason at all he was named Samuel and reduced quickly to Sammy. (He adores my wife, puts up with me, and barks hysterically at the liquor man.)

The names of hound dogs, which have now evolved to the stage of being registered, are earthier. They are not subject to the number-of-letters limitation required of horses by the Jockey Club, but applicants for a name must

— as with the horses — submit not only a first choice but two other possibilities as well, since each name must be unique. The studbooks are maintained by *The Hunter's Horn* and *The Chase*, magazines which also deserve a place, a copy or two at least, in any catholic, eclectic, Americana folklore library.

One of my top-notch students at American University, Lynn Mann, whose family is mixed up in the foxhound breeding and training world, reported via a term paper that

the process of hound-naming among real foxhunters* is nothing more or less than a mnemomic device to keep the lineage of any particular hound in the owner's head. . . . Thus the two pups of a cross between Calico and Lightning would be Cotton and Bolt to keep their parentage straight in the owner's mind. (Calico's littermate, by the way was Gingham.) In the same fashion, littermates, to the extent possible, will have relating names, as when one year a litter of four were named after the four panelists on the "I've Got a Secret" show, or last year's litter of three bitches and four dogs which were named by an Episcopalian huntsman: Faith, Hope, and Charity, and Matthew, Mark, Luke, and John.

Most commonly, names come from physical attributes — size, color, and so forth —, the most famous example being "Old Yeller," both from his color which was "yeller" and his habitual mode of expressing himself. Often, names are just names: Liz, Tom, Lucy, Martin (whose son was Luther). . . .

Lynn Mann cited the "Liquor" breed, or line, from Mississippi to illustrate the transfer of old country ways and talk to the newfangled business of studbook registration and genealogy:

The probable genesis of the name is the hound-man's common term for a hound whose bloodlines are unknown: "pot-licker." Faced with drumming up parentage, the hound's owner or, more likely, the owner of the hound's daddy, who wouldn't have bothered with such foolishness, probably replied, "Oh, he was just some ol' pot-licker, but he run good." And the eager registrant, conscious of sales, wrote down "liquor," which in this case runs on through Mean Liquor, Big Tim Liquor, Ozark Bourbon Liquor, Red Liquor, Hot Liquor, Sel's Diamond Liquor, Big Bill Liquor, Ozark Joy Liquor, Ozark Happy

* Foxhunting: running hounds, without necessarily any reference to the formal mounted hunting of English origin.

Liquor, Ozark Casey Liquor, Big Rowdy Liquor, Wild Cat Kite Liquor, Hardrock Liquor, and Wright's Mean Liquor.

Quite interestingly she points out that

the area in which registered hound-names probably reflect the least commercial influence is in the practice of tacking on the breeder's last name to the hound's own first name. You will remember the passage in *Tom Sawyer* when the two boys are hiding in the barn after witnessing the grave robbery and murder and they hear a dog howl: "Oh, lordy, I'm thankful!" whispered Tom. "I know his voice. It's Bull Harbison." The practice still holds in formal hound registration even though the original name-giver may not now be the owner or breeder. Thus the Goodman line: Lum E. Goodman, Katie Goodman, Joe Goodman Jett, Glassie Goodman, Glasseyed Pat Goodman, Judy Sue Goodman, Cherry's Bigun Goodman, Herbert H. Goodman, Girlie B. Goodman, Blondie B. Goodman, Krantz Be Bee K. Goodman. None of these hounds belong to a Mr. Goodman. In contrast, the following do have the "last names" of their present owners: Wild Bill Stephenson, Cowboy Stephenson, Big Harry Stephenson, Poncho Lloyd, Curley Caudell, Lula Bell Atkins, Dr. Pepper Atkins, Jelly Noblin, James Wings Stanley, Rowdy Sam Morris, Cobbie Shackleford, Rexie Rollins, and Sissy Pusley.

The first foxhounds were landed in America in Calvert County, Maryland, in the seventeenth century and with them came the classic hound names of England: Music, Melody, Fly, Stinger, Frolic, Fancy, Ripper, Terrific. These seldom if ever appear in the formal registry lists, although every informal pack, in Maryland at least, has one or more. The names now, from around the country, have less evident meaning than the older English ones, but, like those of racehorses, in some measure reflect our times and doings, and add color to the pack and conversation about the hounds of the pack: Swiggo Goodman, Rippin' Rachel, Yelling T., Tom McCool, Straw Boss Lee, Hot Shot Buzzard, White Fanny, Rusty Hub, Airplane, Texas Sam Dawson, Greasy Head, Alka Seltzer, Southern Cyclone, Turk Roberts, Big Head, Slow Music, One Red Eye, Razorback Sting, Olive Oil Haggin, Gray Lady Coffin, Pecos Buddy, Him, Tex Ritter, Lonesome Speck, Mean Phantom, Straight Bourbon, Throttle D., Flange D., Valve D., Wheel D., Baham Bilbo Pickett, Halfback Pickett, Shave

Hock, Flapper Lazarus, Squaller, Dixie Dolittle, Sugar Foot Goose, Choctaw McCoy, Perky Godbe, John Foster, Flash Flood, Sterne, Try Courage, Spike Branham, Old Blue, Devil, War Hoss, Hustler, Echo, Sandy Koufax (which should interest him), Possum Grape, Mean Ghost, Scupper Bill, Gangster Jake, Moonlight Swayze. . . .

And so the names go. If you know their voices, you can sit on a hilltop with a mason jar of corn and listen to them at night, in the distance and near distance: Old Yeller, Squaller, Hustler, Sugar Foot. . . .

# 13.

# *Nicknames*

Nicknames are entirely folk. There is no formality or formal organization bringing them into being. They are not at the time of their creation recorded officially in any registers. They are essentially happenstance, informal, accidental, spontaneous.

Except as a person may be addressed in a letter ("Dear Dick:") or referred to in a letter ("Dick told me yesterday . . ."), nicknames are purely oral. They never see the written page except possibly in a court stenographer's transcript of testimony ("I told Dick there shouldn't be no shooting . . ."), or in a frontier account book ("Dick owes two-bits for sugar . . ."), or in those cases where the individual's real name is unknown ("A man by the name of Tex shot and killed . . .") — and in the last case, of course, the nickname ceases to be a nickname and becomes the real name for all intents and purposes.

Nicknames appear in the press and in historical accounts and are remembered there only if the individuals owning them achieve fame in varying ways and carry the nicknames with them to that pinnacle of fame: Dwight D. Eisenhower ("Ike"); Charles Dillon Stengel ("Casey"); William Bonney ("Billy the Kid"). Otherwise they live only during the lifetime of the owners, or until talk and memory of them has ended.

Like the proverb or proverbial phrase, the nickname must not only be created — usually by an individual — but also be recognized, accepted, adopted, and used by the many who hear it. At the very least, it must circulate within a family group. (Normally its circulation is much wider. There can, of course, be two nicknames for a person — one in general use, the other a more personal and "pet" name within the family. In such cases, the two nicknames are apt to be quite separate: the outside group would not be likely to employ a nickname belonging to the intimacy of the family.)

Nicknames are second names, informal ones. They are extraordinarily useful in our casual, daily, social intercourse. Imagine any day without them: the necessity of strictly limiting ourselves to the use of the proper given names and surnames of family, friends, and acquaintances, as well as of persons whom we may not know but about whom we talk. "Charles Dillon Stengel . . ." To speak of him so at any ball park or Third Avenue bar would be meaningless.

Nicknames come into being in several different ways:

— from the common shortening of a name (Dick, Joe, Peg)

— from occupation (Butch, Bedbug)

— from place of origin (Tex, Mex, Nevada)

— from physical characteristics (Red, Shorty)

— from unusual events, actions, or peculiarities
   (Bear Tracks, Christmas Tree)

— from other miscellaneous reasons
   (such as children's malpronunciation of a name: Salga for Sally, Slitch for Richard).

Shortening of a Name

This is the most widespread and accepted form of creating nicknames, and exists on all levels of our society. The use of the diminutive form of the name (usually the given name) is generally limited to friends and reasonably close acquaintances: its use suggests some degree of intimacy and casual association between the person using it and the one to whom the nickname belongs. Except where several drinks may be under the belt and the social gathering is most informal, one would not use even this relatively restrained type of nickname on first meeting. The right to use it is normally accorded by the owner ("Call me Joe"), or by the individual introducing him ("This is Joe McCarthy"). Its use by a stranger, or relative stranger, without such "permission" would cause raised eyebrows at Mike's Bar, let alone the Pavillon.

In any group of twenty persons — cocktail party, classroom, wherever — fifteen of those present will have nicknames based on their given names: Dick, Rick, Peg, Sally, Jack, Lou, Beth, Betty, Betsy, Bitsy, Nell, Sue, Debbie, Jim, Dot, Deedee, Al, Steve, Pam, Joanie, Janie, Judy, Jackie, Jan, Lil, Hank, Bill, and so on indefinitely. There are some names which do not lend themselves to such diminutives: Mary, Marion, George, but they are relatively few. And there are, of course, individuals who never acquire or permit nicknames and who remain Deborah or Elizabeth or William from the registry of birth to the tombstone's chisel. They are not our concern.

## Occupation

In the fluid, melting-pot days of our country, and particularly (by way of example) in the mining camps and growing cities of the West with their swarming, changing populations, something more than the simple diminutive nickname was required. There were too many Joes and Mikes, and they needed further identification. The simplest and most natural way, the very process by which surnames first came into being, was to call each other, or refer to each other, by occupation. There were Daley the Hatter, Axel the Carpenter, Woodchopper Joe, Jim the Smith, Dutch Louis the Butcher, Bill the Bartender, and Louis the Barber. (Not too long ago and over a year's period of time in Virginia City, Nevada — before it went honky-tonk — I had my hair cut by "Louis the Barber" and stood drinks with him several times a week at the Delta Saloon. I never knew any other name for him. Never will. He was never referred to as plain "Louis," always "Louis the Barber." And to the best of my recollection now, there was not another "Louis" in town, and he was the only barber!) There were Sailor Jack, Dan the Paperhanger, Garbage Mike, Butcher John, Big Frank the Carpenter, Eddie the Taylor (and spelled *Taylor* in a grocery account book of the 1870's). There was Bedbug Smith, who was not lousy — like Lousy Dick or Never-Wash — but was the much needed exterminator man for the boardinghouses at Gold Hill, near Virginia City. Old App sold apples. And Snowshoe Thompson carried the mail over the Sierra to Carson, where he was frequently the only winter contact between residents of the Carson Valley and the outside world.

## Place of Origin

Apart from occupations which helped to identify them, men and women were christened for the places and states from which they had come.

A cowboy arrived in camp with no name but Pete. Pete? Just Pete. What camp you from? No camp, just Arizona. OK, Arizona Pete.

There were Telluride Joe and Eldorado Johnny, Frisco Kate and Dublin Dan. Powder River Jack hailed from the Powder River country of Montana, and Dixie Munn Skelly — the "Gold Woman" of Central City, Colorado — came from Louisiana. The mines about which they bragged also gave them names: Cresson Mike, Gold Coin Red, Bullfrog Murphy, and Julia Bob.

Countries of origin enter the nicknames: China Charlie, English George, Nick the Greek, Dutch Louis, Spanish Joe, Frenchy, and plain Swede.

Minnesota Fats carries a double nickname to the pool halls of America, and Casey Stengel was born in Kansas City, known itself by the abbreviated K.C.

## *Physical Characteristics*

There have always been unimaginative, trite, derisive, and frequently cruel nicknames bestowed by youngsters on their fellows because of physical characteristics or habits: Fatty, Skinny, Popeye, Four-Eyes, Dummy, Sissy, Smarty, Pimples, and such. These nicknames are adolescent and pass with adolescence. It is rarely that one hears any of these or comparable others applied to anyone over the age of thirteen. Other nicknames take their place.

But there are solid nicknames based on physical characteristics and used beyond the age of adolescence. Rough, tough ones. Three-Fingered Smith, an early settler on the South Fork of the Salmon River in Idaho, seized an ax and chopped off two fingers that had been bitten by a rattlesnake. Peg-Leg Annie's feet were frozen in a snowstorm on Bald Mountain; she was filled with whiskey, tied down, and her feet amputated above the ankles by Tug Wilson, who used a common meat saw and jackknife. (Consider that, just for a moment.)

There were Crooked-Nose Pete and Baldy Golden, Blind Dick, One-Eyed Murphy, Sleepy Otto, and Dirty-Face Jack. Strawberry Yank sported an alcoholic nose, and Montana's Fat Jack was as lean as a lathe. Johnny-the-Giant wasn't as big as all that by a long shot; Tiny was six feet two and weighed two-fifty; Stuttering Alex had his troubles, and Diamond-Tooth Baker sported his wealth whenever he smiled. Kettle-Belly Brown was prominent on Virginia City's C Street, Shorty Russell still tends bar there, and Slanting Annie walked with a tilt — the result of a slightly crippling accident.

## *Unusual Events, Actions, or Peculiarities*

These nicknames carry with them some sense of local history and incipient legend. There is a story or anecdote implicit in each, and residents of a community will normally oblige with the telling of it. The nicknames are generally good-humored, well intentioned.

Jimmy July, for example, wore an American flag in his lapel and was the only naturalized "Chinaman" in the early days of Butte. Fourth-of-July Murphy raised patriotic Nevada hell on the national holiday. Slot-Machine Ida had a passion for the one-armed bandits, and played the nickel machine whenever she had money. Joe Viani, who owned the Delta, once gave her ten dollars in nickels simply to watch her enjoyment as she whooped, howled, and yelled at the plums, lemons, and bells: it was a long evening, and she danced on the bar before it was over. (Ida froze to death one winter's night in a snowdrift.) Nickel Annie never bummed anyone for more than a nickel, and Shoestring Annie proclaimed her wares simply and directly: "Buy a pair of shoelaces, you God-damned cheapskate!" Christmas-Tree Murphy killed a man with a Christmas tree. And Bear Tracks Murphy acquired his name on the Moffat Tunnel job in Colorado one winter when he made more than passing love to a foreman's wife. The husband returned unexpectedly, and Murphy leaped out a window and across the snow, while the husband demanded to know of his wife who had been there. "Why, nobody." "Well, what are them tracks there then?" "Them? Them's bear tracks."

Hundred-Dollar Jim never wagered more than once a day, but always bet an even hundred in gold, which he played straight up on one number in roulette, stopping — win or lose — with that play. Four-Day Jack never worked more than four consecutive days in the mines, a record better than that of the usual boomer or "ten-day miner." Dead-Shot Reed, Six-Shooter Brown, and Chickie-Thief the Chinaman are obvious. Johnny-Behind-the-Deuce bluffed and died in Tombstone. Crack-'Em-Down Mike was the soul of peace, but once uproariously floored a friend to earn his title.

Wheelbarrow Harbert at first protested vigorously when he was propelled home drunk in a barrow at Tin Cup, Colorado, but soon grew accustomed to it and finally expected the taxi service. And Telephone Tschaikovsky's real name was Matt Konarsky. He earned the "Tschaikovsky" by plinking out two-fingered tunes on a bar piano, and acquired the "Telephone" when a fellow miner in Butte, happily Irish, saw him in the shower wearing newfangled truss equipment to support a rupture: "Lord God, will ye have a look at the tiliphones on old Tschaikovsky!"

The Unsinkable Mrs. Brown in Colorado survived the Titanic disaster. Dinger Williams was proficient in Silver Plume (a beautiful name for a mining camp, drawn from the feathered plumelike ore) at "dinging" pool

*Hayti, Missouri, 1942: Cotton Carnival. Above: hog-calling contest.*
*Below: husband-calling contest*

balls into the pockets, and his brother, Doughbelly Williams, as a youngster, asked his father for a chew of tobacco. "Get away from me, you little dough-belly!" Deacon Blake, an old newspaperman on the Comstock, swore a steady and unprintable streak from the right side of an almost toothless mouth. Skiyoomper bragged about his "ski yoomping" exploits in the old country. And Bronco Lazzeri, who couldn't have known which side of a horse to climb, was the unbroken and irrepressible bartender-owner of the Union Brewery Saloon on the Comstock.

There is a very special Western category of nicknames (preserved for us by Jo and Fred Mazzulla of Denver, Colorado) which speaks for itself, names known throughout the mining camps and in cattle country. They are descriptive and immensely earthy and colorful: Cattle Kate, Rose of Cimarron, Big Matilda, Creede Lil, Prairie Rose, Rotary Rosie, Frisco Sal, Bertha the Adder, China Mary, Ragged Ass Annie, Madame Feather-legs, Sallie Purple, Velvet Ass Rose, The Little Lost Chicken, Three-Tit Tillie, Diamondtooth Gertie, Fatty McDuff, Highstep Jennie, Madame Moustache, Pansy Brasier, Rattlesnake Kate, Little Gertie the Gold Dollar, Josephine Icebox, Latticeporch, Sweet Alice, The Galloping Cow, Wide-Ass Nellie, Red Stockings, Rowdy Kate, Silver Heels, Texas Tommie, Austrian Annie, Spanish Rose, Swede Marie, French Erma, Cornish Queen, Dutch Emma, Italian Rose, Irish Molly, Nigger Elsie, Black Pearl, Jew Jess, Klon-dike Kate, Smooth Bore, The Countess, Cowboy Maggie, Dancing Heifer, Ethel La Moose, Few Clothes Molly, Flora the Ton, Frisco Sal, Foxy Lil, Glassed-eyed Nellie, Grizzly Bear, Lady Godiva, Leo the Lion, Mammy Pleasant, Nellie the Pig, Oregon Mare, Poker Alice, Susie Bluenose, The Mormon Queen, Whispering Mickey, Wicked Alice, Little Egypt, Tit Bit, Lucky Lucy, Red Mountain Hattie, Waddling Duck, Shanghai Kelley, The Roaring Gimlet, Timberline, Queen Gertie, Tin Pot Annie, The Lady in Red, and on indefinitely to include even The Virgin.

A natural outcome of the continued use of such nicknames was to drive men's real names into oblivion. Many a cemetery in the West is filled with otherwise nameless Joes, Mikes, and Jims. When death struck suddenly, there was very often the real problem of any name for the victim. A stranger, who provoked a fight in a San Simon, Arizona, saloon in the 1880's and fell riddled with bullets, was casually buried under a headstone that was partially informative: "He was a dam fule." Lander and Eureka County court records, in Nevada, contain brief entries — "Bull Dog Kate was stabbed and killed by Hog-Eyed Mary"; "Levi Maize, *alias* Buffalo Bill, was shot and instantly killed by Flying Dutchman"; "A man known as Fred. . . ."

And in the town of Austin, Nevada, a stage driver carried a letter for a week, hunting for a Mr. Charles Brown to whom it was addressed. An old friend finally remembered that Charles Brown was the driver himself, locally known as Stub. Stub protested, "Why in the hell can't they write a man by the name he goes by?"

## *Miscellaneous*

The greater number of "miscellaneous" nicknames come into being within a family and are by and large limited to use by it. They are essentially "pet" names, with meaning only for the family circle. Some are accidentally created by children through mispronunciation, while others are very personally fabricated by mother or father for each other or the children. They are, in effect, "secret" names and there are one or two within every family group.

The existence of some other nicknames may be a little more complex. Carl Sandburg, for example, asked General Eisenhower, "Where did the Ike come from?" Eisenhower answered, "All of us, oddly enough, were called Ike. All the brothers. One of us was Ugly Ike, another Big Ike. I was Red Ike, because of my red face. The others outgrew the nickname, but mine always stuck, and it was one of the luckiest things that could have happened to me. A soldier always likes a good name for his officers and generals. Ike was a good name. When they called me Uncle Ike, or during the war just plain Ike, I knew that everything was going well." That nickname, probably the most famous in our century, came out of an Abilene, Kansas, schoolyard and was known with affection and respect around the world by millions.

Eisenhower was, of course, right about the matter of nicknames, as he was about many other down-to-earth and human things about America. Take, by way of example, our national sport. The people have taken their afternoon heroes unto themselves and made them thoroughly human with their nicknames. (This is not true of tennis or golf, nor is it in any comparable degree true of football.) On the basis of nicknames alone, the sport is truly national. And the daily and common use of the nicknames has here very often driven the real names — the given names at least — into oblivion. Even if you know baseball, can you come up with the real names of all the following: Babe Ruth, Ty Cobb, Mickey Mantle, Catfish Hunter, Mudcat Grant, Satchel Paige, Chico Ruiz, Casey Stengel, Bobo Newsom, Goose Goslin, Lefty Groves, Lefty O'Doole (and numerous other Lefties), Whitey Ford, Chichi Rodriguez, Cookie Rojas, Duke Sims, Hondo (Frank Howard), Sandy Koufax, Sudden-Sam McDowell, Pop Haines, Bibb Falk, Irish Meusel? And even where the names are not as colorful, there is certainly no Theodore Williams or Edward Brinkman to be found. (A single-syllable Paul Casanova, yes, but he is also known as Cassy or Cazzy.) They are Mike Epstein, Jim Shellenback, Ted Williams, Reggie Smith, Herb Pennock, Johnny Bench, Ted Uhlaender, Norm Cash, Ken McMullen, Tom Grieve, Jeff Burroughs, Al Kaline, Willie Horton, Denny McLain, Ellie Hendricks, Dave Johnson, Terry Crowley, Don Buford, and so on down the rosters of all the clubs.

The use of nicknames in baseball (as well as their use and non-use within any other group or community) should be of interest to the psychologist and the social historian. Motion picture stars, for example, who are more widely known than baseball players, and about whom people talk and gossip at even greater length, have few *public* nicknames: Robert Montgomery, John Wayne (Duke, by his friends only), Randolph Scott, Alan Ladd, Shirley Temple, Marilyn Monroe, Spencer Tracy, Elizabeth Taylor (rarely Liz), Humphrey Bogart (rarely Bogie), Ava Gardner, Gregory Peck. The difference is one of image: the stars are looked at from a distance, an almost unreal distance, and have not been taken casually and easily into the life of the people. They never will be: they are separated by celluloid and footlights, and one cannot holler and yell at them or joke with them or pound them on the back. They are remote. Olympian shadow figures to be admired, but not touched by the folk.

# Children's Folklore

*Riddles*
*Nonsense Spelling*
*Game Rhymes*
*Autograph Album Rhymes*
*Book Ownership Rhymes*

# 14.

# *Riddles*

A pleasant way of setting the scene for the riddle in America is to go back to winter evenings in Iowa between the years 1873 and 1880 and to listen to Catharine Ann McCollum reminisce about them, as she did in an account reported in the *Journal of American Folklore* (1943). The whole scene is important.

We left the farm when I was only a small girl, but though nearly sixty years have passed, those winter evenings are still clear in my memory, and I often contrast them with the present.

We led the simple life; there was no other. We lived seven miles from a small town (Clarinda, in Page County, southwestern Iowa). A lumber wagon was our only conveyance, there was nothing to go to, and little money for any attraction there might have been. So we had to make our own entertainment.

*Dead Ox Flat, Malheur County, Oregon, 1941:*
*grace before dinner*

Chores done, supper over, and dishes washed, we moved from the "lean-to" which was kitchen and dining room, to the "front room," which was also the bed room for father and mother and the youngest member of the family, myself, who slept in the trundle bed. The room was about fourteen by sixteen feet and the furniture, most of which had been brought from Pennsylvania, was old and of the plainest character. There was no plastering on the walls, just heavy building paper tacked to the studding. There was, however, always rag carpet on the floor, for mother kept herself well supplied in addition to weaving many yards for others. The bed, with the trundle under it, stood in one corner of the room and a lounge in another. A large wood heater was far enough away from the wall so that we could all find places around it (and what quantities of elm, hickory, oak and ash it did consume!), and near the center of the room was a dropleaf table on which stood one or two coal oil lamps.

Iowa winters were very cold and I well remember seeing the coal oil frozen in the lamps in the morning. I can't recall that we thought much about the cold, for we wore warm clothing: long woolen underwear, woolen stockings, and woolen mittens — all knit by mother — heavy shoes, and other garments in keeping with the weather. We certainly were comfortable while in bed, for we slept with a feather bed under us and another over us, with plenty of comforts, some of which were woolen throughout. One of three very large quilts covered the bed, piled high with the big feather ticks. There was the Queen's Fancy quilt, the Grape, and the Rose-in-the-Pattypan, all of which were very pretty and had been beautifully quilted by mother when she was a teacher in Pennsylvania and "boarded 'round" with the "scholars." At the head was a bolster, a long pillow reaching entirely across the bed, and on this were set the two individual pillows. That bed was always perfectly "dressed."

Refreshments of some sort were always provided in the evening. Apples were plentiful and cheap. We raised our own popcorn and never seemed to tire of it. It was fun to scrape out turnips and apples and see who could do the neatest job and leave the thinnest shell. We had plenty of hazelnuts and walnuts. Then, mother's cooky jar never failed. The cookies were by no means rich confections, but they tasted good to us. Nothing but the leavening and the salt had to be bought. Father raised wheat, took it to the mill, had it ground, and brought home flour and bran. He raised sugar cane, took it to the sorghum mill, and brought it home as molasses. Lard was provided by our hogs, eggs by our hens; Elrick, Reddy, and Whitey furnished the milk. These ingredients were combined in proper proportions and the result was plenty of cookies. While eating apples, we sometimes told our fortunes from the seeds, using the rhyme:

*One, he loves,*
*Two, she loves,*
*Three, they both love,*
*Four, he comes,*
*Five, he tarries,*
*Six, he courts,*
*Seven, they marry.*

Sewing carpet rags was the children's usual occupation. Mother paid five cents per pound, and occasionally a bit of stone found its way into the carpet ball, but this was passed by with a smile and taken for the joke it was meant to be. I made a good many balls, but doubt that I ever had the patience to sew one which would weigh a pound. My two brothers earned many a nickel at this job. The woolen mittens and long woolen stockings for the entire family were knitted by my mother largely during those winter evenings, and then, too, there was the never ending patching of trousers and darning of hose. Indeed, I can't remember her sitting down without some work in her hands. Father, before we were able to afford a corn sheller, used to bring in tubs of corn and then by means of a scoop shovel, placed well over the edge of a tub, he would shell corn for seed, using the sharp edge of the shovel to scrape the kernels from the cob. In doing this, father sat on the shovel, a seat made comfortable by putting a coat or two on it for a cushion. He often sewed carpet rags himself, more for a good influence on the boys than anything else. While carpet rags were being sewed, and other work went on, we might ask riddles, and no matter how old they were or how often we heard them, they never lost their interest for us.

We always began with: "What makes a cow look over the hill?" "Because she can't see through it."

Then would follow: "What walks in the water with its head down?" "The nails in a horse's shoe when he walks through the water."

*As I was going to St. Ives,*
*I met a man with seven wives.*
*Each wife had seven sacks,*
*Each sack had seven cats,*
*Each cat had seven kits.*
*Kits, cats, sacks, and wives,*
*How many were going to St. Ives?*

*One. I myself.*

*High as a house,*     *Eye like a barn-door,*
*Low as a mouse,*     *Ears like a cat —*
*Bitter as gall,*     *Guess all night,*
*Sweet after all?*     *And you can't guess that!*

         *A walnut:*          *A big iron kettle,*
*tree, nut, hull, meat.*      *the "eye" being the ball.*

*Chip, chip, cherry,*
*All the men in Derry*
*Can't climb chip, chip, cherry.*

            *Smoke from the chimney.*

"What goes 'round the house and 'round the house, and peeps in at every little hole?" "The sun."

"What goes 'round the house with a harrow after her?" "A hen with her chickens, all engaged in scratching up the ground."

"What's of no use to you and yet you can't go without it?" "Your shadow."

Father always asked this one:

*Twelve pears hanging high,*
*Twelve men came riding by.*
*Each man took a pear*
*And left eleven hanging there.*

        *"Eachman" was a man's name!*

And this was mother's favorite:

*Within a fountain crystal clear*
*A golden apple doth appear,*
*No doors there are to this stronghold,*
*Yet thieves break in and steal the gold.*

               *An egg.*

Other favorites were:

*There was a man who had no eyes,*
*He saw a tree with apples on,*

> *He took no apples off*
> *And he left no apples on.*
>
> > *A man with one eye saw two apples*
> > *on a tree and helped himself*
> > *to one, leaving one.*

> *A man rode over London Bridge,*
> *And yet he walked.*
>
> > *He was accompanied by a dog*
> > *named Yettie!*

These riddles were asked over and over again, night after night, without ever becoming wearisome. Sometimes we tried to invent new ones, but they were very poor as compared to the old, and I can't remember even one of them.

It is valuable to have Catharine McCollum's firsthand account, and we can at the same time be certain that her experience with respect to the riddles themselves was not unique. The riddles have been too widely and readily collected from oral tradition for this to be so: Michigan, Tennessee, Arkansas, New York, Wisconsin, North Carolina, Florida, New Jersey, Maine. Also, beyond the widespread collecting of them by folklorists and others, there is the added assurance of our own family traditions. One can safely wager, for example, that in the 1880's — even earlier and later — riddles were asked or recited at some time during the year, in some quantity or another (perhaps many, perhaps few), within every family in Massachusetts or Maine or Connecticut. (The odds would be 100 to 1 in the case of any family of Scotch-English origin or descent.) The same would hold true in the South. As one moves to the farther West, the incidence might be reduced, but not by a great deal at that time. The knowledge of riddles and riddling was universal.

Catharine McCollum says that the "old" riddles, the tried and true, were the best. Her trial and error affidavit for them ("I can't remember even one of the new ones") confirms the strength of the critical weeding-out and survival process involved in the folk passing of the riddles to us over the years, decades, and centuries. Only the best survived.

Professor Archer Taylor of the University of California, whose book *Eng-*

*lish Riddles from Oral Tradition* is the great work in this field, has grouped riddles into several broad subdivisions: (1) the true riddle, (2) the neck riddle, (3) the puzzle or problem question, and (4) the conundrum and trick question. The divisions make good sense. An understanding of them also makes for appreciation of this fireside pastime.

# The True Riddle

The true riddle deals chiefly with associations and comparisons, where one object or action is described in terms of another in order to suggest something quite different. Frequently also, the first half of the riddle is metaphorical, a misleading decoy or falsehood, while the second half is close to literal fact. A cherry, for example, is described as a man:

> *Come riddle, come riddle my roe-tee-tee-tote,*
> *A little red man in a little red coat,*
> *A stone in his belly, a stick in his throat,*
> *Come tell me this riddle, and I'll give you a groat.*

Another riddle compares a burning candle, which is the correct answer, to a young girl:

> *Little Nanny Etticoat*
> *In a white petticoat*        The girl as misleading decoy.
> *And a red nose;*
> *The longer she stands*       True in fact of a burning candle.
> *The shorter she grows.*

The classic example, of course, is Humpty Dumpty:

| | |
|---|---|
| *Humpty Dumpty sat on a wall,*<br>*Humpty Dumpty had a great fall,* } | Humpty Dumpty, figured as a man,<br>is a misleading decoy. |
| *All the king's horses and all*<br>*the king's men*<br>*Couldn't put Humpty Dumpty*<br>*together again.* } | This is quite true of an egg. |

This first-half falsehood and second-half truth is found in most of the true riddles. There is, for example, the old English riddle: "It runs up the hill and runs down the hill, but in spite of all it still stands still." This same riddle is localized in Maine: "What is it that goes from Windham to Raymond without moving?" The answer to both is: "The road." Like these is another: "What runs all around the yard without moving?" The answer is: "The fence." Very simple also, in form, while retaining the misleading first half and "true" second half: "What has a face and has no mouth?" One thinks immediately of a human being or an animal, misshapen perhaps, but the answer is, of course: "A clock."

One thing about the true riddles: virtually all relate to life around the house, farm, or fields, that is, matters within the full experience of the riddler and the youngster being questioned. There is nothing esoteric about them, nothing of a world beyond the riddlers' immediate knowing. The answers are all: wind, smoke, brook, path, road, fence, hair, bed, fire, chimney, cow, rabbit, blackberry, and other such, all within hand's reach or within the day's doings. However far away a misleading decoy may be ("In marble halls as white as milk . . .") the answer is at home ("Egg").

This is, of course, also the way riddles came into being: the answer first, and the riddle afterwards. A person seeing a familiar or everyday object had his answer, and then worked backward to attempt to create a riddle in which to hide that object — sometimes most successfully, other times not. The successful ones have survived, the poorer have disappeared. Certain objects also lent themselves to the creation of a variety of questions, as in the case of the multiple riddles for a clock, an egg, a bed, a shoe or pair of shoes, a river, and others.

Where several riddles had the same answer, a child questioned might be momentarily caught off balance, believing that he had guessed one object, and that in the natural order of things another object — not the same one — would be the next riddle. But as the riddles were repeated again and again, night after night, with the pleasurable repetition and responses of a litany, the child would shortly know all the answers and there would be no catching off balance. As Catharine McCollum says, the repetition was not boring or dull. It was, on the contrary, exciting. Riddles were asked of a group. There was competition to answer correctly in precisely the same way that there was competition to answer a mathematical question ($8 \times 8 = ?$) or a geographical question (the Sacramento River flows through what state?), the answers in both instances known to all, but repetition bringing its special value to them. Riddles, as with other questions, might go around the circle, one child after another, or they might be tossed to the group as a whole. In either case, all the children were in a state of constant alert. There was the satisfaction of knowing a riddle, or, when a child failed to guess the correct answer, of pleased recognition at understanding the nature of the riddle when the answer was correctly given by the next child.

Of the 1700 true riddles which Professor Taylor studies, I estimate that 400 have had quite wide currency in the United States, and that 200 of these are known — or quickly remembered and actively recognized — wherever riddles are found. Of the selection from oral tradition and widespread sources which follows, for example, I recognize some seventy percent out of my own Massachusetts boyhood.

I have enjoyed them for varying reasons, some for their direct and uncomplicated simplicity:

> *What goes around the house and doesn't make*
> *a track?*
>
> > > *The wind.*

Others because they are complicated:

> *White as snow and snow it isn't,*
> *Green as grass and grass it isn't,*

*Red as blood and blood it isn't,*
*Black as tar and tar it isn't.*

> *A blackberry. First the white blossom*
> *then the green berry which turns red,*
> *and when ripe is black.*

Others for their descriptive humor:

*Four stiff standers,*
*Four down hangers,*
*Two lookers,*
*Two crookers,*
*And one switchabout.*

> *A cow.*

Some few for outlandish humor:

*What wild animal is it that has no head,*
*seven legs, and one tail?*

> *A cat with its head jammed*
> *in a three-legged pot.*

Some for their poetic imagery, and this one bears remembering:

*I washed my hands in water*
*that never rained nor run,*
*I wiped my hands on silk*
*that was neither woven nor spun.*

> *I washed my hands in dew*
> *and wiped them on cornsilk.*

Others because they have a teasing, almost unfair "catch" in them:

*Big as a barn,*

*Light as a feather,*
*And sixty horses can't pull it.*

> *The shadow of the barn.*

And others simply for their tried and true recognition value: everyone must, for example, know:

*On the hill there is a house,*
*In that house there is a closet,*
*In that closet hangs a coat,*
*In that coat is a pocket, and*
*In that pocket is President Lincoln.*

> *A penny.*

A handful of True Riddles:

*What has a head,*
*But has no hair?*

> *A pin, or nail.*

*What has a head,*
*But can't think?*

> *A match.*

*What has teeth,*
*But cannot eat?*

> *A comb, or saw.*

*What has legs,*
*But cannot walk?*

> *A chair, or bed, or table.*

*Four fingers and a thumb*
*Yet flesh and bone have I none.*

> *A glove.*

*Sings and can't talk,*
*Runs and can't walk,*

> *A spinning wheel.*

*Once it was green and growing,*
*Now it is dead and singing.*

> *A fiddle.*

*Black within and red without,*
*Four corners 'round about.*

> *A chimney.*

## CHILDREN'S FOLKLORE

Round as a biscuit,
Busy as a bee,
Prettiest little thing
I ever did see.

           *A watch.*

As long as I eat, I live,
But when I drink, I die.

      *Fire in the fireplace,*
         *or any fire.*

The land is white,
The sea is black,
It'll take a good scholar
To riddle me that.

       *Paper and ink.*

What is neither in the house,
Nor out of the house,
But still is part of the house?

       *A window.*

I walk all day through rain and snow,
I scuff through sleet and hail,
I sleep a-standing on my head,
And my name it rhymes with snail.

      *A nail in a man's shoe.*

Round as an apple,
Black as a bear,
Tell me this riddle
Or I'll pull your hair.

       *An iron teakettle.*

What goes up and down and around
inside the house and then sits in the
corner?

        *A broom.*

A dish full of all kind
   of flowers:
You can't guess this riddle
   in two hours.

        *Honey.*

What is that thing which you cannot
   hold for five minutes,
Yet it is as light as a feather?

       *Your breath.*

Round as a biscuit,
Deep as a cup,
All the Mississippi River
Can't fill it up.

        *A sieve.*

Thirty white horses upon a red hill,
Now they tramp,
Now they champ,
Now they stand still.

        *Teeth and gums.*

*Starke County, North Dakota, 1942: men on the lar*

*What sings morning,*
 *noon, and night,*
*And when the fire's out,*
 *shuts up tight?*

   *A teakettle.*

*It walks east, west,*
 *north, and south,*
*Has a tongue,*
 *but nary a mouth.*

   *A shoe.*

All the preceding true riddles have been in and about the house. The following are, by and large, outside the house and in the fields:

*Round as an apple,*
*Yellow as gold,*
*With more things in it*
*Than you're years old.*

   *A pumpkin.*

*It runs and runs*
*And never tires,*
*Down and down*
*And never up.*

   *A stream or river.*

*Lives in winter,*
*Dies in summer,*
*And grows*
 *with its root upwards.*

   *An icicle.*

*It runs as smooth*
 *as any rhyme,*
*Loves to fall,*
 *but cannot climb.*

   *A stream or river.*

*It goes all over the hills and plains,*
*But when it comes to a river, it breaks its neck.*

   *A path.*

Heraclitus knew the next riddle, and remote tradition has it that Homer, before him, died of frustration at not being able to solve it:

*I went hunting in the wood,*
*And those that I found and killed, I left behind,*
*And those that I could not find*
*I brought home with me.*

   *Lice, or fleas.*

*Up and down,*
*Up and down,*
*Never touches the sky,*
*Never touches the ground.*

*A pump handle.*

*As I went through a field of wheat,*
*I found something good to eat:*
*It was neither flesh nor bone,*
*I kept it till it ran alone.*

*An egg.*

*Goes all over the fields,*
*And leaves a white cap on every stump.*

*The snow.*

*Riddlum, riddlum, raddy,*
*All head and no body.*

*A tadpole.*

*Wanders over the meadow all day long,*
*With a nice little tongue but cannot speak,*
*And goes to the water, but cannot drink.*

*A cowbell.*

The next, although less familiar, is no more fanciful than "Humpty Dumpty":

*As I went down the country road,*
*I met old Granny Gray,*
*I ate her meat and sucked her blood*
*And threw her skin away.*

*A watermelon.*

*It goes through the house*
*And through the barn,*
*Through the woods*
*And around the farm,*
*And never touches a thing.*

*Your voice, or any other sound.*

*Green head, yellow toes,*
*If you don't tell me this riddle,*
*I'll ring your nose.*

                           *A duck.*

*Ears like a mule,*
*Tail like a cotton boll,*
*Runs like a fool.*

                           *A rabbit.*

Last, one of the most famous of all English true riddles, found not infrequently in America, is the beautiful "Riddle Song:"

*I gave my love a cherry without any stone,*
*I gave my love a chicken without any bone,*
*I gave my love a ring without any end,*
*I gave my love a baby and no crying.*

*How can there be a cherry without any stone?*
*How can there be a chicken without any bone?*
*How can there be a ring without any end?*
*How can there be a baby and no crying?*

*A cherry when it's blooming it has no stone,*
*A chicken in the egg it has no bone,*
*A ring when it's rolling it has no end,*
*A baby when it's sleeping there's no crying.*

# The Neck Riddle

The neck riddle has passed out of any extended circulation in America, and finding one in oral tradition is a rarity. This is understandable, since neck riddles do not stand alone but are contained within a story, and were purposely created to be impossible of solution.

A man about to be hanged, for example, is offered the opportunity by his captors or jailors of asking a riddle to save his neck. If none can guess it, he goes scot-free. Otherwise his neck is forfeit.

One condemned man, looking out between bars, saw a crow in a newly planted cornfield. He turned to his executioners:

> *He come, he no come;*
> *He no come, he come.*

No one could solve it, and the prisoner was released. The solution:

> *If the crow comes, the corn will not come;*
> *If the crow does not come, the corn will come.*

Also: Once a man was in jail and was going to be hanged. They told him if he could make a riddle they couldn't guess, they'd set him free. He had a dog named Love, and he killed the dog and tanned its hide. From the hide he made a seat for his chair, a sole for his shoe, and a glove for his right hand. Then he gave this riddle:

> *On Love I sit, on Love I stand,*
> *And Love I hold in my right hand.*

## The Puzzle or Problem Riddle

The puzzle, unlike the true riddle, is stated clearly. All the facts are given, and it is up to the listener to figure them out:

*A man, a woman, and their two sons must cross a river in a boat that will not hold more than 100 pounds. The man and woman each weigh 100 pounds, and each of the boys weighs 50 pounds. How will they get across?*

> *The two boys go over first. One of the boys returns with the boat, and the woman goes over alone. The second boy then returns with the boat, gets the other boy, and they go across together. One of the*

*boys takes the boat back, and waits on the bank while the man goes over alone. The other boy then goes back with the boat and gets his brother.*

The problem riddle frequently contains the solution within the question itself:

*It's between heaven and earth*
*And it's not on a tree,*
*I've told you this riddle*
*As plain as can be.*

   *Knot on a tree.*

*Girls have it,*
*Boys do not,*
*It is in life*
*But not in death.*

   *The letter I.*

*There is a girl in our town,*
*Silk and satin is her gown,*
*Silk and satin, gold and velvet,*
*Can you guess her name?*
*Three times I've telled it.*

   *Ann.*

Arithmetical puzzles all belong here, even though some have a tricky stance to them:

*In what way can you subtract 45 from 45*
*and leave 45?*

$$987654321 = 45$$
$$123456789 = 45$$
$$864197532 = 45$$

*Write down four 9's so that they will total*
*one hundred.*

   *99⁹⁄₉*

The arithmetical puzzles as well as other riddle problems often demand paper and pencil to arrive at a solution. Punctuation, for example, is a requisite in this next in order to make sense out of the statement:

*Charles the First walked and talked half an hour after his head was cut off.*
*Insert a semicolon after "talked."*

A sampling of the Problem Riddles:

*There is a mill with seven corners,*
*In each corner stand seven bags,*
*Upon each bag sit seven cats,*
*Each cat has seven kittens.*
*Then the miller and his wife come into the mill.*
*How many feet are now in the mill?*

*Four. The cats have paws.*

With the solution to a riddle such as this guessed at or given, a youngster was at once initiated into the world of analysis.

*If a room with eight corners has a cat in each corner, seven cats before each cat, and a cat on each cat's tail, how many cats are in the room?*

*Eight cats.*

*A frog started traveling towards the top of a well that was forty-five feet deep. He climbed three feet every day, but fell back two feet every night. How many days did it take him to get out?*

*Forty-three. He gained one foot a day, and in forty-two days he was three feet from the top. On the forty-third day, he leaped out the last three feet.*

*A ship with a crew of thirty men, half of whom were from Maine and half from Connecticut, was in great danger during a fearful storm at sea. The captain, afraid that all would perish unless half the crew were thrown overboard, proposed that every ninth man be thrown overboard until half the crew was destroyed and the ship lightened. It so happened that all the men from Maine were saved, and all the men from Connecticut thrown overboard. Now, what was the order in which the captain placed the crew on deck?*

*With M standing for the men from Maine and C for those from Connecticut, the answer is: M M M M, C C C C C, M M, C, M M M, C, M, C C, M M, C C C, M, C C, M M, C. — This problem may very simply be "proved" by using red and black playing cards laid out on a table, the red standing for the men from Maine, and the black for those from Connecticut. Go through the cards, throwing out every ninth one, and repeating the process until only half of the cards remain, that is, all the red ones standing for the Maine sailors.*

> *A duck before two ducks,*
> *A duck between two ducks,*
> *A duck behind two ducks.*
> *How many ducks?*
>
> > *Three.*

> *There is a lady in the land*
> *With twenty nails on each hand*
> *Five and twenty on hands and feet*
> *This is true without deceit.*
> *How can this be true?*
>
> > Punctuation is the answer:
> > *There is a lady in the land*
> > *With twenty nails; on each hand*
> > *Five, and twenty on hands and feet.*
> > *This is true without deceit.*

*How many feet are there on a lamb if you call a tail a foot?*

> *Four. Calling a tail a foot doesn't make it one.*

*There were seven copy cats sitting on a fence.*
*One jumped off. How many were left?*

*None.*

# The Conundrum
# and the Trick (or Impossible)
# Riddle-Question

The last type includes both the conundrum and the trick, or impossible, question. It involves a play on words, puns — some of them quite terrible — and the combination of farfetched and unrelated ideas. Most of the conundrums and trick questions are modern, within the last century at least, and include incredible items such as: Why is Mr. Timothy More, since he lost his hair, like an American city? (Because he is bald Tim More.) If you wished a doctor of divinity to play on your violin, what would you say? (Fiddle, D.D.) Can a leopard change his spots? (Yes, when he is tired of one spot, he can go to another.) When is a man literally immersed in business? (When he is giving a swimming lesson.) Why do Pennsylvania farmers build their pigsties between the house and the barn? (For the pigs.)

Here also belong those "riddles" or trick questions that hover on the outer fringes of folklore as fads of the moment: The Knock-knocks, the Elephant jokes, the Little Moron jokes, the Sick Jokes, the Dead Baby jokes, the Grape jokes, and the quite numerous other cycle-jokes which pop up, endure for a time, and then disappear — although the life of some can be fairly long, and some may even become fully entrenched in folklore.

A sampling of the Conundrums and Trick Questions:

*What is the difference between a deer fleeing from its pursuers and a decrepit witch?*

*One is a hunted stag, the other a stunted hag.*

*What is the difference between a summer dress in winter and an extracted tooth?*

> *One is too thin, the other tooth out.*

*What is the difference between a ballerina and a duck?*

> *One goes quick on her beautiful legs, the other goes quack on her beautiful eggs.*

*What is the difference between a king's son, a monkey's mother, a bald head, and an orphan?*

> *A king's son is the heir apparent, a monkey's mother is a hairy parent, a bald head has no hair apparent, and an orphan has nary a parent.*

*What is the difference between a glass of water and a glass of whisky?*

> *Fifteen cents.* (That will date that one — and a glass, no less!)

A steady diet of these (even on the vaudeville stage where many of them originated) was enough to drive one right up the wall, and at Brown University, during my undergraduate days, an irreverent, but maturer, balance to these "gags" (and gag they did) was introduced with counter-irritants such as:

*What is the difference between an elephant's ass and a mailbox?*
*I don't know.*
*You'd be the wrong person to send to mail a letter.*

The Why and What queries, all impossible of any rational solution:

*Why is 1860 like 1862?*

> *Because the one is 1860 and the other is 1862.*

*Why can the pallbearers at a young lady's funeral never be dry?*

> *Because they have a gal on a bier between them.*

*Why is Samuel Smith like an underdone cake?*

> *He is not Brown.*

*Why is a poet like a pullet?*

> *Because he chants his lays.*

*Why is a pig with a twisted tail like the ghost of Hamlet?*

> *Because it can a tail unfold.*

*What animals grow on grape vines?*

> *Gray apes.*

*What is a very good definition of nonsense?*

> *Bolting a door with a boiled carrot.*

*What is the most difficult river on which to get a boat?*

> *Arno, because they're Arno boats there. (Eek!)*

*What tricks are most common among New York policemen?*

> *Patricks.*

*What is an old lady in the middle of a river like?*

> *Like to be drowned.*

The Knock-knocks came into being in the 1930 speakeasy days as a veritable craze. For a time it was impossible to attend any sort of party or gathering without being Knock-knocked or Knock-knocking. The craze has died, but the Knock-knocks are still solidly here. Any slight scratching of the surface will bring them out with immediate recognition: no explanation of them is necessary: everyone seems to know the why of a Knock-knock.

## CHILDREN'S FOLKLORE

| First person: | Knock, knock. |
|---|---|
| Second person: | Who's there? |
| First person: | Amos. |
| Second person: | Amos who? |
| First person: | A mosquito bit me. |

Knock, knock.
Who's there?
Andy.
Andy who?
And he bit me again.

Knock, knock.
Who's there?
Tarzan.
Tarzan who?
Tarzan tripes forever.

Knock, knock.
Who's there.
Boo.
Boo who?
What are you crying for?

Knock, knock.
Who's there?
Alfred.
Alfred who?
Alfred the needle if you'll sew the button on.

Knock, knock.
Who's there?
Fiddlestick.
Fiddlestick who?
If the bed's too short, your fiddlestick out.

> *Knock, knock.*
> *Who's there.*
> *Duane.*
> *Duane who?*
> *Duane the bathtub, Mama, I'm dwowning.*

The Elephant riddle-jokes came into being in the early 1960's and are also reasonably well entrenched. They appeal to youngsters and adults alike for their sheer out-of-this-world absurdity.

*Why is an elephant gray?*

> *So you won't mistake him for a bluebird.*

*Why does an elephant have red toenails?*

> *So he can hide in a cherry tree.*

*Why should we never go into the jungle between two and four o'clock?*

> *That's when the elephants come jumping out of the trees.*

*Why do we have Pygmies in the jungle?*

> *Because they went into the jungle between two and four o'clock.*

*Why do elephants wear sunglasses?*

> *If you were the one they were telling all these jokes about, you would want to hide, too.*

Of the three types — the true, the problem, and the conundrum — the true is far and away the best and will last the longest. The conundrum is, literally, a joke and impossible of solution. From the word go, the person questioned knows that he is stooge for the trickster. In the majority of cases, he is not even asked to exercise his wits, but simply to act as straight man to the comic who holds all the cards and controls the laughter. The problem question also does not demand more than a prosaic, analytical approach to the puzzle. It is something to be worked out, and when the answer is arrived at, the solution is recognized, and that's it. The true riddle, however, goes far beyond that. Recognition of the correctness of the answer does not bring the child's enjoyment to an end. Unconsciously he is led into the world of analogy, the world of "this is like that," the realm of symbolism and poetry. A world of beauty:

> *I washed my hands in water that never rained nor run,*
> *I wiped my hands on silk that was neither woven nor spun.*

That came from Illinois: land of Lincoln, Carl Sandburg, Edgar Lee Masters. . . .

# 15.

# Nonsense Spelling

"What's high in the middle and round at both ends? (Ohio)" is by way of being a spelling riddle, just as are also:

> *Two* n's, *two* o's, *an* l *and a* d,
> *Now see what you can spell for me?*
> (*London*)

and

> *Upon the hill there is a mill*
> *Around the mill there is a walk,*
> *Under the walk there is a key,*
> *What is the name of this city?*
> (*Milwaukee*)

A question is posed, and an answer required. But those that follow do not ask a question, and they are, in consequence, not riddles but pure and simple (if complicated) exercises in nonsense-spelling.

Spell Squirrel, for example:

> *Squee diddle R-L,*
> *Squirrel.*

Grasshopper:

> *G-R-A, double S, grass,*
> *H-O-P, hop,*
> *Get on top,*
> *E-R, per,*
> *Grasshopper!*

Mississippi:

> *M-I, crooked letter, crooked letter, I,*
> *Crooked letter, crooked letter, I,*
> *Humpback, humpback, I.*

The origin of these lies in the one-room school spelling drills of the 1800's, where words were required to be broken into syllables in order the better to control the spelled answer, and where the fully spelled word itself was pronounced at the end:

Spell Washington:

> *W-A-S-H, Wash,*
> *I-N-G, ing,*
> *T-O-N, ton,*
> *Washington.*

*San Augustine, Texas, 1939:*
*grade school glee club*

Frolicsome:

> *F-R-O-L, frol,*
> *I-C, ic,*
> *S-O-M-E, some,*
> *Frolicsome.*

The classroom source is clear in "grasshopper" (G-R-A, double S, grass / H-O-P, hop . . .), and the development to fine nonsense is apparent in:

Snapping Turtle:

> *Snee A-P, snap,*
> *Eat a little, tickle E, ortle,*
> *T-L, eetle,*
> *Snapping turtle.*

The debt to the schoolroom spelling exercise and the schoolboy's imaginative spoofing of its method are implicit in others:

Hell:

> *H-E, two hockey sticks,*
> *Hell!*

Woodpecker:

> *W, double O, D, wood,*
> *Sockety peck,*
> *Run around the limb,*
> *And stick his bill in,*
> *Woodpecker!*

Horseback:

> *H-O-R-S-E, horse,*
> *B-A, bick-a-back,*
> *Horseback!*

Aaron:

> *Big A, little a, ron,*
> *Aaron.*

A general favorite in my own youth was Constantinople, with its several variants:

> *With a C and a Si and a Constanti,*
> *With a Nople and a Pople*
> *Spells Constantinople.*
>
> *Can you Con, can you Stan,*
> *Can you Constanti,*
> *Can you Steeple, can you Stople,*
> *Can you Constantinople?*
>
> *C-N-O*
> *And a Constanto,*
> *And a Nople and a Pople*
> *And a Constantinople.*

In the United States, Cincinnati, New York, and, in a rather special way, Chicago bore the brunt of the geographic nonsense-spelling:

> *Cin-Cin, needle and pin,*
> *Gnat and a fly, gnat's eye,*
> *Cincinnati.*
>
> *A needle and a pin spells sin-sin,*
> *A gnat and a fly spells Cincinnati.*
>
> *Cin, Cin,*
> *A needle and a pin,*
> *A skinny and a fatty,*
> *And that's the way to spell Cincinnati.*

New York was ever the land of high living:

> *A knife and a fork,*
> *A bottle and a cork,*
> *And that's the way*
> *To spell New York.*

In prose, Chicago was built up out of portions of words: ³⁄₇ of a chicken, ²⁄₃ of a cat, and ½ of a goat. The rhyme was similar and simpler:

> *Chicken in the car,*
> *The car won't go,*
> *And that's the way to spell*
> *Chi-ca-go.*

Pumpkin and huckleberry pies round out the best of the nonsense-spellings:

> *P-U-N, punkin,*
> *P-U-N, eye,*
> *P-U-N, punkin*
> *Punkin Pie.*
>
> *P-U ennekin, ennekin Y,*
> *Ennekin ennekin, Pumpkin Pie.*
>
> *P-U, double unkin,*
> *P-U, double I,*
> *P-U double unkin,*
> *Punkin Pie.*
>
> *H-U, huckle, B-U, buckle,*
> *H-U, huckle-Y*
> *H-U, huckle, B-U, buckle,*
> *H-U, huckleberry pie.*

Pumpkin and huckleberry as over against mince and peach are readily understandable. But why no Hackensack or San Francisco or Albuquerque or Kalamazoo? Why should the nonsense-spellings of cities have been strictly limited to Cincinnati, Chicago, and New York? They were.

# 16.

# Game Rhymes

## Jump-Rope Rhymes

There is probably nothing in springtime which more joyfully captures that season on the human level (I exclude here Nature's other exclamation points) than the skip-rope games and chants of youngsters (girls) in the fourth and fifth grades, ages nine to eleven, or thereabouts. The whole season is theirs: the wonder of being alive, living and jumping and skipping, with the rhymes and the rhythms of their own making and those inherited from their forebears (now in the sixth grade) to go with them. It is Spring and innocence and exuberance and fearful concentration all wrapped into one. The next time you pass a playground or a schoolyard at recess-time in the months of March, April, or May, pause, look, and listen. If you are over twenty, it will make you feel older than hell.

Jumping rope was once the prerogative of youths and men, and was a game or exercise to test endurance: the one who skipped the longest was winner. The single trace of that early tradition left us is the skip-rope training of boxers, useful for the development of "footwork." At one time also — the entire nineteenth century, to be exact — the dress of "young ladies" sorely inhibited individual skipping, let alone anything approximating "Double Dutch" or "Red Hot Pepper."

The names and the terms of the games today are quite wonderful: grinding coffee, hopsies, swish swosh, sweep the floor, double-French, cut the cheese, split the pie, four no miss, baby in the cradle, bumps, mustard, low water, running through the moon, loops, lift and lay, vinegar, up the ladder, winding the clock, yokey, follow-my-leader, double rope, porridge, scissors, blindsies, climb the stairs, up and down, plain ropes, feet together-and-apart, hot peas, legs crossed, baby's cradle, baking bread. Those come from the youngsters themselves and so do the chants and rhymes.

The now standard reference work on *Jump-Rope Rhymes* is the book of that title by Roger Abrahams, published by the American Folklore Society in 1969. Abrahams gives the texts of 619 separate rhymes (not including variants) culled from published American sources, and also includes an excellent bibliography. He subtitles it *A Dictionary*. It is most useful.

Abrahams' collection, with references, comes from across the country. I add here to it the collection (or parts of it) from the Peabody Elementary School in Washington, D.C., where an imaginative librarian (Miss Jean Alexander) and an understanding principal (Mrs. Florence Radcliffe) "published" a mimeographed few pages of rhymes collected from children in their school: "These jump-rope rhymes were gathered by 18 school children. . . . It was not a class assignment, but purely a library project open to any child who wished to enter the contest for a small prize. . . . One student handed in over 150 rhymes; another, 130." One of my folklore students (Marian Hart) at American University followed this project up in the same school and brought in added rhymes. From this double-barreled collection — thoroughly contemporary yet with traditional base, found in one school in Washington yet largely known around the country — the following are selected. Have you a skip rope? Or memory of one?

> *Grandma, grandma, sick in bed,*
> *Called for the doctor, and the doctor said,*
> *"Grandma, Grandma, you ain't sick,*
> *All you have to do is the seaside six."*
> *Hands up, shakey, shakey, shakey, shake,*
> *Hands down, shakey, shakey, shakey, shake,*
> *Touch the ground, shakey, shakey, shakey, shake,*
> *Turn around, shakey, shakey, shakey, shake,*
> *Stomp around, shakey, shakey, shakey, shake,*
> *Get out of town, shakey, shakey, shakey, shake.*
>
> *Jump a lee,*
> *The rope is so empty.*

> *I'm jumping, I'm jumping,*
> *1–2–3,*
> *I'm jumping, I'm jumping,*
> *4–5–6*
> *I'm jumping, I'm jumping,*
> *7–8*
> *I'm jumping, I'm jumping,*
> *9 and 10,*
> *I'm jumping, I'm jumping,*
> *And that is the end!*

Is that not beautiful?

> *Jaybird, jaybird, sitting on a rail,*
> *Picking his teeth with the end of his tail.*
>
> *Mulberry leaves and calico sleeves,*
> *All school teachers are hard to please.*

*Apples, peaches, pears and plums,*
*Tell me the name of your sweet love.*
*A–B–C–D —*
    *Davey! Do you love me?*
    *Yes, no, maybe so. . . .*
*How many children will you have?*
*1–2–3–4 —*
    *What will you live in?*
    *House, barn, garbage can,*
    *House, barn, garbage can. . . .*

*Eskimo, Eskimo, where have you gone?*
*I've gone to the North Pole.*
*What kind of weather did you have?*
*Hot, cold, hot, cold, hot, cold. . . .*

*Apple on a stick,*
*Five cents a lick,*
*Every time I turn around*
*It makes me sick.*

*"Mother, mother, I am ill,*
*Send for the doctor from over the hill."*
*In comes the doctor, in comes the nurse,*
*In comes the lady with the alligator purse.*
*"Measles," says the doctor, "Measles," says the nurse,*
*"Measles," says the lady with the alligator purse.*
*Out goes the doctor, out goes the nurse,*
*Out goes the lady with the alligator purse.*

I would give a pretty penny to know where that "alligator purse" comes from, and why it persists so. Again, for example:

*Miss Suzie called the doctor,*
*The doctor called the nurse,*

*The nurse called the lady*
*With the alligator purse.*
*In went the doctor,*
*In went the nurse. . . .*

Something a little less traditional? More contemporary?

*Grandma Moses sick in bed*
*Called the doctor and the doctor said,*
*"Grandma Moses, you ain't sick,*
*All you need is a licorice stick."*

*I gotta pain in my side, Oh! Ah!*
*I gotta pain in my stomach, Oh! Ah!*
*I gotta pain in my head 'cause my baby said,*
*Roll-a-roll-a-peep!*
*Roll-a-roll-a-peep!*
*Bump-te-wa-wa, bump-te-wa-wa,*
*Roll-a-roll-a-peep!*

*Downtown baby on a roller coaster,*
*Sweet, sweet baby on a roller coaster,*
*Shimmy shimmy co-co-pop*
*Shimmy shimmy POP!*
*Shimmy shimmy co-co-pop*
*Shimmy shimmy POP!*

Credit where credit is due: the last one was collected from Donna Ashmon, age nine. And a chant of pure and gentle love which comes from her sister, Annette Ashmon, age ten:

*I wish I had a nickel,*
*I wish I had a dime,*
*I wish I had a sweetheart*
*To love me all the time.*

*I'd make her wash the dishes,*
*I'd make her scrub the floor;*
*When she gets finished,*
*I'd kick her out the door!*

And an incredible:

*My name is Wild Bill Jones,*
*And the day they shot me*
*I stood brave and tall,*
*Until the doctor said,*
*"O.K., that's all."*

That must have come from TV and film, but how was it ever capsuled into a jump-rope rhyme? The whole story is in the five lines.

A few more, some traditional, and some not:

*Miss Sue (clap, clap), Miss Sue,*
*The kid from A-la-ba-ma.*
*Let's start to move,*
*START!*
*Chig-a-boo, chig-a-boo,*
*Chig-a-boo-boo-boo.*

*Meet me at the airport,*
*Be on time — Hey!*
*Meet me at the airport,*
*Be on time — Hey!*
*The plane is gonna leave*
*At a quarter to nine!*

*Down by the riverside the green grass grows,*
*Where someone walks, some walk tiptoe.*
*She sings, she sings so sweet,*
*She calls over to someone across the street,*

> *"Tea cakes, pancakes, everything you see,*
> *Meet me at the park at half past three."*

That, of course, is a highly mixed-up (folk transmission) version of "Down by the river/Where the green grass grows/There sat Jennifer/As pretty as a rose. . . ."

This next is very, very nice:

> *Blackbird whistle, woodpecker drum,*
> *"Spring has come, Spring has come."*
> *Cardinal sing in the maple tree,*
> *"Spring is here for you and me."*
> *Longer day and shorter night,*
> *Little boy, bring out your kite.*

Death has its specifics:

> *Little Mrs. Pinky dressed in blue,*
> *She died last night at a quarter of two.*
> *Before she died, she told me this,*
> *"You better run out before you miss."*

And Salome, language and all, is thoroughly updated:

> *Salome was a dancer,*
> *She danced before the king,*
> *And every time she danced*
> *She wiggled everything.*
> *"Stop," said the king,*
> *"You can't do this in here."*
> *"Baloney," said Salome,*
> *And kicked the chandelier.*

I particularly like the poetry of that next to the last line.

The "t" in "señorita" is precisely as collected:

*One day when I was walkin',*          *Oh, shake it sentorita,*
*A-walkin' to the fair,*               *Shake it if you can,*
*I met a sentorita*                    *Shake it like a milkshake*
*With a flower in her hair.*           *And shake it once again.*

*Oh, she wowed 'em to the bottom,*
*She wowed 'em to the top,*
*She turn around and turn around*
*Until she made a S-T-O-P, STOP!*

That was from a nine-year-old. These next two are from an aged ten:

*Piece-a-piece-a-petty*          *'Cause I saw her!*
*Thumbalina!*                     *Piece-a-piece-a-petty*
*Piece-a-piece-a-petty*          *Do a dance!*
*Had a party!*                    *Piece-a-piece-a-petty*
*Piece-a-piece-a-petty*          *How ya do it?*
*How ya know it?*                 *Piece-a-piece-a-petty*
*Piece-a-piece-a-petty*          *Like this!*

*Sandra, somebody's callin' your name.*
*Sandra, somebody's playin' a game.*
*Sittin' at the table*
*Peelin' a boiled 'tatoe*
*Waitin' for the clock to go tick-tock*
*Tick-tock-ta-wada-wada*
*Tick-tock-ta-wada-wada-BOOM!*

"See, saw, Margery Doll" drives completely out of mind the original "Daw" from which it stems:

*See, saw, Margery Doll,*
*Don't you have any master?*

*She shall have but a penny a day*
*Because she can't work any faster.*

"Batman" might well be set to music. And why doesn't a Gershwin capture the playground?

*This way, Batman, Batman, Batman,*
*This way, Batman, all night long.*
*Step back, Sally, Sally, Sally,*
*Step back, Sally, all night long.*
*Lookin' down the alley, alley, alley,*
*What do I see?*
*A big fat man from Tennessee.*
*Betcha five dollars I can beat that man.*
*To the front, to the back, to the side by side,*
*To the front, to the back, to the side by side.*

I very much like "boyfriend" as one word, which, of course, it is in usage. The girl's reaction to love's avowal is a bit unusual:

*One day when I was walkin'*
*I hear my boyfriend talkin'*
*To the pretty girl*
*With the strawberry curl.*
*And this is what he said,*
*"I love you."*
*She jumped in the lake*
*And swallowed a snake*
*And came back with a belly ache.*

*Fudge, fudge, tell the judge,*
*Mama's got a new-born baby.*
*'Tisn't a boy 'tisn't a girl,*
*Just a common baby.*
*Wrap it up in tissue paper,*
*Send it to the elevator.*
*First floor, miss, Second floor miss,*
*Third floor, miss, Fourth floor,*
*Out the door!*

The A, B, C, and one-two-three counts determine the ends of skipping:

*Ladybug, ladybug, turn around,*
*Ladybug, ladybug, touch the ground,*
*Ladybug, ladybug, shine your shoes,*

*Ladybug, ladybug, read the news.*
*Ladybug, ladybug, how old are you?*
*One, two, three, four . . .*

*Light sky, dark sky,*
*Peaches and cream,*
*What are the initials of your dream?*
*A, B, C, D . . . .*

*Jean, Jean, dressed in green,*
*Went up town to eat ice cream.*
*How many dishes did she eat?*
*One, two, three, four . . .*

*Ice cream, soda, Delaware punch,*
*Tell me the initials of your honeybunch.*
*A, B, C, D . . .*

*Apples, peaches, pumpkin pie,*
*How many years before I die?*
*One, two, three, four . . .*

*Raspberry, raspberry, raspberry jam,*
*What are the initials of my young man?*
*A, B, C, D . . .*

*I was born in a frying pan,*
*Can you guess how old I am?*
*One, two, three, four . . .*

*Apples, peaches, cream and butter,*
*Here's the name of my true lover.*
*A, B, C, D . . .*

*Yonder comes the teacher*
*With a great big stick,*
*I wonder what I made*
*On Arithmetic.*
*One, two, three, four . . .*

*Red, white, and yellow,*
*Have you any fellow?*
*Yes, no, maybe so,*
*Yes, no, maybe so,*
*Yes, no, maybe . . .*

*Engine, engine, Number Nine,*
*Running on the Chicago Line,*
*Please tell me the correct time.*
*One o'clock, two o'clock, three o'clock . . .*

And a baker's half dozen:

*Jump, jump, jump,*
*Who can jump the rope?*
*All day long it's*
*Jump, jump, jump.*

*Amos and Andy,*   *Amos and Andy,*   *Amos and Andy,*
*Sugar and candy,*   *Sugar and candy,*   *Sugar and candy,*
*I pop in.*   *I pop down.*   *I pop out!*

*Mable, Mable,*   *Old man Lazy*
*Set the table,*   *Drives me crazy,*
*Don't forget the*   *Up the ladder,*
*Sugar, salt, vinegar, and*   *Down the ladder —*
*RED  HOT  PEPPER!*   *H-O-T spells hot!*

*Spell cat. C-A-T.*
*Spell rat. R-A-T.*
*Now it's time for Exercise:*
*Hands up, hands down,*
*Turn around, touch the ground.*
*Now it's time for Arithmetic:*
*8 plus 8 is 16, 10 plus 10 is 20.*
*Now it's time for History:*
*George Washington never told a lie.*
*He ran around the corner and stole a cherry pie.*
*How many did he steal?*
*He stole one, two, three, four . . .*

*Old lady, old lady, touch the ground,*
*Old lady, old lady, turn around,*
*Old lady, old lady, point your shoe,*
*Old lady, old lady, twenty-three skidoo!*

*Miss, miss, little Miss, miss,*
*When she misses, she misses like this!*

Tired?

# The Counting-Out Rhymes

There are many outdoor games (but chiefly "hide and seek" or some form of it) which require the choosing of one child to be "It." The choosing is usually done by verbal lot, that is, the impartial and indiscriminate counting-out to select one youngster. The one who does the counting may do so as self-appointed leader (excluding himself from the count), or he may include himself as he goes around the group. There is nothing downgrading in being "It": someone must be, in order to get the game started, and there is every likelihood that as the afternoon progresses each child will play his turn.

A counting-out rhyme (they are all rhymes) may be brief and swift in its judgment. In these there is no weeding-out process, no suspense as players are eliminated, but a direct attack upon "It" from which there is no appeal:

*Red, white, and blue,*   *One, two, sky blue,*
*All out but you!*   *All out but you!*

*Ink, pink, penny wink,*
*Oh, how you do stink!*

*Morton County, North Dakota, 1942:*
*children playing "cut the pie" or "fox and geese" at noon recess*

*Roses are red,*
*Violets are blue,*
*When I choose,*
*It will be you!*

More unusual are the longer rhymes which go around the circle or group, taking the individual players out, until the count narrows down to three, and to two, and, finally, to "It."

The majority are well known — in one variant form or another — throughout the United States:

*Onery, twoery, Ickory Ann,*
*Fillison, Follason, Nicholas John,*
*Queevy, Quavy, English Navy,*
*Stinkalum, Stankalum, Buck!*

*Intery, Mintery, Cutery, Corn,*
*Apple seed and apple thorn,*
*Wire, briar, limber-lock,*
*Three geese in a flock,*
*One flew east and one flew west,*
*And one flew over the cuckoo's nest,*
*O-U-T, out!*

*Ibbity, bibbity, sibbity, sab,*
*Ibbity, bibbity, cannaba,*
*Cannaba in, cannaba out,*
*Cannaba over the water spout,*
*O-U-T spells out!*

A suggestion here may be in order. As a youngster I recited this with surety, knowing that the word was "cannaba." I am not so certain of that now, and believe that the rhyme is a corruption of what was clearly known at one time to youngsters along the Erie Canal:

*Ibbity, bibbity, sibbity, sab,*
*Ibbity, bibbity, canal boat,*
*Canal boat in, canal boat out* (of the locks),
*Canal boat over the water spout* (as the water was released, it came out
  with a rushing spout from the lock, and the boat with it).
*O-U-T spells out!*

My own time was much later than that of the Erie Canal and it was also in
Massachusetts, so that a York State "canal boat" was unknown to me and
my friends. The rhyme was a pleasant and meaningless, yet rhythmical,
"cannaba."

> *a, b, c, d, e, f, g,*
> *h, i, j, k, l, m, n, o, p,*
> *q, r, s, t,*
> *u are out!*

> *My mother, your mother,*
> *Live across the way,*
> *Every night they have a fight,*
> *And this is what they say:*
> *Hinkey, dinkey,*
> *Soda crackers,*
> *Hinkey, dinkey, boo,*
> *Hinkey dinkey,*
> *Soda crackers,*
> *Out goes you!*

The "hinkey, dinkey, boo" may well be a child's World War I adaptation of
"hinkey, dinkey, parlez-vous."
  There are other reasonable ones:

*Bee, a bee, a bumble bee*
*Stung a man upon his knee*
*And a hog upon the snout —*
*I'll be dogged if you ain't out!*

*Matthew, Mark, Luke, and John,*
*Saddle the cat and I'll get on,*
*Give me the switch and I'll be gone,*
*Out goes he!*

*Teacups and saucers,*
*Plates and dishes*
*All little boys*
*Wear calico britches,*
*Out goes Y-O-U, sky blue!*

Vance Randolph collected that last from a "little girl in Hot Springs, Arkansas, in 1938," who claimed that it was "the best" of all counting-out rhymes. It may be a hand-me-down corruption of the midwife's rhyme going back to early nineteenth-century Ulster: "Matthew, Mark, Luke, and John / God Bless the bed that she lies on . . ." Anything is possible in folklore — "Saddle the cat and I'll get on!"

The next is a pleasantly complicated (and consequently quite honest) way of selecting the "It" victim.

*Eeena meena dixie dan,*
*Who will be a soldier man?*
*Ride a horse, beat a drum,*
*Tell me when your birthday comes.*

The player on whom the last word falls must name the month and day of his birthday. Then the months and days are counted around. If a player's birthday is on March 4, for example, the count goes around: January, February, March 1, 2, 3, 4, and that player is out.

We come now (and let us take a good look at it) to the "Eeny, meeny, miny, mo" rhyme, which has generally passed all others in popular usage. It was known everywhere, and its popularity in our time (this century and the last) has been due solely to its fantastic rhythm and seemingly wonderful nonsense: "Eeny, meeny, miny, mo . . ." There is a fine beat there. But there is also a strong tradition, going back on the one hand to the days of Druidic human sacrifice, and on the other to the time of the Underground Railroad, when slaves escaped from the South to the North. Neither of these traditions was known, or is known, to youngsters using the rhymes.

Take the Druidic tradition first. An old, old rhyme from Cornwall:

> *Eena, meena, mona, mite,*
> *Basca, lora, hora, bite,*
> *Hugga, bucca, bau;*
> *Eggs, butter, cheese, bread,*
> *Stick, stock, stone dead — O-U-T!*

Charles Francis Potter says:

We are back in Druid times, about the first century B.C., when we chant some of these words. It was in 61 B.C., so Tacitus tells us, that the Roman conqueror Suetonius commanded the holy Druid groves of the sacred isle of *Mona* (now Anglesea) cut down to end the bloody rites of Druidism. To get to that island, even today, from North Wales, you must cross the *Menai* strait. *Hora* and *lora* are Latin for hour and binding-straps and *bucca* was Cornish for hobgoblin or evil spirit.

According to Caesar's chronicles, the Druids resorted to divination by magic rhymes and charms. Potter suggests that our common "Eeny, meeny, miny, mo" was once used (in differerent form, of course: the admixture of Latin comes later in oral tradition) by the Druids to select human victims "to be ferried across the Menai Strait to the isle of Mona to meet a horrible fate under the Golden Bough of the sacred mistletoe amid the holy oaks." One of the Druids' methods of sacrifice was to burn the victims alive in wicker cages. So the chosen victim (or victims) was told that his *hora* had come, was bound with *lora* inside the *stick-stock* wicker cage or *basca*, and burned until he was *stone dead*. The *eggs, butter, cheese,* and *bread* of this particular rhyme reflect the centuries-old belief that those foods have special magic properties.

That the rhyme is ancient, there is no question.

Now we come to the rhyme in America and the interpolation of "nigger." (Parenthetically, folklore carries with it the evils and stupidities and prejudices of humanity as well as the great goodness of the human race. That is an obvious historical fact which it would be senseless to ignore; we can deplore it on the folk level, and thoroughly damn it on any presumed higher level. Anyhow . . .)

Potter offers a most interesting explanation for the second line of our commonly known rhyme. In Canada, he says that children still use a rhyme brought from France:

> *Meeny, meeny, miny, mo,*
> *Cache ton poing derrière ton dos* . . .

"Hide your fist behind your back . . ." The child doing the commanding and ordering then guessed the number of fingers which were held in the fist. If the number was, perhaps, three, then the third player counted 'round was out.

Children in the North — Maine, certainly — hearing this French-Canadian rhyme, attempted in folk etymological fashion to make sense out of the strange, foreign words. "Cache" became *catch* and "dos" became *toe.* The words in between? At this time, slaves were escaping to the North via the Underground Railway. Children heard their parents talking of this, and the missing words were supplied: "Catch a nigger by the toe." *Catch* was there and *toe* was there. (*Negro* in parlance had become *nigra*, then *nigger.* The French use *nègre*, and so does the president of Senegal when he speaks of *négritude.*) The now unsavory term "nigger" filled out the second line. But the creation of the second line, following the "eeny, meeny, miny, mo," was no completion of either rhyme or sense. So we have the third line — "If he hollers, let him go" — which is tied historically to the tribulations and terrors of the escape from slavery through the North to Canada. And the final rhyme, which we all know, runs:

> *Eeeny, meeny, miny, mo,*
> *Catch a nigger by the toe,*
> *If he hollers, let him go,*
> *Eeeny, meeny, miny, mo.*

And so we have Druidic sacrifice in Wales and the terrors of slavery-escape in America of the 1850's reduced (unwittingly, and with no sense of history, or even of the meaning of words) to a children's rhyme. It was my favorite as a youngster in New England, and I had no more understanding of "nigger" than I had of "eeny, meeny." It was a rhyme. I would eliminate the offensive word today, and children themselves and teachers have:

> *Eeny, meeny, miny, mo,*
> *Catch a tiger by the toe,* . . .

But let us not hide our head in the sand and holler *mea culpa* and all that. We were children, growing up, and playing. I would wager that of the millions of children who have used that rhyme less than 1/100 of one percent attached any racial significance whatsoever to it. It was a rhyme, a game rhyme, and had no meaning except for the game, was never used otherwise, and was frequently forgotten (except for nostalgic memory of childhood) by the time we reached the mature age of nine, possibly ten.

# Hide-and-Seek, or I Spy

The game of hide-and-seek is known in all farm communities, villages, and towns throughout the United States. It is a rural or semi-rural pastime (known also in the towns and cities), one for the hot days of Summer when Spring mud has gone and the bushes are in full leaf and the grass high enough to provide cover. Our mental picture of the game is indelibly that of a youngster hiding his head in his arm against a tree trunk, with other children scattering across the field, behind the barn, behind trees and bushes, while the one who is "It" counts to one hundred by ones, or to five hundred by fives, or to any other arbitrarily chosen or agreed-upon number which will give the players reasonable enough time to hide.

> *5, 10, 15, 20, 25, 30, 35, 40, 45, 50,*

*55, 60, 65, 70, 75, 80, 85, 90, 95, 100!*

*5, 10, 15, 20, 25, 30, 35, 40, 45, 50,*
*55, 60, 65, 70, 75, 80, 85, 90, 95, 200!*

*5, 10, 15, 20, 25, 30, 35, 40, 45, 50,*
*55, 60, 65, 70, 75, 80, 85, 90, 95, 300!*
*Ready or not, here I come!*

A quick and tricky way of counting to one hundred, but frowned upon:

*10, 10, 25*
*15 and 40!*

The rhymes are fairly standard and divided into two groups: those which the hunter shouts as initial warning and which give an extension of time to the hiding youngsters, and those shouted shortly after, when "It" gives notice that the hiding time is over and the hunt is on.

The rhymes are all country rhymes: *clover* rhyming with *over*, *rye* with *I*, *cotton* with *trottin'*, *corn* with *born*, *hay* with *away*, and *tree* with *me*. And — clover and hay and cotton and corn — they are summer rhymes.

The "warning" rhymes recall childhood:

*A bushel of wheat,*
*A bushel of rye,*
*All who are not hid*
*Holler, "I!"*

*A bushel of wheat*
*And a bushel of rye,*
*All that aren't ready*
*Holler, "I!"*

*A bushel of wheat,*
*A bushel of cotton,*
*All that are not hid*
*Better be trottin'.*

*A bushel of wheat,*
*A bushel of hay,*
*All who aren't hid*
*Better get away.*

*A barrel of water,*
*A barrel of soap,*
*All that's not hid*
*Holler, "Billy Goat!"*

*A bushel of wheat*
*And a bushel of oats,*
*All that ain't hid*
*Holler, "Billy Goat!"*

*A sack of wheat,*
*A sack of clover,*
*Who ain't ready*
*Can't hide over!*

*A bushel of wheat,*
*A bushel of clover,*
*All who are not hid*
*Can't hide over!*

From Mississippi in 1908 comes a gently worded request, even though it may have been shouted at the top of a child's lungs:

*All that ain't hid*
*Will say, "I,"*
*Those that are hid,*
*Please don't lie!*

The rhymes which give final notice that the hunt is on are direct and forthright:

*One, two, three,*
*Look out for me,*
*For my eyes are open*
*And I can see!*

*A bushel of wheat*
*And a bushel of corn,*
*Here I come*
*As sure as you're born!*

*One, two, three,*
*Look out for me,*
*I'm going to find you*
*Wherever you be!*

*A bushel of wheat*
*And a bottle of rum,*
*You better watch out,*
*For here I come!*

*One, two, three,*
*Look out for me!*
*I see you*
*Behind that big tree!*

*A bushel of wheat*
*And a bushel of rye,*
*All in three feet of my base*
*I spy!*

*One, two, three,*
*Look out for me!*
*I'm coming!*

In my Massachusetts youth in the Berkshires, I can remember ending the game (when two or three of the hunted were so well hidden that I couldn't find them) by yelling: "Olley, olley otts in free!" I had heard the cry "Olley, olley otts," and to me it was just that — "Olley, olley otts" — with no question or doubt about it: an inherited and traditional cry of strange words associated with the end of the game when the last of the hunted were permitted to return free. I realized only recently, some fifty years later, that the magic words I had screamed as a youngster were in actuality: "All the, all the outs in free!" "All the outs in free," standing by itself, was obviously not much of a chant or shout. Preface it with another "all the," and you had something you could really give out with. But I had never heard it that way. Only as "Olley, olley otts. . . ." Which is, of course, an example of folk transmission.

# *Teasing Rhymes*

Children can be rough, tough customers, and it is best on occasion to leave them to themselves to sort out their own problems and relationships:

> *Yah! Yah! Sani-Flush!*
> *Jennie brushes her teeth*
> *With a toilet brush!*

> *Roses are red,*
> *Violets are blue,*
> *When it rains,*
> *I think of you — Drip, drip, drip!*

> *Car, car,*
> *C-A-R*
> *Stick your head*
> *In a jelly jar!*

Those delicate sentiments were given me by students in my folklore class at American University who had collected them (from younger members of the family?) in the New York City area, following brief class consideration of others such as:

> *Ink, ink,*
> *A bottle of ink,*
> *The cork fell out*
> *And you stink!*

> *Stingy gut, stingy gut,*      *Fatty on a steamboat,*
> *Eat the whole world up!*      *Stinks like a nanny goat!*

Taunts are normally made up on the spot by a "clever" youngster, egging on or engaged with others in teasing and tormenting one of his fellows. The life of any teasing rhyme may be as short as morning recess: it can be born during play and die with a return to the classroom. In such cases it is part of spontaneous folk activity, but it does not itself become entrenched in folklore, since it has no continuing life of its own. To become a lasting bit of folklore, it must circulate in time as well as in space — from one playground or street, to another, from one town to another. From England, for example, and known throughout the United States for over a hundred years is:

> *Tell tale tit,*
> *Your tongue shall be split,*
> *And all the dogs in our town*
> *Shall have a bit of it.*

Comparable rhymes with long lives now have a purely American sound:

> *Copy cat, copy cat,*      *Can't catch me,*
> *Run on home and holler "Scat!"*      *Can't catch a flea!*

> *Cry, baby, cry,*
> *Stick your finger in your eye,*
> *Tell your ma it wasn't I!*

It is the catchy ones — those with far-out imagery and a derisive chanting rhythm — that are seized upon, repeated, and preserved:

*Robstown, Texas, 1942: Saturday morning baseba*

*2 and 2 are 4,*
*4 and 4 are 8,*
*8 and 8 are 16,*
*Stick your nose in kerosene!*

*Red head, ginger bread,*
*Five cents a cabbage head!*

Where these rhymes originated or where they even immediately come from, no one knows, and any attempt to find the source for one would be a fruitless and profitless search. They circulate in the folk manner, they are known all over the lot, they are anonymous, and you recognize them. That is enough for our purposes. A child psychologist may wish to fiddle with them, but that is none of our business.

Can you remember your school playground?

*Tattle-tale, teacher's pet,*
*Tell it quick or you'll forget!*

*Suzie, Suzie, sourkraut,*
*Does your mother know you're out?*

*There she goes, there she goes,*
*All dressed up in her Sunday clothes.*
*Ain't she sweet? Ain't she sweet?*
*All but the stink of her dirty feet!*

*Bake a pudding, bake a pie,*
*Did you ever tell a lie?*
*Yes you did, you know you did,*
*You broke your mammy's teapot lid!*

*Green eye, greedy gut,*
*Steal a pig and eat it up;*
*Brown eye, pickey pie,*
*Run around and tell a lie!*

*Goody, goody gout,*
*Your shirt tail's out!*
*Goody, goody, 'gin,*
*Your shirt tail's in!*

*Sugar's sugar, salt's salt,*
*If you get in trouble,*
*It's your own darn fault!*

*'Fraidy calf, fool and a half,*
*Enough to make a monkey laugh.*

*Fiddledy, diddledy, dee,*
*I see something you don't see!*

*Look, look,*
*You dirty crook,*
*You stole your mother's*
*Pocketbook!*

*Noses are red,*
*Noses are blue,*
*Pickles are sour,*
*And so are you!*

*Flypaper, flypaper,*
*Hooey, hooey, hooey!*
*Flypaper, flypaper,*
*Gooey, gooey, gooey!*
*Flypaper, flypaper,*
*Hope it sticks on Looie!*

The tormented had their replies. Sniveling, crying, or shouting with rage and right on their side:

*I'm made of rubber,*
*You're made of glue!*
*Everything you say*
*Bounces from me*
*And sticks to you!*

*Mocking is catching,*
*Hanging is stretching!*

and wherever the English language is spoken:

*Sticks and stones*
*May break my bones,*
*But words will never hurt me!*
*When I die,*
*Then you'll cry*
*For the names you've called me!*

# 17.

# Autograph Album Rhymes

Writing from Great Falls, Montana, at the end of January 1955, Lucille Hardy Birkett said:

Every year when West Junior High School is struck with its annual rash of post-Christmas autograph books, we teachers are expected to sign our share. Usually I sign my name without doing any browsing, but last week I took a look through the pages of an unusually ornate, padded-cover book which had been handed to me, and found on its pastel, colored pages all of the same old verses which we so religiously collected from friends when *I* was in junior high school. Then I got to wondering how long these verses had been in circulation. . . . I know nothing of the history of autograph books, or where they originated, but my aunt has a very grimy old booklet with super-sentimental autographs inscribed in the flowery handwriting of my great-grandparents' time, in ink now brown with age, so the idea must go back quite a few years.

It does.

Autograph albums were first introduced into the United States following their immense popularity — virtually a craze for them — in England in the 1820's. They took hold here slowly, but were firmly entrenched by 1850 and reached their full vogue and flowering in the 1870's and 1880's. The tradition continued strongly through the early decades of this century in all parts of the country, in urban as well as rural and small-town areas. It is still very much alive.

There is a marked difference, though, between the albums of England and those of the United States. In England, they were essentially the property of young ladies whose aim was to obtain the autographs — with appropriate messages — from the great and near great and, particularly, from artists, writers, poets. Charles Lamb and Leigh Hunt, among others, were harassed and bedeviled by young lady petitioners, but complied with their requests even while complaining. The verses which filled the English autograph books were, in consequence, of an elevated character, literary and often lengthy.

When the albums crossed the Atlantic all this changed. The books became the property not of "young maidens" seeking out literary lions, but of youngsters in school, chiefly girls as owners. Boys were self-conscious contributors — sentimental, cynical, smart-alecky — but rarely possessors of albums. And the contributors sought after were not celebrities but friends, classmates, relatives, and teachers. If celebrities happened along, fine, but the autograph albums did not exist for them or because of them. Classmates and undying friendship came first.

It is helpful to sort the album rhymes into their different categories. These are few and fairly obvious. They point up the relatively fixed subjects in the books. They permit us also to participate vicariously in one portion of the adolescent world, and, for some of us at least, to recall our own youth and the albums we signed or owned.

## *Heavenly Guideposts*

"Heavenly Guideposts" were more common in the earlier books, but they still exist today — relics of the past and evidence that this segment of the traditional perpetuates itself. They are inherited, however, rather than being contemporary. They reflect turn-of-the century Sunday School training, family prayers, the strength of New England looking to an assured life after death, and a high moral code. It is most reassuring to find them in the albums of twelve- and thirteen-year-olds.

> *May he who clothes the lillies*
> *And marks the sparrow's fall*
> *Protect and save you, school chum,*
> *And guide you safe through all.*
>
> (Hyattsville, Maryland, 1910)

> *Within this book so pure and white*
> *Let none but friends presume to write,*
> *And may each word in friendship given*
> *Direct the reader's thoughts to Heaven.*
>
> (Kansas, 1905; general)

In the next, the trod-God rhyme is quite wonderful, but, surprisingly, not unique: with slight variations it is found in Montana, the Ozarks, and Maryland.

> *When the golden sun is setting*
> *And your feet no longer trod,*
> *May your name in gold be written*
> *In the autograph of God.*
>
> *In the Book of Life, God's album,*
> *May your name be penned with care,*
> *And may all who here have written*
> *Write their names forever there.*
>
> (General)

The next is possibly the most dolefully hopeful rhyme in the entire lexicon of autograph album verse:

*Oh may I meet you once again*
*When life's sad school is o'er*
*And spend a long vacation*
*Upon the other shore.*

(Missouri, ca. 1900)

## Advice

These rhymes were chiefly contributed by dedicated teachers who did not realize that they were "dedicated," but were simply at all times teaching their best. They came also from mothers and doting aunts, and occasionally from classmates. They are unashamedly admonitory and reflect an era which had a reasonable sense of discipline and a concept of that discipline as an aid to shaping a child's future. They seem to have been thoroughly accepted by youngsters, and no album would be complete without a few.

*Remember, dear, when you grow old,*
*That learning is better than silver or gold,*
*For silver and gold can vanish away,*
*But a good education will never decay.*

(Maryland, 1910, and descended from the English sentiment of 1800: ". . . For learning is better than house or land,/When houses and lands are gone and spent,/Then learning is most excellent.")

*Come when you are called,*
*Go when you are bid,*
*Shut the door after you,*
*And you'll never be chid.*

(New England; fairly general)

*If you wish to be blessed*
*With heavenly joys,*
*Think more of God*
*And less of the boys.*

(New York State, 1875)

*True friends are like diamonds,*
*Precious and rare,*
*False friends are like pebbles,*
*Found everywhere.*

> (Montana, 1955; widely found and often
> with "autumn leaves" instead of "pebbles")

And happily:

*When all your friends have deserted you,*
*Pray do not look for another,*
*But turn to the one who loves you best,*
*Your dearest friend, your mother.*

> (Maryland, 1910)

Pledges of Undying Friendship

With "Undying Friendship" and "Remember Me" we come to the heart of the albums and their virtual *raison d'être* in the schools. "Best Wishes" and "Love" come later and are an integral part of the books, to be sure, but they are frequently diluted with a comic note not generally present in these more serious, everlasting efforts:

*When in my lonely grave I sleep*
*And bending willows o'er me weep,*
*'Tis then, dear friend, and not before*
*I think of thee no more, no more.*

> (Kansas, ca, 1901. Mrs. George H. Tout of Baxter
> Springs says, "I was aged nine to thirteen when this
> and comparable rhymes were the sentiments of my
> friends!")

*Leaves may wither,*
*Flowers may die,*

*Friends may forget thee,*
*But never shall I.*

(New York City, 1909)

*The grapes hang green upon the vine,*
*I choose you as a friend of mine,*
*I choose you out of all the rest,*
*The reason is I love you best.*

(New York City, 1909)

And here belongs the graphic and mouth-watering:

*May our friendship spread*
*Like butter on hot gingerbread.*

(New York City, 1910)

## Remember Me

In the "Friendship" verses, the contributor pledged his or her undying friendship to the owner of the album, while in the more numerous "Remember Me" rhymes, the contributor asks that the owner of the book remember the contributor throughout life. The writer, in effect, is seeking for assurance of identity and some slight touch of immortality.

*Think of me in the hours of pleasure,*
*Think of me in the hours of care,*
*Think of me in the hours of leisure,*
*Spare one thought in the hour of prayer.*

(New York City, 1882; general)

*If apart we two must be,*
*Just read this and think of me.*

(General)

*When the golden sun is setting*
*And your mind from care is free,*
*When of others you are thinking,*
*Won't you sometimes think of me?*

(New York City, 1909; general)

*When this you see,*
*Remember me.*

(Widespread; the Reverend Giles Moore of Sussex, England, noted in his Journal, 1673–74: "I bought for Ann Brett a gold ring, this being the posy [the verse engraved inside the ring]: 'When this you see, remember me.'")

*When this you see,*
*Remember me,*
*A real true friend*
*In Tennessee.*

*In leisure moments cast a look*
*Upon the pages of this book,*
*When absent friends thy thought engage,*
*Think of the one who fills this page.*

(New York City, 1883)

*In the bread box of your affections,*
*Remember me as a crumb.*

(New York, 1930)

With greater surety and poetry from New England:

*In the wood-box of memory,*
*Place one stick for me.*

(Northampton, Massachusetts, 1878)

Death held a romantic fascination for the young and served also to provide the contributor with a Byronic spot on stage center — at the moment of writing, at least, and hopefully thereafter whenever the pages were turned. Both the following are from the Ozarks:

*Remember me when this you see*
*Though many miles apart we be,*
*And if the grave should be my bed,*
*Remember me when I am dead.*

*Remember me when death shall close*
*These eyelids in their last repose,*
*And when the breezes gently wave*
*The grasses on your schoolmate's grave.*

In the "Remember Me" category belongs the fairly extended "Forget Me Not" cycle. One or several are to be found in virtually all the autograph books.

*Your album is a golden spot*
*In which to write Forget Me Not.*

(Missouri, n.d.)

*From memory's leaves*
*I fondly squeeze*
*Three little words —*
*Forget Me Not.*

(New York City, 1883)

The sophistication of the next is greatly to be admired:

*There is a word in English spoken,*
*In French 'tis very dear,*
*In English 'tis forget-me-not,*
*In French 'tis* la souvenir.

(Maryland, 1910)

## *With the Best of Wishes*

All of the autograph albums have verses wishing various degrees and kinds of happiness to the owners. Most of the rhymes are, in effect, toasts. A very personal one comes from St. Louis, Missouri, dated 1884:

> *May you grow fair,*
> *Have long curly hair,*
> *Never use vile slang,*
> *And marry a nice man.*

For its practicality as well as accidents of spelling, I also like from Montana:

> *May the angles round*
> *Your bedside hover,*
> *And keep you*
> *From kicking off the cover.*

The well-wishing takes a variety of forms, and some of the concepts are quite pretty:

> *May the larkspur with its eyes of blue*
> *Look upon no purer, happier girl than you.*
>                 (Kansas City, Missouri, ca. 1900)

> *May your wing of happiness*
> *Never lose a feather.*
>                         (New York City, 1909)

> *May blessing attend you*
> *Both early and late,*
> *And heaven assist you*
> *In choosing a mate.*
>
>                         (Kansas, 1882)

*I wish you love,*
*I wish you plenty,*
*I wish you a husband*
*Before you're twenty.*

(New York City, 1909)

*I wish you luck, I wish you joy,*
*I wish you first a baby boy,*
*Then when his hair begins to curl,*
*I wish you then a baby girl.*

(Maryland, 1910)

## Love

Love, of course, has its place in the autograph books, and the daring entries
were undoubtedly made with many a self-conscious giggle:

*Don't make love*          *Some kiss behind a lily,*
*By the garden gate,*      *Some kiss behind a rose,*
*Love may be blind,*       *But the proper place to kiss*
*But the neighbors ain't.* *Is right beneath the nose.*

*Good little girls love their brothers;*
*So good have I grown*
*I love other girls' brothers*
*As well as my own.*

*My heart to you is given,*
*O! do give yours to me.*
*We'll lock them up together*
*And throw away the key.*

(Pendleton, Indiana, 1890)

*The sea is wide*
*And you can't step it,*

> *I love you*
> *And you can't hep it.*
>
> > (Tennessee, 1950; proof in writing
> > of the rural pronunciation of "help")

And with poetic irreverence but rural sincerity:

> *Cows love punkins,*
> *Pigs love squash,*
> *I love you,*
> *I do, by gosh.*
>
> > (Pendleton, Indiana, 1890)

And a roundabout offer of marriage: the "poetry" of some of these is really touching:

> *The road is wide*
> *With many a crook,*
> *I hope someday*
> *You'll be my cook.*

Where there is love, heartbreak follows, and the tragedies of the seventh grade also appear:

> *Your heart is not a plaything,*
> *Your heart is not a toy,*
> *But if you want it broken,*
> *Just give it to a boy.*
>
> > (Montana, 1955)

> *Fall from an apple tree,*
> *Fall from above,*
> *But for the love of Mike, May,*
> *Don't fall in love.*

The philosophical summing up of the bitterness of life in the next cannot leave us untouched:

> *To meet, to love, and then to part*
> *Is the sad, sad story of a school girl's heart.*
>
> (Pendleton, Indiana, 1890)

## *Marriage*

There is a curious contradiction with these rhymes; in earlier rhymes well-wishers hope that the owner of the book will not "be an old maid," will be married "before you're twenty," and will be happily assisted by heaven "in choosing a mate," but when it comes to the actual institution of marriage, then it becomes fashionable in the seventh grade (or ages nine to thirteen) to look upon it with a jaundiced eye — and to take realistic note of sewing stitches in britches, cleaning house, keeping "squalling brats" very quiet, and, above all, to keep husbands from gallivanting around and to rule them, in no uncertain terms, with broom and slipper. Love and courtship is one thing: marriage is definitely another:

> *When you get married*
> *And your husband gets cross,*
> *Pick up a broom*
> *And show him who's boss!*
>
> (Widespread, regrettably)

> *If you get a husband*
> *And he is a clipper,*
> *Get him acquainted*
> *With the end of your slipper.*
>
> (Baxter Springs, Kansas, 1905)

227

*When you are single*
*It's sugar and pie,*
*When you are married*
*It's root hog or die.*

(This one and the following are from the Ozarks.)

*When you get married*
*And have squalling brats,*
*Just cut off their heads,*
*And feed 'em to the cats.*

## Authorship

Many a youngster paled at the prospect of producing an acceptable verse for a classmate's album, and a goodly number sought refuge in widely spread and traditional rhymes such as:

*It tickles me,*
*It makes me laugh*
*To think you want*
*My autograph.*

*Autograph writing*
*Is very tough;*
*Here's my name*
*And that's enough.*

*Some write for pleasure,*
*Some write for fame,*
*I write simply*
*To sign my name.*

*My pen is poor,*
*My ink is pale,*
*My hand shakes like*
*A monkey's tail.*

*I thought, I thought*
*I thought in vain,*
*At last I thought*
*I'd write my name.*

*Head weak,*
*Brain numb,*
*Inspiration*
*Won't come.*

When authorship was a problem, contributors also avoided creativeness by resorting to the rhymes associated with the placement of names on special pages or places in the book:

*By hook and by crook,*
*I got the last (first) page in your book.*

*Way back here and out of sight,*
*I'll write my name in just for spite.*

*If anyone loves you more than I do,*
*Let them write on the last page!*

(This, of course, completely filled the last page.)

In most albums there is usually one entry which requires the reader to revolve the book: each separate line of the verse occupies one edge of the page, with the third line written upside down on the bottom of the page.

*When you are in the country*
*Sitting on the hedges,*
*Remember it was me*
*Who wrote around the edges.*

And there is always:

*By writing upside down.*
*Remember the boy who ruined your book*
*Remember the boy from the town,*
*Remember the boy from the country,*

All of these are escape hatches for the non-creative, unless, of course, they have been preempted by earlier contributors. In which case there remain the relatively standard "Gigglers."

## Gigglers

The "Gigglers" can be reasonably gentle:

*I see you in the ocean,*
*I see you in the sea,*

*I see you in the bathtub —*
*Oh! — Pardon me!*

(Montana, 1931)


*Yours till the ocean waves at you.*


*Yours till China gets Hungary*
*and eats Turkey fried in Greece.*
                (How very clever and cosmopolitan
                we thought that was!)


*You asked me to write in your album,*
*I've nothing new to put in,*
*For there's nothing original in me*
*Except original sin.*

With the "Gigglers" also belong the trick combinations of letters and numbers cryptically forming words:

| | |
|---|---|
| *2 big U R,* | U R |
| *2 big U B,* | 2 Good |
| *I C U R* | 2 B |
| *2 big 4 me.* | 4 gotten. |


*If U B U and I B I,*
*It's EZ to C the reason Y*
*I like U and U like I.*


## Smart Alecks and Thumb Noses

But with the "Smart Alecks" and "Thumb Nosers," gentleness flies rapidly out the window. With cynical realism they not only deflate true sentiment, sentimentality, the Byronic poses, and the forget-me-nots and I-love-you's of the generality of the rhymes, but they carry their rhymes further into open attack upon the owners of the books.

The traditional

> *Roses are red,*
> *Violets are blue,*
> *Sugar is sweet,*
> *And so are you,*

for example, takes a fearful beating:

> *Roses are red,*
> *Violets are yellow*
> *You're the girl*
> *That stole my fellow.*

> (Indiana, n.d.)

> *Roses are red,*
> *Violets are blue,*
> *If I looked like you,*
> *I'd join the zoo.*

> (Tucson, Arizona, 1955; that and the
> following "Roses" were sent to me by
> a young girl in the seventh grade.)

> *Roses are red,*
> *Violets are black*
> *You would look better*
> *With a knife in your back.*

> *Roses are red,*      *Roses are red,*
> *Violets are black,*    *Violets are blue,*
> *A face like yours*     *Skunks have instincts*
> *Belongs in a sack.*    *And so do you.*

Poetic concepts of Life and Love are brought squarely down to earth:

> *Life is like a rose,*
> *Love is like a blossom,*
> *If you want your finger bit,*
> *Stick it at a possum.*
>
> > (The Ozarks, n.d.)

> *I love you, I love you,*
> *I love you so well,*
> *If I had a peanut,*
> *I'd give you the shell!*
>
> > (Washington, D.C., n.d.)

And advice from aunt and teacher is parodied:

> *Remember well*
> *And bear in mind*
> *That an old cow's tail*
> *Hangs down behind.*

The weeping-willow view of death is thoroughly mocked:

> *When I am dead and laid to rest,*
> *Stand on my grave and yell your best.*
>
> > (Missouri, n.d.)

> *When I am dead and in my box,*
> *You can have my dirty sox.*
>
> > (Montana, 1955)

Some of these rhymes surely provoked crises between contributors and owners of books, and one such reaction of a lasting character is described in a letter (1955) from Elizabeth H. Warner, of Northampton, Massachusetts, who vividly — seventy-one years after the event! — remembers:

This rhyme, inexpressibly vulgar, was actually written in my own album in 1884, and I suppose it stuck in my mind because I was so angry. The boy

*San Augustine, Texas, 1943:*
*schoolboys*

writer lived in a barn, on "the edge of town," and used to chase us barefoot girls with a switch of nettles, so that we were afraid always. How he got hold of my album in school, I never knew, but I tore the leaf from my book, but, strangely enough, not from my memory. His name was "Speely" W———, and I still hate him.

> *Ain't she sweet?*
> *Ain't she sweet?*
> *Striped stockings*
> *And dirty feet.*

The rhymes are perhaps trite and obvious to us, now. But they were not so once, nor are they to the youngsters who still collect them in grammar school and junior high. They have meaning and import to the pre-teenager (a word I never knew). If you were lucky enough to have been school-raised in a town or small city, you will remember them. The nostalgia is there — the school itself, your classmates (whatever became of them?), the street on which you lived, the games you played, picnics, first love, the long summer vacations. These are all captured on the autograph pages, fixed in time, forever part of America.

# 18.

# Book Ownership Rhymes

The mere flyleaf entry of name indicating ownership of a book is not of itself folklore:

> *William Orne's    1799*
>
> *Eliza Lee's property*
> *cost of it 3/ Hartford 10th Dec. 1798*
>
> *Miss Jane Elizabeth Smith her book*
> *Price 37½ Cnts    January 1st    1833*
> *Miss Nottinghams Seminary for Young ladies*

When ownership, however, is attested by traditional rhyme — or by original rhyme which becomes traditional — then we do have folklore:

> *I pity the river,*      *This book is one thing,*
> *I pity the brook,*      *My fist is another,*
> *I pity the one*      *Touch this one thing,*
> *That takes this book.*      *You'll sure feel the other.*

> *If perchance this book should roam,*
> *Box its ears and send it home.*

Three from the nineteenth century:

> *Steal not this Book*
> *For fear of Shame*
> *For hear you read*
> *The owners name*
> *Asa Stebbins Book*

> *Steal not this book, for if you do,*      *Steal not this book for fear of strife*
> *Tom Harris will be after you.*      *For the owner carries a big jackknife.*

And three from our beginnings as a nation:

> *Steal not this book my honest friend*
> *For fear the gallos will be your end*
> *The gallos is high, the rope is strong,*
> *To steal this book you know is wrong.*

> *Let every lerking thief be taught,*
> *This maxim always sure,*
> *That learning is much better bought*
> *Than stolen from the poor*
> *Then steel not this book.*

*Whosoever steals this*
*Book away may*
*Think on that great*
*judgement day when*
*Jesus Christ shall*
*come and say*
*Where is that book you*
*stole away.*
*Then you will say*
*I do not know*
*and Christ will say*
*go down below.*

One can fairly believe that book was safe!

# *Street Cries and Epitaphs*

# 19.

# *Street Cries*

I n the days of intinerant commerce in our cities, street cries were the
advertisements of the time, equivalent to radio and TV commercials
today. They differed in that they were simpler, more personal, more direct.
The wares also were more basic and were available on the spot. The cry
was immediate: "Here I am! Buy now!"

At one time the cries — or some at least — served a distinct municipal
purpose, and crying was not only countenanced but ordered. Boston select-
men in 1655 directed Robert Wyatt and William Lane, duly appointed
chimney sweepers, "to cry aboutt streetes that they may be knowne." In
1686, Mayor Barnard of New York ordered chimney-sweeper William Butler "to passe through all the streetes, Lanes and Passages . . . with such
noise or Cry as may Discover yow to the inhabitants thereof." Times
changed, however, and on September 20, 1908, the New York *Sun* reported

*New York City, Harlem, 1943:*
*woman with her pet dog*

that "with the passing of the street cry, recently forbidden by Commissioner Bingham's order for the suppression of unnecessary noises, New York has lost one of the familiar activities of a bustling city, the thing which for more than a century has individualized its lower strata of commerce." Such city edicts, plus chamber of commerce protests against the competition of itinerant vendors, have wiped the cries out as an institution, although some few — but far between — may occasionally be heard to this day.

The cries were specialized. In any given community there was no confusing of individual vendors, nor the vendor of one item with the vendor of another, no matter how garbled the shouts or cries might become. In New Orleans,

*Oyta! Sally! Oy — ta! Sally!*

was just as clearly "oysters" to customers along that particular vendor's way as the more intelligible cry from the same city:

*Oyster Man! Oyster Man!*
*Get your fresh oysters from the Oyster Man!*
*Bring out your pitcher, bring out your can,*
*Get your nice fresh oysters from the Oyster Man!*

In Baltimore it was:

*Oy' ee! Oy' ee!*
*Some t' stoo, en some t' fry,*
*En some t' make de oystuh pie!*
*Oo — oy! ee!*

And in New York:

*Oysters: Oysters: here's your beauties*
*of Oysters: here's your fine,*
*fat, salt Oysters!*

No one of these, of course, could possibly be confused with:

> *'Ta – toes!*
> *Peach  – es!*
> *'N cents a basket!*

or with:

> *Yed-dy go, sweet potatoes, oh!*
> *Fif-en-ny bit a haf peck!*

As in the case of "oysters," the cries were highly individualized. Each vendor screamed his own, varied them, changed them, shortened or lengthened them, sang, chanted, or shouted them. There was variety within the frame of the tradition.

The merchandise of the vendors was made up chiefly of staples and most of it seasonal — vegetables, fruit, fish, cooked foods.

The cries were colorful:

### The Crab and Deviled Crab Vendors

> *Ah, I have 'em hot,*
> *Ah, I have 'em brown,*
> *Ah, I have 'em long,*
> *Ah, I have 'em roun',*
> *Dey's nice en fat, dey weighs a poun',*
> *Daibble!*
>
> *Da-aibble! Debble, Daibble Crab!*
> *My ol' man makes me mad,*
> *Sen's no me out widde Develish Crab!*
>
> *Hard fried, crab cakes, en daibble crabs!*
> *Hard fried, er yawl wide!*

244

*Crab-by Crab!*

*Keep yo' haid levvul!*
*Tom de devvul!*
*Ah on'y has de kin' de ladies oughter buy.*
*Ef yo' don' come soon ah'm ergoin' by.*
*Daibble! Debble Crab!*
*Crab-man's goin' 'way — Good-bye!*
              (All the above from Baltimore)

*Crabs!*
*Red hot crabs!*
*Get 'em while they're hot!*
                            (Texas)

*Fresh, fresh crabs,*
*Fresh Baltimore crabs!*
*Put them in the pot*
*With the lid on top,*
*Fresh Baltimore crabs!*
                        (Philadelphia)

*She Craib! She Craib! She Craib!*
                        (Charleston)

## Fish

*Mullet! Mullet! Mullet!*
*Flounder and Black Fish!*
*Shark steaks for dem what likes 'em;*

*Sword Fish for dem what fights 'em.*
*Fish-ee! Fish-ee!*
                        (Charleston)

245

*Here comes the fishman!*
*Bring out your dishpan,*
*Porgies at five cents a pound!*

(Charleston and South)

*Porgy walk and porgy talk,*
*And porgy eat with knife and fork,*
*Get yer nice por-gy!*

(Charleston)

*Fine Clams: choice Clams: Here's your*
*Rock-a-way beach Clams: here's your*
*fine young, sand Clams.*

(New York)

*Raw! Raw! Raw Swimp!*

(Charleston)

And also from Charleston, Harriette Leiding reports a young shrimp-seller who first identified himself before calling his wares:

*An' a Daw-Try Daw! An' a swimpy Raw!*
*An' a Daw-Try Daw-Try! Daw-Try!*
*Raw Swimp!*

## Watermelons

The vendor of watermelons was as normal a part of Summer in American towns and cities as the iceman with wagon, leather shoulder apron, tongs, and scale. July and August without him would have been unthinkable. His wagon was piled high with the green serpent-striped fruit, and there were always one or two melons cut open to show their "red-ripeness." As if such evidence were not enough, he "guaranteed" his wares and stated his willingness to "plug" any particular melon to prove its ripeness. The first four cries are from Texas, collected by Elizabeth Hurley:

*Watermelons, watermelons,*
*Fresh off the vine,*
*Get your watermelons,*
*A nickel or a dime.*

*Wa-ter-mel-ons, come and see-ee,*
*Ev-'ry-one sold on a guar-an-tee-ee!*
*Red ripe wa-ter-mel-ons! Sweet and jui-cy,*
*Fit for you and fit for Lu-cy!*

*Oh, good old red ripe watermelons!*
*Oh, they're red and ripe and sweet as honey.*
*You can save money.*
*You can cut 'em and plug 'em,*
*They are red ripe.*
*Oh, lady, lady, you can eat the meat*
*And pickle the rind*
*And save the seed 'til plantin' time!*

*Big like a barrel and red ripe!*
*We plug 'em and we cut 'em,*
*And they've got to be good.*
*And I know you'd buy one if you could.*
*They are home-grown.*
*They are the Hempstead melon and red to the rind,*
*And you'll never eat a good one 'til you've had one of mine.*
*They are red ripe!*

And from New Orleans:

*I got water with the melon, red to the rind!*
*If you don't believe it, jest pull down your blind.*
*You eat the watermelon and preee — serve the rind!*

*Watermelon, Lady!*
*Come and git your nice red watermelon, Lady!*
*Red to the rind, Lady!*
*Come on, Lady, and get 'em!*
*Gotta make the picnic fo' two o'clock,*
*No flat tires today.*
*Come on, Lady!*

## Other Fruits

*Cantal — ope — ah!*
*Fresh and fine,*
*Just offa the vine,*
*Only a dime!*

(New Orleans)

*Bring your dishpan!*
*Here's your banana man!*
*Lady! Lady!*

(Texas)

*Anran-le Straw-aw-aw-berries!*

(Baltimore. Anran-le:
for Anne Arundel, the County)

*I got strawberries, Lady!*
*Strawberries, Lady!*
*Fifteen cents a basket —*
*Two baskets for a quarter!*

(New Orleans)

*Oh well, oh well, who wouldn't buy?*
*Just came in from Sandy Lake*
*And hand picked, right off the ground.*

(Troy, New York. Sand Lake strawberries
are still preferred in Rensselaer County.)

*Blackber—reeees! Fresh and fine,*
*I got blackber—reeees, Lady!*
*Fresh from th' vine!*
*I got blackberries, Lady!*
*Three glass fo' a dime.*
*I got blackberries!*
*I got blackberries!*
*BLACK—BERRIEEEEEEEEEES!*

(New Orleans)

*Pieappleeeeeeee, Pieappleoooooo!*
*Hand-picked, right off the ground!*
*One for the lady, the rest for the baby,*
*Hand-picked, right off the ground.*
*Pie apples, sour apples, eating apples, apples for pie,*
*Come out, all you young ladies, and buy.*
*They are hand-picked, right off the ground.*
*Two quarts for five cents, hand-picked right off the ground!*

(Troy, New York)

And Elizabeth Hurley reports a news "butch" on a Texas and Pacific run through West Texas who puzzled customers with:

*Apples, oranges,*
*Two for a nickel apiece!*

There was also "old App," the street vendor in Virginia City, Nevada, who sold fruit and garbled his wares:

*Grapples and Apes!*

## *Vegetables*

Sweet Potatoes, Carolina Potatoes!        *Lou-is-i-an-a yel-low yams,*
*Here's your Sweet Carolinas!*           *Sweet po-ta-toes, here now!*

          (New York)                    (Texas)

*Okra, cucumbers, squash and sweet potaters,*
*And look at these good old red ripe tomaters!*

                  (Texas)

*Nice little snapbeans,*
*Pretty little corn,*
*Butter beans, carrots,*
*Apples for the ladies!*
*Jui—ceee lemons!*

                  (New Orleans)

*Sweet corn, as long as your arm,*
*Hand-picked, right off the ground!*

     (This Troy, New York, vendor picked
     everything "right off the ground.")

Hot, roasted corn was also sold — with salt and butter on the side — at picnics and in the streets, just as roast chestnuts are sold today in the Winter streets of our cities:

*Here's your nice Hot Corn!*
*Smoking hot! Piping hot!*
*Oh what beauties I have got!*

                  (New York)

*Hot corn! Hot corn!*
*'Ere's yer lily-white hot corn!*

                  (Philadelphia)

## *Cooked Foods*

Elizabeth Hurley says that "shortly after the turn of the century a Mexican vendor sold his tamales and enchiladas through the streets of San Antonio. He carried them in buckets, one in each hand. His tamales, which he sold at ten cents a dozen, were so moist they would melt in your mouth and so hot they would burn your fingernails. To dispose of his cornhusk-enveloped treat he sang a simple tune:

> *Hot tamales and enchilollies,*
> *Get 'em while they're hot!*

Other Texas vendors:

> *Hot tamales!* Tamale caliente!

> *Hot tamales, floatin' in gravy,*
> *Suit ya taste and don't mean maybe!*

> *Hot tamales, two in a shuck!*

And poetically:

> *The world goes around*
> *And the sun comes down,*
> *And I got the best*
> *Hot tamales in town!*

> *Menu-u-do-o-o,*
> *Enchila-a-a-das,*
> *Ta-a-a-a-cos,*
> *Chi-i-i-i-i-le!*

## STREET CRIES AND EPITAPHS

Texas doughnuts, Southern hominy, and Philadelphia pepper-pot:

*Doughnut, doughnut, doughnut man!*
*Get 'em hot while you can!*

*Home-made doughnuts! Home-made doughnuts!*
*Can't you hear that dough-ough-nut man?*
*Ma-a-a-ma! Ma-a-a-ma!*
*Won't you buy my home-made doughnuts?*

*Hom-in-y man, hom-in-y man,*
*Com-in' a-round on time!*
*Hom-in-y man, hom-in-y man,*
*Com-in' down the line!*
*Two quarts for fif-teen cents,*
*One quart for a dime!*

*Hominy! Beautiful hominy!*

*Peppery pot! Peppery pot!*
*All hot! All hot!*
*Makee back strong!*
*Makee live long!*
*Come buy my pepper pot!*

Saturday afternoon ball games and Sunday picnics:

*L-l-l-l-l-l-l-l-lem-men Ice Cream!*
*La-la-la-la-lemmun Ice Cream!*

(Baltimore)

*Ice cold lemonade!*
*Made in the shade,*
*Stirred with a silver spade!*

(Texas, and also the two following)

*Ice cold lemonade!*
*Made in the shade,*
*Stirred with a spade,*
*Sweetened with the fingers*
*Of a pretty little maid!*

*Ice cold lemonade!*
*Freeze your teeth, curl your hair,*
*Make you feel like a millionaire!*

Before cones were first introduced at the St. Louis World's Fair in 1904, ice cream was either sold in oblong blocks in a sort of oil paper or, frozen, was cut off in pieces through which a stick was pushed, making a "hokey-pokey," or primitive sort of popsicle:

*Ice-cream biscuits!*

*Hokey-pokey ice-cream,*
*Five cents a stick!*

*Hokey-pokey ice-cream,*
*Cry for it, little girl, cry for it!*

## Charcoal

Charcoal for lighting fires and cooking was once an urban necessity:

*Char-coal, Lady! Char-coal! Chah-ah-coal, Lady!*
                    (New Orleans)

*Char-coal! Charcoal!*
*My horse is white, my face is black,*
*I sell my charcoal, two-bits a sack —*
*Char-coal! Char-coal!*

                    (New Orleans)

*Charcoal by the bushel,*
*Charcoal by the peck,*
*Charcoal by the frying pan,*
*Or any way you lek!*

> (Philadelphia, with the blowing of a horn
> prior to 1835 and, by edict, the ringing of
> a handbell thereafter)

Lyle Saxon in his *Gumbo Ya-Ya* gives us Lafcadio Hearn's superb report of the cry of a New Orleans vendor of charcoal, a local mixture of French and English. Try speaking it: you cannot: it sings:

*Black — coalee — coalee!*
*Coaly — coaly; coaly — coaly — coal — coal — coal.*
*Coaly — coaly!*
*Coal—ee! Nice!*
*Chah—coal!*
*Twenty-five! Whew!*
*O Charco-oh-oh-oh-oh-oh-lee!*
*Oh — lee — eee!*
*(You get some coal in your mout', young fellow,*
*    if you don't keep it shut!)*
*Pretty coalee — oh — lee!*
*Charcoal!*
*Cha—ah—ahr—coal!*
Charbon! Du charbon, Madame! Bon charbon?
    Point! Ai-ai!
Tonnerre de dieu!
Cha-r-r-r-r-r-rbon!
A-a-a-a-a-a-aw!
Vingt-cinq! *Nice coalee! Coalee!*
*Coaly-coal-coal!*
*Pretty coaly!*
Charbon de Paris!
De Paris, Madame! De Paris!

## Services

The chief services offered by the wandering hawkers were the grinding of scissors, the mending of umbrellas, and the sweeping of chimneys:

> *Scis-sors to grind!*
> *Scis-so-so-o-r-s to grind!*
>
> (New York)

> *Um-brel-las to mend!*
>
> (New York)

And the small and pitiful urchins (God help us, at what age did they die of dust on the lungs?):

> *Sweep, O-O-O-O-O!*
> *From the bottom to the top,*
> *Without a ladder or a rope,*
> *Sweep, O-O-O-O-O!*
>
> (New York)

> *Sweep 'em clean! Sweep 'em clean!*
> *Save the fireman lots of work,*
> *We hate soot, we never shirk,*
> *Sweep 'em clean! Sweep 'em clean!*
>
> (New Orleans)

In New Orleans the French *ramineau* (chimney sweep) was mixed with the cry:

> Ra-mi-neau! Ra-mi-neau! Ra-mi-neau!
> *Lady, I know why your chimney won't draw,*
> *Oven won't bake and you can't make no cake,*
> *An' I know why your chimney won't draw!*

255

And in Charleston, Harriette Leiding reported that "even the chimney-sweeps are musical, and as their tiny faces appear at the top of the chimney they are sweeping, you hear 'Roo roo' sung out over the sounds of the street below."

A vestige of the cries remains today at the ball parks. At the RFK Stadium on Saturday, August 8, 1970, at a game between the Washington Senators and the Cleveland Indians, I heard and patronized the vendors crying their beer. I mention this because it is pleasant to remember and record such days (I have forgotten what the score was):

> *Beer man! Beer man!*    *Cold beer!*
> *Get your cold beer!*    *Cold beer!*
> *Cold, cold beer!*    *Beer man!*
>
> *Beer man! Beer man!*    *Get your beer!*
> *Coldie-cold beer!*    *Get your beer*

And, for the record, when I used to sell *The Saturday Evening Post* (about 1918) in Berkeley, California, I hawked its literature with an irresistible scream:

> Saturday Evening Post,
> *Best paper on the Coast,*
> *Only a nickel, half a dime,*
> *Keeps you reading all the time!*

It was a more lively business than selling vanilla extract from door to door in Framingham, Massachusetts.

# 20.

# *Epitaphs*

I remember as a youngster in New England how, after church, the townspeople stood around outside the white doors talking, some of them wandering off among the graves quite as casually as though they were strolling in a garden, others standing by two's and three's on the grass along the walk. All the graves at some time of day — morning or hot afternoon — lay under the reach of the tall steeple. The churchyard was home to the living and the dead, and the living knew the dead, and the dead, the living. It was all very natural and pleasant.

The dead talked to us and told us about themselves, as they continue to do on their stones across the land.

The epitaphs run the gamut of life — and death. They range from admonition and warning to rough and macabre humor. Some are pathetic; others move to tears; some are thumb-nosingly caustic; all are informative.

## STREET CRIES AND EPITAPHS

It is a pity that the custom has died out and that there are no more epitaphs today, but instead only the perfunctory markers: Smith 1906–1964, Braddock 1910–1958. Monument makers (I doubt that there are "stonecutters" any more) in Washington did not even know what I was talking about, and when I explained said they had never had a call for an epitaph and would not know to whom to refer me. They were the purveyors to the newer cemeteries, younger men whom tradition had not touched, believers in the mortuary ads in the public buses.

There are stones left, however, out of the American past.

The greatness of New England comes thundering down the years to us in the timeless warnings:

> *Keep death and judgement always in your eye,*
> *None's fit to live but who is fit to die.*
>
> *Behold and see as you pass by,*
> *As you are now, so once was I.*
> *As I am now, so you must be,*
> *Prepare for death and follow me.*

*No age nor sex can death defy;*       *Death is a debt to Nature due,*
*Think, mortal, what it is to die.*      *Which I have paid & so must you.*

And from Hayground Cemetery in Bridgehampton, Long Island:

> *Hark from the tombs a doleful sound!*
> *My ears attend the cry,*
> *Ye living men come view the ground*
> *Where you must shortly lie.*
> *Princes, this clay must be your bed*
> *In spite of all your towers,*
> *The tall, the wise, the reverend head*
> *Shall lie as low as ours.*

In much the same vein, but considerably more conversational and personal in tone are others. It is as though friends or neighbors were gently admonishing:

> *This turn is mine:*
> *The next may be thine.*

> *We must all die, there is no doubt;*
> *Your glass is running — mine is out.*

> *Time was, I stood where thou dost now,*
> *And look'd, as thou look'st down on me;*
> *Time will be, thou shalt lie as low,*
> *And others then look down on thee.*

> *Beneath these clods in silent dust,*
> *I sleep where all the living must:*
> *The gayest youth, the fairest face*
> *Must shortly lie in this dark place.*

And in question-and-answer form there is an epitaph that comes to us from England (as many of the early ones did) which can be read backwards and forwards, up and down, but whose message in any direction is inevitably the same:

| | | | |
|---|---|---|---|
| SHALL | WE | ALL | DIE? |
| WE | SHALL | DIE | ALL. |
| ALL | DIE | SHALL | WE? |
| DIE | ALL | WE | SHALL. |

Various epitaphs, obviously written before death, thumb skeletal noses (why not?) at the curious passerby, telling him to be on his way, to mind his own business, or to admit his earthly idiocy. The first is from New Jersey, the second from Vermont, and the third from Charleston, South Carolina:

*Reader, pass on! don't waste your time*
*On bad biography and little rhyme,*
*For what I am this crumbling clay insures,*
*And what I was is no affair of yours!*

*I was somebody*
*Who, is no business*
*of yours.*

*Reader, I've left this world,*
*In which I had a world to do:*
*Sweating and fretting to get rich —*
*Just such a fool as you!*

And so, in a measure, we are fools, all of us, and Death comes "slily" while we act at being so. There is an epitaph that puts it very nicely:

*Death is a fisherman. The world we see*
*A fishpond is, and we the fishes be.*
*He sometimes angler-like doth with us play,*
*And slily takes us one by one away.*

There are epitaphs composed with a wry sense of humor by the grave's occupant before death, many of which describe his one-time work or occupation. On an angler, for example, the one word: HOOK'D. On a farmer from Eastport, Maine: TRANSPLANTED. On a doctor from Brookland, Arkansas: OFFICE UPSTAIRS. A high school principal in Elkhart, Indiana: SCHOOL IS OUT, TEACHER HAS GONE HOME. A traveling salesman buried in Burlington, Iowa: MY TRIP IS ENDED, SEND MY SAMPLES HOME. On a newspaperman in Atlanta: COPY ALL IN. On a bartender: THIS IS ON ME. A photographer: TAKEN FROM LIFE.

Virtually every occupation lends itself to a pertinent epitaph, and I offer these as possibilities (you will think of more of your own): For a newscaster or sports announcer: TIME FOR STATION IDENTIFICATION. For a baseball player: STRIKE THREE! Or: SAFE AT HOME! For an automobile salesman:

RECALLED FOR INSPECTION. For a politician: ELECTED! Or: DEFEATED AT LAST. For a travel agent: ANYWHERE BUT HERE. And for a housewife? The possibilities are limitless.

Interestingly enough — and this might bear a little poking into — the great majority of epitaphs appear to have been the creation of men, not women. Possibly because in the past men controlled the purse strings. Possibly because they were more familiar with death and viewed it with an easier, more realistic eye. Possibly because they felt a greater sense of history. The tombstones in any case were ordered by the men from a stonecutter and carver, not by the women. Which gave some husbands the opportunity to assert themselves, and — reversing all normal laws — they, at the last, had the last word.

The epitaphs they created reflect, to put it mildly, marital uproars and differences:

*Here lies my wife*
*Here lies she.*
*Hallelujah!*
*Hallelujee!*

*Here snug in grave my wife doth lie,*
*Now she's at rest, and so am I!*

*I laid my wife beneath this stone*
*For her repose and for my own.*

Others are more explicit about the wife's character:

*Here lies my wife in earthly mould,*
*Who, when she lived, naught did but scold;*
*Peace! wake her not! for now she's still:*
*She had, but now I have my will.*

*Here lies my dear wife,*
*A sad slattern and shrew,*
*If I said I regretted her,*
*I should lie too!*

Not all husbands, however, were cynical and bitter. One extraordinarily lovely tribute to love, sufficiently beautiful to outbalance all others, comes from Long Island, from Nathaniel T———, to his wife, Michal, who died February 15, 1765:

> *Beneath this little stone*
> *Does my beloved lie,*
> *O pity, pity me, whoever passeth by,*
> *And spend a tear at least,*
> *Or else a tear let fall*
> *On my sweet blooming rose*
> *Whom God so soon did call.*

The words are not easily forgotten: "Beneath this little stone / Does my beloved lie, / O pity, pity me. . . ."

Strong individualists remained so to the end, and their individualism lasts in epitaphs of their making. Their no-nonsense directness is refreshing. One of these is forthrightly described:

> *He lived and died a true christian,*
> *He loved his friends and hated his enemies.*

Another, John Custis of Virginia, a landed gentleman who died in 1750, directed and insisted that his epitaph read:

> *Here lies the body of John Custis,*
> *who died aged 77 years; and yet lived but 7,*
> *being the time of his keeping a bachelor's house,*
> *at Arlington,*
> *on the eastern shore of Virginia.*

That one certainly took care of all those involved in the other 70 years of his existence — and conjures up also visions of the 7.

But my favorite among all individualists (French in this case, and not American) is a wealthy Parisian who, bored with the petty routines of daily

*Morehead, Kentucky, 1940:*
*Primitive Baptist Church members attend a baptismal service*
*held in a creek*

life, committed suicide after penning the words now gracing his tombstone:

> *Tired of this eternal buttoning*
> *and unbuttoning.*

I suggest that your next stroll, outing, walk, even picnic, be in the direction of the oldest cemetery near you. And that you take the time there to move slowly between the tombstones, and read there the long past, the story of the men and women who made your community, who lived once upon this land.

You may come across a single line as incredibly moving as that over Lizzie Angell's grave in East Derry, New Hampshire:

> *I don't know how to die.*

You may find a stone which tells you, once and for all, that your credit cards are no longer of any use:

> *This world's an Inn, and I her guest*
> *I've eat and drank and took my rest*
> *With her awhile, and now I pay*
> *Her lavish bill and go my way.*

Or you may, by great chance, find poetry:

> *Stranger, pause and think of me,*
> *Who once did move and breathe like thee,*
> *Who knew the grass and tree-lined sky,*
> *And now in eyeless dust must lie.*

And the leaves will be greener and the sky, for the moment, brighter for the finding and the reading of it. Death will come — but later.

The tradition of the epitaph itself goes back to the funeral tablets of Persia, the pyramids and obelisks of Egypt, the monuments of Greece, the catacombs of Rome. Countless centuries: "More than two hundred generations of mortal men lie buried in this vast cemetery of land and ocean that we call the earth." Until Elizabethan times in England, however, epitaphs were in general reserved "to those eminent in public service or distinguished by extraordinary virtues and talents . . . valiant and most worthy men." And, until the time of Elizabeth I, epitaphs were chiefly inscribed in Latin or French and engraved on brass. Thereafter they were more commonly cut in stone, and it was this tradition that passed the Atlantic to the cemeteries of Massachusetts, Rhode Island, Pennsylvania, Virginia, and the other colonies with the early settlers and their immediate descendants.

Of epitaphs, Thomas Fuller said that "the shortest, plainest, and truest are the best." Puttenham, in the *Arte of English Poesie*, agrees thoroughly, and lambastes the windy and wordy:

An epitaph is but a kind of epigram applied to the report of the dead person's estate and degree, or of his other good or bad partes, to his commendation or reproach: and is an inscription such as a man may commodiously write or engrave upon a tombe in few verses, pithie, quicke and sententious, for the passer-by to peruse and judge upon without any long tariaunce: so as if it exceede the measure of an epigram, it is then (if the verse be correspondent) rather an elegy than an epitaph, which errour many of these bastarde rimers commit, because they be not learned, for they make long and tedious discourses, and write them in large tables to be hanged up in churches and chauncells over the tombes of great men and others, which be so exceeding long as one must have halfe a daye's leisure to read one of them, and must be called away before he come halfe to the end, or else be locked into the church by the sexton, as I myself was once served reading an epitaph in a certain cathedrall church of England.

W. H. Beable in his work on epitaphs also agrees with the view "that while *epitaph* etymologically means strictly an inscription upon a tomb, by a natural extension of usage the name is applied to anything written ostensibly for that purpose whether actually inscribed upon a tomb or not." Which opens a vast field.

Fuller, Puttenham, and Beable would be very happy with the pithiness (if not the entire spirit) of a group of "epitaphs" collected from film stars by Homer Croy in Hollywood in 1932 and published there in a small booklet, *The Last Word*. These epitaphs were composed by the celebrities for their own gravestones, but to the best of my knowledge only that by W. C. Fields was actually used:

*Clark Gable: Back to the silents.*
*Eddie Cantor: Here in Nature's arms I nestle,*
                     *Free at last from Georgie Jessel.*
*Marie Dressler: Just a lonely trouper starting on a new circuit.*
*Polly Moran: I'm on my way to the biggest Preview I ever attended.*
*Walter Winchell: Here lies Walter Winchell*
                     *— in the dirt he loved so well.*
*Fredric March: This is just my lot.*
*Rex Bell: After Hollywood, nothing is a surprise.*
*George Gershwin: Here lies the body of George Gershwin,*
                     *American composer.*
                     *Composer? American?*
*Clive Brook: Excuse me for not rising.*
*Fontaine Fox: I had a hunch something like this would happen.*
*Will Irwin: At last he is catching up on his sleep.*
*Edward G. Robinson: X marks the spot.*
*Charles Bickford: Strike the set.*
*W. C. Fields: On the whole, I'd rather be in Philadelphia.*
*Douglas Fairbanks: Home, James.*
*Dorothy Parker: Excuse my dust.*
*Joan Bennett: It was fun while it lasted.*
*Constance Bennett: Do not disturb.*
*Edna May Oliver: It might have been worse.*

With two exceptions, all are now gone, but their willingness not to take themselves too seriously as they looked to the end of the road is refreshing. Was then, and still is now.

The best recent work on American epitaphs is Charles L. Wallis's *Stories on Stone*. He has some twenty-seven chapter headings, ranging from "Home Is the Sailor," "Out Where the West Begins," and "Freed from Bondage," to "Crime and Punishment," "Doctors and Patients," "A Word or Two for Mother," and "The Course of True Love." The collection of epitaphs is a solid one, but I would myself reduce the number of divisions to nine, giving each one at the same time broader scope for the inclusion of closely related materials. These divisions, with illustrations from cemeteries across the land, are:

## *Epitaphs Warning of Death*

*Dear friends who live to mourn and weep*
*Behold the grave wherein I sleep*
*Prepare for death for you must die*
*And be entombed as well as I.*

> (Old Cemetery,
> Bridgehampton, Long Island, 1848)

*Draw near, ye fair, as in a mirror see,*
*What you tho' e'er so lovely soon must be.*
*Tho' beauty with her rosebuds paint each face,*
*Approaching death will strip you of each grace.*

> (Common Street Cemetery,
> Watertown, Massachusetts, 1792)

## *Epitaphs Expressing Hope and Assurance of the Hereafter or Philosophical Acceptance of Death*

*This body sleeps in dust*
*Immortal joys await the host*
*In perfect beauty may it rise*
*When Gabriel's trumpet shakes the skies.*

> (Old Cemetery,
> Bridgehampton, Long Island, 1833)

*With patience having run his race*
*Now death hath set him free*
*We wish he does enjoy the place*
*Of true Felicity.*

(Newport, Rhode Island, 1736)

*A coffin, sheat & grave's*
*My earthly store*
*'Tis all I want: & kings*
*Can have no more.*

(East Hill Cemetery,
Peterborough, New Hampshire, n.d.)

And this exceptional one I cannot resist including: it comes from New Brunswick, just north of us:

*The earth goeth on the earth*
*Glittering like gold*
*The earth goeth to the earth*
*Sooner than it would*
*The earth builds on the earth*
*Castles and Towers*
*The earth says to the earth*
*All shall be ours.*

(Melrose, New Brunswick, 1751)

## Epitaphs of Infancy, Childhood, and Youth

*I in the Graveyard too may see*
*Graves shorter there than I*
*From death's arrest no age is free*
*Young children too may die.*

(From *The New England Primer*)

*Bernalillo County, New Mexico, 1940: adobe church with graves*

*Our child has gone to heaven to rest*
*For God alone does what is best.*

(Boylston Street Cemetery, Boston, 1800)

*We loved her.*

(On a child aged seven, Sagg Cemetery,
Bridgehampton, Long Island, 1861)

*Here did she go*
*Just as she did begin*
*Death to know*
*Before she knew to sin.*

(New Preston, Connecticut, 1777)

*Ere sin could blight or sorrow fade,*
*Death came with friendly care*
*The opening bud to Heaven conveyed*
*And bade it blossom there.*

(Rose Hill Cemetery,
Chicago, 1848,
on a child died age eleven months)

*Beautiful flower of Middletown,*
*How art thou cutted down! cutted down!*

(Middletown, Connecticut, n.d.)

## Epitaphs on Women

I have mentioned the satiric, humorous, misanthropic epitaphs on women, but they are, of course, few in actual number. Collectors gather them because they are unique, and because they stand out "shockingly" from their more traditional and respectable neighbors. This one for "mrs. Elizabeth Davis" of Fairfax, Virginia, refutes them and stands squarely on the best traditions of Virginia:

*She was related to several of the most respectable families*
*in Virginia and Maryland,*
*lived deservedly esteemed by all the worthy of her acquaintance,*
*and died greatly lamented. . . .*

(Alexandria, Virginia, 1803)

What better recommendation to her Maker!
The epitaphs of death in childbirth pathetically reflect their times:

*Died leaving an infant four days old,*
*And with her rests that sweet babe.*

(Wisconsin Avenue Cemetery,
Georgetown, District of Columbia, 1863)

*In the circle of one little year*
*Maiden, wife, and mother:*
*Sweet changes, but another*
*Leaves thee lamented here. . . .*

(Oak Hill Cemetery,
Georgetown, District of Columbia 1856)

*Though she was fair while she had breath*
*And on her cheeks the rose did bloom*
*Yet her dear Babe became her Death*
*While she became the infant's Tomb.*

(Harvard, Massachusetts, 1776,
died age twenty-four)

From the following, one wonders how many Buels there are in Connecticut today: there are other stones of this sort around the country, but Mrs. Buel's is quite sufficient:

*Here lies the body of Mrs. Mary, wife of Dr. John Buel, Esq.*
*She died Nov. 4, 1778, AEtat 90,*

*having had 13 children, 101 grand-children,*
*274 great-grandchildren, 22 great-great-grandchildren;*
*total 410;*
*surviving, 336.*

(Litchfield, Connecticut, 1778)

Near Silver Lake, New York, there is a backhanded compliment:

*She never done a thing to*
*displeas her Husband.*

(Cemetery near Silver Lake,
New York, 1859)

And Jane Bent must have been a strong and sprightly New England character:

*In memory of Jane Bent,*
*who kicked up her heels and away she went.*

(Rockville, Massachusetts, n.d.)

## Epitaphs Citing the Occupation of the Deceased

I would include here also those epitaphs which cite some special work or action for which the deceased hopes to be deservedly remembered, such as:

*Ephraim Wales Bull*
*The originator of the Concord Grape*
*He sowed, others reaped.*

(Concord, Massachusetts, 1895)

*Stephen F. Fassett*
*I began the preserving*

*of cow's milk with white*
*sugar for the use of steamers*
*crossing the Atlantic Ocean.*

(Winchendon, Massachusetts, 1856)

On a sailor:

*Landsmen or sailors*
*For a moment avast,*
*Poor Jack's main topsail*
*Is laid to the mast,*
*The worms gnaw his timbers,*
*His vessel a wreck,*
*When the last whistle sounds,*
*He'll be up on deck.*

(Young Street Cemetery,
East Hampton, Connecticut, 1883)

And another most eloquent on a seaman:

*Though Boreas' blasts and Neptune's waves*
*Have cast me to and fro;*
*Yet, in spite of all, by God's decree,*
*I anchor here below,*
*Where I do here at anchor ride,*
*With many of our fleet;*
*Yet once again, I must set sail,*
*My adm'ral, Christ, to meet.*

(Hanover, New Jersey, 1768. A quite similar
epitaph is found in Stepney churchyard,
England, 1697)

On a cooper, whose epitaph needs quoting in full:

> *Here lies the body of Richard Thomas,*
> *an inglishman by birth*
> *A Whig of '76.*
> *By occupation a cooper*
> *Now food for worms.*
> *Like an old rum puncheon*
> *Marked, numbered and shooked.*
> *He will be raised again*
> *and finished by his creator.*
> *He died Sept. 28, 1824; aged 75.*
> *America my adopted country*
> *My best advice to you is this*
> *take care of your liberties.*

(Windsor, Maine, 1824)

## Epitaphs Describing the Manner of Death

These normally reflect a tragic or sudden, unlooked-for death, as, for example:

. . . *who was drowned while bathing in the ocean* . . .

. . . *who was accidentally killed on board the ship* Henry Lee . . .

. . . *who died suddenly of Apoplexy* . . .

. . . *was instantly killed by falling from aloft on board of Whaling Bark* Nimrod, *on the 18th of Sept. 1860. Ae. 19* . . .

. . . *she was suddenly cut down without warning amidst earthly enjoyments* . . .

Some point the finger of responsibility:

*AE 6 yrs*
*He was instantly killed*
*by a stagecoach passing*
*over him*

(Putney, Vermont, 1845)

And later:

*Born Nov. 18, 1912*
*Killed by an automobile*
*September 1, 1915*

(Dublin, New Hampshire, 1915)

And more directly and bitterly:

*In memory of*
*Ellen Shannon*
*Aged 26 Years*
*Who was fatally burned*
*March 21st 1870*
*by the explosion of a lamp*
*filled with "R. E. Danforth's*
*Non Explosive*
*Burning Fluid"*

(Girard, Pennsylvania, 1870)

The date on this next does away with any need for enlarged explanation:

*His death was occasioned by*
*an accidental blast of powder*
*on July 4th.*

(Putney, Vermont, 1838)

A country tragedy:

> *Died on the 4th of May, 1831, by the kick of*
> *a colt in his bowels.*
> *Peaceable and quiet, a friend to*
> *his father and mother, and respected*
> *by all who knew him, and went*
> *to the world where horses*
> *don't kick, where sorrows and weeping*
> *is no more.*

> (Williamsport, Pennsylvania, 1831,
> for a ten-year-old boy)

On the stone is engraved a diabolical picture of the colt in the act of planting his hooves on the abdomen of the boy, who, as the epitaph reads, was a friend to his mother.

## Epitaphs Associated with Historic Events

> *In Memory of M$^r$*
> *Benadam Allyn who died*
> *Sep 6th 1781 In fort Griswould*
> *by traitor arnolds murdering*
> *Corps in y$^e$ 20th year of his Age.*

> *To future ages this shall*
> *Tell This brave youth*
> *in fort griswould fell*
> *For amaricas Liberty*
> *He fought & Blead*
> *Alas he die$^d$.*

> (New London County,
> Connecticut, 1781)

*A devoted martyr to the*
*Cause of his Country.*
*Reader, Art thou possessed of Liberty?*
*He died for thee.*

(On tombstones throughout New England)

My favorite from the Revolutionary period is one to have been inscribed on a monument erected to the memory of the Honorable Job Pray, a member of the executive council of Georgia and, during the Revolution, a brave naval commander. It was most certainly composed by a naval man:

*Sunk at his moorings, on wednesday, the 29 of April, 1789, one, who never struck his flag, while he had a shot in the locker; who carried sail in chace till all was blue; in peace, whose greatest glory was a staggering topsail breeze; in war, to bring his broadside to bear upon the enemy; and who, when signals of distress hove out, never stood his course, but hauled, or tacked, or wore, to give relief, though to a foe; who steered his little bark full fifty annual cruises over life's tempestuous ocean, and moored her safe in port at last; where her timbers being crazy and having sprung a leak in the gale, she went down with a clear hawse. If these traits excite, in the breast of humanity, that common tribute to this wreck, let thine be borne upon the breeze, which bends the grassy covering of the grave of old JOB PRAY.*

Others, simpler, are equally moving:

*Lost in the North Atlantic*
*when his ship was torpedoed*
*on the way to Greenland.*

(McKinley, Maine, 1943)

*Vicinity of Jackson, Kentucky, 1940:*
*the preacher, with mother, widow, and other relatives*
*at a memorial service*

*Orrin Rice*
*81st Airborne Division*
*Died of Wounds, Normandy*
*June 7, 1944*

## *Satiric Epitaphs*

These are the epitaphs of the non-believers and of those who, with dying wish, mock the serious. Prizes of a sort belong to all of them. Take Arthur Haine, who was buried in City Cemetery, Vancouver, Washington, in 1907. In his will written two years before his death: "Know everybody by these presents that I, Arthur Haine, knowing what I am about, make this my last will and testament. . . . My funeral is to be of the cheapest kind and I don't want my body to be transported but buried in the vicinity where I may die. As I have lived an Infidel, I must be buried as such without any monkey business." His wishes were carried out. His coffin was taken to the cemetery in a beer truck while a band played popular tunes, and kegs of beer were spigotted for friends and spectators. His epitaph reads briefly:

*Haine Haint.*

A similar non-believer (and read this very carefully):

*Who never sacrificed his reason*
*at the alter of superstitious God,*
*who never believed that Jonah*
*swallowed the whale.*

(East Thompson, Connecticut, 1872)

One who led a bitter life comments:

*Cold is my bed, but ah I love it,*
*For colder are my friends above it.*

(Calvary Cemetery,
Chicago, 1859)

A curious gentleman was Daniel Emerson, who wanted to be buried with his head sticking out of the ground, so that he could keep a watchful eye on his neighbors. His wish was not granted, but when he died at the age of eighty-two, his epitaph did warningly read:

THE LAND I CLEARED IS NOW MY GRAVE
THINK WELL MY FRIENDS HOW YOU BEHAVE.
(Marlboro, New Hampshire, 1829)

In any old and large cemetery there will be found a few of these, each reflecting a quaint, crotchety, or fiercely independent individual or character.

## *Humorous Epitaphs, Intentional and Unintentional*

The intentionally humorous epitaphs are for the most part the creations of the deceased, such as those of the movie stars collected by Homer Croy, or those relating death itself to one's occupation in life, as the journalist's "Copy All In." The unintentionally humorous result chiefly from accidents of spelling and phrasing, and come to us from country stonecutters and rural cemeteries:

*Gone to be an angle.*
(White Horn, Tennessee, n.d.)

*My glass is Rum.*
(East Derry, New Hampshire, 1781)

*Lord, she is Thin.*
(Cooperstown, New York, 1825)

*Let the dead and the beautified rest.*
(Virgil, New York, 1871)

*To the Memory of Abraham Beaulieu*
*Born 15 September 1822*
*Accidentally shot 4th April 1844*
*As a mark of affection from his brother.*

(Catholic Cemetery,
La Pointe, Wisconsin, 1844)

I close with the newspaperman's

30

# Legends and Tales

*Legends*
*Urban Belief Tales*
*The Jack Tales*
*Tales Told in the Gullah Dialect*
*"Tall" Tales: Jim Bridger*
*The* Cante-Fable

# 21.

# *Legends*

In the mainstream of American folklore, we have no myths. Myths (in the folk and literary sense) deal with stories about the Creation, of how man came into being, how fire was brought to earth, and such. When the first ships from Spain and England touched shore in Florida, Virginia, and Massachusetts, they brought with them passengers who had passed well beyond any Greek need for such beautiful believings. Myths had died with the generations of their ancestors.

Myths belong to a primitive people or the beginnings of a people: the Greeks, the Teutonic peoples, the Jews, the Indians. Myths are beyond man's present experience: they are of awe and terror: darkness, the Flood, the outer gods. Some may suggest that the Negro brought with him from Africa myths in the form of the Br'er Rabbit stories ("How the Rabbit Got His Short Tail") and comparable stories of beginnings, but take a look at them. The stories were told here for full fun. There is no sense of fear in them, no awe. They are as sophisticated in their way as the shipboard anecdotes of Virginia settlers who had lived (albeit many in jail) in Shakespere's London before setting forth on the iron-gray seas.

Legends, yes. We have our legends. Not of Roland, Charlemagne, the Cid, Virgil, and Avicenna, but of our own kind: Crockett, Carson, Bridger, Boone. Not of Ararat and Roncesvalles, but of the Rockies and Raton. Not of Tours and its great battle, but of Concord and a small skirmish. Not of Salamis and Lepanto, but of Erie and the Old Head of Kinsale. We have our legends.

Legends may be big or little, have a long life or a short one, be told over a lot of territory or limited to a small town. They are of several types.

Some legends are based on generic characters, and these are essentially local: one never remembers the names, but the characters: the village idiot, the town drunk. In New England, I remember in Framingham a harmless and pathetic village idiot who was deathly afraid of dogs; children barked at him from across the street and terrified him. In Virginia City, Nevada, I remember (but not his name) a "character" (the town was full of them) who lived on a hillside remote but visible from C Street, and who, morning and evening, raised and lowered the American flag from a pole in his front yard and at the same time fired off a small cannon in honor of the flag and nation. It woke us up and sent us to the saloons (the Brewery, the Bucket of Blood, Delta, Old '62, Sazerac, Crystal, and others), or if already there, stirred us into hoisting a glass in patriotic confirmation of the event.

Some legends stem from greatness: Washington, Lincoln, Babe Ruth, "Snowshoe" Thompson, Man O'War, Truman, Eisenhower, *The Twentieth Century Limited*, *The Flying Cloud*.

Legend may grow out of romanticized outlawry: Jesse James, Sam Bass, Cole Younger, the Daltons. There are necessary ingredients here: the outlaw was always kindhearted, generous to the poor, chivalrous to the ladies; driven to outlawry by accident or forces beyond his control (outlawry was never *chosen*); betrayed by one close to him (Robert Ford, Frank Murphy); and dead before his time — with boots on, never in bed.

Legend may grow out of stupidity or evil, the deeds magnified heroically, the stupidity and evil softened with time and telling: General George Custer, Clay Allison, Billy the Kid.

Legend may grow out of great disaster: the *Titanic*, the Old '97; Casey Jones, the Santa Barbara earthquake, the Chicago fire, the blizzard of 1888, the Dust Bowl.

Legends are all over the place, and the chief touchstone to them is that they relate — or are presumed to relate — to actual persons, events, and places. They are, in effect, for the folk, historical accounts, even though the folk in the telling or hearing of them may be aware that the basic historical facts are being embroidered upon or are even dubious in origin. The presumption is that there is truth somewhere in the telling. As Richard Dorson of Indiana University points out, the difference between the legend and the tale can be summed up in what might always be the opening words of each. The legend: "There was once . . ." The tale: "Once upon a time . . ." The legend refers to specifics and history; the tale to a fanciful, never-never land. (The deadpan telling of a "tall tale" is, of course, wonderful and conscious American confusion and admixture of both, the setting of an unbelievable tale within the framework of believable truth.)

Our "personal" legends are close to us; they are not remote on the heroic national heights of the Cid or St. Patrick. We can touch our legendary figures: they are within reach, like our baseball players. All of our history is close to us, and the legends that go with it. John Paul Jones: "I have not yet begun to fight!"; Washington and the "silver dollar o'er Rappahannock's tide"; Weems and the cherry tree; the Battle of the Bulge, Bastogne, and "Nuts!"; Boone returning from a frontier forest trip and being asked if he was ever lost: "Lost? No, I was never lost, but I was bewildered once for three days"; Crockett and the almanacs and "Remember the Alamo!"; the terrors of the Donner Party; Al Packer in Colorado, who ate five of the seven Democrats in Hinsdale County; John Henry, who burst his heart driving steel in competition with a newfangled steam power drill; Roy Bean and the legends of The Law West of the Pecos; Julie Bulette — Queen of the Comstock "Red Light" — carried to her grave by the men of Engine Company No. 1 with bands playing traditional dirges, and returning to the romping tune of "The Girl I Left Behind Me"; and, found here, Santa Claus, The Cowboy, Jesse James, Sam Bass, Colonel George A. Custer, Frankie and Johnny, and Professor George Lyman Kittredge of Harvard. Some of them legends, continuing fact; some, trimmings on fact.

The greatest of our great legendary figures are two. They are our creation and ours only, and they have passed to every nation and people on this earth. The Iron Curtain cannot keep them out. They are heard of and known everywhere: Santa Claus and the Cowboy. More than any other legendary figures in the entire history of the world these are better known. And they are ours. And they reflect us as a nation: generosity and individualism, gentleness and honor. (There are those who would sneer and denigrate, but they will pass: Santa Claus and the Cowboy remain.)

# *Santa Claus*

The St. Nicholas–Santa Claus legend has its religious-miracle beginnings in medieval Europe with St. Nicholas, and its secular-magical growth in nineteenth-century America (and specifically New York) with Santa Claus. The two figures are now sharply separated, but were once — happily and almost accidentally — brought together by Washington Irving (*The Knickerbocker History*) and Clement C. Moore ("The Night Before Christmas") to make our present roly-poly Salvation Army and department store symbol.

The facts about the saint are very brief: Nicholas was born in Patara, Asia Minor, early in the fourth century, moved as a young man to the nearby city of Myra, attended the Council of Nicaea in 325 as Bishop of Myra, was imprisoned under the reign of the Emperor Diocletian, released under the more tolerant Constantine, and died on December 6 — his saint day — 343 A.D. That is all that we know of him, and even some of that little is in doubt — his birthplace, for example, is not proven, and his name is not mentioned in accounts of those attending the Council. But he did exist. He lived and died, and until the Catholic Church recently — for reasons known only to

God and itself — dropped him from its preferred roster of saints, St. Nicholas' Day was observed on December 6 as one of the greatest in all Christendom.

Veneration of him, in terms of saintly time, was almost immediate. Within less than a hundred years of his death, the Emperor Justinian erected a church in his honor in Constantinople, and a basilica was built in Myra to guard his body. His cult spread throughout the East, and he became the patron saint of Moscow and (with Mary) of Russia, giving his name to five czars and, by unholy chance, to commissars — Nikita is a diminutive form of the name. In the West, merchants of Bari — competing with those of Venice — landed from seven ships, seized his bones in a surprise attack on Myra, and returned them in triumph to their city in 1087. On October 1, 1089, Pope Urban II consecrated the altar in the crypt of the cathedral being built to honor his bones. The cathedral at Bari became one of the greatest of pilgrimage centers in the Middle Ages, equal to St. James of Compostella, to Tours, Rome, and Cologne.

The cult spread: consider the honors and the devotion: patron saint of Russia, Greece, Norway (with Olaf), Sicily, Apulia (ĕastern Italy), Lorraine in France; patron saint of the cities of Moscow, Aberdeen, Bari, Corfu, Amiens, Civray in Poitou, Ancona, Fribourg in Switzerland; patron saint of virgins, unwedded maidens, schoolchildren, wandering scholars, students, and vagabonds, sailors, fishermen, lawyers, thieves, pirates, pawnbrokers, grocers, apothecaries, oil merchants, grain merchants, carriers of coal, dockers (longshoremen), prisoners (particularly those awaiting execution), bakers, cobblers, coopers, tailors, dyers, shopkeepers, and shepherds. Before the year 1500, there were more than 3000 churches dedicated to St. Nicholas in Germany, France, Belgium, and Holland alone. St. George is the patron saint of England: there are 204 churches dedicated to him there, but there are 446 to St. Nicholas.

There are legendary reasons for his patronage of all these varied countries, cities, crafts, and peoples. (He preserved mariners caught in terrible Mediterranean storms, and today Greek sailors wish well to others when a sailing caïque moves out: "May St. Nicholas hold the tiller!" He saved three innocent men from execution, and lawyers and condemned prisoners alike adopted him as patron in consequence.) There are upwards of fifteen miracles ascribed to him in the *Legenda Aurea* of Jacob de Voragine and in the medieval French of Wace's poem celebrating him. Of these legends, two have direct meaning for the later creation of Santa Claus: (1) his dowry-gifts to three virgins, saving them from lives of prostitution, and (2) his restoration to life of three young students who had been killed by an inn-keeper.

One, the giving of gifts: As a young man, Nicholas (the sole son of wealthy parents) learned to his horror that three virgins, the unwedded daughters of a respectable but impoverished citizen of Patara, were about to become prostitutes out of desperate necessity. Rather than see this happen, Nicholas on three successive nights passed by the unhappy house and on each occasion tossed in the window a ball of gold wrapped in a linen cloth. Each gift was dowry in plenty for one of the young women. They were saved from lives of sin, and all married happily. We have here one Santa Claus element, the secret giving of gifts. (And, incidentally, we have also the origin of the pawnbrokers' three balls, the symbol and sign found over every pawnshop around the world. The three gold balls will save. . . .)

Two, the protector and patron of children: Two young students (sometimes three) returning on holiday to their homes from boarding school, stopped at an inn for the night, were murdered by the innkeeper, chopped up into small pieces, and salted down into a tub of pork. Nicholas learned of the missing youths, confronted the innkeeper, and miraculously restored the youngsters to whole life out of their tub pieces. In consequence, Nicholas becomes the patron saint of (students, wandering scholars, vagabonds, and) children.

As the secret giver of gifts and the special patron of children, we have the basic characteristics of Santa Claus-to-be. But he is still St. Nicholas.

Nicholas moves now through the centuries. He is under attack during the Reformation (all saints were), but he manages to survive in disguise (as Father Christmas, Père Noel, Kris Kringle), and the date of his gift-giving shifts from his saint day and gravitates naturally toward the great feast of Christmas.

In Holland *Sinta Nikolaas* is readily corrupted into *Sinterklaes*, and the Dutch presumably bring this with them to New Amsterdam. But they actually pay very little attention to Nicholas — he is all but forgotten — and he would have gone completely down the drain had it not been for Washington Irving. The Dutch provided Irving with the inspiration for his *Knicker-bocker History*, which appeared in 1809, and in that work there are some twenty-five references to St. Nicholas and Santa Claus. The immense popularity of the book served to introduce — or reintroduce — St. Nicholas to the American public. Without Irving there would certainly be no Santa Claus today. But still, in Irving, St. Nicholas is a figure of the church, bringing his gifts — as he did in Holland — with horse and cart. Contemporary engravings depict him as a bishop with long black robes, austere in aspect. Without another step or two in his development, St. Nicholas again might have died — or Santa Claus never been born.

A short decade later, in 1821, there appeared an anonymous and tiny juvenile called *The Children's Friend*, which consisted of eight quatrains devoted to "Santeclaus," and which pictured him riding on a rooftop in a sleigh drawn by exactly one prancing reindeer. The first two quatrains go:

> *Old Santeclaus with much delight*
> *His reindeer drives this frosty night.\**
> *O'er chimney tops, and tracks of snow,*
> *To bring his yearly gifts to you.*
>
> *The steady friend of virtuous youth,*
> *The friend of duty, and of truth,*
> *Each Christmas eve he joys to come*
> *Where love and peace have made their home.*

We have "Santeclaus" bringing gifts secretly to children on Christmas Eve. He has a sleigh and a reindeer, rides over the rooftops, and is wearing a big fur cap, a flowing robe with a fur collar, and over-the-calf leather boots. But the doggerel is just that, and again Santa might have died a-borning. We are on the threshold, however.

At the next Christmas season, in 1822, the Reverend Clement C. Moore, an Episcopal clergyman in New York City and the son of the Bishop of New

---

\* This is the first reference to the reindeer and sleigh now associated with Santa Claus. They are both purely American inventions, and never existed in any European tradition.

York, wrote a private, family poem for his children. The poem was "A Visit from St. Nicholas," or "The Night Before Christmas." Aside from its family use, Moore thought the poem beneath his dignity and was ashamed of it. He would not permit it to be published, but a relative surreptitiously sent it to an upstate newspaper. In 1837, Moore finally acknowledged authorship when it appeared in a compilation of local poetry. He is now, of course, remembered for nothing else at all.

Moore had certainly read Irving, but in his creation of the poem he did one thing which seems not to have been noted. From Irving and the Dutch tradition he drew St. Nicholas, the traditional St. Nicholas. But from his past reading of the *Knickerbocker History*, Moore remembered most vividly the descriptions of the fat and jolly Dutch burghers with their white beards, red cloaks, wide leather belts, and leather boots. So, when he came to write a poem for his children, the traditional and somewhat austere St. Nicholas was transformed into a fat and jolly Dutchman. Also, from *The Children's Friend* of the year before, which he had probably purchased for his own youngsters, he drew not one lone reindeer, but created the now immortal and fanciful eight.

In the same year, 1837, when Moore's poem appeared in book form, Santa Claus sat for his first portrait in oil, at — of all places — the United States Military Academy at West Point. The painting was done by Robert W. Weir, professor of art at the Academy, and shows a fat and jolly Santa with a "finger aside of his nose" about to ascend a chimney after filling the stockings beside it. His cape is red and white-furred, and the bag on his back is full of presents.

In the years immediately following, Santa Claus appeared at Christmastime on the small pocket-sized advertising cards of New York business firms. It was not until 1863, however, that he showed signs of becoming a truly national figure. In that year Thomas Nast, the great cartoonist of the century, began drawing annual Christmas pictures of him for *Harper's Weekly*, the most notable popular magazine of the era. And Santa finally, of course, reached the White House. In 1891, President Benjamin Harrison told an inquiring newspaperman, "We shall have an old-fashioned Christmas, and I myself intend to dress up as Santa Claus for the children. If my influence goes for aught in this busy world, I hope that my example will be followed in every family in the land."

Santa Claus is now thoroughly and completely secular. The medieval legends about St. Nicholas are gone, and Santa bears no relation to him whatever. Every so often — every Christmas, actually — some member of the clergy (I remember a Baltimore bishop a few years back) rises to deplore the secularization of Christmas and the Santa-symbol of commercialization. The clergy should think twice before doing so, because Santa as the gift giver removes all such commercial taint from the Christ-child and leaves Him the sacred and religious aspect of the season which is His due. Were it not for Santa there might be some very messy confusion.

In its beginnings as St. Nicholas, the religious legend is purely folk. No matter whether some of the stories were created by a monk in his cell. They circulated orally and passed by word of mouth across the Continent and to the islands, and were believed. The Santa Claus transformation in America is not, however — in the early 1800's — folk, but sophisticated (Irving, Moore, Weir) and popular (advertisements, cartoons).

With his full adoption by Americans, however, Santa Claus does again become folk: in stories told of him by parents to children, in "dressing up for the children," and in the starry-eyed belief of youngsters in him. This was so, more so in the early part of this century than it seems to be today. As with the disappearance of home-made toys and our purchase of them ready-made for us, we tend also to sit back and let someone else do it: George Gobel on TV. The "folkness" of Santa in our own homes is somehow less. (I can remember at Christmas trying to puzzle out who was playing Santa Claus — an uncle, my grandfather, a neighbor. They "ho-ho'd" very realistically, and I was never quite sure. The youngsters were delirious, but I knew there was someone behind that beard. Someone who liked us and liked what he was doing.) All families have something of the Santa Claus tradition in their heritage. And so does the United States as a nation. It has been a good heritage, for us as a people, and for the world.

# The Cowboy

It is very difficult to capsule the legendary figure of the cowboy. A full book on him *as legend alone* at least is wanted. Into the making of it would go Owen Wister, B. M. Bowers, Zane Grey, Luke Short, *The Illustrated Police News*, *Harper's Illustrated Weekly*, Theodore Roosevelt, Frederick Remington, Willard Thorpe, Con Price, Will Rogers, Charlie Russell, Tom Mix, Buck Jones, Hoot Gibson, John Wayne, millions of American youngsters playing cowboys and Indians, millions of American men (some of whom should know better) wearing cowboy boots and ten-gallon hats, and millions of American men, women, and children watching him at the movies or on TV (half a dozen shows per week, or more?), and innumerable other matters — his speech, his food, his clothes (and as the folk say, and I am glad to be able to put this in somewhere) *and etcetera.*

Why all this, and why the legend? Because the cowboy is a symbol of what we as a people and nation have wished as our way of life. He is a projection of our hopes and desires, a projection of our best code of ethics, of our wished-for *mores.*

Santa Claus is a projection of certain of our characteristics — generosity, gift giving, kindness, thoughtfulness — but he is a one-shot annual occurrence. We go all out with him at Christmastime, but the cowboy is with us the year 'round. And the cowboy symbolizes much more of us and for us than Santa.

Let me summarize some of the cowboy's greatness.

[But before doing so, a sideswipe at his denigrators. The little "researchers" are coming along (there have been nitpickers in every generation) saying that the cowboy was in literal fact lousy, often a drunkard, uneducated and illiterate (like Jim Bridger), had himself no concept of anything beyond his forty-dollars-and-beans a month, raised payday hell out of sheer boredom, and so on and on. Let us readily admit every bit of this as it applied to some, and even a goodly number, of cowboys: and sailors, and farmers, and

railroaders, and newspapermen, and workers of every sort, and United States senators (percentagewise), and mothers of our children. But let us also quickly reverse tracks and say that on balance the symbol of goodness and greatness in the cowboy knocks all that nitpicking into a cocked hat. — It would amuse me, if it weren't all so boring, to note that Soviet Russia attacks Santa Claus as "a tool of American capitalist interests." And that Soviet Russia praises (follow this) Paul Bunyan because he is a symbol for the American worker of the power of the American worker in the face of bourgeois, ideological, capitalistic oppression. When will they ever learn that Paul Bunyan is a "capitalistic" chamber of commerce creation and is no symbol of anything whatsoever to the worker other than a grand-scale picnic, rib-roast, log-rolling, outdoor jamboree competition or holiday? (I wonder who feeds Moscow its pap?) — And the cowboy. I have not myself seen an attack upon the cowboy. And yet if the Russians had any sense they would attempt to undermine him in every possible way, because the cowboy is us. I have the feeling that they may have considered doing so. Considered attacking him and reducing him with their monstrous machine to something *bourgeois, etc., etc.* . . . , to a nothingness. (How would you feel about that, Tex? Up on the Cimarron? Would you go with it in the Judith Basin? What about around Winnemucca? Along the Ruidoso? Down Durango way?) I think that the Soviets and their representatives here may have considered it, but that even they, in the face of their audience, may have backed away from such idiocy. Every child from the age of seven or eight on up in the United States would have laughed themselves silly, which would have been only a beginning of the snickering assault upon such obscenity. I think we'll keep the cowboy. And I do not feel that Russia will ever attempt to touch him. To attempt to take him for themselves (along with the electric light bulb and radio) would at once deny their "collectivism." To attack him would make everyone forever aware of their humorless, insensitive bureaucracy. Ah, to hell with them.]

Anyhow, these it seems to me are the attributes and attractions going to make up the cowboy, in fact and legend. Many overlap, but that is reinforcement, not repetition. Add your own beliefs and affections in the event I have missed some. The cowboy as legend (and legend based on fact):

Individualism: *"I am my own man. I speak for myself. . . ."*

Independence: *"Nobody owns me. I can pick up my saddle and go. . . ."*

Freedom: *"Don't fence me in!"* (How about *that* phrase over East Berlin way?)

Close to the land, but not bound by it, as a farmer is: *One sees the cowboy against the great spaces of the West, the mountains, the plains, the distances. There is freedom on the land that he sees and rides.*

Not given to bragging: *Very great understatement in his speech and description of anything unusual he may have done:* *"They just would not go across that swollen river, and it took us four days, and finally we got the fifteen hundred head over by not letting them drink, and then they made a rush for water, and we just kept driving them. . . ."*

Courage: *"Men who followed this life wouldn't tolerate a coward . . . one coward endangered the whole group. He had to have bones in his spinal column and know how to die standin' up."*

Cheerfulness: *"The bigness of the country . . . wouldn't let him listen to the whimpers of a mere human. . . . No one knowed a man was tired; sickness or injury was his own secret unless it couldn't be hid any longer. You'd never know but what he was as happy as a lost soul with hell in a flood, and he was usually grinnin' like a jackass eatin' cactus."*

Pride: *There is no prouder soul on earth than a cowboy.* *"The man on hossback has always held himself above the man on foot."*

Loyalty: *"He was one class of worker who didn't have to be watched to see that he did his work well. The nature of his work demanded that he be trusted. He took a pride in being faithful to his 'brand' and in performing his job well. He needed no overseer, or advice. He worked long hours and packed no timepiece. He belonged to no union, and no whistle was blowed orderin' him to knock off work. He worked from before dawn to after dark, and even later if need be. His loyalty to the boss came first, and he'd ride night herd on the cattle as faithfully on a rainy night, or in a stingin' sleet, as he would on starry, moonlight nights. . . . He'd lay down his life, if necessary, for the privilege of defendin' his outfit. Once a cowhand had throwed his bedroll into the wagon and turned his private hoss into the remuda of an outfit he'd pledged his allegiance and loyalty."*

True to his word: *His word was as good as law. It had to be. One did not survive on that harsh land on false promises. One did not question a man's word. One never forced him into defensively saying, "If I say so, I'll do it." It was said, and believed implicitly, and done. No questions. Complete faith, complete honesty.*

Generosity: *"The true old-time cowhand had a heart in his brisket as big as a saddle blanket." He shared with friends and strangers, and even enemies when the occasion demanded. "Hearing of some puncher being sick or broke or needing medicine, the whole range would empty its pockets." And this next I have seen: "Far out on the range, a long way from where he could buy more, his supply of 'makin's' might run low, but he never refused another a smoke unless he wanted to offer a direct and intentional insult." It was so natural that I have forgotten now whether I was the giver or the recipient.*

Women: *"One of the strictest codes of the West was to respect women. No other class of men looked upon women with greater reverence. . . . No matter who she was, or her station in life, the cowman held her with respect. . . . A woman might live alone, miles from anyone but she had no fear of any true cowman. She was as safe as in a church, and she knowed it. If any man, at any time, under any circumstances, mistreated a woman, he was culled from society. Men refused to speak to him, doors were shut aaginst him, and he was an outcast. In spite of the movies, if one insulted a woman he was probably killed sooner or later, even if somebody had to get drunk to do it."*

Kindness: *Of course. A basic American trait. You don't think it was invented by GI's giving chewing gum and chocolate to children, do you? They simply carried the tradition.*

The equal of any man: *Fighting fair and square, could anyone beat the cowboy? Impossible.*

*SMS Ranch, near Spur, Texas, 1939:*
*cowboy cinching up his saddle*

Nicknames: *They are good. Tex, Nevada, Luke, Shorty, Red, Mex, Whitey, Bronc. . . .*

The names of their ranches and brands: *These are enough to make the men stand separate from the rest of us: Rocking X, Lazy L, Flying W, R Bar Z, Running M. We envy them for the names. . . .*

Their clothes and gear: *These set the men apart: chaps, sombreros, leather jackets, bandanas, boots, spurs, jeans (Levi's), gloves, saddle, lariat, six-shooter, Remington, blanket, slicker. . . .*

Their way of life: *bunkhouse, corral, range, roundup, trail-herding, fence-riding, cutting out, branding, night-herding, chuckwagon, their special speech and their Western words. . . .*

All of these attributes and individual characteristics go into the making of the cowboy legend and become an inextricable part of it. At random ask any person to describe a cowboy (what makes him different?) and see what you come up with. On balance, it will be good and with elements of legend.

These things are the legend, the base of the legend, but there is more, certainly. The legend grows and is carried in all of the cowboy songs: each one of them is the stuff of legend: "The Streets of Laredo," "The Dying Cowboy," "The Trail to Mexico," "The Chisholm Trail," "Little Joe, the Wrangler." Legend lies back of every cattle brand. Legend rides every one of the great trails. Legend rides every range. Legend is in every cowtown. Legend is at every bar and in every saloon still standing. Legend is in every saddle.

To pick out one or half a dozen tales or legends is not the purpose here. (Read J. Frank Dobie, Con Price, Ramon F. Adams, Will James, and all the others for that.) The purpose here is to give the cowboy — as legendary figure — the greatness which is his due. Legendary and very human.

I am glad that he rides our land.

# *Jesse James*

Jesse James was looked upon as a combination Robin Hood and frontier adventurer, and the legends about him are for the most part generous and hero-worshipping. Starting his career with Quantrill's bushwhackers, he became in the fifteen years following the Civil War the most notorious train and bank robber in the country, and a price of $10,000 was placed on his head by the governor of Missouri. James hid out under the alias of Thomas Howard, but Robert Ford, a member of the gang, was tempted by the reward and killed Jesse in St. Joseph, Missouri, on April 4, 1882. The story has it that James was hanging a picture in the front room of the house on Lafayette Street with the doorway open to the street. Rather than attract the attention of passersby with his weapons, he removed both pistols and placed them on a chair while he stood on a bed to fix the picture. Robert Ford had never seen James off his guard before, and seized the opportunity to kill his companion from behind. James heard the click of Ford's pistol as he cocked it and turned to receive the pistol ball over his eye. Ford, fearing the revenge of James's friends, left Missouri for Colorado to run a saloon and gambling house in Creede. Here he was shot to death one night by Ed Kelly, a friend of James's.

As H. M. Belden points out in his *Ballads and Songs Collected by The Missouri Folk Song Society*, Jesse's betrayal and killing at the hand of a traitor was all that was needed to set the seal on the legend. It is one of the necessary and stock ingredients: Roland had his Ganelon, Arthur his Modred, Sam Bass his Jim Murphy, and Jesse James his Robert Ford.

Vance Randolph reports that the song swept the whole Middle West like wildfire, and he quotes the reminiscence of Mr. Robert L. Kennedy, writing in the Springfield, Missouri, *Leader*, for October 18, 1933:

Soon after the killing of James a ten-foot poem, set to music, came out and was sung on the streets of Springfield quite frequently. It told how Jesse James had a wife and she warned him all her life and the children they were brave and the dirty little coward who shot Mr. Howard and they laid poor Jesse in the grave. It caused tears to be shed. . . . An old blind woman used to stand in front of the court house in Springfield and sing it by the hour; mourners would drop coins in her tin can. She went up to Richmond, Missouri, and was singing her sad song with tears in her voice when she found herself slapped and kicked into the middle of the street. Bob Ford's sister happened to be passing that way.

Haldeen Braddy of Texas Western in El Paso contributed a note on Jesse James's chivalry to the *Journal of American Folklore:*

According to a report by my former student, Ray Gregory of Columbia, Missouri, his grandfather, Cliff Gregory, once encountered the notorious hold-up artist, Jesse James, on a train going from Columbia to Kansas City. Having heard that the outlaw was chivalrous to women, Gregory slipped his wallet to his wife for safekeeping when he saw Jesse board the train. Thus he saved his greenbacks, and all the robber got were the few loose coins Gregory had in his pockets. Jesse made no demands for money from the grandmother; instead, he gave her a kiss. The outlaw repeated this performance, of robbing the men and kissing the women, with all of the train passengers. The grandfather, therefore, had only kind memories of the James boys, for he was proud of having outwitted Jesse and glad to retain possession of his money. The grandmother enjoyed remembering her experience, too. In the opinion of the Gregory family, Jesse James measured up to the best traditions of the gentlemanly badman.

All of the ingredients are here, and "Jesse James" has become, without question, the best-known American outlaw ballad. It has a good tune, and the repetitious refrain (it may vary from version to version) imprints itself on the memory. Jesse will be around for a long time.

The version here was recorded by Artus M. Moser from the singing of Bascom Lamar Lunsford at Swannanoa, North Carolina, in 1946. Lunsford himself introduces the song: "This song is 'Jesse James.' I heard it when I was a boy in many different ways, but this text is the one I learned from Sam Sumner who lives just across Hickory Nut Gap next to Bat Cave in Henderson County, North Carolina, in 19 and 03."

I went down to the station not many days ago,
Did something I'll never do again,
I got down on my knees and delivered up the keys
To Frank and his brother, Jesse James.

*Poor Jesse, goodbye Jesse, farewell Jesse James,*
*Robert Ford caught his eye and he shot him on the sly,*
*It laid poor Jesse down to die.*

Oh, the people in the West when they heard of Jesse's death,
They wondered how he came to die;
It was Ford's pistol ball brought him tumbling from the wall,
And it laid poor Jesse down to die.

Oh, Jesse leaves a wife, she's a mourner all her life,
And the children they were brave;
But the dirty little coward, he shot Mr. Howard,
And he laid poor Jesse in his grave.

Oh, Jesse was a man and a friend to the poor,
And little did he suffer man's pain,
But I know with his brother Frank, he robbed the Chicago bank,
And he stopped the Glendale train.

Now Jesse goes to rest with his hands on his breast,
And the Devil will be upon his knees;
He was born one day in the county of Clay,
And he came from a great, great race.

*Poor Jesse, goodbye Jesse, farewell Jesse James,*
*Robert Ford caught his eye and he shot him on the sly,*
*And he laid poor Jesse down to die.*

# Sam Bass

"Sam Bass was born in Indiana — that was his native home . . ."

From the opening words through to the end of the ballad, there is as full a biographical account of the protagonist as one is likely to find in any ballad anywhere.

The story moves in an unbroken line: Sam Bass came from Indiana to Texas; in Texas he raced a good mare in Denton, made her locally famous, won money on her, and spent the money as freely as it easily came; drank nothing but the best whiskey, a high accolade in the days of rot-gut and 40-rod; went north to the Dakotas with a trail herd from the Collins ranch, sold the herd, and lost the sale money gambling and carousing; started back broke to Texas and on the way robbed a U.P. train (of $10,000 or more, it is reported); arrived back in Texas with his cowboy companions, and took to robbing stages and trains near Dallas (two stagecoaches and four trains in the spring of 1878). A reward was placed on his head; Jim Murphy, a member of his "gang," betrayed him and sold him out to Major John B. Jones, adjutant-general of Texas; in consequence Sam Bass, Seaborn Barnes, and Frank Jackson were met by Texas Rangers at Round Rock, Texas, where they had planned a bank holdup on Friday, July 19, 1878. Barnes was instantly killed by the Rangers and Bass was mortally wounded, but with Jackson escaped into the brush. Jackson wished to stay with Bass, but Sam persuaded him to leave. Jackson saved himself, and was never heard of after. Bass was captured the following day, July 20, and died on Sunday, July 21. Barnes and Bass are buried at Round Rock.

Walter Prescott Webb was a small participant in the making of the legend. He writes in *Texas Folk and Folklore* that he learned the ballad

at the age when it was a great privilege to be permitted to pad along in the freshly plowed furrow at the heels of the hired man, Dave. Not only was Dave the hired man, he was a neighbor's boy, and such a good poker player that he developed later into a professional gambler. But at the time I write of, Dave was my tutor in Texas history, poetry, and music, all of which revolved around Sam Bass. To me and to Dave, Sam Bass was an admirable young man who raced horses, robbed banks, held up trains, and led a life filled with other strange adventure. At length, this hero came to an untimely end through a villain named Murphy, "who gave poor Sam away." It was a story calculated to capture the imagination of young men and small boys. All over Texas, hired men were teaching small boys the legend of Sam Bass, a story which improved in the telling according to the ability of the teller.

Not only was the story thus told. Men of high station in life — the lawyers, judges, and old-timers — congregated around the courthouse of this western county and told of how Sam rode through the country at night after one of his daring robberies. Once a posse organized to go out and take Sam Bass. The leader of the posse was a lawyer, a smart man, and he knew exactly where Sam could be found and how he could be taken. He bravely placed himself at the head of a group of heavily armed men; he assured them that they would take the bandit and share the liberal reward that had been set on his head. They rode away into the night, they approached the lair of the fugitive; they *knew* they had him — at least the leader knew it. But that was the trouble. Sam did not run; therefore, the posse could not pursue. Sam seemed too willing to be approached; that willingness was ominous. Sam was such a good shot, so handy with a gun. The posse paused, it halted, consulted with the leader. The leader's voice had lost its assurance. The posse that had ridden up the hill now rode down again. Sam Bass *could not be found!* And until this day, when old-timers get together in that county, someone is sure to tell the story of that hunt. The wag of the courthouse, a lawyer, reduced it to writing, and on such public occasions as picnics and barbecues, he will read the account of "How Bill Sebasco Took Sam Bass." It was cleverly done and made as great a hit with the public as did Dave's rendition of the song and story to the small boy. In both cases all sympathy was with Sam Bass, all opinion against Murphy and Bill Sebasco.

Thus in West Texas, from the judge in the courthouse to the small boy in the furrow behind the hired man, was the story of Sam Bass told. What was taking place in this county was occurring, with proper variations, in every other county in the state, especially in those of the north and west. The legend of Sam Bass was in the process of becoming. Today it would fill a volume.

Webb gives a brief resume of Sam Bass's life, concluding with:

Bass died gamely, as he lived. He refused to give any of his comrades away, though he was rational until the end. "If a man knows any secrets," he said, "he should die and go to hell with them in him." Bass said that he had never killed a man, unless he killed the officer in Round Rock. [In the shooting at Round Rock, a Ranger had been killed.] Frank Jackson wanted to remain and help Bass, but the latter, knowing he was near the end, persuaded Jackson to leave, and gave him his horse to ride.

Bass and his men had camped near some Negro cabins at Round Rock, not far from the cemetery. Bass had an old Negro woman, Aunt Mary Matson, to cook some biscuits for him and to grind some coffee. When she had done this, Bass gave her a dollar. He then asked, "Have you ever heard of Sam Bass?" She told him she had. "Well, you can tell them you saw Sam Bass," he said, and went away.

His generosity was well known. He always paid for what he got from individuals. He was particularly considerate of poor people. He would give a poor woman a twenty-dollar gold piece for a dinner and take no change. He paid the farmers well for the horses he took from them, though sometimes he did not have time to see the farmer.

Sam Bass relics are scattered over the country, everywhere. Some say that he gave his gun to Frank Jackson. Others declare he surrendered it to the officers who found him. His belt with some cartridges in it is in the library of the University of Texas. A carpenter at Snyder has a horseshoe from Bass's best race horse nailed to the top of his tool chest. Near Belton are some live oak trees that Bass is said to have shot his initials in while riding at full speed. Horns of steers supposed to have been killed by Bass sell over the country at fancy prices. In Montague County there is a legend of $30,000 of loot buried by Sam Bass. Again, he is supposed to have left treasure in the Llano country. At McNeill, near Austin, there is a cave in which Sam Bass hid when he was in retirement. There he kept his horses and from there he made his forays.

Finally, when Sam was dead, legend wrote an epitaph on his monument which is not there. The legendary epitaph reads: "Would That He Were Good as He Was Brave." No such inscription can be deciphered on Bass's monument. The monument has been badly mutilated by souvenir collectors, but the inscription remains:

SAMUEL BASS
BORN
JULY 21, 1851
DIED
JULY 21, 1878
AGED 27 YEARS

In the lower right hand corner of the block on which the inscription appears is the name of the maker, C. B. Pease, Mitchell, Indiana. The people of Round Rock say that the monument was erected by a member of the family about a year after Bass's death.

More interesting than Bass's rather pretentious monument is that of his comrade, Seaborn Barnes, who sleeps the long sleep by his side. A rough sandstone stands at the head of this grave. It has been chipped away until the name is gone. The inscription, however, remains along with the date of his death. Were there no legend of Sam Bass in Texas, this inscription would make one. It is written in language Bass would have loved: it has a certain impertinence to law-abiding people in the near-by graves, a certain pride in the leader at whose heels Barnes died. The epitaph contains seven words. The spirit of the person who wrote the seven words of that epitaph is the spirit that created the legend of Sam Bass in Texas.

### HE WAS RIGHT BOWER* TO SAM BASS

From the details in the ballad, it must be obvious that it came into being very shortly after the events, within weeks even. "Jack" Thorp first heard it at a dance hall in Sidney, Nebraska, in 1888. But this is late. Austin Fife says that C. F. McCarty wrote Robert Gordon telling him that he (McCarty) was around Texas, Kansas, and the Indian Territory "in '79 or '80, maybe '81, when the song was sung night after night around the cattle, in the gambling halls, saloons, and other places where the boys and girls congregated."

---

* The bower in card games is the jack. In certain games, the jack is the next highest card to the king.

Sam Bass was born in In-di-an-a, that was his na-tive home, When
at the age of sev-en-teen, young Sam be-gan to roam; He
first came out to Tex-as a cow-boy for to be, A
kind-er heart-ed fel-low than Sam you nev-er see.

Sam Bass was born in Indiana, that was his native home,
When at the age of seventeen, young Sam began to roam;
He first came out to Texas a cowboy for to be —
A kinder-hearted fellow than Sam you never see.

Sam used to deal in race stock, one called the Denton mare,
He matched her in scrub races and taken her to the fair;
Sam used to coin the money and spend it very free,
He always drank good liquor wherever he may be.

Sam left the Collins ranch in the merry month of May
With a herd of Texas cattle the Black Hills for to see,
Sold out in Custer City and there got on a spree —
A harder set of cowboys you hardly ever see.

Sam had four companions, four bold and daring lads,
There was Richardson, Jackson, Joe Collins, and Old Dad;
A daring set of cowboys than Texas ever knew,
They whipped the Texas Rangers and run the boys in blue.

On their way back to Texas they robbed the U.P. train,
And then split up in couples and started out again;
Joe Collins and his partner was overtaken soon,
With all of their good money they had to meet their doom.

Sam had a good companion, called Arkansas for short,
He was shot by a Texas Ranger by the name of Thomas Floyd;
Old Tom's a tall six-footer and think's he's mighty fly,
Though I can tell you his racket — he's a deadbeat on the sly.

Sam got back to Texas all right side up with care,
Rode into the town of Denton his friends all there to share;
Sam's life was short in Texas for the robbery he did do,
He robbed all off the passenger, mail, and express train too.

Jim Murphy was arrested, and then released on bail,
He jumped his bond at Tyler and taken the train for Terrell;
Old Major Jones had posted Jim, and that was all a stall,
It was a plan to capture Sam before the coming fall.

Sam met his fate at Round Rock, July the twenty-first,
They pierced poor Sam with rifle ball and emptied out his purse;
Poor Sam is now a corpse and a-molding in the clay,
While Jackson's in the bushes a-trying to get away.

Jim borrowed Sam's good gold and did not want to pay,
The only way Jim thought to win was to give poor Sam away.
He give poor Sam away and left his friends to mourn —
Oh, what a scorching Jim will get when Gabriel blows his horn!

# Custer's Last Charge

This gory account of the Battle of the Little Big Horn elevates "blond-haired Custer" to the rank of hero, whereas, militarily, he made virtually every wrong decision possible and, had he survived, should have been court-martialed for them and the loss of his troops. Smarting from his reduction in rank from brigadier general to lieutenant colonel following the Civil War, Custer sought fame and promotion on the Indian frontier. He found both, but not in any way he had hoped for.

Consider the four glaring mistakes he made — but first, the setting.

Word had gone out among the Sioux to gather at the Little Big Horn in Montana in June 1876. Whether they came there for a last buffalo hunt, as has been claimed by some, or to meet in warlike council, is disputed. Certainly the tribulations that had fallen upon the Indian were discussed.

Whatever the reasons for the gathering, the tribes and the greatest of their warriors met on the banks of the Little Big Horn, where their lodges stretched unbrokenly for a distance of four miles. It was perhaps the largest and most important meeting in the history of the Indian nation. There were the great tribes of the Sioux — the Brules, the Minneconjous, the Sans Arcs, the Oglalas, the Uncpapas, and the Blackfeet. With them were the allied tribes of the Cheyennes and Arapahoes. Their war chiefs and medicine men were legend: Crazy Horse, Big Road, and Red Horse of the Oglala Sioux; Gall, war chief of the Uncpapa Sioux, Crow King, his lieutenant, Sitting Bull, medicine man; and Two Moon, leader of the fierce Cheyenne.

Against this encampment of the Sioux, numbering thousands, marched Colonel George A. Custer with six hundred men. Custer was overly ambitious and sure of himself, and he underestimated the enemy and his strength. Like Fetterman, who had had an easy way with a few Indians who "ran like rabbits," Custer felt that he could march through all the Indians in the West with his small force. Like Fetterman, he was to die.

Custer marched — *as the advance party of General Terry's force* — from the mouth of the Rosebud toward the Little Big Horn. His scouts told him that there were many Indians ahead, but Custer chose to disbelieve them (first mistake), and gave a "senseless order" which split his command in two, sending Captain Benteen, with 125 men, on a scouting expedition up an adjacent valley to the left (second mistake). Thus weakened, Custer moved steadily forward, still confident that there was no enemy and that, even if there were, the enemy would run or be slaughtered. On the morning of June 25, 1876, Custer was informed that his scouts had made contact with the Sioux and that the Sioux knew of his approach. Belatedly, Custer recognized the presence of the enemy. But, rather than assume a defensive position with his command and wait for the reinforcements of General Terry *with whom he was to rendezvous on the next day, the 26th,* Custer, still confident, moved against the encampment without bothering to ascertain its size (third mistake). At the bank of the Little Big Horn, Custer ordered Major Reno to attack across the river. Again he split his force (fourth mistake).

What Custer did after Reno attacked has been a subject of raging debate ever since. Some say that he circled behind a ridge, distant from the river and out of sight of it, in order to attack the encampment from the far end, and that in doing so he deliberately left Reno and his men to their fate without waiting to observe the result of Reno's attack. Others claim that Custer moved forward to attack on the flank, but that as he progressed with his troops, he remained in sight of the battle across the river and below him.

What he saw, or learned, appalled him. Reno and his three troops forded the stream toward the Sioux lodges, riding at a fast trot across the level flat beyond the Little Big Horn. On one side was the stream, and on the other, low brush. On both sides and in front of Reno were the waiting Sioux, and when he was sufficiently advanced, the Indians attacked. Reno and his troops were cut to ribbons and had to retreat across the Little Big Horn to a low hill where they entrenched themselves, to fight there a night and a day until reinforcements came. And to lose fifty-six dead and fifty-nine wounded.

Custer, aware now of the terrible danger in which he stood, sought to secure a position on the most elevated hill in order to defend himself and his men. Custer may have been foolhardy to this point — Westerners assert that he was — but he died bravely: there was no other way. The odds were so great that nothing availed him. The Oglalas, the Uncpapas, and the Cheyennes, under Crazy Horse, Gall, and Two Moon struck with fury, and the battle was over in less than half an hour. Two hundred and twenty-five soldiers, with Custer, died without having had time to form in anything resembling a defensive battle line. Hoka hey! "It was like chasing buffalo!"

The death of Custer and his men, however, was not a massacre. He and his men were soldiers on a mission of war, well-armed, hunting for the enemy, and precipitating the attack. They found what they had come for. And the victorious Sioux, as they packed their lodges and trailed into the Big Horn Mountains from the battleground, composed a song of victory which has been chanted by the Sioux ever since:

"Long Hair, you have found what you were seeking — Death!" (This song, by the way, is in the Archive of Folk Song at the Library of Congress and was sung for us by a Sioux chief who would not record it until he had decorated himself with war paint.)

"Custer's Last Charge" was recorded from the singing of Warde H. Ford at Central Valley, California, in 1938, by Sidney Robertson. The text appears to be not far removed from "literary" creation. I know of no other collection of it. The making of "heroic" legend is apparent in it and it complements, with equally colorful inaccuracy, the Anheuser-Busch lithograph of "Custer's Last Stand."

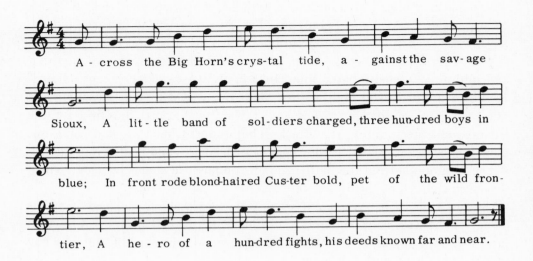

Across the Big Horn's crystal tide, against the savage Sioux;
A little band of soldiers charged, three hundred boys in blue;
In front rode blond-haired Custer bold, pet of the wild frontier,
A hero of a hundred fights, his deeds known far and near.

"Charge, comrades, charge! There's death ahead, disgrace lurks in our rear!
Drive rowels deep! Come on, come on!" came his yells with ringing cheer.
And on the foe those heroes charged — there rose an awful yell,
It seemed as though those soldiers stormed the lowest gates of hell.

Three hundred rifles rattled forth, and torn was human form,
The black smoke rose in rolling waves above the leaden storm;
The death groans of the dying braves, their wounded piercing cries,
The hurling of the arrows fleet did cloud the noonday skies.

The snorting steeds with shrieks of fright, the firearms' deafening roar,
The war song sung by the dying braves who fell to rise no more;
O'er hill and dale the war song waved 'round craggy mountain side,
Along down death's dark valley ran a cruel crimson tide.

Our blond-haired chief was everywhere 'mid showers of hurling lead,
The starry banner waved above the dying and the dead;
With bridle rein in firm-set teeth, revolver in each hand,
He hoped with his few gallant boys to quell the great Sioux band.

Again they charged — three thousand guns poured forth their last-sent ball,
Three thousand war whoops rent the air, gallant Custer then did fall;
And all around where Custer fell ran pools and streams of gore,
Heaped bodies of both red and white whose last great fight was o'er.

The boys in blue and their savage foe lay huddled in one mass,
Their life's blood ran a-trickling through the trampled prairie's grass,
While fiendish yells did rend the air, and then a sudden hush,
While cries of anguish rise again as on the mad Sioux rush.

O'er those strewn and bloodstained fields those goading redskins fly,
Our gang went down, three hundred souls, three hundred doomed to die;
Those blood-drunk braves sprang on the dead and wounded boys in blue,
Three hundred bleeding scalps ran high above the fiendish crew.

Then night came on with sable veil and hid those sights from view,
The Big Horn's crystal tide was red as she wound her valleys through;
And quickly from the fields of slain those gloating redskins fled —
But blond-haired Custer held the field, a hero with his dead.

*South Side, Chicago, Illinois, 1941:*
*Saturday night*

# *Frankie and Johnny*

This is one of the greatest of American indigenous ballads. It is direct and forthright, with no holds barred. It is Greek in its simplicity and cleanness of line, wholly American in language and place. The scene is set in the sharp opening stanza: the protagonists are placed on stage with the first five words, while the last line of the stanza suggests the inevitable tragedy to follow.

Carl Sandburg recognized its dramatic power and sang and talked it to small groups and larger audiences around the country. John Huston turned it into a play, *Frankie and Johnny*, in New York in 1930. Robert W. Gordon collected more than a hundred texts of it. It is certainly of Negro origin. There are various suggestions as to its ultimate source, Phillips Barry even claiming that it goes back to the killing of Charles Silvers by his wife Frankie at Toe River, North Carolina, in 1831. There seems to be no textual or musical relationship whatsoever between the two, but Barry suggests that the ballad based on the Silver killing was subsequently reworked for other comparable killings, thus accounting for its reappearance (in altered form) in various regions and at various times up to the killing of Allen Britt by Frankie Baker in the Negro underworld of St. Louis in 1899. In any event, "Frankie and Johnny" (also known as "Frankie and Albert") is now associated with St. Louis, and this version of it comes from that city.

1. *Frankie and Johnny were lovers, oh Lordy, how they could love,*
   *Swore to be true to each other, just as true as the stars above.*
   *He was her man, but he done her wrong.*

2. *Frankie she was a good woman, just like everyone knows,*
   *She spent a hundred dollars for a suit of Johnny's clothes.*
   *He was her man, but he done her wrong.*

*North Platte, Nebraska, 1938:*
*entertainer in a saloon*

3. *Frankie and Johnny went walking, Johnny in a brand-new suit,*
   *"Oh, good Lord," says Frankie, "but don't my Johnny look cute?"*
   *He was her man, but he done her wrong.*

4. *Frankie lived in the crib house, crib house had only two doors,*
   *Gave all her money to Johnny, he spent it on those call-house whores.*
   *He was her man, but he done her wrong.*

5. *Johnny's mother told him, and she was mighty wise,*
   *"Don't spend Frankie's money on that parlor Alice Pry.*
   *You're Frankie's man, and you're doing her wrong."*

6. *Frankie went down to the corner to buy a glass of beer,*
   *Says to the fat bartender, "Has my lovingest man been here?*
   *He was my man, but he done me wrong."*

7. *"Ain't going to tell you no story, ain't going to tell you no lie,*
   *I seen your man 'bout an hour ago with a girl named Alice Pry.*
   *If he's your man, he's doing you wrong."*

8. *Frankie went down to the pawn shop, she didn't go there for fun;*
   *She hocked all her jewelry, bought a pearl-handled forty-four gun,*
   *For to get her man who was doing her wrong.*

9. *Frankie she went down Broadway, with her gun in her hand,*
   *Saying, "Stand back all you living women, I'm looking for my gambling*
       *man;*
   *For he's my man, won't treat me right."*

10. *Frankie went to the hotel, looked in the window so high,*
    *There she saw her loving Johnny a-loving up Alice Pry.*
    *He was her man, but he was doing her wrong.*

11. *Frankie went down to the hotel, she rang that hotel bell,*
    *"Stand back, all you chippies, or I'll blow you all to hell!*
    *I want my man what's doing me wrong."*

12. *Frankie threw back her kimona, she took out her forty-four,*
    *Root-a-toot-toot three times she shot, right through that hotel door.*
    *She was after her man who was doing her wrong.*

13. *Johnny grabbed off his Stetson, "Oh, good Lord, Frankie, don't shoot!"*
    *But Frankie pulled the trigger, and the gun went root-a-toot-toot.*
    *He was her man, but she shot him down.*

14. *First time she shot him he staggered, second time she shot him he fell;*
    *Third time she shot him, oh Lordy, there was a new man's face in hell.*
    *She killed her man who had done her wrong.*

15. *"Oh, my baby, kiss me, once before I go.*
    *Turn me over on my right side, the bullet hurts me so.*
    *I was your man, but I done you wrong.*

16. *"Roll me over easy, roll me over slow,*
    *Roll me over on my left side, for the bullet hurts me so.*
    *I was your man, but I done you wrong."*

17. *Johnny he was a gambler, he gambled for the gain;*
    *The very last words that Johnny said were, "High low Jack and the*
        *game."*
    *He was her man, but he done her wrong.*

18. *Bring out your long, black coffin, bring out your funeral clothes,*
    *Bring out Johnny's mother, to the churchyard Johnny goes.*
    *He was her man, but he done her wrong.*

19. *Eleven mack a-riding to the graveyard, all in a rubber-tired hack,*
    *Eleven mack a-riding to the graveyard, only ten coming back.*
    *He was her man, but he done her wrong.*

20. *Frankie went to the coffin, she looked down on Johnny's face.*
    *She said, "Oh, Lord have mercy on me, I wish I could take his place.*
    *He was my man, and I done him wrong."*

21. *Frankie went to Mrs. Holcomb, she fell down on her knees;*
    *She said to Mrs. Holcomb, "Forgive me, if you please.*
    *I've killed my man for doing me wrong."*

22. *"Forgive you, Frankie darling, forgive you I never can,*
    *Forgive you, Frankie darling, for killing your only man?*
    *He was your man, though he done you wrong."*

23. *The Judge said to the jury, "It's as plain as plain can be.*
    *This woman shot her man, it's murder in the first degree.*
    *He was her man, though he done her wrong."*

24. *Now it was not murder in the second degree, it was not murder in the*
    *third;*
    *The woman simply dropped her man, like a hunter drops his bird.*
    *He was her man, and he done her wrong.*

25. *"Oh, bring a thousand police, bring them around today,*
    *Oh, lock me in that dungeon and throw the key away.*
    *I killed my man 'cause he done me wrong.*

26. *"Oh, put me in that dungeon, oh, put me in that cell,*
    *Put me where the northeast wind blows from the southeast corner of*
    *hell.*
    *I shot my man 'cause he done me wrong."*

27. *Frankie walked up to the scaffold, as calm as a girl can be,*
    *And turning her eyes to heaven she said, "Good Lord, I'm coming to*
    *Thee.*
    *He was my man, and I done him wrong."*

# Harvard's Kittredge

Among the greatest of the "greats" at Harvard was George Lyman Kittredge, full professor in the Department of English, Shakesperian scholar, Chaucerian, medievalist, and authority on early New England. He took his Bachelor's degree at Harvard College in 1882 and earned no advanced degree beyond that. He was honored, however, with LL.D.'s from the University of Chicago, 1901; Johns Hopkins University, 1915; McGill University, 1921; Brown University, 1925; with Litt.D.'s from Harvard itself, 1907; Yale, 1924; and Oxford University, 1932. He was, in addition, an Honorary Fellow of Jesus College, Cambridge, and of the Royal Society of Literature. (The varied robes that he might have worn at commencements boggle the mind.) His publications included *The Old Farmer and His Almanack*, *Chaucer and his Poetry*, *Shakespere*, *A Study of Gawain and the Green Knight*, *The Language of Chaucer's Troilus*, *Sir Thomas Malory*, and *Witchcraft in Old New England*. He lived at 8 Hilliard Street in a gray clapboard house off Brattle Street, mid-distance between the Yard and Radcliffe.

He was a strict disciplinarian, yet at the same time extraordinarily human in the fine New England sense. He was affectionately known to graduate and undergraduate students as "Kitty." He was a gentleman in the true sense of that word, and universally respected.

He became a legend in his lifetime.

I was most fortunate to be a student of his and by the chance of time to be his last Ph.D. candidate. In the process of obtaining my doctorate under him, I had occasion to sit with him before his fireplace, smoke his famous slim cigars, discuss my dissertation and — in relaxing moments — recount to him the lively legends circulating in the Yard about "Kitty." I was in the happy and enviable position of checking the legends with the legend himself.

As a scholar, "Kitty" knew what I was doing and was appreciative and amused.

The stories were fun — and attached with adulation by Harvard to Kittredge the Great. "Kitty," with his snow-white beard (he was seventy-seven at the time), his cane, immaculate dress, unequaled knowledge, New England heritage, his wit . . .

"Professor Kittredge, the Yard has it that you were walking down Brattle Street one quiet evening, returning to your house from a late dinner, and that you heard and saw three or four undergraduates loudly and raucously singing 'The Bastard King of England.'

"The story goes, sir, that you rapped your cane sharply on the brick sidewalk, confronted them, and asked them to stop their singing. They recognized you and — aware of your absolute authority over their Harvard lives — immediately became quiet.

"You are reported to have told them that it was ungentlemanly and highly inconsiderate of them loudly to abuse the night: 'Behind those open windows are ladies in bed who cannot help but hear the words you are singing, who are subjected to those words even against their will. . . .'

"The thoroughly abashed students apologized to you, and to themselves hoped that you would not recognize or remember them the following day. Having reprimanded them, you released them.

"But it is reported that as they were leaving, you turned, tapped your cane again on the sidewalk, and said: 'Gentlemen, by the way, the words you were singing to that last stanza were not quite correct. They should go like this. . . .'"

"Kitty" said, "Yes, that is an approximately correct version of what happened."

"A second one, Professor Kittredge:

"This story has it that you were away from your summer house on the Cape on a lecture engagement. And that you returned rather unexpectedly. And as you were walking down the road towards your house, you met a horse and wagon. And on the wagon was a privy. And that you recognized — or felt you recognized — your own privy. So you stopped the driver, whom you knew, and spoke to him, asking him whose privy he was hauling away.

"And the driver said, 'It's yours, Mr. Kittredge.'

"And you are supposed to have said, 'By whose authority are you hauling my privy away?'

"And the driver replied, 'Mrs. Kittredge told me to do so, Mr. Kittredge.'

"And then you said, 'You turn right around and take it back. I have had my best thoughts on Chaucer in that privy, and I am not going to part with it now.'"

"Kitty" thought a moment, "The moving of the privy did happen while I was away, and I was not altogether happy about it. But since Mrs. Kittredge had ordered it, I would not, of course, have changed her instructions. The privy was removed.

"The 'thoughts on Chaucer,' I think, must have been thoroughly apocryphal." [But I know that "Kitty" was pleased.]

"A third, Professor Kittredge:

"Yard tradition has it that all Harvard professors lacking a Ph.D. were to be examined to check their qualifications. This was under President Lowell, I believe. President Lowell is reported to have spoken to you about it, and you presumably replied, 'But who will examine me, Mr. President?' "

"Kitty" commented: "This did not happen, and if the situation had arisen where it might have happened, I certainly would not have replied in that fashion. There were, of course, men who could well have examined me, learned men. But as I say, the situation did not arise."

"Kitty" used to insist that we all be in class and in our seats ahead of him. He was there on time, always. And when his lecture had begun and a late-comer straggled in — perhaps one minute late — the lecture stopped dead until the delinquent had slunk into the nearest available seat.

There was this discipline of time and of presence. It was as it should be; we knew it and we observed it. We were at Harvard, and Kittredge was perhaps in our time the greatest of the greats. (Oh, there were others, but not touching him.) He could demand of us, and we expected of him.

I will not forget the morning class when he lectured to us about some aspect (I have forgotten now what) of Chaucer. He was sitting behind his desk, and as the hour drew to its exact close, he stood and picked up his cane and briefcase. (It was spring, I remember, and he was wearing a pale gray suit that day with a starched collar, and a conservatively patterned gray tie.) Lecturing all the time, casually and learnedly, he walked with precise timing towards the classroom door, which was midway up the room on our right.

"And, gentlemen, this French scholar who foolishly made these absurd observations on the matter ["Kitty's" hand is on the doorknob], neverthe-less, knows more about the subject [the door is open and "Kitty" is halfway out] than anybody in this room." ["Kitty" is over the threshold and is speaking the final words from the corridor to a temporarily stunned and permanently delighted class of students.]

One class. And there were many, year after year.

*Professor George Lyman Kittredge*

Kittredge believed, as all New England did before him, that where books were, that place should be honored. And the great center for such worship at Harvard was Widener Library. I never witnessed it myself, but I have heard it reported frequently enough to believe it implicitly: whenever Kittredge, in Widener, saw a student with his hat on, up would come "Kitty's" slim cane and the student's hat would leave his head instanter. (It is perhaps as well that "Kitty" cannot see what goes in and out of the Library today.)

"Kitty" may, in one sense, have died in 1941. But he lives in his students and their students who serve on staffs and faculties from the University of California to Florida, from Harvard to Chicago, from the Library of Congress to Nebraska, from Indiana to the Smithsonian. . . .

He lives in them — and in his living legend.

# 22.

# *Urban Belief Tales*

### *The Rape Trial*

Bill Gold contributes a sensitive, amusing and homey column daily to *The Washington Post* called "The District Line." It is full of odds and ends of the little things about Washington and makes interesting reading for residents of the capital. Every so often he includes a wandering story such as the one in the issue of Monday, March 30, 1970:

Several readers have told me about an incident that took place during a rape trial. The young victim had taken the stand to identify the accused, and did. "Now then," said the prosecutor, "tell us what this man said to you when he first approached you."

The girl lowered her eyes, then shook her head. Gently with understanding, the prosecutor explained to her that it was her duty to testify, but the girl just bit her lip and shook her head.

Finally the judge suggested that the girl could write her reply, and to this she agreed. She wrote it out on a piece of paper, and the bailiff carried it over and handed it to the foreman of the jury.

The foreman read the message and passed it to the next juror in stony silence. The next passed it to the next, and so it went until it reached the end of the second row. When the woman there tried to pass the piece of paper to the last juror, she found that he had been dozing. So she nudged him awake and handed him the girl's testimony.

The startled man's eyes popped, and he quickly folded the piece of paper and shoved it into his pocket.

"Mr. Bailiff," called out the alert judge, "get that piece of paper from that juror and bring it here."

The juror's astonishment turned to panic. "Oh, no, Your Honor," he protested, "that note is a personal matter between this here lady and me."

With the end of the story, Gold continues:

All of the readers who have told me this story have assured me it is true, and their reports on it have agreed in almost all details. However, there are a few discrepancies, and they speak for themselves.

Some readers say the incident took place last week during a trial in Arlington, some say I'll find it in the records of a trial held a long time ago in Prince George's County, one woman says she heard it from a woman who was on the jury and that it happened in Washington, and a man says he had heard the story in California last year before moving here. So this one may have more miles on it than that other great "true" story about the woman who drives away and leaves her husband stranded in his underdrawers after he has jumped out of the family trailer to find out the cause of a sudden stop.

Staff writer Martin Weil didn't have to hear conflicting versions of the story to doubt its veracity. His logical mind zeroed in at once on the story's obvious weaknesses.

"In the first place," he said, "we're asked to believe that this alert judge hadn't noticed that one of his jurors was sleeping. Very far-fetched. But there's something worse, something that rings false at once."

"What's that?" I asked.

"This was the high spot of the trial," Martin explained. "This lovely, innocent, shy girl was on the stand — the one witness whose story everybody on

*Cimarron, New Mexico, 1939: statue by a local art*

the jury was waiting to hear. Whatever else that guy might have slept through, he didn't sleep through the girl's appearance on the witness stand."

No cross-examination, Mr. Weil, you have made your point and may step down.

In spite of Martin Weil's puncturing of the story (a very dirty, antifolklore trick), the story will continue its rounds. Folklorists have termed such wandering stories "urban belief tales" and "migratory legends," which seem to me fairly high-powered terms, but, nevertheless, let us accept them. They are certainly not jokes, and they are a good cut above simple anecdotes. They have a "cycle" life of their own, and the touchstone to them is that they are either actually believed by the teller or reported by him as being the true experience of someone else. Whether they are full tales and legends is another matter, but they travel like wildfire and in the manner of folklore. It is virtually impossible to trace any one of them to a specific source, any more than one can trace a bawdy joke or story to an individual.

## The Second Blue Book

In any event, a favorite of mine is what Professor Lew Girdler of San Jose State College calls "The Legend of the Second Blue Book," dealing with very clever trickery at final exam time at college. I quote his report of it from *Western Folklore:*

I heard this story late in 1937 from a brilliant graduate student named Ed Schaefer, then about twenty-two years old, in a boarding house where we both lived in Berkeley, California. This version, told about an anonymous student at the University of California at Berkeley, is the simplest I have encountered. It went something like this:

This student went into his final examination with an A— average. There were two essay questions. He knew nothing about the first one, but he was primed on the second. He filled his first blue book with just anything he thought of. Then he labeled his second blue book II and began it with what appeared to be the last sentence or two of the answer to the first essay question. Then on the second page of this second blue book he put down 2 for the second essay question, and he wrote a beautiful answer. He turned in only the second blue book. A few days later he got a postcard from the instructor saying he got an A in the course and apologizing for having lost the first blue book.

In lecturing on the migratory legend in my folklore course in spring 1969 I mentioned this story, along with such classics as the black widow spider hair-do and the hitchhiking ghost. After class a student came up to report that he had heard a more complicated version. I asked him to write it out and to tell what he could about the conditions under which he heard it. He turned in this version:

The student takes a test which is composed of two pages. Realizing that he doesn't know much, he spends all of his time on the second page. When the period ends, he slips the first page into his notebook and only hands in the second page.

Once outside the classroom, he hurriedly looks up the answers and fills in the first page. Then he takes and steps on the page. He gives this page to a friend who [has] a later class in the same room. The friend approaches the teacher after class and says that he found this 'in the back.' The teacher takes it, checks through the papers collected in the morning class, and sure enough, the student's first page is missing. He grades all the papers and the student gets an A.

My student was Algis Sketeris, age twenty-four, who heard the story at Lincoln High School in San Jose from a fifteen-year-old boy whose name Sketeris could not remember. It was told in 1960, and the event was said to have occurred in 1959.

The Sketeris version enchanted me, especially the details of the footprint on the page and the accomplice in a later class. I told both my simple Schaefer version and the Sketeris version in another class studying migratory legends, and still another student reported after class that she had heard a more recent version. Again I asked for a written account, which again I quote verbatim:

A friend of mine tells this about her brother Jack, a sometime student. Jack found himself sitting in the classroom during an important examination with two blue books, a pen, and a question he couldn't answer. Being naturally bright, if lazy, he thought of the following solution. In one of the blue books he wrote a letter to his mother, telling her that he had finished writing his exam early but was waiting for a friend in the same class and so was taking the opportunity to write to her. He apologized for not writing sooner but said he'd been studying very hard for this instructor, who was a nice guy but had pretty high standards. When the time was up he handed in this blue book and left in a hurry with his unused one. He hurried to his text, wrote an answer, and then put the blue book in an envelope and mailed it to his mother in Boston. When the instructor found the letter, he called Jack, who explained that he had written in two blue books and must have got them mixed up and if the instructor had the letter, the answer must be in the mail on the way to Boston. He offered to call his mother in Boston and have her send the envelope back as soon as she got it. He did, she did, and the blue book was sent back with the inner envelope postmarked the day of the test and the outer envelope postmarked Boston.

The student who wrote this version was Mrs. Gladys Hart of Santa Cruz. She heard it at San Jose College in autumn 1967 from Mrs. Katherine Arnsdorff of San Jose.

Such deception of innocent professors is greatly to be deplored, and the ingenuity of students equally to be admired.

A representative group of added belief tales have been gathered by members of the Hoosier Folklore Society and students of Indiana University and its affiliates. They have been consummately edited by Linda Dégh, editor of *Indiana Folklore*, a journal which maintains high standards of scholarship and yet is at the same time very readable — as the following tales bear chilling witness. (Sir Graves Ghastly, move over.)

The student collectors of the tales have taken them down in on-the-spot writing from their student informants, preserving as closely as possible the exactness of speech and telling. One tale ("The Hook") is clearly from a tape recording, and gives us some idea also of contemporary campus idiom. Folk language on the college level. . . .

## The Runaway Grandmother

Well, I heard this true story from my neighbor. I don't remember which neighbor, but I believe it was my neighbor called Mary Randolf. Mary is of Polish descent and is the widow of a Gary policeman. Mary called up one day and was almost in a state of shock. She told Mama this story and Mama didn't believe it. Later Mary came over to our house and repeated the story to me.

It happened to her friend's family (I don't know their name) as they were traveling across the desert to California. Within this station wagon there was a father, a mother and their children, and the mother-in-law who every-one called "Grandma." And as they were going across the desert Grandma became sick and she died. Now they didn't want to alarm the children and they didn't want to leave Grandma out in the desert so the only place they had room for her where she — her smell wouldn't bother the children — was to strap her on top of the station wagon along with the baggage with a tarp over her, of course. And as they were traveling across the desert they kept looking for a town where they could deposit Grandma. They finally arrived in a small town in Arizona where they stopped at a filling station and they went in to report Grandma's death. And while they were within the filling station somebody stole the station wagon and when they went out — no station wagon and no Grandma! Well, it wasn't very funny even though it sounds like it because they have to wait seven years now to prove that Grandma is dead before they can collect any insurance. And they've never been able to find either the car or Grandma. This actually happened.

They couldn't leave Grandma out in the desert. Not only because — uh — it wasn't right to leave a body out in the desert but also for insurance and also to prove it wasn't murder and also to prove there was a body in any court proceedings.

## The Hook

I heard this story at a fraternity party. I heard this. This guy had this date with this really cool girl, and all he could think about all night was taking her out and parking and having a really good time, so he takes her out in the country, stops the car, turns the lights off, puts the radio on, nice music; he's really getting her in the mood, and all of the sudden there's this news flash comes on over the radio and says to the effect that a sex maniac has just escaped from the state insane asylum and the one distinguishing feature of this man is that he has a hook arm, and in the first place this girl is really, really upset, 'cause she's just sure this guy is going to come and try and get in their car, so the guy locks all the doors and says it'll all be okay, but she says he could take his arm and break through the window and everything and she just cries and cries and goes just really frantic and the guy finally consents to take her home, but he's really mad 'cause you know he really had his plans for this girl, so he revs up the car and he goes torquing out of there and they get to her house, and he's really, really mad and he's not even going to get out of the car and open the door for her, and she just gets out on her own side of the car and as she gets out she turns around and looks and there's a hook hanging on the door.

## The Boyfriend's Death

Don Smith told me this story; actually a friend of his told him it, so you are getting it second-hand. There was this local Moses Lake couple who went out and parked one night. They were in the country on a road that leads to a dead-end right under a big weeping willow tree. It is about four or five miles from town, and there is no one around. The tree was the only one there, it was standing all alone. They were there until late in the morning, and a . . . when they decided to leave the car wouldn't start, they were out of gas. The young man decided that it would be best if he went back and got some gas. He told her to lie down on the seat and not to look up, and keep all the doors locked and the windows rolled up . . . an' everything . . . an' he left. And a . . . she was very scared most of the night, she was very scared, and she blew up everything out of proportion. She heard all sorts of strange things, like things on the roof . . . all sorts of sounds, but she didn't look up. Toward morning she saw the shadow of some sort of liquid on the window shield. But she still didn't look up. Just after the sun had risen, she heard the sound of a siren, someone had seen the car parked out under the weeping willow tree, and reported it to the police, they had been looking for the two kids all that night. Her parents had called because they were worried about the pair. The police came up to the car, they told her to unlock the doors, come out and go with them. The police told her not to look back, but she did anyway. And there on the branch of the willow tree was her boy-friend, his hand was dangling in the breeze scraping the top of the car with his finger nails. He was hanging upside down, but he didn't have a head, it was as if it had been tore off. The police looked around for feet prints, but they only saw the footprints of the boy.

I heard it when I was back in Washington, probably around the first part of this last December. Don Smith heard it from this chick, who it supposedly happened to. I really believed that it happened. This girl is so afraid of boys now, that she won't go out with anyone.

## The Roommate's Death

This story takes place in a sorority house on this campus, during Christmas vacation when most of the girls had gone home. There were two or three girls left in the sorority house. It was late at night and the girls decided that they were hungry, so two of the girls went downstairs to the kitchen. One of the girls went back to the room to rejoin the other girl, leaving one girl downstairs in the kitchen. A little bit later on, say about half hour later, the two girls in the room started wondering about the other girl 'cause she hadn't come back yet. So they went out on the landing and they heard something moving around downstairs. So they called down and nobody answered, the person or what ever it was moving around was still heard. They were afraid to go downstairs, so they locked themselves in their room and waited for morning. They actually waited about an hour when they decided to try it again. They were going to open the door, when they heard a noise outside — like scratching, so they got scared and didn't open the door. The scratching was like somebody dragging somebody down the steps. They were afraid to leave the room 'cause someone was out in the hall. They stayed in their room till early the next morning until the mailman came around, and they hailed the mailman out the window. He came in, and during the night, they had heard a scratching on their door. The mailman came in the front door and went up the stairs, and told the girls to stay in their room that everything was all right but that they were to stay in their room. But the girls didn't listen to him 'cause he had said it was all right, so they came out into the hall. When they opened the door, they saw their girlfriend on the floor with a hatchet in her head.

## The Decapitated Victim

This happened at Ball State. I guess some girl had gone out on a date, but her roommate stayed in that night. When the girl returned, her roommate was in bed all covered up so she didn't turn on any lights but just got ready for bed. Then her roommate started humming. For a while she just ignored it. Then she really became angry and asked the girl if she would please be quiet, that she was tired and had to get to sleep. The roommate kept humming. Finally, the girl became furious — she went over and pulled the covers off the roommate, only to find that she was decapitated. But there was still humming. She looked over and right by the door stood a man holding a big butcher knife and the roommate's head.

## The Furry Collar

Two girls were home on vacation from school and were staying alone in one of the girls' homes. It was storming and the electricity went out. While they were lying in bed upstairs, in the dark, they heard a noise. One was frightened, but the other jumped out of bed and put on her robe. The robe had a furry collar around the neck. She went downstairs. Quite a bit of time elapsed and the girl upstairs got more and more frightened. At last she heard the shuffle of feet coming down the hall. At first she was relieved and then she began to worry that it might not be her girl friend, but someone else. She finally decided that when the person came in she would reach up and touch the person's neck and if she felt the furry collar, she would know it was her friend. The steps came closer and closer. The door creaked open and at last the person was right next to her. She reached with both hands and felt the fur and then touched a little higher. All she felt was a bloody stump where her friend's head had been. . . .

## The Ghostly Hitchhiker

And then there is, of course, the very widely known "Ghostly Hitchhiker," considerably less bloody, but nevertheless shivery. This version, reported by Richard K. Beardsley and Rosalie Hankey in the *California Folklore Quarterly*, comes from that State:

This is the story just as we heard it several months ago, from a level-headed, conscientious businessman. "I've never been able to understand this," he began hesitatingly. "It happened to a friend of mine, Sam Kerns, a fellow who went to Cal with me. He can't explain it either.

"Kerns and another man were driving home from a party in San Francisco. It was a wretched night, bitingly cold and raining with such violence that driving was difficult. As they drew near a stop sign on Mission Street they made out the indistinct form of a woman standing on the corner, quite alone, as if she were waiting for someone. Since it was after two o'clock in the morning and they knew that streetcars no longer were running, they stared at her curiously as they drew up to the corner. Then Kerns brought the car to a sharp halt, for standing in the pouring rain without a coat or an umbrella was a lovely girl, dressed in a thin white evening gown. She was evidently in some embarrassment or trouble so without hesitation they offered to take her home. She accepted and got into the back seat of their two-door sedan. Realizing that she must be chilled, they wrapped her in the car blanket. She gave them an address near Twin Peaks and added that she lived there with her mother. However, she made no attempt to explain her presence on Mission Street in the pouring rain, without coat or umbrella. The men started toward Twin Peaks making some effort at conversation, to which the girl responded politely but in a manner which showed plainly that she did not care to talk. When they reached Fifth Street, Kern's friend looked around to see if she were comfortable. There was no one in the back seat. Startled, he leaned over to see if she might have fallen to the floor, but, except for the crumpled blanket, there was nothing to be seen. Amazed and frightened, he made Kerns stop the car. Without doubt the girl was gone.

"The only possible explanation of her disappearance was that she had slipped quietly out of the car; but they had not stopped since picking her up. That she could have jumped from the car while it was moving and closed the door behind her was almost impossible. Thoroughly puzzled and not a little worried, they decided to go to the address she had given. After some difficulty they found the house, an old ramshackle building with a dim light showing from the interior. They knocked and after a long wait the door was opened by a frail old woman, clutching a shawl over her shoulders. As they began their story they were struck by the complete incredibility of the entire business. Feeling more and more foolish, they stumbled on as best they could. The old woman listened patiently, almost as if she had heard the same story before. When they had finished, she smiled wanly, 'Where did you say you picked her up?' she asked. 'On First and Mission,' Kerns replied.

" 'That was my daughter,' the old woman said. 'She was killed in an automobile accident at First and Mission two years ago.' "

There are many variants of this, and it is found virtually everywhere. Louis Jones of Cooperstown, New York, has one in which the girl "in a white dress" is picked up near Graceland Cemetery. As the young man attempts to explain his story, the "woman in a flannel bathrobe" interrupts him: "You don't need to go on, young man. I know what happened. It's my daughter again. It often happens on rainy nights; that's when she seems to want to get home. You understand, of course, that she has been buried up there for nearly four years now." And in still other variants, the girl disappears with the young man's coat, which he finds later draped over her tombstone in the cemetery.

There are many others: the woman in the Midwest store who feels she has pricked her finger on a pin while turning over pieces of cloth (from Hong Kong), only to find her arm swelling, and to be told by her doctor that she has been bitten by a poisonous snake (frequently the arm is amputated); the Kentucky (why Kentucky, I don't know) fried rat that is served up in a Washington, D.C. restaurant (named, but here nameless); the child killed on a railway trestle whose screams can be heard each time a train passes over it; the high school or college girl who goes into a coma (and occasionally dies) because black widow spiders have nested in her uncombed bouffant hairdo; the "death car," a late-model automobile sold for pennies because the smell of a corpse cannot be washed from it; the would-be murderer hiding on the back-seat floor of an automobile, whose plans to kill the girl driver are thwarted by a following car which flashes its bright lights on whenever the murderer rises from the floor — while the girl, unaware that she is being protected, is driven almost insane with fear at being so closely followed; the decapitation in an elevator accident; and so on pleasantly into the small hours.

They are all told as true. Some of them may be.

# 23.

# The Jack Tales

Mrs. Maud Long of Hot Springs, North Carolina, visited the Library of Congress in 1947 and recorded at the time a very considerable body of folksongs as well as several of the rare and charming Jack Tales. All of this material came to her in a direct line of folk transmission — Mrs. Maud Long heard the tales from her mother, Mrs. Jane Hicks Gentry, who had learned them from her mother, who had in turn heard them from her father, Council Harmon. In a recent letter, Mrs. Long describes the transmission:

Jane Hicks Gentry — spoken of by Irving Bacheller as "The Happiest Person I Ever Knew" in a short story published in March, 1925, *American Magazine*, and later included in his book of short stories, *Opinions of a Cheerful Yankee* — was born in Watauga County, N.C. Dec. 18, 1863. Her father Ransom Hicks, a minister and Federal soldier at that time, moved his family to Madison County at the close of the war and it was in this county that my parents brought up a family of nine children to maturity, the first death coming in the dreadful Flu epidemic of 1918. — They moved to Hot Springs in Madison County in 1898 so that their children could attend a Presbyterian Mission school for eight months (later nine) instead of the 3 or 4 months public school. — My mother had a wonderful memory and she was always interested in a new song or story. . . . She would sing the old ballads she knew or tell the marvellous Jack, Will and Tom Tales that she had learned from her mother whose father Council Harmon had told her when a little girl.

It may be noted that Cecil Sharp, the great English folksong collector — who collected in the Appalachians in the early part of this century before American collectors were even stirring — transcribed many songs from the singing of Mrs. Jane Gentry, Mrs. Maud Long's mother. It is also of interest to note that the liveliest and purest record of the Jack Tales in America lies with Council Harmon and his descendants. They are virtually non-existent outside this line of transmission.

Jack the Giant Killer is, of course, English prior to appearing in Tennessee and North Carolina, but he becomes thoroughly localized in short order. Lions, unicorns, and giants remain in the tales for the delight and astonishment of children, but when Jack kills any of them he is paid off in understandable coin of the realm — a hundred dollars a head for giants — and when he starts on an adventure he cooks himself a little ash cake before "going up the road a piece." This happy combination of the old and the new — a unicorn and a Carolina country road — is a delightful example of the lively continuity and adaptability of folk tradition.


## Mrs. Maud Long Introduces the Jack Tales

I cannot remember when I heard the Jack, Will and Tom tales for the first time. For we just grew up on them like we did the mountain air and the lovely old ballads that my mother used to sing to us.

But the occasion for the tales is a very vivid memory:

It would be on a long, winter evening when, after supper, all of us were gathered before the big open fire, my mother taking care of the baby or else the baby was in the cradle very near to mother. And she would be sewing or carding.

My father would be mending someone's shoes or maybe a bit of harness. The older girls were helping with the carding or the sewing. And all of us little ones would either have a lapful or a basket full of wool out of which we must pick all the burrs and the Spanish needles and the bits of briars and dirt against the next day's carding.

For my mother wove all of this wool that had been shorn from the backs of our own sheep — raised there on the farm that was in the heart of the Great Smoky Mountains in North Carolina — into linsey-woolsey, or hers and our dresses, or into blue jeans for my father's and brothers' suits, or into blankets to keep us warm, or into the beautiful patterned coverlets, to say nothing of all of the socks and stockings and mitts and hoods that it took for a large family of nine children. And so she needed every bit of the wool that she could get ready.

And to keep our eyes open and our fingers busy and our hearts merry, my mother would tell these marvellous tales — the Jack, Will and Tom tales.

## *Jack and the Giants' New Ground*

This is the story of Jack and the giants' new ground.

A long time ago Jack and his folks lived way back in the mountains and they were just as poor as people could be. Will and Tom, the two older brothers, were just fine workers — they helped in everything. But Jack was just so lazy — half the time they couldn't get a lick of work out of him. Now, of course, this made for a lot of quarreling and fussing with the two older brothers and his father and mother.

So one day Jack said, "You know what I'm going to do? I'm going to clear out of this place. I'm going out into the world and see if I can't find me a fortune. I'm tired of this little old rocky farm."

So his mother fixed him up a poke of vittles and he threw 'em over his back and away he went. He walked and he walked, and the sun just a-beating down on him so hard. He got hungry and ate up his poke of vittles, and went a-walking on, and the sun getting hotter and hotter every step he

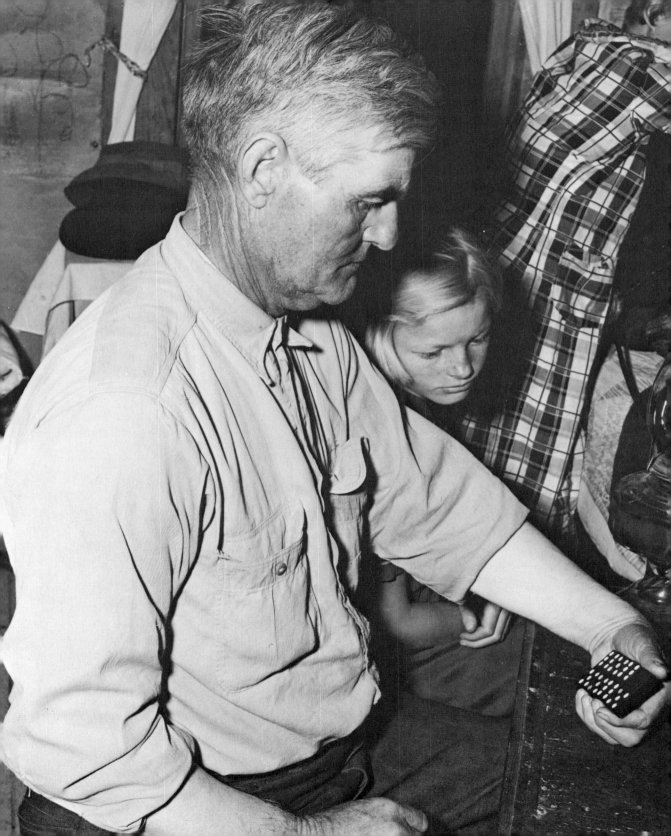

took. And yet it wasn't twelve o'clock. And he thought, "I wonder where I'm gonna get a bite of dinner . . . for I sure am getting hungry."

Just then he noticed a nice-looking road that turned off from the main highway and he thinks to himself, "I'll just follow this a little way and see where it leads to." And pretty soon he came to a great big rock wall with a gate of pure gold. "Hm-m-m," said Jack to himself, "they's well-doing folks a-living here. I just wonder if they'd give me a bit of dinner. I believe I'll holler and find out."

"Hello-o-oo!"

Pretty soon a man came out on the porch and said, "Hello, stranger. What are you doing, what are you looking for?"

"Well, I'm a-lookin' for a job of work," says Jack.

"Well, I don't know as I'm hiring anybody right now, but come on in anyway, stranger, and sit a while."

Jack pushed that gate open and walks right in. And the man reached around and brought out two chairs, and says, "Come on, sit down, I reckon you can rest a little while, can't you? You're not in much of a hurry."

"No," Jack says, "I guess I can rest a little while anyway." So he took out his old corncob pipe and leaned back and went to smoking. Looked around after a while and he says, "And what did you say your name was, Mister?"

"Why, I'm the King. What's your name?"

"Jack's my name. Now, Mister King, I'm just mighty glad to know you. I'm mighty glad. And I know with all of this land that you have around here, you've got a sight of work. Don't you want to hire somebody?"

"Well," the old King says, "now Jack, I'd like to know, are you a good worker?"

"Oh, yes sir," Jack says, "I'm the finest worker there is back home."

"Well, can you plow?"

"Sure I can."

"Well, can you clear a new ground?"

"Why, you know, King, that's just all I do back home, I just clear new ground."

"Well, can you kill a giant?"

"Huh?" says Jack. Dropped his old pipe and he reached down and picked it up. Said, "Well, I ain't never killed one yet, but I guess I could try."

343

"Well now," the King says, "if you can clear a new ground and if you're a giant killer, you're just the man I've been looking for. But I tell you, Jack, I have a new ground at the top of that mountain yonder that I've been trying to get cleared for a year. I've sent more than a dozen men up there, and they've every one been killed by that giant. Because you see, down in that other holler, there lives a family of giants that claim that new ground is theirs and they won't let anybody clear it. Well, if you can go up there and kill them, and then clear that new ground, Jack, I tell you, you're the man I'm looking for. Besides paying you good wages for clearing that new ground, I'll pay you a thousand dollars for every giant head you bring here to the house. And I'll give you ten cents a hour for every bit of work you do besides. And that's a good price."

"Yes, sir," Jack says, "that's a good price and that just suits me fine. I'll be ready to go up there and see what I can do."

"Yes," the King says, "after you eat a bite of dinner. Now come on in, I think the old woman has us some dinner ready. And let's see if we can't eat a little, and then you can go up there and see what you can do."

Jack went in to the table and, my! — it was just loaded wih good things to eat. Chicken and ham and pie and cake, and biscuit and butter and honey. Oh, Jack just ate *such* a dinner!

But he looked across and the old King was still eating, and the Queen just piled his plate up full of food again and, lord, Jack didn't want those folks to think that he couldn't eat as much as the King.

So he reached down under the table and drew up that old leather apron that he always wore, fastened it good in his pants-belt, and drew his belt right good and tight to hold it down good and strong, and he begun eating all over again. He'd take a bite and then he'd slip a whole lot down into that leather apron. Poured four or five glasses of milk down in there, bread and chicken and cake — just everything.

After a while, the King pushed back his chair and said he was through. And Jack pushed back his chair, went out on the porch and he said, "Now I guess, bedads, I'd better be about that giant killing."

"Yes," the King said, "go on down yonder to the woodpile and you'll see there some axes. Pick you up the sharpest-edged looking one you can find, and go on. Up on the top of the mountain there, you'll find the tree with a chip or two taken out of it, where the other fellows have tried to begin chipping. But just about the time you begin a-whacking, Jack, right then the giants will be a-coming."

Well, Jack went on down to the woodpile, looked back and waved to him and said, "I'll be back in time for supper."

Picked him up a little old bit of a tommy-hatchet there, and the King said, "Jack, Jack! you'll need one of them big axes! Don't take that little old thing."

"No," Jack says, "bedads, this axe is just what I want." Stuck it in his belt and went a-climbing on to the top of the mountain.

Now when Jack got up there, he was sure worried. He didn't know what he was going to do. Gracious sakes, he didn't want to begin a-hacking on that tree, for those giants'ud come a-running up on him. And he knew that if he didn't hack some, the King would know that he hadn't been doing any kind of work and he wouldn't give him any supper. Well, he thought and he thought. What could he do? He just didn't know.

He looked around and he saw a tall slim poplar tree, the highest thing on the mountain. Climbed into the very tip top of that, took off that little old tommy-hatchet from out of his belt and begun hacking at the little bitty limbs. Ka-whack! Ka-whack!

He hadn't made more than six whacks till he heard something coming through the underbrush, and he looked down there and, gracious sakes alive, there was that two-headed giant that the King had told him about! (Yes sir, this one just had two heads, but the twins had three heads apiece, the old mother had three heads, and the old daddy had four.)

"Oh, boy," Jack says, "there comes $2000, but do you reckon I'll ever get 'em?"

He just kept right on a-whackin', though, just like he didn't know a thing was down underneath.

The old giant came right up to the very tree where he was a-whackin' and looked up at him, and he says, "Howdy, stranger, what in the world are you doin' up there?"

"Ah," Jack says, "bedads I'm clearing the new ground."

"Clearing the new ground!"

"Yes, I'm clearing the new ground for the King."

The giant said, "Now lookee here, stranger, what's your name?"

"Jack's my name, bedads."

"Well, Jack, you must be plumb crazy. Clearin' a new ground and a-beginnin' at the top of the tree. I never heard tell of no such."

"Why," Jack says, "that's the way we clear the new grounds back home all the time."

"Well," the giant says, "listen, Jack, we're not havin' that new ground cleared. No siree, we're not! This new ground belongs to us, and the King or nobody else is goin' to clear it. Now you just come down on out of that tree and go on home with me for supper."

Well, the old giant thought Jack wouldn't understand what he meant. But Jack did. But he came sliding down the tree, but he stayed well up in the limbs above that old giant's reach. He looked down at him and he said, "I tell you, I've always heard that giants is powerful strong. How 'bout it, sir?"

"Well," the old giant said, "some of us is and some of us ain't. Now as for me, I can kill any thousand Englishmen that ever dare face me, just bare-handed."

"Well," Jack says, "I tell you what, I bet you I can do something that you can't do."

"Huh," the old giant says, "what is that?"

"Why," says Jack, "I can squeeze milk out of a flint rock."

"Now you can't do it, and I know it!"

"Well," Jack says, "just a-hunt me up a flint rock down there and chunk it up here, and I'll show you."

So while the old giant was hunting around to find an old flint rock, Jack took a little old knife — the sharp point of it — and jabbed a little old hole in that little leather apron. The giant threw him up the flint rock and Jack caught it in his hand, squeezed it right up tight next to that little old hole in that leather apron, and

drip

    drip

        drip went the milk right down at that old giant's feet.

"Well," he says, "lands sakes, Jack, do that again."

So Jack pushed it up good and tight against the little old apron and squi-i-i-r-rt the milk came out just like you was a-milking a cow.

346

"Well," that giant says, "throw that rock down here to me. If you can do that, I can do it."

Jack threw the rock down to the giant, and he squeezed down on it and he didn't get a drop of milk. And he squeezed again, and there didn't any milk come. And the old giant got so mad, he just squeezed down with all his might and just ground that flint rock into powder in his hands.

"Well," Jack says, "I can do something else you can't do, too, giant."

"Now," the giant says, "what can you do this time?"

"Why, laws a-massy, I can just take my knife and rip my stomach right open, sew it up again, and I'm just as good as new."

"Hah, now," the old giant says, "now I know you're lying, Jack."

"All right," Jack says, "bedads, just watch me."

Took his knife and he ripped open that little old leather apron and out came pouring milk and chicken and everything. And Jack just took him a little old rawhide string that he had, and punched him some holes, and sewed that old leather apron right back up again.

The old giant says, "Jack, for lands sakes, throw me down that knife. I know if you can do that, I can do it."

Jack threw him down the knife and the old giant picked it up and r-r-ripped open his stomach, and blood and everything come flying out — and first thing you know the old giant just reeled around there and keeled over dead.

Jack slid down that tree, took his little old tommy-hatchet, hacked off those two heads, and went a-dragging them down to the King's house.

Well, when the King saw him coming he says, "Land a-sakes, Jack, if you're not the finest killer I ever saw! You're sure the man I've been a-lookin' for. And here's your $2000 for those two heads. Now come on in, Jack, and eat you some supper and rest up a bit."

Well, Jack went in and he had him a good supper. And he had a good bed to sleep in and, oh!, he had $2000. "Ho," Jack thinks to himself, "boys, as soon's I can get away from here, I'm a-lightin' back out home."

After breakfast he said to the King, "Now I tell you, I'd better be going home. The folk's are missing me powerful back there, and I betcha my pappy's a-wanting me to help him set out tobacco. I'd better just be goin' on back."

"Oh, no," the King says, "Jack, you can't go back now. Why, gracious sakes, you're the finest giant-killer that there is. No sir, you go back up in that new ground and kill me some more of those giants. That's what you do. Why, I believe you can destroy the whole bunch of them."

"Well," Jack says, "bedads, I guess I can go back and try."

So he started back up the mountain.

Oh, my, how he wished he could get out of there without passing back by the King's house. He didn't want to mix up with those giants any more.

But he didn't have much time to think, because just about the time he reached there, a-coming up the holler he heard tramp! break! scrape! down through the thicket there. He looked and there came the twins with the three heads, just a-stepping over those big old rocks and thickets, coming just a-brushing up that mountain.

"Law," Jack thought, "what will I do! what will I do?" He was just shaking all over.

He saw a great old big hollow log over there, and ran into that just as hard as he could go, scooping his shirt-tail up full of rocks as he went in. Got in there and laid down. It was so big, why, he could stand right up in it. He just crawled down among some of the big old leaves and things that had blown in there, and lay as still as a mouse.

When those two giants came up and saw their brother lying there with his heads cut off, oh, my land, such taking on you've never heard! They screamed and they cried, and they said, "Oh, what will Pappy and Mammy say when they know about this! And don't we wish we knew who did it! Look, the ground's not tore up a bit. It don't look like there's been a sign of a fight, and yet his head's whacked clear off and gone. Oh, if we could just find the feller that did that, wouldn't we go for him! You know, he could have killed a thousand Englishmen if every one of them had come at him at one time. Now who do you reckon could have done that? Well" they said, "we'd better pick him up and take him on down home."

And one of them said, "You know what, Mammy sent us up here for some firewood. We'd better not go back without it either. But let's just pick the handiest thing there is. Let's just take this hollow log over there. That'll be just fine."

All right, one of the twins got at one end of it and the other at the other.

*Carroll County, Georgia, 1941:*
*the Lemuel Smith family saying grace*
*before the afternoon meal*

Of course Jack got jostled around a good bit laying in there, but finally they kind of got it up on their shoulders and settled down a little bit.

The giant in front had it just laying right up on his shoulders, just right with his head showing right square to Jack.

Jack waited until they got down the hill a little ways.

He picked him out one of those pretty good sized rocks and with all his strength — kavim! — he took the old giant right in the back of the head.

The old giant stumbled a little and he said, "Looky here, don't you be a-rocking me! Goodness knows we've got enough carrying this old log with brother laying on top of it. Don't go a-rocking me now, sir!"

"Oh," the other giant said, "why I didn't touch you with no rock. What's the matter with you? I've not got a rock anyway." He said, "Go on down that mountain."

Well, they started on down the mountain a little.

Traveled a little bit further, and Jack picked him out a little bit bigger rock. And ka-whack! he took him right in the back of the head. Oh, boy, that hurt, I know!

The old giant stumbled around and he said, "Now listen here, that's the second time you've done it. You hit me with another rock, and if you don't take a lickin' it will be because I can't give it to you. Now you mind what you're doing."

His brother said, "Well, what in the world are you a-talkin' about? I've not hit you with no rock."

Well, they just fussed and quarreled and gave each other the lie and everything you could think about. They finally started on down the hill, though, carrying the big old log with the brother laying on top.

Well, Jack reached around in among his rocks and got a real sharp-edged one, the biggest one of the whole bunch. And just let go with it — ka-wham! — right in the same spot. And just cut that old giant's head till the blood begun to ooze down there. Oh, it just almost knocked him down!

And he threw down that log and he took back at that other giant, and he said, "I tell you, I told you I'd whip you if it was in me if you hit me with another rock — and you've cut the blood out of my head!"

And such a fight you've never seen.

Why, they clawed and kicked and bit and pulled hair, and finally they just got clinched so tight, they rolled over and over on the ground. They kicked up great trees and rocks, and they just fought until they were so weak they couldn't even let go of each other.

When Jack saw them in that kind of a fix, he just crawled out of the end of that old log and — ka-whack, ka-whack, ka-whack, ka-whack, ka-whack, ka-whack! — the six heads of those giants were off.

Jack took the six heads and he went a-walking back down to the King's house.

Well, there was $6000 more. Oh, boy, Jack was feeling good.

The King says, "Now, Jack, you've killed all the young ones. There's just the old man and the old woman, and I know good and well you can go back up there and get them."

"Well," Jack says, "I tell you, this is enough. I guess I'd better be going for home, sure. I know my folks is worried about me by now. They're expecting me back to the house. I'd better go on."

"Not now, Jack," the King says, "go on back up there and kill the rest of those giants. And then the only thing in the world you'll have to do will be to clear that new ground."

"Well," Jack says, "bedads, I'll go on back up there and try."

So back up the mountain he started. And this time he didn't climb no trees. He wasn't a-shaking, he wasn't scared. He just took his little old tommy-hatchet and he begun a-hacking on that tree — ka-whack, ka-whack! And my land, it sounded like thunder coming up that mountain — this old big giant with four heads, just right charging on him. And he saw his boys lying there dead, their heads cut off.

He said, "Huh, stranger, howdy. What's your name?"

Says, "Mister Jack is my name, sir."

"Well," he says, "Mister Jack, do you know anything about who's killed my boys here?"

"Yes, sir," Jack says, "you're looking right at the man now. I killed 'em. Come up here sassin' and a-cussin' me around. I'm not takin' that off of anybody. And you want to be mighty careful, sir, what you say to me or I'll fix you the same way."

"Oh, yes," the old giant pappy says, "come on, Mister Jack, and come on down to the house with me and meet the old lady. Why no, I'm not going to sass you nor say nothing bad at all. I'm going to be powerful careful of what I say."

"Well," Jack says, "bedads, I don't care if I do, then. Let's go." And down the mountain they started to the old giant's house.

The old giant said when he got pretty close, he said, "Now, Jack, you'd better wait out here and let me go in, for when I tell the old woman about these boys being killed and your being out here, she's a-going to take on powerful. Law, they's no telling what she might do. So, Jack, you just stay out here and wait on me a little while, and I'll go in. And then if it's all right, why, we'll be glad to have you come in for some supper."

"Well," Jack says, "bedads, I'll just wait out here on you."

He just waited until the old giant got in the house and he went a-slipping up to the door as fast as he could and put his ear right to the keyhole, and he heard the old man say, "Old woman, they's a little old man out there named Mister Jack. Jack's killed all three of our boys. He's cut their heads off. You've never seen such a fight in your life as they fit up on that mountain . . . it's just cleared up pretty near!" And he said, "This Mister Jack says he done it. Now I don't know whether he did or not. He don't look powerful strong to me, but out there's the boys. I brought 'em down. They're laying out there in the yard."

Well the old woman *did* throw a fit. She screamed and she cried and she raved, and then she said she'd kill Mister Jack. . . .

"Now, now, now," the old man said, "don't you go out there. He's killed those three boys. Now don't you dare go. Old woman, you're a-kind of weak and feeble compared to them. Don't you go out that way. You just wait. I'll test out Jack's strength, I'll see if he's as strong as he says he is."

So the old woman calmed down a little.

And the old giant said, "I'm going out and find out about him, and you just kind of straighten up the house in here — and get the oven good and hot! I think maybe we might have him for a little supper."

So Jack went a-pounding back out into the yard and was a-standing out at the edge, just like he was a-walking up to where the old giant and the house was.

The old giant came out and he reached down in the yard and he picked up four great big old buckets. You've never seen such things! Slung 'em on his arm and said, "Come on, Jack, let's go down here to the creek and bring the old woman up a little bit of water so she can get her some supper."

So they went down to the creek and the old giant reached in with one hand and he dipped up one big piggin full, and he reached in the other hand and he dipped up the other. And he said, "Now, Jack, over there's your two buckets."

Jack didn't pay him a bit of attention. He just rolled up his britches-legs and rolled up his shirt-sleeves way up to his elbows, and he went a-wading right out into the middle of that creek, feeling around in under a big old rock that was out there.

And the old giant says, "Jack, what in the world are you doing out there?"

"Why," he says, "bedads, just as soon as I can find a place to take hold of, I'm going to tote this creek up there to the old woman so we won't have to be a-toting loads of water up there. She can just come out there and get it when she wants it."

"Oh, law, no," the old giant says, "don't be getting this creek up there, Jack. No, no, don't do that." Says, "Land sakes, don't you know it would ruin my cornfield. And besides, the old woman's getting kind of old and tottery. She might fall in and get drowned. Come on, come on back to the house."

"Well," Jack says, "bedads, if I can't take the creek up there, I'm not taking no little old piggin of water."

"Well," the old giant says, "just leave the creek alone, Jack, and you don't need to mind about the little old buckets of water. Come on. These two's enough for her anyway." And on back up to the house they went.

The old man went in the house again, and he said, "Land sakes, old woman, I had the hardest time in the world getting Jack not to bring that creek up here. Lord, he's the mightiest man I ever did see or hear tell of. I just had to beg him to leave it down there." Said, "Now listen, you see if you can't do something with him. I'll get him to come on in the house here, and you see if you can't get him in that oven over there. I'll go out, and I'll be out here somewhere. Well, wait," the old man said, "wait a minute. Let me . . . let me try him first with throwing that crowbar. Just wait a minute, I'll see what he can do with that."

So he comes on back out. And Jack had heard every word that he said, but he was standing way off down in the yard just like he hadn't heard a thing.

The old man says, "Come on, Jack, this is what me and the boys used to do while the old woman was a-getting supper. We'd pick up this crowbar here and see who could throw it the furthest. Now come on, I'll give it a send way out yonder in the field, and you go out there and get it and bring it on back over here. Throw it on back over here to me."

So the old man picked up this great old big crowbar — why, it must have weighed a half a ton! — and give it a sling through the air. Went about a hundred and fifty feet out there.

Well, Jack went a-running on out to where the old crowbar lit up in the ground. Just standing there. He didn't even pay a bit of attention to the old giant. He cupped his hands up to his mouth and shouted: "UN-N-CLE! UN-N-CLE!"

"Ah!" the old giant says, "what'd you call me 'Uncle' for?"

"Oh," he says, "I'm not a-talking to you, I'm not a-talking to you at all . . . UN-N-CLE! . . . I'm a-hollerin' to my uncle way over yonder in Ohio. Why I've got a uncle over there that's a blacksmith, and he needs this here crowbar about making some horseshoes. The very thing. I'm just getting ready to throw it over to him, and I want him to be ready to catch it. UN-N-CLE!"

"Listen, Jack, Jack, don't throw that crowbar away! Why, that's all the one I've got. Don't do that. Now take your hand off of that crowbar and come on back here. Come on to the house and let's go on in. I think the old woman's got some supper ready. If she hain't, she pretty soon will have."

So the old giant took Jack into the house and said, "Now, old woman, here's Mister Jack, and he's going to come and have a little supper with us. I'll go out and split you up a little bit of wood while you go on finish the supper."

Well, the old woman she made like she was real glad to see Jack, and she picked up a comb and a washrag and said, "Come on here now, Jackie, let me comb your hair and wash your face and get you nice and cleaned up, ready for supper."

"Oh, no, bedads," Jack says, "I can wash my own face, and I can comb my own hair, too."

"Oh, no, no, now," the old woman says, "come on and just let me do it. This is the way I always fixed up my own boys. Now come on and let me do it, Jackie. Just get right up there on that shelf, and I can just reach right over and get you without having to stoop over a bit."

And Jack looked — and he saw that that shelf was right where it could be tipped right off into the old oven.

Well, Jack he acted like he'd like to get up on the shelf and he couldn't. And he'd wiggle off and he'd get always off on the wrong side.

And the old woman said, "Well, Jack, didn't you ever sit on a shelf before in your life?"

"No, sir," Jack says, "bedads, I never did. I don't know a bit more know how to sit on this shelf than anything. You get up here and show me."

"Well," the old woman says, "I'm kind of heavy to get up on that little shelf. But you just put your shoulder right under the edge of it there and hold it up so it won't break, and I'll get up there and show you how to sit on a shelf."

So the old woman, the old giant, got up on that shelf, and Jack just gave his shoulder a little hunch and a good push and right into that old oven he threw the old giant mother. And he worked around there with a great old big iron hook and he finally pulled the lid on it. Went over and hid in behind the door.

After a while the old man pushed open the door, come walking in, and says, "Old woman, old woman! Jack's a-burning, I smell him, I smell him!"

Jack didn't say a thing.

The old man run over and pulled the top off of that big old furnace there . . . "Law have mercy," he says, "that's not Jack. That's my old woman, and she's burned to a coal! There's your three heads, there's your three heads! That's her!"

"Yes," and Jack stepped from behind the door. And he said, "Mind what you say to me, I'll just sure put you in there, too."

"Oh, yes, Jack, I'm a-minding what I say to you. I'm not going to say a thing in this world out of the way. No, sir, Jack, I'm not!" But he says, "Listen, Jack. Help me get out of this country some way." He said, "Here you've killed the boys and now you've killed the old woman . . . just help me get out of the country."

"Well," Jack says, "I'd be glad to, sir, but, you know, I'm afraid it's a little too late."

"Too late? What do you mean?"

"Why," Jack says, "the King's a-sending a thousand soldiers down here right now, maybe two or three thousand of them. And they're going to kill you just as soon as they get down here."

"Oh, Jack, Jack! Can't you hide me somewhere? Can't you do something for me, Jack?"

"Yeah," Jacks says, "get into that old big chest over there and I'll see what I can do."

So he got the old giant down in the chest, and Jack ran out on the back side of the house. And he took up big sticks of wood, and he thumped and he beat on the old house, and he hollered and he whooped. And you'd have thought there was two or three thousand men out there, the noise Jack was a-making.

And he was a-fussing with them: "Now go on back, go on back. I tell you I've done away with all of them. You go on home and tell the King he didn't need to send you over here. Go on back, every one of you!"

But he acted just like they'd pushed right on into the house. And Jack came on in the house, throwing over the chairs, and breaking up the tables, and ker-whacking and ker-banging. And finally Jack acted like he was just driving them every one back out, and he took up a big stick and he said, "Now, if you don't get out of here, I'm going to do you just like I did the giants. Get out, I tell you! I've already killed the old giants."

Finally it went like they'd all went off and the noise kind of died down. And Jack went over to the chest and raised up the lid a little bit, and said, "Now crawl out there," he said, "the last one of 'em's gone. You get out of there easy like, and get away from here."

The old giant came out. He was just a-trembling and a-shaking. "Oh, Jack," he said, "what'll I do for you, what'll I do? Here you've saved my life from all them three thousand Englishmen." Said, "I know they'd a-killed me, they'd a-tore me limb from limb. Now, Jack, now, Jack, what do you want me to do?"

Jack says, "Mister, just start right over that mountain and don't let me see you stop anywhere. Just keep a-walkin' and that'll be all I ever ask of you. Just don't you ever come back here!"

The old giant said, "Jack, I'll be so glad to get away from here I'll never want to come back." And great steps he went taking right over that mountain.

And the last Jack saw of him, he just tipped the ridge and went right down on the other side.

Well, Jack looked around. There was the three old heads of the old woman giant. He could take them in . . . but, boys, what was he going to do about the old man? He'd sent him away.

Took those three heads back down to the King, and the King says, "Now, Jack, I just owe you $3000 more, but I sure can't pay you a thing for them giant's heads that went walking off over the mountain. You just lost $4000 right thataway."

"Well, Jack says, "bedads, this is plenty to do me and my folks the rest of our lives anyway." And he says, "Now listen, King, I'm kinda tired and wore out fightin'. I'm goin' on back home, and tomorrow I'll send Will and Tom to clear that new ground for you."

## *Jack and the Varmints*

Jack was one of those boys that just simply didn't like to work. He could do most anything in the world to get out of it.

And one day as he was walking along the road, he had a little old stick — a-whittling along on it. Nice little old soft piece of pine. Didn't know what he was making, he was just a-whittling. But the first thing he knew he had a good-looking little paddle made out of it.

He came alongside of a good cold spring and he knelt down to get him a drink, and there was a whole lot of little blue butterflies flew up as he laid down to drink.

And he thought, "I'm going to watch and let them settle again. And I'm going to see how many of them I can get at one whack."

Took his little paddle, and the butterflies settled down, and *slam!* he came down. Raised up his paddle, and there were seven of the little butterflies he'd killed.

"Hmm-m," he said, "I know what I'll do. I'll go down here to this black-smith and get him to make me a nice big broad belt. And on it he'll say 'Little Man Jack Killed Seven at a Whack.' Won't that look good on that belt? My, that will make me look like something and somebody!"

He went down to the blacksmith's shop and, sure enough, the blacksmith said, "Sure, I can make that kind of a belt." And in just no time Jack put on his new belt and went strutting on down the road, feeling mighty fine and big.

After a while he said, "Well . . . believe I'll just walk up to the King's house and see what I can do for him."

When the King saw him, he said, "Jack, I like the looks of that belt . . . 'Little Man Jack Killed Seven at a Whack' . . . do you really mean that you can do that?"

"Well," Jack says, "bedads, I've done done it. Sure I can kill seven at a whack. What is it you'd like to have killed, King?"

"Well," the King said, "I'll tell you something I'd like to have killed. Way back over here in the north part of the kingdom, there's a big wild hog that is just ruining everything. Why, people are getting scared to go out, Jack! They're afraid of that wild hog. I guess he just wandered over from Tennessee, but they sure are scared of him, and he's causin' a lot of trouble. Now, Jack, listen . . . if you'll get on my horse, I'll take you over there, pretty close to the place where he's been a-workin'. And then I'll let you off. And you go on and kill that hog for me, come back to the palace, and I'll pay you $1000."

"Well," Jack says, "bedads, let's get going. Where's your horse?"

So Jack climbed up behind the King on his horse, and he rode away into the north country.

The King was beginning to get pretty nervous. Jack could tell that. He came to a certain place and he said, "Now listen, Jack, I can't take my horse and go any further. You slide off. And now be careful, Jack, for that hog is a monster and, I'm telling you, he's a mean one."

"Oh," Jack says, "don't you worry about me and that hog. We'll get along all right."

King turned around and whippity-cut back down the road he went just as

*359*

hard as he could, 'cause he didn't want that hog to get wind of him and that horse.

Jack went a-walking on a little ways and he said, "Now, bedads, how can I get out of this country? I'm not a-going to mix up with no big hog, I can tell the world that! But I don't know where to go. I'll just ease along and maybe he'll never even hear me."

So Jack was walking along just as soft as he knew how — when all of a sudden up through the brush he heard a mighty crashing and a-tramping and a-scraping.

"Oh, law," he said, "he's smelled me, he's smelled me, sure as anything! Now what can I do?! I don't know a thing in the world but just to take to my heels."

He turned around and back down the mountain he went, just as hard as he could go, and right behind him coming through the brush and breaking the dead limbs and all, he could hear this monster of a hog. He looked over his shoulder one time and . . . oh my! . . . he didn't take time to look any more. That was the biggest hog he'd ever seen in his life — great long tusks and just coming right straight at him, just a-snorting. Oh, Jack just stirred up the ground! He just flew!

And as he was going by, he saw an old kind of a waste-house, and he thought "Well, I'll run in there and maybe I can get away from that hog."

He ran into this little old house, but right behind him he heard that hog coming.

But the top had all been blown off of the old house and it was just great high walls, without any roof. Jack was going so fast, he just gave one mighty leap and right up the wall he went, sitting on the top. And the old hog run right in at the door after him, right behind him.

Oh, Jack just fell off of that wall, and around and slammed that door as quick as could be! There he had the big old hog all just fastened up in that little old house.

Turned around and begun kind of whistling and walking on back towards the palace. He walked and he walked, and finally the King saw him coming and came running out. He said, "Jack, Jack, did you see that hog?"

"Oh, well," Jack said, "there was a little old shote up there come running around after me, messing around, wanting like it wanted to play. Is that what you're talkin' about, you reckon, King?"

"Why," King said, "I guess that's what it is, that's the only hog up there that I know anything of. What did you do with him, Jack? What did you do with him?"

"Why, I picked him up by the tail and flung him into the little old shed up there. If you want him, send your soldiers up there and let them kill it."

The King called twelve soldiers and gave them guns and sent them up to the little old house to see, sure enough, if Jack had put that big wild hog in there. When the men came and looked in, they just couldn't believe their eyes. There he was, just charging and snorting and . . . oh my! . . . he looked like he could tear all twelve of them up.

Finally they got him killed.

When they got that hog out of there, and scalded him and dressed him, cut him up, he made a wagon-load of the finest hog meat you've ever seen in your life. They went hauling it on back down to the palace.

Well the King paid Jack his $1000, and Jack thanked him and was ever so much obliged to him. Says now he'd better be getting on his way.

"Oh no, no," the King says, "you just wait a minute, Jack. I tell you, we've got another varmint. It is just worrying the people down in the south part of the kingdom to death. They can't stay there, their horses can't get out, their cattle can't get out, they're afraid to go work their farms. It's just awful, Jack. You'll have to go down there and try to kill that unicorn."

"Oh," Jack says, "a little old unicorn . . . who's scared of that?"

"Well," the King said, "you'll be when you see him. But now listen, get up on my horse here, and I'll take you just as far as I dare go. And then, Jack, you'll just have to do the rest of it on foot."

"Oh, yes," Jack said, "bedads, that's all right. Come on, let's get going." So Jack climbed up on the horse.

The King went riding off, and rode just as far as he dared into the country where that unicorn was loose. He said, "Now, Jack, slide off, and the rest of it's up to you, son. And I just wish you the best of luck in the world. But you be careful of that unicorn. I'm tellin' you that horn's killed more men than you can think of. Now you just be careful."

"Oh, yes," Jack says, "bedads, I'll be careful. I know how to do that."

And the King left him, turned on his horse and clickity-cut! back down the road he went just as hard as he could tear, leaving Jack standing there.

After the dust had kind of died down, Jack looked around and he thought, "Unicorn, you can stay right here for all I care. I've got a $1000 and that's all I want. I'm leaving here, too. But I'll wait till the King's out of sight."

Well, he didn't have time to wait till the King was out of sight. Just as he turned around, he heard a great noise and a pawing, and there came the unicorn charging down the mountain on him just like a streak of red lightning. Oh, my, but Jack took to his heels again! And down he went just as hard as he could go through this big field, around this tree and over that one, and the unicorn right behind him. He was getting so close, he could almost feel his breath on his back.

Out in front of Jack there, he saw a little young tree. Too little to climb, but he thought, "I believe I'll dodge behind it. Maybe it might save me."

And as he dodged right behind that little tree, *kerslam!*, the old unicorn just rammed his horn right through it.

Now you know a unicorn's old horns has rings all on it. And it just fastened in there just exactly like a screw had fastened it. And the unicorn couldn't get loose. He just pawed and he snorted.

Jack stood off and looked at him a little while, picked him up a little brush, and gave him one good little lick to see if he'd hold. And that unicorn was fast. Right there by his horn.

Jack went on to the palace.

The King said, "Jack, did you find that unicorn?"

"Huh, well yes, I guess I did. I found a little old pony up there with a horn out in the middle of his head. I tied him up and fastened him up there to a little sapling. If you want him, let your men go up there and get him."

"Well," the King says, "come on. Take fifty of the soldiers out there and go and see if you can find him."

Well when they came near, that unicorn was just pawing and snorting and cutting up so, the men were just scared. They were scared almost to get close enough to him to kill him.

Jack picked him up a little switch and walking up and he gave him a switch or two on the rump, and said, "See, he can't hurt you. Come on up here and shoot him." Well, the men came up, killed the little old unicorn.

"Well," the King says, "Jack, I'm telling you, you're the finest feller to go out after varmints that ever I seen. Now, listen, we've got one more thing. Over on the east side of the kingdom, there is a lion loose. A lion that has eaten up men that I've sent over there to kill him. Now I want to know if you think you can go over and kill that lion."

"Oh, why, law yes," Jack says, "a little old lion. Huh, anybody can kill a lion if they just know how."

"Well, all right," the King says, "here's your $1000 for the unicorn. Now just go on over there and make away with that lion for me. And that's the last varmint that I know of that you'll have to kill."

So Jack got started. The King didn't even take him on the horse that time. He said, Jack, you'll just have to go ahead on foot. That lion has killed too many men. I'm not goin' over there."

"Ho," Jack says, "bedads, I don't mind a bit in the world. I'll just go over on foot." And so he went walking away.

He waited until he got good and out of the sight of the King and he said, "Hm-m-m, lion, no, I'm not looking for you. And I hope you're not looking for me, 'cause if I can get past you, I'm leaving this country."

He was walking along just as soft and easy as he knew how to walk. But he couldn't walk soft enough to get past that lion.

With an awful roar, Jack heard him coming!

"Oh," he says, "I'm gone for now! What'll I do, what'll I do? . . . I'll climb up this tree." And up the tree he went, just as hard and as fast as he could go.

The old lion had seen him.

He reached up just as high as those long sharp claws of his could reach and scraped down the bark of that tree. And growled and roared. My gracious, he roared until he just shook the earth!

Jack just sat up in that tree and trembled. "Phe-e-ew," he said, "I just don't know what I'm a-going to do, but just as long as that lion stays here, I'm staying here." So he sat down on a limb.

Well, then, he waited, and the old lion run around that tree, and he'd reach up and he'd roar and he'd pull off more bark. And finally he was just given out. Layed down right at the foot of the tree and went sound asleep.

"Boy," Jack says, "here's my chance. If I can just light down out of this tree and get away from that lion while he's asleep and worn out, I'll be all right."

So he was slipping down the tree with his eye right on that old lion all the time. He wasn't looking where his feet was a-going. And the first thing you know, one foot went right down on a little old dead limb and *ker-whack!* it broke off, and Jack dropped right down on the back of that lion.

Oh, with an awful roar that lion was up and just flying! Jack holding on to his mane just as hard as he could, just laying there. Didn't know what in the world was going to happen, but anyway, he was hanging on to that lion. And the lion just ripping right down through the road, just as hard as he could go, right into the town and right 'round and 'round the palace, and the people all scared to death. They just fell into the houses, and the men hollering "Get your gun, get your gun!"

Here the men were all running out, peeping around to see where in the world Jack was riding that lion. Round the palace they went, Jack just holding on to his mane for dear life.

Well, the men were just so excited! Finally one of them got a good aim and *ker-bang!* killed that lion dead — with just one shot.

When the lion fell out from under Jack, Jack stood up there, and by that time all the noise and confusion had brought the King. The King came walking over and he says, "Jack, what in the world were you doing?"

"Well," Jack says, "what I was doing is nothing to what I'm a-going to do now. For I'm mad, and I'm plenty mad."

"Well, what are you mad about, Jack?"

"Good land, what in the world did they go and kill that lion for? My lands, don't you know I was a-breaking that lion for you a ridey-horse? Great day, what did they go and kill him for! I just had him pretty near tame, and he'd 'a made you the finest ridey-horse. I'm mad. I tell you, they'll pay me, and they'll pay me plenty. They can just fork over $3000 for killing that lion on me."

So the King went over to the men and he says, "I tell you, Jack is mad, and he's plenty mad."

And he said, "We've got to give him $3000 extra dollars for you shooting that lion. He was breaking that lion for me a ridey-horse. Now, I tell you, there's just nothing to do. Let's pay him and get rid of him."

And the men all began chipping in their money.

First thing you know they had $3000 made up for Jack. The King paid him the $1000 he owed him, and gave him that other $3000.

Well, Jack told them all "good-bye" and went a-walking off down the road.

And ever after that, Jack was known as —

"Little Man Jack, Killed Seven at a Whack!"

# 24.

# Tales Told
# in the Gullah Dialect

lbert H. Stoddard (1872–1954), the teller of these "Buh Rabbit" tales, was born and brought up on Daufuskie Island off the South Carolina coast. In the days preceding and following the Civil War, his family owned a plantation on the island, where young Stoddard grew up as a child with the Gullah Negroes and acquired their speech and manner of telling stories as naturally as any person acquires the language and accent heard daily around him. Leaving the island for college and then returning to it, Stoddard recognized the distinct folk value of both speech and stories, and then consciously began to preserve the tales, writing them down with great fidelity. The texts which follow are his own, taken down from the Gullah at the turn of the century, seventy years ago: there were no recording machines then.

In 1949, Mr. Stoddard, aged a sprightly seventy-seven, visited the Library of Congress and recorded for us some fifty tales, of which thirty belong to the "Buh Rabbit" or animal story cycle, while the remaining twenty are local Daufuskie stories. Twenty-eight of the former have been issued by the Library on three long-playing records, and each one is a delight. Mr. Stoddard was a born storyteller, a person whose cadence, rhythm, and sense of timing in the telling of the tales is extraordinary. Although at "second hand," his telling of the tales is quite authentic (there is no sense of "outside" mimicry whatever) and about as close to any Gullah "original" as it now seems possible to come. In a recorded interview at the Library of Congress in 1949, Mr. Stoddard said that "as a result of schooling and communication with the outside world, the Gullah dialect has changed greatly, and one can no longer hear it as I heard it as a youngster. The only exception to this is to get the very older Negroes excited — they then occasionally lapse into the old Gullah." That was in 1949.

The word "Gullah" itself is generally presumed to be a shortening or corruption of Angola, and the Gullah dialect is one which flourished on the once-isolated coastal islands of South Carolina and Georgia. The very isolation of the islands made possible the preservation of the dialect and the creation of a folk culture unlike any other to be found in the South.

In general, the Gullah dialect is a shortcut to the use of the English language and represents the effort of the early slaves to acquire the language of their masters, often with the happiest results. Examples of this shortcutting are found in the use of *e* as a pronoun to stand for "he, she, him, her, it, his, hers, and its," and in the use of *shum* to stand for "see them, see him, see her, see it" and also, in the past, for "saw them, saw him, saw her, and saw it." *E shum*, for example, can stand for "she saw it, he saw them," or any other combination of the words given. The persons and objects involved in the different stories determine the reading. When S'Allegetter (Suh Allegetter: Sister Allegetter) appears in one of the following tales the pronoun is *e*, as always, and stands for "she," just as in the same tale it stands for "he" for B'Allegetter as well as for Buh Rabbit. Similarly, the verb may be shortcut, and a single form stand for both the present and past, as *yeddy* stands for both "hear" and "heard" in the same tale.

As Mr. Stoddard tells them, the stories move with a mellifluous, hypnotizing, continuing sound and motion like that of an even and steady stream. One can imagine the spellbound children listening to the stories told with the same intonation Stoddard gives them in his telling. There is tremendous art in these tales: there is no fat on them, they are spare and lean and direct; the dialogue never interrupts the tale, but always moves it along; the characters are sharp and clear. Try reading one aloud, but better still hear one of Stoddard's records from the Library of Congress — and then try reading the tale aloud.

Don't let the dialect bother you. After a twice-over reading of the first tale, you will be trapped by the four stories *and* the dialect.

## How Buh Houn Got His Long Mouth

[Buh Rabbit is, of course, the greatest trickster of all, and some of his "tricks" come close to pure deviltry. In this story, he gives the hound his long mouth and unwittingly sets the hound-dog to chasing him for all time. The hound's baying after Buh Rabbit and his howling at the moon are very satisfactorily explained.]

When Farrer [God] fus bin mek Buh Houn e mout ain stan [look] sukka [such as, like] yo shum [see it] stan now. E bin roun sukka e yie [eye], ondly e bin mo bigger.

Buh Rabbit bin een e rice fiel duh habes [harvest] e rice en de sun git berry hot en Buh Rabbit lef e fiel en gone up on de flood bank whey some bush dey en e set down on-neet one bush een de shade, en biggin fuh whistle.

Dem days Buh Rabbit en Buh Houn bin good frens. Buh Houn come long en yeddy [heard] Buh Rabbit duh whistle. E say Buh Rabbit uh wish uh could uh whistle lukka younna [like you].

Buh Rabbit tell um say e mout ain stan [made] fuh whistle. "Roun mout ain fuh whistle. Ef yo had long mout lukka mine yo could uh whistle."

Buh Houn tell Buh Rabbit say e wish e had uh long mout en e could uh whistle.

Buh Rabbit tell Buh Houn say e could uh gie um long mout.

Buh Houn ax Buh Rabbit say ef e does gie um long mout es e gwine hut [hurt] um.

Buh Rabbit tell um say e ain hut um none tall when e git a long mout.

Buh Houn say, "Do, Buh Rabbit, gie me long mout en teach me fuh whistle."

Buh Rabbit had e reap hook wid um whey e bin uh cut rice with. E tell Buh Houn fuh hole e head high es e kin is, en e fuh shet e yie tight, en e fuh draw long bret.

Buh Houn hole e head high es e kin is, en e shet e yie, en e draw uh long bret. Buh Rabbit tek de reap hook een all two e hans en come down puntop [on top of] Buh Houn mout en cut um mos' back tuh e yays [ears].

When Buh Houn feel Buh Rabbit reap hook duh cut um e holler, "Wow."

E open e yie fuh see wuh Buh Rabbit duh do. E see Buh Rabbit duh stan dey duh laugh puntop um. E try fuh talk tuh Buh Rabbit but e mout hut um summuch tell all e could uh say duh [was], "Wow, Wow." E sta-a-t fuh go tuh Buh Rabbit en Buh Rabbit tink say e duh comin fuh hut um en e run off.

Buh Houn run at [after] Buh Rabbit en does try fuh talk tur um but all e could uh say duh, "Wow, Wow." Ebber sence dat when Buh Houn see Buh Rabbit e does run um en e holler, "Wow, Wow, Wow, Wow." En ebby time Buh Houn does hole e head high, lukka when he does look puntop [at] de moon, e mek um membunce uh how Buh Rabbit reap hook hut um en e holler, "Wow-wow-wow-wow-ough-ough-o-o-o."

## *How Buh Wasp Gets His Small Waist*

[Buh Wasp almost splits in two laughing at Buh Skeeter's "leetle dry bone shank leg," and even though today he would like to laugh like everyone else, he cannot, but must always be cross and angry in order not to finally break himself in half. Buh Skeeter's "biggety" pose and explanation of the fine potatoes in his father's potato field could set him off into hysterics again, and together they account for the wasp's present small waist, which was, originally, quite as fat and normal as anyone else's.]

Een de fus off sta-a-tin [in the beginning] Buh Was' wais ain bin lettle lukka how yo shum [see it] stan now. E bin big ez anybody wais. En de way

*McIntosh County, Oklahoma, 1940:*
*guitar player and singers at a play party*

Buh Was' come fuh git e leetle wais e bin uh walk long de road en e see Buh Skeeter duh hoe tutter [potato] een e fiel.

E tell um say, "Good Mawnin, Buh Skeeter, how all uh younna?" Buh Skeeter gie um answer say, "We all duh mekkin out berry well, tank Gawd. How all uh younna?"

Buh Was' tell um say all uh dem dey dey [are there] tank Gawd.

Buh Was' lean e self on de fench [fence] en dem biggin talk. Buh Was' say, "Buh Skeeter, e look luk yo got uh berry fine crop uh tutter een yo fiel dis ear [year]."

Buh Skeeter tell um say, "Yeh, dis de bes crop uh tutter uh ebber raise een muh life. All duh good fine tutter."

Buh Was' tell um say da's fine fuh e ha sischa good tutter.

Buh Skeeter tell um say e ha good tutter fuh true, but ef e wa' see big tutter fuh true, e fuh go een e Pa fiel [in his Pa's field]. Ebby one dem duh big fine tutter, ent uh leetle tutter dey een e whole Pa fiel.

Buh Was' ax Buh Skeeter how big de tutter dey een e Pa fiel.

Buh Skeeter bin bayfoot [barefoot] en e put e foot puntop de tutter hill en pull up e pantloon laig, en e tell Buh Was' say, "Buh Was', yo see muh laig yuh so?"

Buh Was' tell um say yeh, e shum.

Buh Skeeter tell um say, "Buh Was', ebby one de tutter een muh Pa fiel dis [just as] big ez muh laig yuh so. Ent uh leetle tutter dey een e Pa whole fiel."

Buh Was' look puntop [at] Buh Skeeter duh stan up dey so biggety duh show a leetle dry bone shank fuh show how big de tutter een e Pa fiel dey [is], en e tink say ef de tutter ain big mo'n uh dat dey'd be uh powerful po chance uh doin enny eatin, en e bus out laff [burst out laughing].

Buh Was' laff. E laff tell e side hut [hurt] um. E mash e han een e side fuh keep e side fuhm hut um. E roll all erbout on de groun duh laff. Ebby time e wa' [want] stop laff e study [think] bout Buh Skeeter duh stan up dey so biggety duh show e leetle dry bone shank fuh show how big de tutter een e Pa fiel is, en e haf fuh bus out laff gen.

When Buh Was' bin able fuh stop laff, e had uh mash e wais een leetle lukka how yo shum stan now. En de cayjon [this is the occasion/reason] fuh Buh Was' be so cross all de time. Buh Was' does wa' laff lukka some body, but Buh Was' faid, say ef e ebber sta-a-t laff gen e duh gwine bruk e self een two, so e haf fuh keep e self cross fuh keep fuhm laff.

## *Man Git E [His] Adam Apple*

[The localizing of God in this story is delightful: God has the garden, but has so much business to take care of that he needs a hand to work it, so creates Adam, who then, in turn, needs Eve to help him. (She talks-talks-talks so much that Adam has to go out in the field to rest his ears!) Then God has to go to town on business, but delays his going, out of consideration for the oarsmen (we are on Daufuskie Island) so that they will not have to row against the tide. In consequence of this delay, God catches Adam eating the apple, and we have the apple bobbing up and down in Adam's throat. God is so vexed with them both, Adam and Eve, that to punish them he not only drives them out of the garden, but creates mosquitoes, sand gnats, and all kinds of comparable things for the "bodderation" of man and beast. I particularly like the serpent's laugh: "S-s-s-s-s. . . ."]

When Farrer fus mek de wul e [it] bin all kibber ober wid watuh, en e ain bin no fitten place fuh eeder man uh eeder creetur fuh lib.

Farrer see e ain bin no fitten place en e mek canal en ditch en quatuh dreen [drain] fuh dreen de watuh off, en when de yut [earth] done dry e tek en plant grass en all kine uh beyobs [herbs] en ting fuh be bittle (victual) fuh man en beas.

Farrer yet see dey ain no light puntop de yut fuh ting fuh see fuh git bout, so e mek de sun fuh de day, en de moonshine en de sta fuh be light een de night.

Farrer mek one good ga-a-den en put all kine ub uh ting een dey. Den e come fuh fine out e had summuch uh binnis tell e ain ha time fuh mine [mind] de ga-a-den, en e does wa' one hans [hand] fuh ten de ga-a-den fuh um.

Farrer tek some de dut [dirt] een de ga-a-den en mek um een de shape ub uh man, en e breeze [breathe] e bret een e noshril en e mek um come libe.

When e come libe Farrer tell um say e name duh Adam en e fuh ten de ga-a-den fuh um.

Adam ten de ga-a-den en try fuh do e wuk faitful, but Adam hads summuch uh time fuh min' roun e house en cook e bittle tell when dem June rain come Adam ain bin able fuh keep up wid e wuk.

Den gen de p'yo [pure] lonedly git um down. E ain hads no one fuh talk tuh en fuh be comp'ny fuh um.

Adam gone tuh Farrer en at [after] e done mek e mannus [manners] Farrer ax um wuh e does wa'. Adam tell Farrer say, "Please, suh Farrer, uh does try fuh do muh wuk faitful, but it tek me summuch uh time fuh sweep en ten roun de house en fuh cook muh bittle tell uh ain able fuh be een de fiel nuf, en dem June grass duh gwine git uh me. Den, suh Farrer, de p'yo lonedly done git me down. Please, suh Farrer, see ef yo could gie me nedder hans fuh help me."

Farrer tell Adam say he would uh see wuh e could uh do bout um, en Adam tun en sta-a-t fuh go back tuh e wuk.

Farrer call um, "Adam!"

Adam tun en e gone back tuh Farrer, en Farrer tek um en mek um fuh drop sleep, en when e duh sleep Farrer tek out one e leases [smallest] rib en mek ooman, en when Adam wake up, de ooman dey dey side um.

Farrer tell Adam say, "Adam, dis yuh duh Ebe. Uh mek um fuh be comp'ny fuh yo en fuh mine de house en fuh cook yo bittle en fuh help yo een de fiel when e does ha time."

Adam tek Ebe home wid um en de ooman is bin nuf uh help tuh Adam en e bin good comp'ny fuh um, but e berry lub compersation [conversation].

E dunk'yer [she doesn't care] who e duh talk tuh dis so e'd yeddy [listen] tur um. E talk summuch tell Adam hads fuh lef de house dis fuh res' yays [ears], en e tell de gal say, "Summuch uh compersation duh gwine git yuh een trouble one uh dese days."

One time Farrer hads fuh go town on binnis en e come een de ga-a-den en call Adam en tell um say, "Adam, uh gots fuh go town on binnis en uh gwine be gone two tree day. You en Ebe fuh tek chage de ga-a-den en mine um good while uh dey-dey [there], en enny ting wuh dey een de ga-a-den duh younna fuh nuse [use], scusin [except] tuh one ting. Da nyung [young] apple tree wuh dis duh beer [bear] younna ain fuh tetch dat. Sho es yo tetch dat, yo duh gwine dead."

Adam tell Farrer say, "Yes, suh Farrer." En e tun en gone back tuh e wuk.

De sarpint bin eed de grass en e yeddy [heard] whu Farrer tell Adam, en when Adam done gone een de fiel e gone tuh Ebe. E put on e sweet mout en e tell um say, "Good mawnin." Suh [sister] Ebe tell um say, "Good mawnin, suh."

De sarpint tell Ebe say dey hads one pooty ga-a-den, en Farrer mus be tink well uh dem fuh do all uh da ha-a-d wuk.

Ebe say, "E is tink well uh we. E duh gwine town en e tun de whole ga-a-den ober tuh we fuh we fuh tek enny ting wuh diddy [here] scusin tuh one lone ting." De sarpint ax um, "Wuh dat?", en Ebe tell um duh [was] da nyung apple wuh dis duh beer fuh de fus. "Ef we tetch dat we duh gwine dead."

De sarpint laugh, "S-s-s-s-s. Farrer tell yo dat case e know duh de sweetes ting een de ga-a-den en e want um fuh e self. Tek one en tase um. E ain duh gwine dead yo. Farrer ain duh gwine miss one leetle ole leetle apple."

Ebe tell um, no suh, him ain duh gwine tek no apple, him ain wa' dead.

De sarpint sweet mout um en sweet mout um tell Ebe tek one de apple en tase um. En de ting sweeten e mout tummuch [very much].

Dis e [she] bin uh nyam [chew] de fus moutfull Adam come out de fiel en Ebe chook [put] de apple behime e back.

Adam say, "Gal, wuh da yo duh hide behime yo back?" Ebe say, "E ain duh nuttin suh." Adam say, "E is duh suppin, show me wuh yo got."

Ebe pull out de apple en when Adam shum [saw it] e holler. "Gal, trow dat ting way fo yo dead. Fuh whuf fuh yo gone done de ting Farrer tell yo yo en fuh do?"

Ebe tell um say ain duh him tek de apple, duh de sarpint mek um tek de apple.

Adam gen tell um fuh trow de ting way, but Ebe tun en sweet mout um tell Adam tek one bite de apple.

Farrer ain bin gone [hadn't gone to] town soon es e tought. E bin uh wait [had waited] fuh de tide fuh tun [turn] so e oasmen wouldn' uh had summuch uh ha-a-d pullin fuh go gen tide, en e tek uh walk en gone een de ga-a-den.

Dis Adam tek e fus big bite de apple, Farrer call um, "Adam!"

Adam ain bin ha time fuh n'yam [chew] de apple en e try fuh swaller um. De ting gone down een e trote en come up, gone down een e trote en come up. En ebber sence dat, man bin ha adam apple.

Farrer git bex [vexed] fum dem do wuh e tell dem dey ain fuh do, tell e run all two uh dem out de ga-a-den, en Adams hads fuh tek up new groun en wuhk so hahd fuh mek out, en Farrer bin dat bex tell fuh punish dem e mek out fuh git een dem hay [hair] en skeeter [both mosquitoes] en san' nat en all kine ub uh ting fuh bodderation man en beas.

## B'Allegetter Sees Trouble: How B'Allegetter Git E Ma'kin*

[Buh Rabbit introduces B'Allegetter to trouble, which he has never seen before. S'Allegetter and all the little children allegetters insist on going along, and B'Allegetter — to keep them quiet and to keep from being driven crazy — permits them to come along. The little children make their curtseys to Buh Rabbit, they all stand in the center of a dry-grass field, Buh Rabbit rings them all with fire — and they see trouble! In the process of escaping through the flames, their backs become burned and ridgy — just as they are now — while their bellies, next to the ground and untouched by the fire, remain white. Buh Rabbit, his normal self, hoots at them as they run off to the safety of the creek. I like the little alligators going Shu-shu-shu-shu-shu-shu into the water after the tremendous SPASHOWS! of their parents.]

B'Allegetter lib een de watuh whey nuf uh fish dey [there] fuh e eat en e don' does haffuh wuk fuh e libbin, en e nebber meet up wid trouble.

Buh Rabbit lib on de lan en e meet up wid nuf uh trouble.

One time Buh Rabbit bin uh project* on de crick sho [shore] whey B'Allegetter house dey, and Buh Rabbit meet B'Allegetter duh set on e poach en e tell um say, "Good mawnin, B'Allegetter, how all uh younna."

* His markings.
* Project: lighthearted wandering, often connoting mischievous intent.

375

*Delacroix Island, St. Bernard Parish, Louisiana, 1941:*
*Spanish muskrat trappers playing cache*
*in their camp in the marshes*

B'Allegetter tell um say all duh gittin on bery well, en e ax Buh Rabbit how all uh dem tuh him house.

Buh Rabbit tell um say dey all duh mekkin out, "But summuch uh trouble, B'Allegetter. Summuch uh trouble."

B'Allegetter ax Buh Rabbit wuh duh trouble. How e stan [looks]?

Buh Rabbit ax B'Allegetter say, "B'Allegetter, yo ain nebber see trouble? Uh kin show you trouble."

B'Allegetter tell Buh Rabbit say him would uh like fuh see trouble fuh see how e stan. Buh Rabbit tell um say ef e would meet um een de broom sage fiel nex mawnin time de sun done dry de jew [dew] off de grass good, e would showed um trouble.

Nex mawnin time de sun bin git hot, B'Allegetter tek e hat en sta-a-t fuh lef de house. When S'Allegetter [Sister or Mrs. Allegetter] shum [saw him] duh gwine e [she] ax um whey e duh gwine. E tell S'Allegetter say him duh gwine fuh meet Buh Rabbit fuh him fuh show um how trouble stan.

S'Allegetter tell um say ef him duh gwine see trouble, him [she] duh gwine too. B'Allegetter tell um say, "Shet yo mout, gal. Yo ain duh gwine no whey. Yo bes fuh lemme go see how trouble stan fus. Den uh kin show yo."

S'Allegetter qua'il [quarrel] en tell B'Allegetter ef him duh gwine, him duh gwine too. All de leetle allegetter yeddy [heard] dum duh qua'il en all uh dem holler say, "Ef younna duh gwine us duh gwine too. Ef younna duh gwine us duh gwine too."

Dem all mek summuch uh racket tell B'Allegetter git tire fuh yeddy [hear] dem en e tell dem all fuh shet dem mout en come on den.

Dey all gone cross dem ma-a-sh en time dem git een de broom sage fiel dem meet Buh Rabbit duh set puntop one stump duh wait fuh dem.

Dem all tell Buh Rabbit good mawnin en de leetle allegetter mek dem curtschey [curtsy].

At [after] Buh Rabbit done tell dem all good mawnin, e ax B'Allegetter say, "Younna all come fuh see trouble dis mawnin, entty [ain't it]?"

B'Allegetter tell um say, yeh, when him bin uh gwine leff de house dis mawnin dem all baig fuh come, en dem all mek summuch uh racket tell fuh sabe e yays [ears] e haffuh le' dem come too.

Buh Rabbit tell dem stan out een de middle uh de fiel en tell dem fuh wait dey en him would go git trouble en bring um.

Buh Rabbit gone on de aig [edge] uh de fiel en e cut uh han uh broom sage en e put fire tuh um en e run um roun en roun de fiel so de fire dey roun en round de fiel.

Turrecly S'Allegetter see de fire duh jumpin up red en de smoke duh gwine up, en e say, "B'Allegetter, wuh da yonder?" Dem lib een de ribber en de wet ma-a-sh, en ain nebber see fire.

B'Allegetter tell um say e dunno whu duh him.

S'Allegetter say, "Uh tink da's trouble Buh Rabbit duh bring fuh show we."

All de leetle allegetter jump up en down en holler, "Ain strubles pooty, ma? Ain strubles pooty?"

Turrecly de fire hot [heat of the fire] git close, en de smoke git bad en dem tek out fuh one side de fiel. Dey meet de fire. Dey tun roun gone tarrer [to the other] side. Dey meet de fire.

De fire git so close e feel luk e duh gwine bun [burn] dem.

Dey all shet dem yie [eyes] en trowed dem head close tuh de groun en bus' troo de fire en ain nebber stop tell B'Allegetter gone SPASHOW! een de crick. Right behine um S'Allegetter SPASHOW! een de crick. All de leetle allegetter come, Shu, shu, shu, shu, shu, shu, een de crick.

When dem duh comin out de fiel Buh Rabbit bin uh set puntop one stump en e holler, "Yo done see trouble now B'Allegetter, yo done see trouble."

De fire ain bin git tuh de belly pa-a-t [part] wuh bin nex tuh de groun, en e yet white. But all dem back done bun tell e black en ridgy lukka how yo shum stan tell yet.

# 25.

# "Tall" Tales:
# Jim Bridger

The "tall tale" in America is very close to the land and frequently has elements in it of both fact and legend. Crockett is a good example of this three-way being, and so are the seacoast exaggerations of Nantucket sleigh rides, the "tallest" of which is reported by J. Ross Browne in his *Etchings of a Whaling Cruise*, in which the struck whale gives John Tabor a ride from the south coast of Africa, up and across the Atlantic to Buzzard's Bay and Taborstown, and on to the Allegheny, Ohio, and Mississippi Rivers, down the Gulf of Mexico to South America, across the Andes, and on crazily around the world, winding up at Algon Bay beyond the Seychelles and down the Mozambique Channel. Nantucket sleigh rides there were, of course, in fact and legend, but John Tabor's was a "tale" set within the legendary-factual experience of whalers. Any seaman of the time appreciated it fully. Just as men in other parts of the country and other occupations immediately appreciated the "tale" quality of stories about the Mississippi River boatmen, impossible deeds of cowboys, lumbermen, miners, as well as the incredible wonders of the land itself. Fiction in a setting of fact. The dividing line between legend and tale is occasionally a slim one.

Then why not allow Paul Bunyan to join the group? Simply because the Paul Bunyan stories (with very few exceptions) never have circulated as folklore. They have been the creation of newspapermen, writers, public relations men for the lumber companies, local chambers of commerce, and others. They have circulated in print, and rarely orally. A very cursory reading (three or four pages) of James Stevens's (no relation to the poet) *Paul Bunyan* will clear the air in this respect. The person looking for folklore in the tales will back away from them in sharp anguish. (There is, to return to an earlier observation, no folk language or speech in them. It is impossible to believe that these stories were ever told.)

The "tall tales" I like best are those which have come down to us from Jim Bridger, and I like them doubly for the wonderful irony of their being. First, a few facts about this extraordinary frontiersman.

Jim Bridger was born in 1804 in Richmond, Virginia, lived there until the age of eight, then traveled west with his parents to the booming town of Kansas City, where they acquired a small and profitless farm. The town was rough and harsh on these innocents. The father earned some extra money surveying in the outlying country, but on one of his trips his wife and a daughter died, and he himself died shortly after. Young Bridger, at the age of fourteen, farmed himself out as a four-year apprentice to a blacksmith, and at the end of his apprenticeship in 1822, at the age of eighteen, signed up with a large trapping expedition going up the Missouri. The advertisement for hands and volunteers had to be read to him: Bridger was totally illiterate and could never read or write.

From the time of his signing on until his death in 1881 Jim Bridger was West. Mountain West. As a hunter, trapper, fur trader, and guide, he was unequaled. The details of his greatness are elsewhere: sufficient to say here that he discovered the Great Salt Lake in 1824 (twenty years old!), the South Pass in 1827, and what is now Yellowstone Park in 1830 or thereabouts — the exact year is open to discussion. He opened the Overland Route by Bridger's Pass to Great Salt Lake, founded Fort Bridger, and guided General Dodge's Union Pacific surveys and Indian campaigns in 1865–66. He knew the western United States from the Canadian border into Mexico, from Wyoming to California. Major General Grenville Dodge had this to say of him:

He was a born topographer; the whole West was mapped out in his mind, and such was his instinctive sense of locality and direction that it used to be said of him that he could smell his way where he could not see it. He was a complete master of plains and woodcraft, equal to any emergency, full of resources to overcome any obstacle, and I came to learn gradually how it was that for months such men could live without food except what the country afforded in that wild region. . . . Nothing escaped their vision, the dropping of a stick or breaking of a twig, the turning of the growing grass, all brought knowledge to them, and they could tell who or what had done it. A single horse or Indian could not cross the trail but that they discovered it, and could tell how long since they had passed.

While Bridger was not an educated man, still any country that he had ever seen he could fully and intelligently describe, and could make a very correct estimate of the country surrounding it. He could make a map of any country he had ever traveled over, mark out its streams and mountains and the obstacles in it correctly, so that there was no trouble in following it and fully understanding it. . . .

He was a good judge of human nature. His comments upon people that he had met and been with were always intelligent and seldom critical. He always spoke of their good parts, and was universally respected by the mountain men, and looked upon as a leader, also by all the Indians. He was careful to never give his word without fulfilling it. . . .

A great man. King of the Mountain Men.

The Overland Trail, which he laid out in practical fact, was the great Western highway over which thousands of wagons passed. In some places it was a hundred yards wide, and the wagon ruts were deep in the earth. When Indians came across it, they gazed on it with utter astonishment. He was asked once by a colonel of cavalry, "Is there any chance of my missing the trail when I come to it, not seeing it? What then?" Jim Bridger simply looked at the colonel and did not answer. The question was beyond belief!

To the tales. Hiram Martin Chittenden, who wrote the *History of the Fur*

*Trade*, also wrote *The Yellowstone National Park*, published in 1895. He states that Bridger's first personal knowledge of the wonders of the park

is believed to date from 1824, when he is supposed to have been upon the upper Yellowstone. It is certain that before 1840 he knew of the existence of the geysers in the Firehole Valley. . . . Between 1841 and 1844 Bridger was leader of a grand hunting and trapping expedition, which for upward of two years, wandered over the country from the Great Falls of the Missouri to Chihauhau, Mexico. At some time during this expedition he entered the region of the upper Yellowstone and saw most of its wonders. His descriptions of the geysers and other remarkable features of that locality can be traced back nearly to this period and present an accuracy of detail which could only come from personal observation.

But would you have believed Bridger's account of these things (the Cinnabar Mountains, the Obsidian Cliffs, the Falls, the geyser basins, geysers spouting seventy feet high, the Mammoth Hot Springs, water so hot that meat or fresh-caught fish could be cooked in it, bubbling mud) if he had told them to you? You would have figured him to be as daft as I if I were to tell you that there is a mountain pass at an elevation of 8,150 feet where two streams (one from the north, one from the south) meet and become one, and that this one stream flows both into the Atlantic via the Yellowstone and into the Pacific via the Snake, and that fish coming from one stream pass into the other, so that a fish "predestined" for the Atlantic is not actually so, but can flop over and go on to the Pacific if he chooses. You would consider me at least lightheaded if I claimed any such nonsense. But it is true. Bridger discovered the pass, the streams and stream, observed the fish, and told the story. No one believed it. (If you don't believe me, by the way, write to the Yellowstone National Park people.)

Bridger described the Yellowstone Park as "a place where hell bubbled up." We know that now. Bridger described the Yellowstone in detail to Colonel R. T. Van Horn, editor of the *Kansas City Journal*, in 1856, and Horn wrote the account up and was about to publish it when "a man who claimed to know Bridger, told him that he would be laughed out of town if he printed 'any of old Jim Bridger's lies.' " Horn did not print the story, thereby missing one of the greatest scoops in journalistic history: what one would not give to have a fairly verbatim account of Bridger's report! Horn had the decency later (in 1879) to apologize editorially to Bridger, and that apology presumably is in some library which has a file of the KCJ. I have not seen it. (Bridger at the same time also "drew with a piece of charcoal on a piece of wrapping paper an outline of the route necessary to be taken by a railroad should it ever cross the continent, which route is exactly on the line that is now crossed by the Union Pacific.")

A prophet is not without honor save in his own country. So Jim Bridger said the hell with them, if they think I'm telling them a pack of lies, then, by God, I'll give them some that they can really believe are lies. The god-damned hell with them! And so, building on the base of the actual Yellowstone, he created his whoppers. Chittenden says that his tales "were generally based upon fact, and diligent search will discover in them 'the soul of truth' which, according to Herbert Spencer, always exists 'in things erroneous.' These anecdotes are current even yet among the inhabitants of the Yellowstone, and the tourist who remains long in the Park will not fail to hear them." That was in 1895, and gives us proof positive of their folk circulation. Chittenden comments, before giving us the tales, that "the persistent incredulity of his countrymen, and their ill-concealed suspicion of his honesty, to say nothing of his mental soundness, were long a cloud upon Bridger's life. . . . Whether from disgust at this unmerited treatment, or because of his love of a good story, Bridger seems finally to have resolved that distrust of his word, if it must exist, should at least have some justification."

Chittenden reports Jim Bridger:

When Bridger found that he could not make his hearers believe in the existence of a vast mass of volcanic glass, now known to all tourists as the Obsidian Cliff, he supplied them with another glass mountain of a truly original sort. Its discovery was the result of one of his hunting trips and it happened in this wise.

Coming one day in sight of a magnificent elk, he took careful aim at the unsuspecting animal and fired. To his great amazement, the elk not only was not wounded, but seemed not even to have heard the report of the rifle. Bridger drew considerably nearer and gave the elk the benefit of his most deliberate aim; but with the same result as before. A third and a fourth effort met with a similar fate. Utterly exasperated, he seized his rifle by the barrel, resolved to use it as a club since it had failed as a firearm. He rushed madly toward the elk, but suddenly crashed into an immovable vertical wall which proved to be a mountain of perfectly transparent glass, on the farther side of which, still in peaceful security, the elk was quietly grazing. Stranger still, the mountain was not only of pure glass, but was a perfect telescopic lens, and, whereas, the elk seemed but a few hundred yards off, it was in reality twenty-five miles away!

Another of Bridger's discoveries was an ice-cold spring near the summit of a lofty mountain, the water from which flowed down over a long smooth slope, where it acquired such a velocity that it was boiling hot when it reached the bottom.

An account, in which the "soul of truth" is not so readily apparent, is that of a mining prospector of this region, who, in later times, met a unique and horrible fate. He had for days been traveling with a party toward a prodigious diamond set in the top of a mountain, where, even at noonday, it shone with a luster surpassing the sun. He arrived at length on the top of the mountain only to see the diamond on another summit apparently as far away as ever. Disheartened and weary, he thought to save the labor of descent by taking advantage of an extremely smooth face of the mountain, and accordingly sat down upon his shovel, as upon a toboggan, and let slide. There was a vacant place around the camp-fire that evening, and next day the rest of the party, passing along the base of the mountain, found an infusible clay pipe and the molten remains of a shovel. Warned by the fate of their comrade, the superstitious survivors forbore any further search for the diamond.

To those who have visited the west shore of the Yellowstone Lake, and know how simple a matter it is to catch the lake trout and cook them in the boiling pools without taking them from the line, the ground work of the following description will be obvious enough. Somewhere along the shore an immense boiling spring discharges its overflow directly into the lake. The specific gravity of the water is less than that of the lake, owing probably to the expansive action of heat, and it floats in a stratum three or four feet thick upon the cold water underneath. When Bridger was in need of fish it was to this place that he went. Through the hot upper stratum he let fall his bait to the subjacent habitable zone, and having hooked his victim, cooked him *on the way out!*

In like manner the visitor to the region of petrifactions on Specimen Ridge in the north-east corner of the Park, and to various points in the hot springs districts, will have no difficulty in discovering the base material out of which

Bridger contrived the following picturesque yarn. According to his account there exists in the Park country a mountain which was once cursed by a great medicine man of the Crow nation. Every thing upon the mountain at the time of this dire event became instantly petrified and has remained so ever since. All forms of life are standing about in stone where they were suddenly caught by the petrifying influences, even as the inhabitants of ancient Pompeii were surprised by the ashes of Vesuvius. Sagebrush, grass, prairie fowl, antelope, elk, and bears may there be seen as perfect as in actual life. Even flowers are blooming in colors of crystal, and birds soar with wings spread in motionless flight, while the air floats with music and perfumes siliceous, and the sun and the moon shine with petrified light!

In this way Bridger avenged himself for the spirit of distrust so often shown for what he had related. The time presently came, however, when the public learned, not only how large a measure of truth there was in his stories, but also how ingenious a tale he could weave from very inadequate material.

There were other tales in the same tradition, brief because American speech is given to brevity. South of the Slot in San Francisco, bedbugs were so large that when they were routed out of bed they grew indignant and jumped up on the chandeliers and barked at the men. Jersey mosquitoes moved west: settlers in Montana and Idaho thought to protect themselves from the insects by sleeping under iron kettles, but the mosquitoes drilled holes in the kettles, hooked their bills through them, and hoisted them off the quaking pioneers. Lake fishing was difficult: "Constable Baldwin says the mosquitoes are bigoted and revengeful. You can do nothing with them. When you get after them with a brush of boughs, they get mad at not being allowed to have their own way. They then get up on the hillside and throw rocks." Grasshoppers were big enough to drive as horses for spring plowing, and trained pet snakes were used by stage drivers to link front and rear wheels and brake the stages going downhill.

It is so hot in Yuma that its residents are buried in overcoats to protect them from freezing when they reach Hell. When a storm sets in Montana, the wind strips the feathers off chickens, pins cats and dogs against the barns ten feet off the ground, and snaps wagon chains. Nebraska tornadoes raise real hell. Caroline Smith, a student at the University of Denver in 1941, reported that straws were driven through two-by-fours and toothpicks halfway into tree trunks. Also, that a woman who was sitting in her rocking

chair on the second floor of a house before a tornado was still rocking unharmed after it, but was in the basement. A rooster was blown into a gallon
jug and was found after the storm with its head sticking out of the opening
crowing for all it was worth. A woman claimed she had her clothes washed
and in the basket out in the yard before the tornado struck, and after the
tornado passed she found them neatly pinned to the line. And after one storm
a man who thought his house was unharmed checked carefully and found
that only the paint was standing. The rest of the structure had been blown
away.

In the hot country of New Mexico, a prospector's fierce comment to a
buzzard adequately expressed his feelings: "You damned black bird, you've
got wings and you stay here!" Places in the West were described as being "a
thousand miles from hay and grain, seventy miles from wood, fifteen miles
from water, and only twelve inches from Hell." In such country lived Dick
Wick Hall, in the town of Salome, Arizona, midway between Wickenburg
and the California line. His gas station sported a sign: "Smile. You don't
have to stay here but we do." And his mimeographed newspaper, *The Salome Sun*, brought him local (Salome: population, one hundred) and state-
wide recognition as a humorist. He bragged of the fertility of the soil: "Melons don't do very well here because the vines grow so fast they wear the
melons out dragging them around the ground." And he told the story of
Mac, the Yale sprinter and track star, who took a job herding sheep before
the lambing season, and was warned by Reed, his boss, not to lose any of the
lambs during the upcoming season:

The sheep and Mac soon disappeared in the brush and nothing more was
thought of them until suppertime came and no sign of Mac or the sheep. Reed
commenced to worry — about the sheep — and about seven o'clock was about
to start out looking for them when Mac at last came driving them up through
the brush into the corral, and, after shutting them in, came up to the chuck
tent, streaked with dust and perspiration and, from all appearances, tired out.
Before Reed could say anything Mac burst out:
"Boss," he said, "I'm through. They thought back East that I was a foot
racer, but I'm not. Almost any sheepherder that can herd that band for a week
and not lose those lambs can beat all the world's records. I didn't lose any
today and I ran every one of those damn lambs back into the band every time

they tried to get away, but one day is enough for me. I'm all in, but they are all there. Go and count them up and then give me my time. I'm done."

Reed, knowing that there were no lambs in the band and that none of the ewes could have lambed yet, went down to the corral to investigate and, off in one corner, huddled up by themselves, he counted 47 jackrabbits and 16 cottontails.

The loneliness of certain occupations forced men to become humorists to retain their sanity, and one such was Sergeant John T. O'Keefe, who spent three years in the 1870's on Pikes Peak recording wind velocities, rain and snowfalls, temperatures, and other phenomena for the United States Signal Corps. He reported two violent eruptions that turned the Peak into a flaming volcano. The second of these "began with a tremendous burst which shook Pikes Peak to its very foundations, hurling into the air dense clouds of ashes and lava. The explosions succeeded each other with rapidity and increased in violence for about an hour, when the volcano seemed to enter a profound sleep. No doubt Colorado Springs will meet the same fate as Pompeii and Herculaneium."

One evening, alarmed by screams, the same Sergeant O'Keefe rushed into his bedroom to find his wife being besieged by an enormous number of ferocious, carnivorous pack rats. With rare presence of mind he encased her in zinc roofing material and then, to protect his legs, thrust them into two lengths of stovepipe and began to battle the rats with a heavy club. He was making very little headway against the army of rodents, who had already eaten a quarter of beef and his small daughter, when his wife, also with great presence of mind, threw a wire loop over her husband and attached it to a powerful storage battery. The heavy current electrocuted the rats nibbling at the sergeant and made it possible for him, by alternately electrocuting some and clubbing others, to rout the enemy.

Certain of these reports astonished Washington. Perhaps because of them or because of the intrepid sergeant's battle with pack rats, he was removed to less dangerous climes.

Like Bridger, whose truth was not believed, a Nevadan returned East on a visit and casually described a prospecting trip of two days during which he and his partner traveled with their wagon through rain, mud, freezing weather, dust, snow, and blistering heat. For this account he was made an honorary member of the local liar's club and disgustedly returned West, resolved never to tell the truth again. Where truth would not go down, however, the tall tale did. An old lady from California visited a Nevada town and expressed her astonishment at the rapid flight of time. "I do declare," said she, "I get up, breakfast, and have hardly time to turn around before it is noon." "It is always so here," said her host, "time passes very rapidly here. It is on account of the extreme rarity of the atmosphere, you know." "La, yes," said the old lady, "I did know that once, but had forgotten it."

Similarly, the proprietor of a Western hotel, constructed in the last century without fire escape or other special egress in the event of disaster, was asked by a visitor (myself) occupying a third-floor room what the procedure was in case of fire. To which the owner replied, "Jump out of the window and turn left." This satisfied me completely. It still does, a perfect and spontaneous answer to an idiot question.

# 26.

# The Cante–Fable

The *cante-fable* is a combined song-and-tale form which comes to us in European tradition from the Middle Ages, and which reached its greatest literary peak in the French "Aucassin and Nicolette" of the twelfth century.

In the *cante-fable*, verse-with-music is mixed with prose, and each is dependent upon the other to move the story forward, dependent to such a degree that either one standing alone would be meaningless — hence *cante-fable*, or song-story. The prose requires the song to make full sense, and the song requires the prose or otherwise the story is nothing.

In the United States, the form is rare, and to the three given here I would add only two more, "No Use Knockin' on the Blind" and "The Parson Tricked by Boy's Song."

## Little Dickie Whigburn

["Little Dickie Whigburn" was recorded from the recitation and singing of Mr. Samuel Harmon of Cade's Cove, Blount County, Tennessee, by Herbert Halpert in 1939.]

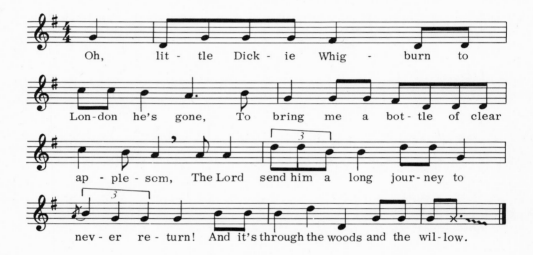

Oh, lit-tle Dick-ie Whig-burn to Lon-don he's gone, To bring me a bot-tle of clear ap-ple-som, The Lord send him a long jour-ney to nev-er re-turn! And it's through the woods and the wil-low.

Well, one time there's a little town by the name of Whigburn, and there's a little man lived in that town by the name of Dickie Whigburn. And there was an applesom spring away far off in the wilderness where, when one got sick, they'd go there and get this water to cure them. And little Dickie Whigburn's wife got bad one time, and she wanted him to go to the applesom spring and get her some water.

And so he got the bottle and started, and he goes on and gets out in the wilderness a piece, and he meets up with a pedlar that he was well acquainted with once, and he asked him where he was going. He told him he was going to the applesom spring to get some water for his wife, and she was bad off.

Well, the pedlar got to talking to him and told him that there wasn't anything wrong with his wife, that she just wanted to get shet of him, and that the old parson was going to be there that night and she didn't want him to be there.

Well, he couldn't believe it for a long time, but the pedlar he kept on arguing with him and finally got him to agree to go back with him. He told him to go back with him, and he could fix it so he'd see the whole thing with his own eyes. Well, he agreed to go at last. And he told him he'd put him in one of his goods sacks, and he put him in a sack and carried him up and went on. And he got to little Dickie Whigburn's about sundown and called to stay all night. And his wife said she hardly ever kept anybody when her husband was gone — he wasn't there — but being she was well acquainted and he'd stayed there so much, why, to drive out to the barn and put up his team and come on in.

Well, he done so, and come in. Why, there wasn't a thing the matter with the woman! She's all rigged up, you know, so fine a fly couldn't stick to her hardly, you know. And the preacher was there, you know, fixing to have a good time.

Well, this pedlar says to Mrs. Whigburn, says, "Mrs. Whigburn, I got a sack of goods wet in crossing the river today. If you have no objections, I'd like to set 'em in by the fire and let 'em dry out tonight." She told him to go bring 'em in, and he took little Dickie and set him up in the corner over by the fire. And they ate supper, and after supper Mrs. Whigburn says, "Suppose we all sing a verse of a song apiece tonight, being we're all here by ourselves." They all agreed, and they says, "Well, you're the woman of the house, you sing the first one."

> *"Oh, little Dickie Whigburn to London he's gone,*
> *To bring me a bottle of clear applesom.*
> *The Lord send him a long journey to never return!*
> *And it's through the woods and the willow."*

"Pretty good, Mrs. Whigburn, sing that again."

> *"Oh, little Dickie Whigburn to London he's gone,*
> *To bring me a bottle of clear applesom.*

> *The Lord send him a long journey to never return!*
> *And it's through the woods and the willow."*

"Well, now Mr. Preacher, comes to your turn."

> *"Oh, little does Dickie know or little does he think*
> *Who eats of his eats and drinks of his drinks,*
> *The Lord spared my life this night to lie with his wife.*
> *And it's through the woods and the willow."*

"Pretty good, Mr. Preacher, sing that again."

> *"Oh, little does Dickie know or little does he think*
> *Who eats of his eats and drinks of his drinks,*
> *The Lord spared my life this night to lie with his wife.*
> *And it's through the woods and the willow."*

"Well, Mr. Pedlar, it comes to your turn."

> *"Oh, little Dickie Whigburn he is not far,*
> *And out of my hopsack I'll have him to appear,*
> *And if a friend he does lack, I will stand at his back.*
> *And it's through the woods and the willow."*

The old preacher looked up when he heard this and said, "I guess I'd better be going." "Oh, no! Oh, no!" the pedlar said. "You can hear mine twice, too."

> *"Oh, little Dickie Whigburn he is not far,*
> *And out of my hopsack I'll have him to appear,*
> *And if a friend he do-eth lack, I will stand at his back.*
> *And it's through the woods and the willow."*

Then little Dickie he walked out:

*"Good morning, fair gentlemen, all in a row,*
*The chief of your secret I very well know,*
*And the tongues of the guilty before you doth go.*
*And it's through the woods and the willow."*

*They beat the old parson right straight away,*
*And spanked Dickie's wife on the very next day,*
*And Dickie and the pedlar together did stay.*
*And it's through the woods and the willow.*

## *The Irresistible Captain*

[Herbert Halpert gives this descriptive but certainly non-folk title to a delightful *cante-fable* he collected in 1939 from the recitation and singing of Charles Grant at New Egypt, New Jersey. It might well have come to us from the times of Chaucer or Boccaccio. Any landsman trusting his wife to a sea captain deserved whatever he got. This one, to boot, loses his fiddle!]

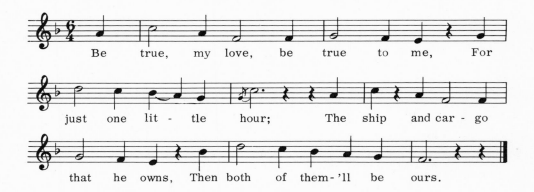

Be true, my love, be true to me, For just one lit - tle hour; The ship and car - go that he owns, Then both of them - 'll be ours.

This sea captain fell in with an old violin player. He was makin' his brags what he could do with the women, and the old fiddler told him he didn't have anything to bet, but he'd be willing to bet his life that his wife was true and virtuous. But the captain he offered to bet his ship and cargo against the old man's fiddle that he could do as he pleased with her. So the old fiddler went home and told his wife, and made arrangements for the captain to be with his wife for an hour in the settin' room alone. Then the old fiddler he got a chair and set down right by the door so she could hear him play on the violin. And this is what he played. And as he played, he sung — he was a great singer, too. He begin to play and sing:

> "*Be true, my love, be true to me,*
> *For just one little hour;*

> *The ship and cargo that he owns,*
> *Then both of them'll be ours."*

He was a-singin' this and playin' it over to remind her of what there'd be. They'd be rich. After a while she answered him. She begin to sing:

> *"Too late, my love, my love, too late,*
> *His arm's around my middle;*
> *He's kissed me once and f——— me twice,*
> *You've lost your damned old fiddle."*

# Mr. Garfield

[James A. Garfield was inaugurated President in March 1881, and, a few months later, was shot in the Baltimore and Ohio railway station in Washington, D.C., while on his way to attend the commencement ceremonies at Williams College. The shooting took place on July 2, but Garfield did not die until September 19, at Elberon, New Jersey, where he had been removed on September 6. The assassin was Charles J. Guiteau, a disappointed office-seeker, whose act was probably influenced by the abuse heaped upon the President by his opponents within the Republican party. Guiteau had come to Washington from Chicago, hoping to receive the appointment as American consul at Marseilles, and committed his crime after being rebuffed. His trial and appeal were unnecessarily lengthy, and the sentence of death was not carried out until June 30, 1882. He was hanged at the District of Columbia jail.

Bascom Lamar Lunsford of South Turkey Creek, North Carolina, first heard the rare *cante-fable* relating to the Garfield assassination in 1903, and recorded it at the Library of Congress in 1949. Mr. Lunsford introduces "Mr. Garfield" with an account of his learning of it and moves then directly into the *cante-fable*.]

The title of this song is "Mr. Garfield." I first heard it about 19 and 03 when I visited the home of Mr. A. W. Williams, who lived on the edge of Henderson County, North Carolina, when I was selling nursery stock. And the boys played it there. Anderson Williams, a young man, picked it and played it on the banjo. First I'd heard it. Afterwards his sisters and Anderson visited our home in Rabbit Ham Creek section of Buncombe County on Hamlin Mountain, where I grew up. Then in 19 and 25, the eminent folk-song collector, Dr. R. W. Gordon, came to the mountain country, and I traveled with him some. And I took him to the home of Anderson Williams, at that time a man of some age, and we went to his home one night, and Anderson picked and sang this song. Once after that I heard one stanza by another person. That's the only two people I've ever heard sing the song, besides myself. I sing this and record it here March the 23rd complimentary to Mrs. Emrich, who has been transcribing some of my records and likes the song.

Going down to the station the other day, and I heard the report of a pistol. And I said to a friend of mine, I says, "What does that mean?" He looked rather excited like, and he give me something sort of like this:

> *"Oh, they tell me Mr. Garfield is shot*
> *And a-laying mighty low, mighty low,*
> *They tell me Mr. Garfield is shot."*

Well, I went down the street. I saw a large crowd gathering up over there, many people around the house. I went on over, went in, and I saw Mr. Garfield laying there on the bed. I walked up. About that time, the doctor come. He walked in, set his saddle box down beside the bed, went over, and picked up his hand, felt his pulse, says, "How are you feeling, Mr. Garfield?" He looked up kind of sad like, and give him something sort of like this:

> *"Oh, I'm shot down very low down low,*
> *Oh, I'm shot down very low."*

Doctor says, "Mr. Garfield, you're in pretty bad shape. Better send for a preacher. This is serious." They sent for the preacher. The preacher come after a while. He walked in, stepped over to the bedside, said, "Mr. Garfield, how are you feeling?" Mr. Garfield looked up kind of sad like, give him something sort of like this:

> *"Oh, I'm shot down very low down low,*
> *Oh, I'm shot down very low."*

Preacher said to him, he says, "If you should die tonight," says, "where do you think you'd spend eternity?" He looked up kind of sad like, and give him something sort of like this:

> *"Oh, I'd make my home in hell, Lord, Lord,*
> *Oh, I'd make my home in hell."*

Preacher said, "This'll never do. You better get your heart right. Better pray." So he got down and prayed a long prayer, got up wiping the sweat off his face, says, "Now, Mr. Garfield, if you should die, where do you think you'd spend eternity?" This time he looked up with a smile on his face, and he give him something sort of like this:

> *"Oh, I'd make my home in heaven, Lord, Lord,*
> *Oh, I'd make my home in heaven."*

Good many people called there that day, and they all stayed for dinner. They called 'em on to eat. There was one town dude there. Asked him what he'd have. He leaned back, give 'em something sort of like this:

> *"You can pass around your ham and your eggs, Lord, Lord,*
> *You can pass around your ham and your eggs."*

Then there was a country fellow there. They asked him what he'd have. He leaned back and he says, "I want something I'm usen to." And he give 'em something sort of like this:

> *"Oh, bring on your bacon and your beans, Lord, Lord,*
> *Oh, bring on your bacon and your beans."*

Well, after Mrs. Garfield got through washing the dishes, she come on in, sit down on the bedside where her husband was. She says, "Mr. Garfield, if the worst should come to the worst, and you shouldn't get well, would you be willing for me to marry again?" He looked up, this time with a little smile on his face, and he give her something sort of like this:

> *"Don't you never let a chance go by, Lord, Lord,*
> *Don't you never let a chance go by."*

I was going down the street a couple of days after that. I saw a strange looking fellow going down on one side of the street, and the sheriff going down on the other side. The sheriff hollered, "Hands up, over there!" The fellow stopped, turned around. Sheriff walked over and stuck a .44 in his face. Says, "Your name Guiteau?" He says, "Yes, pacifarm [peace officer, pacifier?]." Sheriff looked him right in the eye, and he gave him something sort of like this:

> *"You're the very man I want, Guiteau,*
> *You're the very man I want."*

Sheriff put the handcuffs on him, took him down to jail. Of course, a big crowd followed along down there. I went on down, went on in, walked up to the cell, looked in through the bars, and saw Guiteau sitting there. I says, "Mr. Guiteau, how are you feeling?" He looked up to me kind of sad like, and he gives me something sort of like this:

> *"Going to hang on the 10th of June, Lord, Lord,*
> *Going to hang on the 10th of June."*

Next day I was going down the street, and I saw Mrs. Garfield all dressed in black, tears in her eyes, carrying a large bunch of roses. I says, "Mrs. Garfield, what're you going to do with those roses?" She looked up kind of sad like, and she give me something sort of like this:

> *"Going to place them on my husband's grave, Lord, Lord,*
> *Going to place them on my husband's grave."*

I says, "Mrs. Garfield, where are you going to bury him at?" She looked up kind of with a smile on her face, and give me something sort of like this:

*"Going to bury him on that long Flowery Branch, Lord, Lord,*
*Going to bury him on that long Flowery Branch."*

# Folksongs and Ballads

*Historical Songs*
*Sea Shanties*
*Cow-Country Songs*
*Love Songs*
*Murder Ballads*

# 27.

# Historical Songs

## Free America

It was my good fortune once to introduce two great Americans to each other, Carl Sandburg and General Eisenhower. This was during the time when Luther Evans was Librarian of Congress and when Sandburg used to stop over between trains from New York on the way to his home in North Carolina. On one occasion Evans and Sandburg got around to discussing men of stature, men who were the living embodiment of American tradition. Dr. Evans asked Sandburg whom he placed at the top of the list.

"Eisenhower."

It developed that Sandburg had never met his number one American. Dr.

Evans asked me to arrange a talk between the two and, in SHAEF parlance, it was "laid on" for 10 A.M. Friday, July 25, 1947, in the General's office at the Pentagon. I reported the meeting in an article, "The Poet and the General," in the *Saturday Review* for March 20, 1948. It was a wonderfully human and memorable meeting and conversation, but the part that concerns us here came towards the end when Sandburg — who had brought his guitar along — but let me quote:

Carl Sandburg had been seated for some time, and I suggested that the General might like to hear one of his songs. He walked across the office to his guitar, took it out of the case and returned to the General's desk, where he had stood when he first came in. He looked beyond Eisenhower sitting relaxed at his desk. He looked beyond the American flag in its stand by the window, and out across the great view of the nation's capital. He looked across the Potomac to the Lincoln Memorial and the Washington Monument. Strumming the guitar slowly, he spoke in his deep resonant voice, "I'm going to sing you an old song about America. It was written by Joseph Warren, a Boston physician who died in the Battle of Bunker Hill. It is a genuine antique. The pronunciation of the word then was 'Americay.' And yet it is an appropriate song today. It is called 'Free Americay.' The tune is 'The British Grenadiers.' "

Then Sandburg sang for General Eisenhower:

*The seat of Science, Athens, and earth's proud mistress, Rome —*
*Where now are all their glories? You scarce can find a tomb.*
*Then guard your rights, Americans, nor stoop to lawless sway.*
*Oppose, oppose, oppose, for North Americay.*

*We led fair Freedom hither, and lo, the desert smiled,*
*A paradise of pleasure was opened in the wild.*
*Your harvest, bold Americans, no power shall snatch away!*
*Huzza, huzza, huzza, for free Americay.*

*Torn from a world of tyrants, beneath this western sky*
*We formed a new dominion, a land of liberty.*
*The world shall own we're masters here, then hasten on the day,*
*Huzza, huzza, huzza, for free Americay.*

*Lift up your hands, ye heroes, and swear with proud distain,*
*The wretch that would ensnare you, shall lay his snares in vain;*
*Should Europe empty all her force, we'll meet her in array,*
*And fight and shout, and fight for North Americay.*

*Some future day shall crown us the masters of the main,*
*Our fleets shall speak in thunder to England, France, and Spain;*
*And the nations over the ocean spread shall tremble and obey*
*The sons, the sons, the sons of brave Americay.*

By way of footnote, it was my impression at the time that General Eisenhower liked it all except for the "tremble and obey." He said, "Warren certainly didn't have any mean idea of empire!"

## Washington the Great

"Washington the Great" was, as Mrs. Morgan says, a grade-school song designed to instill the nobler feelings of patriotism and ambition in young scholars, whose country itself was still young enough to remember vividly its immediate origins. Feeling against the British still runs high in the song, reflecting its closeness to the Revolution itself and our own adolescent period of growth. There is no cherry tree, but the silver dollar of Rappahannock fame becomes entrenched in American legend. Mrs. Minta Morgan recorded the song for John A. Lomax at Bells, Texas, in 1937, and introduces it herself:

Well this song has been in our immediate family for a hundred years. My father was borned in 1824. He said he learned it when he was about thirteen years old at a country school that he went to, Cogshill school in East Tennessee, McMinn County.

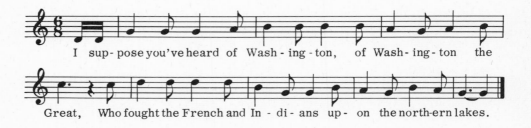

I suppose you've heard of Washington, of Washington the Great, Who fought the French and Indians upon the northern lakes.

I suppose you've heard of Washington, of Washington the Great,
Who fought the French and Indians upon the northern lakes,
And when King George of Eng-e-land oppressed our lovely land,
Our country fought for freedom under Washington's command.

He captured British battleships, and tore their ensign down,
And raised our banner in its place, our banner of renown,
He drove the British from our shores, he whipped them good and strong,
And sent them back to Eng-e-land, the place where they belonged.

He was the first great President, the first to rule the land,
And all the people honored him down to a single man;
He taught the people to be good, and love their country, too,
And everybody sings his praise, as loudly as we do.

He loved the little children, too, and took them out to ride,
And he threw a silver dollar o'er bold Rappahannock's tide;
And when he died, they buried him beside Potomac's waves,
And raised a marble monument to mark a hero's grave.

If all the boys throughout the land his deeds would emulate,
They'd grow to be like Washington, like Washington the Great.

## *Hunters of Kentucky*

The War of 1812 had ended, but news traveled slowly then, and there was, in consequence, time for another battle — the Battle of New Orleans, where word of the peace had not come. The battle itself took place on January 8, 1815, and Packenham, the British commander, was killed in the action. Andrew Jackson commanded the American force, composed chiefly of volunteer frontiersmen from Kentucky.

Samuel Woodworth's song on the battle was a great stage success in New Orleans, was printed in a New York collection in 1826, and frequently reprinted thereafter. It passed into oral tradition (the tune is a catchy one and the words equally so), and the song has been collected from Tennessee, Wisconsin, Missouri, and — reasonably enough — Kentucky. Sam Hinton of La Jolla, California, sang it for the Library of Congress in 1947.

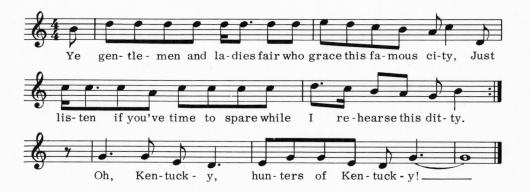

Ye gentlemen and ladies fair who grace this famous city,
Just listen if you've time to spare while I rehearse this ditty;
And for the opportunity conceive yourselves quite lucky,
For 'tis not often that you see a hunter from Kentucky.

*Oh, Kentucky, hunters of Kentucky!*
*Oh, Kentucky, hunters of Kentucky!*

I suppose you've read it in the prints, how Packenham attempted
To make old Hickory Jackson wince, but soon the scheme repented;
But Packenham he made his brags, if he in fight was lucky
He'd have our girls in cotton bags in spite of old Kentucky.

> *Oh, Kentucky, hunters of Kentucky!*
> *Oh, Kentucky, hunters of Kentucky!*

Old Hickory led us to the swamp, the ground was low and mucky,
There stood John Bull in martial pomp, and here was old Kentucky.
But steady stood our little force, none wished it to be greater,
For every man was half a horse and half an alligator.

> *Oh, Kentucky, hunters of Kentucky!*
> *Oh, Kentucky, hunters of Kentucky!*

And when so near we saw them wink, we thought it good to stop them,
It would have done you good, I think, to see Kentuckians drop them.
And so if danger e'er annoys, remember what our trade is,
Just send for us Kentucky boys and we'll protect you ladies.

> *Oh, Kentucky, hunters of Kentucky!*
> *Oh, Kentucky, hunters of Kentucky!*

*Pvt. Edwin Francis Jamison,*
*Georgia Regiment, C.S.A.*

## The Southern Soldier

"The Southern Soldier" is a song clearly contemporary with the Confederacy and reflects the immediate bitterness of that period. With the passage of time, we may look upon it with historic interest. For another song presenting the strong Southern point of view, see "Good Old Rebel."

I'll place my knapsack on my back, my rifle on my shoulder,
I'll march away to the firing line, and kill that Yankee soldier,
And kill that Yankee soldier,
I'll march away to the firing line, and kill that Yankee soldier.

I'll bid farewell to my wife and child, farewell to my aged mother,
And go and join in the bloody strife, till this cruel war is over,
Till this cruel war is over,
I'll go and join in the bloody strife, till this cruel war is over.

If I am shot on the battlefield, and I should not recover,
Oh, who will protect my wife and child, and care for my aged mother,
And care for my aged mother,
Oh, who will protect my wife and child, and care for my aged mother.

And if our Southern cause is lost, and Southern rights denied us,
We'll be ground beneath the tyrant's heel for our demands of justice,
For our demands of justice,
We'll be ground beneath the tyrant's heel for our demands of justice.

Before the South shall bow her head, before the tyrants harm us,
I'll give my all to the Southern cause, and die in the Southern army,
And die in the Southern army,
I'll give my all to the Southern cause, and die in the Southern army.

If I must die for my home and land, my spirit will not falter,
Oh, here's my heart and here's my hand upon my country's altar,
Upon my country's altar,
Oh, here's my heart and here's my hand upon my country's altar.

Then Heaven be with us in the strife, be with the Southern soldier,
We'll drive the mercenary horde beyond our Southern border,
Beyond our Southern border,
We'll drive the mercenary horde beyond our Southern border.

## *The Bonny Blue Flag*

After "Dixie," "The Bonny Blue Flag" was the most popular song of the Confederacy. It came into being on January 9, 1861, at the Mississippi Secession Convention at Jackson, Mississippi. Belden reports in *North Carolina Folklore* that a "Mr. C. R. Dickson entered the hall bearing a beautiful silk flag (blue) with a single white star in the center. . . . Upon leaving the hall, Harry McCarthy, a comic actor who had witnessed the scene, wrote . . . 'The Bonnie Blue Flag, that Bears a Single Star.' The next day it was printed by Col. J. L. Power, and that night it was sung in the old theater in Jackson by its author." Within a week it had circulated in the chief cities of the South. There was, of course, no Confederate flag — other than the individual flags of North Carolina and Texas — which bore a single star. Following the fall of New Orleans to Northern troops, the song so incensed General Butler that he issued an order "that any man, woman, or child that sang that song, whistled or played it, should be fined twenty-five dollars." The tune was a catchy one, and other songs — "The Southern Girl's Reply" and "The Homespun Dress" — were sung to it as well.

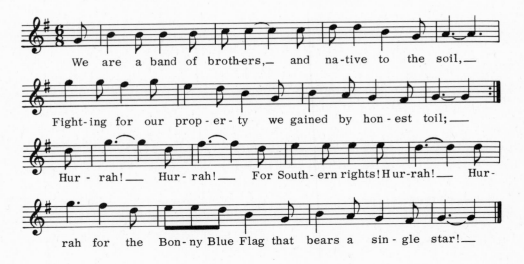

We are a band of brothers, and native to the soil,
Fighting for our property we gained by honest toil;
And when our rights were threatened, the cry rose far and near:
Hurrah for the Bonny Blue Flag that bears a single star!

*Hurrah! Hurrah! For Southern rights! Hurrah!*
*Hurrah for the Bonny Blue Flag that bears a single star!*

As long as the Union was faithful to its trust,
Like friends and like brothers, kind were we and just;
But now that Northern treachery attempts our rights to mar
We'll hoist on high our Bonny Blue Flag that bears a single star!

Come all you men of valor, now rally the banner of our right,
For Texas and fair Louisiana will join us in the fight;
With Davis, our loved President, and Stevens, a statesman rare,
Now rally round our Bonny Blue Flag that bears a single star!

Now here's to brave Virginia, the Old Dominion State,
With the young Confederacy at last has linked her fate;
Impelled by her example, now other States prepare
To hoist on high the Bonny Blue Flag that bears a single star!

And here's to our Confederacy! Strong are we and brave;
Like patriots of old, we'll fight our heritage to save,

And rather than submit to shame, to die we would prefer;
So cheer for the Bonny Blue Flag that bears a single star!

Then cheer, boys, cheer, and raise the joyful shout,
For Arkansas and North Carolina have both now gone out.
Then let another rousing cheer for Tennessee be given,
For the single star of the Bonny Blue Flag has grown to be eleven!

We cast our eyes far northward and lo! Missouri comes
With roar of dread artillery and sound of martial drums;
Through fire and smoke with martyr tread she braves the god of war,
So hoist on high the Bonny Blue Flag that bears a single star!

Then cheer, boys, cheer, for the dark and bloody ground
Awaking from her lethargy has caught the inspiring sound;
For noble old Kentucky shouts from her vales so green:
Make room upon the Bonny Blue Flag — Kentucky makes thirteen!

Maryland looks southward with supplicating eye
And listens with breathless haste to catch the battle cry.
When Beauregard shall tread her soil all panoplied in war,
She'll hoist on high the Bonny Blue Flag that bears a single star!

Maryland, we'll think of thee, we'll heed thy supplicant's calls
As mournfully they float from out McKenny's walls;
One corner shall be kept for thee through all the blaze of war
Upon our noble Bonny Blue Flag that bears a single star!

## The Homespun Dress

This is one of "the most beloved and best-remembered songs of the Confederacy." One account of its origin is given in *North Carolina Folklore* (vol. III) where it is suggested (among other possibilities) that the words were written by a Lieutenant Harrington, of Alabama, riding with Morgan's cavalry, who penned them in Lexington, Kentucky, in late September 1862, following a ball there at which all the ladies wore homespun dresses. Harrington was so impressed by their fortitude that he composed the poem immediately thereafter. The words are sung to the tune of the equally popular "Bonny Blue Flag." Lieutenant Harrington was killed in the battle of Perryville, October 3, 1862, only a few days after the ball.

Our text comes from a Mrs. Rebecca Simmons's scrapbook with the notation: "Carrollton, Arkansas    Transcribed by Becca May 24th 1863."

*Oh, yes, I am a Southern girl, I glory in the name*
*And boast it with far greater pride than glittering wealth or fame.*
*I envy not the Northern girl, her robe of beauty rare,*
*Though diamonds grace her snowy neck and pearls bedeck her hair.*

> *Hurrah, hurrah,*
> *For the sunny South so dear;*
> *Three cheers for the homespun dress*
> *That Southern ladies wear!*

*This homespun dress is plain, I know; my hat's quite common, too.*
*But then it shows what Southern girls for Southern rights will do;*
*We've sent the bravest of our land to battle with the foe,*
*And we would lend a helping hand — we love the South, you know.*

*The Southern land's a glorious land and hers a glorious cause.*
*Then here's three cheers for Southern rights and for the Southern boys!*
*We've sent our sweethearts to the war, but, dear girls never mind,*
*Your soldier love will not forget the girls he left behind.*

A soldier lad is the lad for me, a brave heart I adore;
And when the sunny South is free and fighting is no more,
I'll choose me then a lover brave from out that gallant band;
The soldier lad I love the best shall have my heart and hand.

And now, young men, a word to you, if you would win the fair.
Go to the fields where honor calls and win your lady there;
Remember that our brightest smiles are for the true and brave,
And that our tears fall for the one who fills a soldier's grave.

Hurrah, hurrah,
For the sunny South so dear,
Three cheers for the uniforms
That Southern soldiers wear!

## Good Old Rebel

The "Good Old Rebel" was written by Innes Randolph, poet and friend of Sidney Lanier, who served "in the Confederate Army throughout the whole of the great struggle." The poem "was written . . . while Reconstruction held sway in the South." It was printed in its original form in *Poems by Innes Randolph*, edited by Harold Randolph, Baltimore, 1898, but appeared, of course, prior to that as well as being reprinted subsequently. It can be sung with great bitterness, but it can also be sung with a sense of history past. Booth Campbell, recording it in 1942 for Vance Randolph, said, "It don't hardly seem right to go singing songs agin the Government." It might have eased his mind to know that I heard it sung with great good humor by two officers — one from Massachusetts, the other from Virginia — at the officers' club at Supreme Headquarters in France during World War II, where it was enjoyed by very loyal Americans around the table and momentarily stunned some Britishers. The version given here was sung for the Library of Congress by Eugenia and Charles Anderson of Ruxton, Maryland.

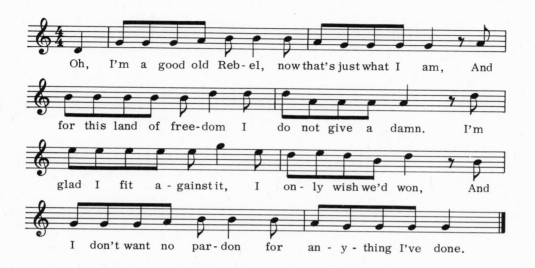

Oh, I'm a good old Reb-el, now that's just what I am, And for this land of free-dom I do not give a damn. I'm glad I fit a-gainst it, I on-ly wish we'd won, And I don't want no par-don for an-y-thing I've done.

Oh, I'm a good old Rebel, now that's just what I am,
And for this land of freedom I do not give a damn.
I'm glad I fit against it, I only wish we'd won,
And I don't want no pardon for anything I've done.

I hate the Constitution, this great Republic, too,
I hate the Freedmen's Bureau in uniforms of blue,
I hate the nasty eagle with all its rare and fuss,
Oh, the lying, thieving Yankees, I hate 'em wuss and wuss.

I hate the Yankee nation and everything they do,
I hate the Declaration of Independence, too,
I hate the glorious Union, 'tis dripping with our blood,
Oh, I hate the stripéd banner, I fought it all I could.

I followed old Marse Robert for four years near about,
Got wounded in three places and starved at Point Lookout,
I cotched the rheumatism a-camping in the snow,
But I killed a chance of Yankees and I'd like to killed some more.

Three hundred thousand Yankees lie stiff in Southern dust,
We got three hundred thousand before they conquered us,
They died of Southern fever, of Southern steel and shot,
Oh, I wish it was three million instead of what we got.

I can't take up my musket and fight 'em any more,
But I ain't a-going to love 'em, now that is sartin sure,
And I don't want no pardon for what I was and am,
And I won't be reconstructed — and I do not give a damn!

## *Phil Sheridan*

Historically, the Valley of Virginia or the Shenandoah Valley was a natural, protected gateway for Southern troops moving north, or for Northern troops moving against the South. Several battles took place in it during the Civil War, and Winchester was a frequent battleground. In 1864, General Grant, who recognized the strategic value of this avenue of attack for the Confederacy, ordered General Sheridan to march, with heavy cavalry support, through it as part of the large enveloping movement against Southern forces and against Richmond. General Sheridan did and rendered it useless to the Confederacy, so useless that "a crow flying through the Valley would have had to carry its own rations."

As noted in the opening chapter, "Phil Sheridan," sung by Judge Learned W. Hand, is an excellent illustration from the folklorist's point of view that traditional songs are transmitted in the folk manner on all levels of our society.

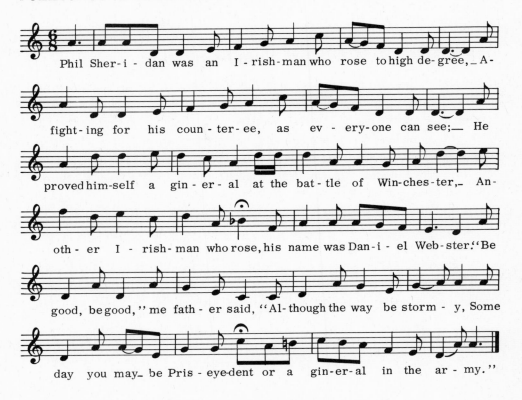

Phil Sheridan was an Irishman who rose to high degree,
A-fighting for his counteree, as everyone can see;
He proved himself a gineral at the battle of Winchester,
Another Irishman who rose, his name was Daniel Webster.

*"Be good, be good," me father said,*
*"Although the way be stormy,*
*Some day you may be Priseyedent*
*Or a gineral in the army."*

JUDGE HAND: "That song I first heard in the Harvard Law School sometime about 1895 or 6. It was then sung by a man named George B. Eliot, who was afterwards general counsel of the Atlantic Coast Line, and has since died. He was from North Carolina."

ALAN LOMAX: "Is that all there was to the song?"

JUDGE HAND: "That was all there was to the song, except he had a way . . . he would sit and cross one leg over the other and keep time with the free leg. And then at the end, after he said 'general of the army,' he would say, 'One, two, three, shift!' And when he shifted, he would cross the . . . take the free leg and put it down, and put the other leg over the free leg, and it was quite . . . it had to be quite quick to do it and keep the time. But I know of no more of the song, never heard him sing any more of the song, nor have I any idea where it came from or where he got it."

## *The Iron* <u>*Merrimac*</u>

The following two songs — "The Iron *Merrimac*" and "The *Cumberland*'s Crew" — recount, in different manner, the epic sea battle which changed the whole course of naval history, marking as it did the advent of the ironclad gunboat and the immediate obsolescence of the old, towering, wooden ships of war. The *Merrimac* — originally a Union vessel burned by the retreating Northern forces at Gosport Navy Yard, and reconditioned as the *Virginia* by the South — looked like "a terrapin with a smoke-stack on its back." On March 8, 1862, this strange ironclad craft, with engines that could make no more than five knots and with a hull depth of twenty-three feet, slowly crept forward against the massed strength of the Union fleet in Hampton roads. Commodore Buchanan, commanding the *Merrimac*, first sighted the *Congress*, a fifty-gun frigate, and the *Cumberland*, thirty guns. The *Congress* and *Merrimac* exchanged broadsides, the *Congress* receiving the full effect of the guns, while the shot bounced harmlessly off the *Merrimac*. Buchanan then turned to the *Cumberland*, rammed her, and cut a deep hole in her side. The *Cumberland* went down with guns firing to the last, and the colors flying from her tall masts. Buchanan then turned slowly back to the *Congress*, and inflicted terrible losses on her. The *Congress* finally struck her colors with the death of her commander. The Union *Minnesota* also was driven aground in the battle.

The following day, the *Merrimac* returned to do more battle and damage, but as she moved against the *Minnesota* and the other warships, confidently expecting to pick them off one by one, there appeared against her a craft as strange as herself — a vessel described as "a tin can on a shingle," the Union *Monitor*, commanded by Lieutenant John L. Worden. The two pounded each other with shell to no avail whatsoever, and the battle ended as a draw.

While it was a draw in terms of the actual sea contest between the two ships, the victory actually lay with the North, since the mere presence of the *Monitor* from this moment forward protected the great fleet of four hundred transports and supply ships carrying McClellan's forces along the coast against the South.

The i-ron *Mer-ri-mac*, with_ oth-ers at her back, Com-mand-ed by Bu-chan-oy and the Gran-dee - O, From Nor-folk start-ed out for to put us all to route, And to cap-ture lit - tle Yan-kee Doo - dle Dan - dy - O.

The iron *Merrimac*, with others at her back,
Commanded by Buchanoy and the Grandee-O,
From Norfolk started out for to put us all to route,
And to capture little Yankee Doodle Dandy-O.

The *Cumberland* went down, *Minnesoty* fast aground,
Which made the Yankee cause look quite disastee-do,
When, hark three hearty cheers, and the *Monitor* appears,
And the music struck up Yankee Doodle Dandy-O!

The rebel shot flew hot, but the Yankees answered not
Till they got within a distance neat and handy-O,
Then said Worden to his crew, "Boys, let's see what we can do,
Oh, we'll fight for little Yankee Doodle Dandy-O!"

JUDGE HAND: "That song I learned about, I should suppose 60 years ago in Elizabethtown, which is a very small village in the Adirondack Mountains, Essex County, New York, about eight miles from Lake Champlain. It was then sung by boys of my own age, a few, and I know nothing more about it than that. I think possibly it was sung by my uncle's hired man, who had been in the Civil War, but that I'm very uncertain of. I don't know where we boys picked it up."

# The *Cumberland*'s Crew

Oh, com-rades, come lis-ten and join in my dit-ty Of a ter-ri-ble bat-tle that hap-pened of late, Makes Un-ion tars shed (a) sad tear of pi-ty, When they think of the once gal-lant *Cum-ber-land's* fate; For the eighth day of March told a ter-ri-ble sto-ry, The most of our seamen to the swells bid a-dieu, Our flag it was wrapped in a man-tle of glo-ry By the he-ro-ic deeds of the *Cum-ber-land's* crew.

Oh, comrades, come listen and join in my ditty
Of a terrible battle that happened of late,
Makes Union tars shed a sad tear of pity
When they think of the once gallant *Cumberland*'s fate;

For the eighth day of March told a terrible story,
The most of our seamen to the swells bid adieu,
Our flag it was wrapped in a mantle of glory
By the heroic deeds of the *Cumberland*'s crew.

On the eighth day of March, about ten in the morning,
The sky it was cloudless and bright shone the sun,
When the drum of the *Cumberland* sounded the warning,
Which told every seaman to stand by his gun;
When an ironclad came bearing down on us,
And high in the air the rebel flag flew,
The pennant of treason soon proudly was waving,
Determined to conquer the *Cumberland* crew.

Then up steps our captain with firm resolution,
Saying, "Boys, by this monster we'll ne'er be dismayed,
Let us fight for the Union's beloved Constitution,
To die for the Union we are not afraid;
Let us fight for the Union's own cause, it is glorious,
For the stars and the stripes we will always prove true,
Let us die at our quarters or conquer victorious!"
Was answered with cheers from the *Cumberland*'s crew.

When our port we flew open, and our guns we let thunder,
Broadsides on the enemy like hail did pour,
Our seamen they stood wrapped in great wonder
When the shot struck her side and glanced harmlessly o'er.
The pride of our navy could never be daunted,
The dead and the dying our decks they did strew,
And the Star-Spangled Banner so proudly kept waving,
And stained by the blood of the *Cumberland* crew.

When traitors found cannon no longer availed them
For fighting those heroes with God on their side,
The cause of Secession no longer to quail them,
The blood of our seamen it crimsoned the tide,
She struck amidship, our planks did quiver,
Her sharp iron prow pierced our noble ship through,
And as we were sinking in the dark rolling river,
"We'll die at our guns," said the *Cumberland*'s crew.

Slowly she sank in Virginia's dark waters,
Our voices on swell shall ne'er be heard more,

May we [be] wept by *Cumberland*'s brave sons and proud daughters,
By the blood of the . . . avenged . . . Virginia's shore;
In the battle-stained river so silently sleeping,
The most of our heroes and swells bade adieu,
And the Star-Spangled Banner so proudly was waving,
Was hailed by . . . nailed to the mast by the *Cumberland*'s crew.

Columbia, the gem of the brightest communion,
No flag ever floated so proudly before,
Now while those heroes who fought for the Union,
Beneath those bright stars so exultingly soar,
When any brave heroes in battle assemble,
God bless that dear banner, the red, white, and blue,
For beneath its proud folds we'll cause tyrants to tremble,
Or die at our guns like the *Cumberland* crew.

Captain Pearl R. Nye, who recorded this for the Library of Congress in 1937, is a little forgetful, and the text — particularly in the last two stanzas — is a bit confused.

*Portrait of a child*
*found on the battlefield at Port Republic*
*by Thomas W. Timberlake, 2nd Virginia Infantry,*
*between the bodies of a Union soldier and a Confederate soldier*

## *We Are Coming, Father Abraham*

I hesitated for some time before deciding to include this and the following song in this book. There is no proof — from collectors, archives, or elsewhere — that either of the songs passed into oral folk tradition, yet it seems to me highly probable that they must have, along with the more widely known "John Brown's Body," "Dixie," and "Battle Hymn of the Republic." I include them here, therefore, to test that hypothesis, and would welcome a note from any reader indicating that either of the songs or parts of them were known in the folk manner to his grandparents, or other relatives, or their acquaintances. I think it quite possible that many "war" or "patriotic" songs such as these have been overlooked or rejected by collectors simply because the songs did not at the time fit their concept of "traditional English" folksong, and also because the songs may have seemed to be too readily at hand in print. I may be quite wrong in this; if so, I shall readily admit it.

The two songs are powerful, and must have had tremendous influence over the emotions of the North.

In the dark days of 1862, when the Union cause seemed dangerously close to disaster, Abraham Lincoln issued a call for 300,000 volunteers. James Sloane Gibbons, a New York Quaker, Abolitionist, and banker, was inspired to write one of the most famous poems of the Civil War, "We Are Coming, Father Abraham, Three Hundred Thousand More." It was printed anonymously in William Cullen Bryant's *New York Evening Post*, July 16, 1862. The poem was greeted with tremendous enthusiasm, reprinted widely, and set to music by many composers, among them Stephen Foster. Gibbons's abolitionist sympathies did not pass unnoticed by the anti-Negro element in New York. He illuminated his house in January 1863 in honor of Lincoln's Emancipation Proclamation. In July 1863, when the draft riots raged through New York, his house was one of the first to be sacked by the mob, and he and his family had to flee for their lives. The drive for volunteers was quite successful, however, and Gibbons's song undoubtedly deserves a share of the credit.

We are coming, Father Abraham, three hundred thousand more,
From Mississippi's winding stream and from New England's shore;
We leave our plows and work-shops, our wives and children dear,
With hearts too full for utterance, with but a silent tear;
We dare not look behind us but steadfastly before,
We are coming, Father Abraham, three hundred thousand more.

> We are coming, coming our Union to restore,
> We are coming, Father Abraham, three hundred thousand more.

If you look across the hilltops that meet the northern sky,
Long moving lines of rising dust your vision may descry;
And now the wind an instant, tears the cloudy veil aside,
And floats aloft our spangled flag in glory and in pride;
And bayonets in the sunlight gleam, and bands brave music pour,
We are coming, Father Abraham, three hundred thousand more.

If you look all up our valleys, where the growing harvests shine,
You may see our sturdy farmer boys fast forming into line;
And children from their mothers' knees are pulling at the weeds,
And learning how to reap and sow, against their country's needs;
And a farewell group stands weeping at every cottage door,
We are coming, Father Abraham, three hundred thousand more.

You have called us and we're coming, by Richmond's bloody tide,
To lay us down for freedom's sake, our brothers' bones beside,
Or from foul treason's savage grasp to wrench the murderous blade,
And in the face of foreign foes its fragments to parade;
Six hundred thousand loyal men and true have gone before,
We are coming, Father Abraham, three hundred thousand more.

*Union soldier from Ohio*

## *Father Abraham's Reply to the Six Hundred Thousand*

Of the many replies to "We Are Coming, Father Abraham," George F. Root's "Father Abraham's Reply to the Six Hundred Thousand" is equal in dignity and spirit to Gibbons's poem. It was published by the important and prolific firm of Root and Cady in 1862. Root, the most famous of all Civil War songwriters, also wrote "The Battle Cry of Freedom," "Just Before the Battle, Mother," and "Tramp, Tramp, Tramp, the Boys Are Marching." The figure of three hundred thousand in Gibbons's song and the six hundred thousand of Root's is a discrepancy accounted for by the fact that in the many published versions of Gibbons's work the figure varied. The poetic use of the names of the states is both moving and powerful.

*I welcome you, my gallant boys, from Maine's resounding shore,*
*From far New Hampshire's granite hills I see your legions pour;*
*From Massachusetts' fertile vales, from old Vermont they come;*
*Connecticut wheels into line at rolling of the drum,*
*And little Rhody springs to arms, like David in his might,*
*Upon rebellion's giant front to strike one blow for right,*
*One blow for right, my hero boys, for right and Uncle Sam,*
*Strike and receive the blessings of the God of Abraham.*

*'Tis glorious, 'tis glorious, to see your legions pour,*
*I welcome you, my gallant boys, six hundred thousand more!*

*I see from all her boundaries the glorious Empire State*
*A countless host is sending forth with freemen's hopes elate;*
*From Delaware there comes a gleam of white and crimson bars,*
*Where faithful hands are holding up the banner of the stars;*
*New Jersey answers to the call, as if along her shore,*
*Each grain of sand had said, we come, six hundred thousand more,*
*We come to strike for liberty, for right, and Uncle Sam,*
*Who gives us all the blessings of the God of Abraham.*

*And Pennsylvania, keystone of this glorious Union arch,*
*Is sounding through her thousand caves the thrilling order, March!*
*I see her dusky sons come forth from every darkened mine,*
*And, like the clouds along her hills, swift forming into line;*
*Their eyes have such a fiery gleam from glowing forges caught,*
*Their arms such strength as if they were of iron sinews wrought;*
*I think, when on Secession's head they strike for Uncle Sam,*
*Each blow will fall like vengeance from the God of Abraham.*

*I see a-down our Western vales your legions pour, my boys;*
*Ohio, Indiana, and my own loved Illinois,*
*And Iowa and Michigan and Minnesota, too,*
*And far Wisconsin's prairies send their heroes tried and true.*
*Come on, oh, living avalanche! break into floods of light,*
*And roll your waves of truth along Secession's shores of night;*
*Drown out rebellion, as of old, and then with Uncle Sam,*
*Safe in the Ark of State, we'll praise the God of Abraham.*

## *Mademoiselle from Armentières*

This World War I song is based on the earlier British "Skiboo." As "Mademoiselle from Armentières," however, it came into being with the British at Armentières itself in 1915, was subsequently taken over by American troops, sung by them during the War, and continued to be popular with them on their return to America in A.E.F. and American Legion gatherings.

Like "The Old Chisolm Trail" and some of the sea shanties, "Mademoiselle from Armentières" is a song into which one can throw any likely or unlikely stanza at will or at random. It is a marching or cadence song and was shouted out by both British and American troops as they trained in England and in France, before moving up into the lines and the hell of the Meuse, the Somme, the Argonne, Ypres, Château-Thierry, Belleau Wood, and the other names of death in France. It was a cocky, thumb-nosing song. The end might be around the corner, but in the meantime . . .

The English are a funny race,
  Parlez-vous,
The English are a funny race,
  Parlez-vous,
They fight like hell 'till half past three
And then knock off for a cup of tea,
  Hinky-dinky parlez-vous.

Oh, farmer, have you a daughter fair,
Who can wash a soldier's underwear?

Oh, Mademoiselle from Armentières,
She hasn't been kissed in forty years.

The M.P.s say they won the war,
Standing on guard at a café door.

Oh, Colonel Jinx was a hell of a guy,
He stayed in Toul while his men
  marched by.

Mademoiselle is as bright as a jewel,
She knows some things not taught in
  school.

The General won the Croix de Guerre,
  Parlez-vous,
The General won the Croix de Guerre,
  Parlez-vous,
The General won the Croix de Guerre,
But the son of a bitch wasn't even there,
  Hinky-dinky parlez-vous.

Mademoiselle from Armentières,
She ain't even heard of underwear.

The officers get the pie and cake,
And all we get is the belly ache.

When we're mustered out we'll tell
The regular army to *go to hell!*

She might have been young for all we
  know
When Napoleon flopped at Waterloo.

There are more than a million married
  men
Who want to go back to France again.

The ration cart comes up each day,
We get what the officers throw away.

The captain he's carrying the pack,
Hope to the Lord it breaks his back.

'Twas a hell of a war, as we recall,
　Parlez-vous,
'Twas a hell of a war, as we recall,
　Parlez-vous,
'Twas a hell of a war, as we recall,
But still, 'twas better than none at all.
　Hinky-dinky parlez-vous.

You might forget the gas and shell,
　Parlez-vous,
You might forget the gas and shell,
　Parlez-vous,
You might forget the gas and shell,
But you'll never forget the mademoi-
　selle.
　Hinky-dinky parlez-vous.

# 28.

# Sea Shanties

T here are four distinct types of shanties, each — by virtue of beat and tempo, shantyman's line and sailors' chorus — geared to special work aboard the merchant sailing ships.*

The *capstan* or *windlass shanty* ("Amsterdam Maid," "Shenandoah," "Rolling Home") was lengthy and employed chiefly to weigh anchor, to warp the ship from one berth to another in port, and also, as necessary, to load and unload cargo. The shantyman sat on the capstan head or stood to one side on the deck, and the sailors, pushing on the capstan bars, turned the capstan slowly to the rhythmic beat of the song. The capstan shanties

* Shanties were never used in the Navy. Silence aboard a man of war was essential in order to hear commands, and meant the difference between life and death when moving into battle. Tight discipline, constant drill, and spoken, cadenced commands took the place of shanties.

were the most tuneful and, in general, the shanties which maintained the strongest story line or central theme.

The *halyard* or *long-haul shanty* ("Blow, Boys, Blow," "Roll, *Alabama*, Roll") was used with any heavy work demanding a long pull, such as the hoisting of a yard or heavy sail. These shanties were also lengthy because of the nature of the work, but unlike the steady marching-tempo of the capstan shanties, emphasized two heavily accented beats in the chorus lines of each stanza when the men pulled in unison on the rope, resting briefly between pulls and waiting for the next beat.

The *short-haul shanty* ("Paddy Doyle," "Haul the Bowline"), on the other hand, had only one accented beat and pull, coming with the last word of each stanza, and was a very brief shanty used only when a short and hard pull was needed — for bunting up a sail when furling it, or for hauling aft the foresheet.

The last type of shanty was the *walkaway, stamp-and-go,* or *hand-over-hand*. Its use as a hand-over-hand shanty was restricted to the unbroken hand-over-hand hoisting of a light sail by two or three men who sang the shanty in unison, pulling steadily on the rope, much as landsmen might do in the hoisting of a bucket from a well. As a walkaway or stamp-and-go shanty, its use was limited to the cleaning of barnacles and weed from the ship's bottom when at sea. A rope or "purchase" thrown over the stern of the ship was held by men on each side of the deck, and as they marched forward scraping the bottom with the rope, they sang the walkaway in unison. The best-known walkaway or hand-over-hand was "The Drunken Sailor."

The Library of Congress has issued two long-playing records (L26 and L27) of "American Sea Songs and Shanties," containing some twenty shanties representing the four types. All of the songs on these two records are sung, without exception, by men who used them in the days of sail. These men have since died, and in the near future — if not already — there will be no man living who actually used these songs in the traditional folk manner within a folk industry. The days of sail are gone, and with them the men who sailed the great ships. There have been excellent book collections of the shanties, to be sure, and a record of them in that form will always be preserved. But there have been few actual recordings made of the men themselves singing these songs. I believe these two records are the first such to have been presented to the public. The Library of Congress also, very happily, has other recordings in its Archives, so that our loss of the past is not a total one.

It is most fortunate — for one reason alone — that this is the case: our awareness of the true tempo of the songs. When one now hears these songs over the radio, on TV, from a hopped-up singer with an electric guitar, or from a professional choral group, one hears them in a thoroughly falsified fashion. The tempo is too fast:

> *InAmsterdamtherelived a maid*
> *Andshewasmistress ofher trade*

This is nonsense. The men sang it at the capstan:

> *In Am ster*
>           dam
> *there lived*
>       *a*
>          maid
> *And*
>    *she*
>      *was*
>        mis   *tress*
> *of her*
>    trade

This tempo is true to the tradition, and any faster tempo is false. The shanties were work songs, and the work was slow and arduous. The work would have been impossible at a faster tempo. Richard Maitland, Captain Leighton Robinson, Noble Brown, and others on these records set us straight in this respect. And in doing so, they lend dignity and power to the songs, recovering them from the bastardization of footlights, and returning them to the tremendous seas of yesterday. The voices of the men may be tired and edging toward the grave, but the spirit, thank God, is true. I recommend that you listen to them — with considerable humility, and pride.

There is dispute over the origin of the word "shanty." Some suggest that it comes from the French *chanter* and, specifically, from the imperative "chantez!" as ordered by the mate or other officer to beef up work with song. Others suggest that it comes from the lumberjack tradition and refers to the shanties in which the men lived, relaxed, sang. "That's a shanty song. . . ." It is possible that it stems from both, and that the use of the one reinforced the other. Let us let it go at that. One thing, however, is certain: the pronunciation was always *sh* as in *shanty* and never *ch* as in English *chant*. The *chantey* spelling is written and bookish; it was never the spoken language of the ships.

# Capstan Shanties

## A-Roving, or the Amsterdam Maid

"A-Roving," or "The Amsterdam Maid," is perhaps the oldest of the great capstan shanties, going back in time at least to 1630, when it appeared in Thomas Heywood's *Rape of Lucrece* as performed on the London stage. At its point of origin, it was probably not a shanty, but a shore song whose rhythm, however, lent itself to immediate adaptation at sea. The shanty recounts shore-leave love in some detail, and stanzas (as in many other shanties also) were rough and bawdy. Some are included here that do not appear on the Library of Congress record issued for general sale.

In Amsterdam there lived a maid,
And she was a mistress of her trade,
I'll go no more a-roving with you, fair maid.

*For a-roving, a-roving, since roving's been my ruin,*
*I'll go no more a-roving with you, fair maid.*

Her eyes were like twin stars at night,
And her cheeks they rivalled the roses red,
I'll go no more a-roving with you, fair maid.

*For a-roving, a-roving, since roving's been my ruin,*
*I'll go no more a-roving with you, fair maid.*

I asked this fair maid where she lived,
She rooms up on Skidamsky Dyke,
I'll go no more a-roving with you, fair maid.

I took this fair maid for a walk,
For I liked to hear her loving talk.

I placed my hand upon her knee,
Says she, "Young man, you're getting free."

I placed my hand upon her thigh,
Says she, "Young man, you're rather high."

443

I placed my hand upon her thatch,
Says she, "Young man, that's my main hatch."

I placed my hand upon her breast,
And now, my boys, you know the rest.

This last six months I've been to sea,
And, boys, this gal looked good to me.

In three weeks time I was badly bent,*
And then to sea I sadly went.

On a red hot Yank bound 'round Cape Horn,
My clothes and boots were in the pawn,
I'll go no more a-roving with you, fair maid.

*For a-roving, a-roving, since roving's been my ruin,
I'll go no more a-roving with you, fair maid.*

* "Bent": slang, equivalent to present-day "broke."

## Shenandoah

American sailors pronounced it "Shanandore," and it is perhaps the loveliest — if one may use that word to the men of these ships — of all the capstan shanties. Its origin is in doubt, but it probably was a shore song first (out of the Canadian-American voyageur tradition or from Ohio River boatmen), drifted to the sea as a forecastle song, and then gradually came above decks to become the hauntingly greatest of all capstan shanties. It was sung on English as well as American ships, and the stanzas — as in all other shanties — differ from variant to variant.

Oh, Shen - an-doah's my na-tive val-ley,_____ A - a - way,_____ you rol-lin' riv-er! Shen - an - doah is my na-tive val-ley, Ah - way, we're bound to go 'cross the wide Mis - sou - ri.

Oh, Shenandoah's my native valley,
    Away, you rolling river!
Oh, Shenandoah's my native valley,
    Away, we're bound to go
'Cross the wide Missouri!

Oh, Shenandoah, it's far I wander,
    Away, you rolling river!
Oh, Shenandoah, it's far I wander,
    Away, we're bound to go
'Cross the wide Missouri!

*445*

Oh, Shenandoah has rushing waters,
  Away, you rolling river!
Oh, Shenandoah has rushing waters,
  Away, we're bound to go
  'Cross the wide Missouri!

Oh, Shenandoah, I love your daughters,
  Away, you rolling river!
Oh, Shenandoah, I love your daughters,
  Away, we're bound to go
  'Cross the wide Missouri!

Oh, Shenandoah, I long to see you,
  Away, you rolling river!
Oh, Shenandoah, I long to see you,
  Away, we're bound to go
  'Cross the wide Missouri!

Oh, Shenandoah, I'm bound to leave you,
  Away, you rolling river!
Oh, Shenandoah, I'm bound to leave you,
  Away, we're bound to go
  'Cross the wide Missouri!

Oh, Shenandoah, I'll never grieve you,
  Away, you rolling river!
Oh, Shenandoah, I'll never grieve you,
  Away, we're bound to go
  'Cross the wide Missouri!

## Rio Grande

"Rio Grande" is one of the great outward-bound capstan shanties, sung as the men were heaving up the anchor prior to leaving for the outward voyage. The Rio Grande referred to is not the Texas-Mexican river, but the port of Rio Grande do Sul in Brazil, a favorite with sailors the world over. And the pronunciation is not Ree-o Grand-eh, but the sailors' straightaway Rye-o Grand.

Oh, Rio Grande lies far away,
    'Way Rio!
Oh, Rio Grande lies far away,
    And we're bound for the Rio Grande.

*And away Rio,*
*It's away Rio!*

*Sing fare you well, my bonny young girl,*
*And we're bound for the Rio Grande.*

I thought I heard our old man say,
    'Way Rio!
I thought I heard our old man say,
    And we're bound for the Rio Grande.

Two dollars a day is the sailor's pay,
    'Way Rio!
Two dollars a day is the sailor's pay,
    And we're bound for the Rio Grande.

So it's pack up your donkey and get under way,
    'Way Rio!
So it's pack up your donkey and get under way,
    And we're bound for the Rio Grande.

Oh, I left my old woman a month's half pay,
    'Way Rio!
Oh, I left my old woman a month's half pay,
    And we're bound for the Rio Grande.

So heave up your anchor, away we must go,
    'Way Rio!
So heave up your anchor, away we must go,
    And we're bound for the Rio Grande.

*And away Rio,*
*It's away Rio!*
*Sing fare you well, my bonny young girl,*
*And we're bound for the Rio Grande.*

## *Rolling Home*

Although this song is sometimes classified as a forecastle song and not a shanty, the words of the opening stanza indicate the specific capstan shanty use to which "Rolling Home" was also put. Captain Robinson's " 'Vast heaving!" at the end bears this out also. "Rolling Home" was the sailors' farewell to the foreign shores they were leaving for the homeward voyage, often sung on British vessels bound from Australia to England, but easily adapted by American sailormen to their own land — with the substitution for "old England" of "New England," "old 'Frisco," and "New York City."

Pipe all hands to man the windlass,
See our cable run down clear,
As we heave away our anchor,
For old England's shores we'll steer.

*Rolling home, rolling home,*
*Rolling home across the sea,*
*Rolling home to merry England,*
*Rolling home, dear land, to thee.*

Man your bars, heave with a will, lads,
Every hand that can clap on,
As we heave away our anchor,
We will sing this well known song.

*Rolling home, rolling home,*
*Rolling home across the sea,*
*Rolling home to merry England,*
*Rolling home, dear land, to thee.*

Fare you well, Australia's daughters,
Fare you well, sweet foreign shore,
For we're bound across the waters,
Homeward bound again once more.

Up aloft amongst the rigging,
Where the stormy winds do blow,
Oh, the waves as they rush past us
Seem to murmur as they go.

Twice ten thousand miles before us,
Twice ten thousand miles we've gone,
Oh, the girls in dear old England
Gaily call us way along.

*Rolling home, rolling home,*
*Rolling home across the sea,*
*Rolling home to merry England,*
*Rolling home, dear land, to thee.*

### 'VAST HEAVING!

## *Homeward Bound, or Goodbye, Fare You Well*

This capstan shanty is another homeward-bounder. Originally English, it becomes, with changes of place, American, and was beloved of sailors on both sides of the Atlantic. Richard Terry in *The Shanty Book* (London, 1921–1926) says that "so strongly did its sentiment appeal to sailors that one never heard the shantyman extemporize a coarse verse to it."

We're homeward bound, I hear them say,
    Goodbye, fare you well, goodbye, fare you well,
We're homeward bound, I hear them say,
    Hurrah! my boys, we're homeward bound.

We're homeward bound this very day,
    Goodbye, fare you well, goodbye, fare you well,
We're homeward bound this very day,
    Hurrah! my boys, we're homeward bound.

We're homeward bound for 'Frisco town,
    Goodbye, fare you well, goodbye, fare you well,
We're homeward bound for 'Frisco town,
    Hurrah! my boys, we're homeward bound.

Oh, heave away, she's up and down.

Those 'Frisco girls, they've got us in tow.

And it's goodbye to Katie and goodnight to Nell.

Oh, it's goodbye again and fare you well.

And now I hear our first mate say.

Her anchor, boys, we soon will see.

We're homeward bound, 'tis a joyous sound.

I thought I heard our old man say,
  Goodbye, fare you well, goodbye, fare you well,
I thought I heard our old man say,
  Hurrah! my boys, we're homeward bound.

Oh, 'Frisco Bay in three months and a day,
  Goodbye, fare you well, goodbye, fare you well,
Oh, 'Frisco Bay in three months and a day,
  Hurrah! my boys, we're homeward bound.

We've got the fluke at last in sight,
  Goodbye, fare you well, goodbye, fare you well,
We've got the fluke at last in sight,
  Hurrah! my boys, we're homeward bound.

### 'VAST HEAVING!

# Halyard Shanties

## The Dead Horse

The "dead horse" in this halyard shanty was the thirty-day advance in wages which the men received before sailing on a long voyage. It was spent in short order paying off the boardinghouse master, buying sea clothes, or carousing in the taverns. Not a penny of it saw the ship. Until this advance had been paid off, the sailor touched no cash and earned no money for the future. He was simply working off a debt and paying for "a dead horse." When the thirty-day "dead horse" period was over, the horse was buried with seagoing ceremony, and the captain, in honor of the occasion and to cheer the crew, usually issued grog. Captain Leighton Robinson, who sang for the recording transcribed here, introduces the song:

They would get a tar barrel and get "Chips" to make a horse's head to it, and put a tar brush in the stern of it and for a tail . . . and then they would mount it on this thing [a sort of cart], and generally the shantyman would get astride of it and, as I say, it being fine weather, why they'd start and pull this thing along the deck. And then the shantyman would sing the song, what they called "Poor Old Man" or "The Burying of the Dead Horse." Having worked up thirty days, why, then the next day they were going on pay. They were really earning some money then. 'Course they'd be into the slopchest probably for a few beans, but at the same time they'd feel that they'd begun to earn their money. And this is the way that that went. . . .

Poor old man came riding along, And we say so, and we hope so, — A poor old man comes riding along, Oh, poor old man.

Poor old man came riding along,
   And we say so, and we hope so,
A poor old man comes riding along,
   Oh, poor old man.

Poor old man, your horse he must die,
   And we say so, and we hope so,
Poor old man, your horse he must die,
   Oh, poor old man.

Thirty days have come and gone.

Now we are on a good month's pay.

I think I hear our old man say.

Give them grog for the thirtieth day.

Up aloft to the main yard arm.

Cut him adrift, and he'll do no harm.
   Oh, we say so, and we hope so,
Cut him adrift, and he'll do no harm,
   Oh, poor old man.

## Captain Robinson adds:

   I might explain to you that we hoisted him up to the main yard arm, and then there was a fellow up there . . . we generally used the clew garnet, you know, just to hoist him up there, we had to put a strop around the barrell . . . and then they would just cut him adrift. And then you'd see this old thing floating astern.

## *Blow, Boys, Blow*

Both William M. Doerflinger and Joanna C. Colcord, two of the major collectors of shanties, are in agreement that this great halyard shanty is purely American in origin, and came into being during the days of the North Atlantic packet trade with Liverpool, shortly after the War of 1812. There is pride in the Yankee ship and its flag ("the stars and bars" were synonymous then with "stars and stripes"); there are the derisive comments about the skipper, the chief mate, and the food; there are the oft-stated hopes for fair winds during the long, long voyages; and there is the realistic play on words in the matter of blowing ashore and blowing hard-earned pay. It is a rousing song and was immensely popular.

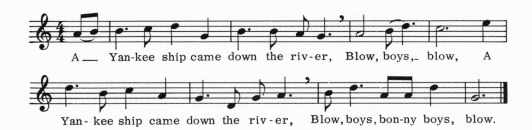

A Yankee ship came down the river,
    Blow, boys, blow,
A Yankee ship came down the river,
    Blow, boys, bonny boys, blow.

And how do you know she's a Yankee clipper?
    Blow, boys, blow,
Oh, how do you know she's a Yankee clipper?
    Blow, boys, bonny boys, blow.

The stars and bars they flew behind her,
The stars and bars they flew behind her.

And who do you think was the skipper of her?
A blue-nosed Nova Scotia hardcase.

And who do you think was the chief mate of her?
A loud-mouthed disbarred Boston lawyer.

And what do you think we had for breakfast?
The starboard side of an old sou'wester.

And what do you think we had for dinner?
We had monkey's heart and shark's liver.

Can you guess what we had for supper?
We had strong salt junk and weak tea water.

Then blow us out and blow us homeward,
Oh, blow today and blow tomorrow.

Blow fair and steady, mild and pleasant,
Oh, blow us into Boston harbor.

We'll blow ashore and blow our pay day,
Then blow aboard and blow away.

We'll blow until our blow is over,
    Blow boys, blow,
From Singapore to Cliffs of Dover,
    Blow boys, bonny boys, blow.

# *Roll, Alabama, Roll!*

This halyard or long-haul shanty is one of the few shanties celebrating or commemorating an historical event. (The majority of the shanties deal with the sailor's life on shore or at sea, and generally relate directly to his work, and often very specifically to the work immediately at hand.) The Confederate cruiser *Alabama* was built by William and Jonathan Laird in the yards of the Birkenhead Iron Works at Liverpool and launched on May 15, 1862. She sailed down the Mersey and to the Azores, which were called by sailors the "Western" or "Westward Islands." At Fayal she was clandestinely fitted out and armed. During the next two years the *Alabama* sank, burned, and otherwise destroyed all "Federal comers" that came her way, that is, some seventy unarmed merchant vessels, including returning whalers totally unaware that any war was going on.

Early in the summer of 1864, Captain Raphael Semmes, CSN, docked the *Alabama* at Cherbourg for repairs. Its arrival there was reported, and the United States sloop of war, *Kearsarge*, Captain Winslow commanding, proceeded to Cherbourg and waited outside the harbor for the *Alabama*. Semmes, not dodging the issue, sent Winslow a message challenging him to a fight (the shanty has it the other way around). News of the impending battle reached both Paris and London, and fashionable French sightseers came to watch the battle from the Cherbourg cliffs, while pleasure yachts brought the English over. (An excellent excuse for an outing!) The battle took place on Sunday, June 19, 1864. It lasted forty minutes, when the *Alabama* began taking water, and Semmes struck his colors. The British yacht *Deerhound* rescued Semmes and some forty of his officers and men and landed them at Southampton, rescuing them not only from the sea but from the *Kearsarge* as well. This violation of neutrality further inflamed American bitterness over England's role in the matter of the *Alabama*, a bitterness that was not settled until 1872, when a tribunal adjudicated the so-called "*Alabama* claims," finding against England and awarding the United States $15,500,000 in damages.

When the *Alabama*'s keel was laid,
    Roll, *Alabama*, roll!
They laid the keel at Birkenhead,
    Oh, roll, *Alabama*, roll!

She was built in the yard of Jonathan Laird,
    Roll, *Alabama*, roll!
She was built in the yard at Birkenhead,
    Oh, roll, *Alabama*, roll!

And away down the Mersey she sailed one day,
    Roll, *Alabama*, roll!
And across to the Westward she ploughed her way,
    Oh, roll, *Alabama*, roll!

'Twas at the island of Fayal,
    Roll, *Alabama*, roll!
Where she got her guns and crew on board,
    Oh, roll, *Alabama*, roll!

Then away cross the watery world,
    Roll, *Alabama*, roll!
To sink, to burn, and to destroy,
    Oh, roll, *Alabama*, roll!

All the Federal comers that came her way,
    Roll, *Alabama*, roll!
'Twas in the harbor of Cherbourg one day,
    Oh, roll, *Alabama*, roll!

There the little *Kearsarge* she did lay,
    Roll, *Alabama*, roll!
When Semmes and Winslow made the shore,
    Oh, roll, *Alabama*, roll!

Winslow challenged Semmes out to sea,
    Roll, *Alabama*, roll!
He couldn't refuse, there was too many around,
    Oh, roll, *Alabama*, roll!

Three miles outside of Cherbourg,
    Roll, *Alabama*, roll!
There the *Kearsarge* sunk her down below,
    Oh, roll, *Alabama*, roll!

## Hanging Johnny

In *A Sailor's Garland* John Masefield said of the halyard shanty "Hanging Johnny":

It has a melancholy tune that is one of the saddest things I have ever heard. I heard it for the first time off the Horn, in a snowstorm, when we were hoisting topsails after heavy weather. There was a heavy, grey sea running and the decks were awash. The skies were sodden and oily, shutting in the sea about a quarter of a mile away. Some birds were flying about us, screaming.

I thought at the time that it was the whole scene set to music. I cannot repeat those words to their melancholy wavering music without seeing the line of yellow oilskins, the wet deck, the frozen ropes, and the great grey seas running up into the sky.

Oh, they call me Hang-in' John-ny,— A - way,— John-ny,— Oh, they call me Hang-in' John-ny,— Oh, hang, boys,— hang.

Oh, they call me Hangin' Johnny,
   Away, Johnny,
Oh, they call me Hangin' Johnny,
   Oh, hang, boys, hang.

And they said I hanged me daddy,
   Away, Johnny,
And they said I hanged me daddy,
   Oh, hang, boys, hang.

Me daddy and me mammy,
   Away, Johnny,

Me daddy and me mammy,
　Oh, hang, boys, hang.

And they say I hanged for money,
　Away, Johnny,
And they say I hanged for money,
　Oh, hang, boys, hang.

But I never hanged nobody,
　Away, Johnny,
But I never hanged nobody,
　Oh, hang, boys, hang.

Oh, we'll hang and swing together,
　Away, Johnny,
Oh, we'll hang and swing together,
　Oh, hang, boys, hang.

Oh, we'll hang for better weather,
　Away, Johnny,
Oh, we'll hang for better weather,
　Oh, hang, boys, hang.

*Astride a yard on the bark* Garthsnaid:
*furling a sail*

# Short-Haul Shanties

## Paddy Doyle

This short-haul shanty was used, as the singer, Richard Maitland, indicates, solely for the purpose of bunting up a sail when furling it. Colcord says that the song was sung in chorus from the beginning "through the last syllable, when all hands gave a tremendous lift to the heavy roll of canvas to get it on top of the yard, being simply a yell." Paddy Doyle, for whom the song is named, was a Liverpool boardinghouse master, and the "*poor* Paddy Doyle" is heavy satire, since it was the poor sailor who suffered at the hands of the boardinghouse masters, generally known around the world for their selfish and grasping natures. Colcord reports that Paddy Doyle kept a cow's horn in the back yard, round which he solemnly marched "green hands," so as to be able to tell a doubting skipper that they had "been three times around the Horn!" The boardinghouse masters sold boots and clothes to the men (advanced out of their pay), and often sold the men (many of them shanghaied) at so much a head to the mates and skippers.

As Maitland explains on the record: "Now this is a song that's just used in the one place . . . on the . . . when the men are all together on the yards, one of the lower yards . . . they call it the main or foreyard . . . and they're rolling up the sail. They get the sail all ready for one big bowsing up, and the man in the bunt will sing . . .

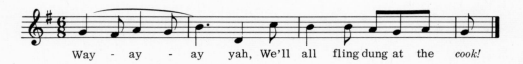

Way - ay - ay yah, We'll all fling dung at the cook!

> *Way ay ay yah,*
> *We'll all fling dung at the* cook!

"With that last word, 'cook,' all hands gives a bowse on it, and that hauls the sail up . . . but you'll never get it up with one pull, so the man sings out then . . .

> *Way ay ay yah,*
> *Who sold poor Paddy Doyle's* boots?

"And another pull. Well, if it isn't satisfactory, if you want one more . . .

> *Way ay ay yah,*
> *We'll all go down and hang the* cook.

"Well, if the sail is bowsed up, that's all there is to be said about it . . . but there's never any more than about six verses to that same song."

## *Haul the Bowline*

This is the oldest known short-haul shanty and, according to John Mase-field, goes back to the days of Henry VIII. Its age is proven by the text itself, since the "bowline" as a term on sailing vessels has not been used since the late sixteenth or early seventeenth century. At that time, the bowline was the equivalent of the present-day foresheet, and the latter-day use of the bow-line shanty with respect to the foresheet is clearly described by Frederick P. Harlow:

The topsails having been set, the ship once more heeled over in her accustomed manner, and by dropping and hauling aft the sheet of the foresail she carried about as much sail as she wanted. Here Brooks brought out another old-timer [shanty] when the sail refused to flatten with our combined effort. All hands available strung forward, along the deck, with feet braced and arms extended, our calloused hands gripping the foresheet awaiting the final word of the chorus, in which all hands give one sudden strong pull while singing "Haul the bowline, the bowline, haul!" This chantey is sung by the chanteyman without a pull from anyone until the final word of the chorus *"Haul!"* Then everyone pulls his mightiest and the clew of the sails comes down foot by foot, until the mate sings out, "Belay! That'll do the foresheet!"

Richard Maitland: "Now this is a short song that's usually used in pulling aft a sheet or hauling down a tack."

Haul the bowline, the long-tailed bowline,
Haul the bowline, the bowline, *haul!*

Haul the bowline, Kitty, oh, my darling,
Haul the bowline, the bowline, *haul!*

Haul the bowline, we'll haul and haul together,
Haul the bowline, the bowline, *haul!*

Haul the bowline, we'll haul for better weather,
Haul the bowline, the bowline, *haul!*

Haul the bowline, we'll bust, we'll break or bend her,
Haul the bowline, the bowline, *haul!*

# *Walkaway,*
# *or Stamp-and-Go Shanty*

## *The Drunken Sailor*

The special use for this walkaway shanty is clearly described by Richard Maitland. Because the men stamped on the deck with the words "Way hey and up she rises," it was also known as a stamp-and-go shanty.

Now this is a song that's usually sung when men are walking away with the slack of a rope, generally when the iron ships are scrubbing their bottom. After an iron ship has been twelve months at sea, there's a quite a lot of barnicles and grass grows onto her bottom. And generally in the calm latitudes, up in the horse latitudes in the North Atlantic Ocean, usually they rig up a purchase for to scrub the bottom. You can't do it when the ship is going over three miles an hour, but less than that, of course, you can do so. But it all means a considerable walking, not much labor, but all walking. And they have a song called "The Drunken Sailor" that comes in for that.

Now what shall we do with the drunken sailor,
What shall we do with the drunken sailor,
What shall we do with the drunken sailor
Early in the morning?

Oh, chuck him in the long boat till he gets sober,
Chuck him in the long boat till he gets sober,
Chuck him in the long boat till he gets sober
Early in the morning.

Ay hey and up she rises,
Ay hey and up she rises,
Ay hey and up she rises
Early in the morning.

Oh, what shall we do with the drunken soldier,
What shall we do with the drunken soldier,
What shall we do with the drunken soldier
Early in the morning?

Oh, put him in the guardhouse and make him bail her,
Put him in the guardhouse till he gets sober,
Put him in the guardhouse till he gets sober
Early in the morning.

Way hey and up she rises,
Way hey and up she rises,
Way hey and up she rises
Early in the morning.

Oh, here we are nice and sober,
Here we are nice and sober,
Here we are nice and sober
Early in the morning.

Oh, way hey and up she rises,
Way hey and up she rises,
Way hey and up she rises
Early in the morning.

# Forecastle Songs

With the work done, men relaxed in the forecastle and there (on occasion at least) sang songs unrelated to their work. They did so also on shore. These songs might be of any kind — ballads of love and disaster, hymns, sea songs, the popular tunes of the day. A forecastle song might be sung by one man or by a few or the entire group, depending upon the song. It might have to do with the sea, or have nothing to do with it. The three here, by virtue of the fact that the sea is under consideration, do deal with the sea. The first was certainly sung by the group, the below-decks "shantyman" giving out with the stanza and the rest coming in with the chorus. It is an "Alphabet Song" of the sea, comparable to other such "alphabet songs" of lumbermen and soldiers.

## The Sailor's Alphabet

So mer-ry, so mer-ry, so mer-ry are we, No mor-tal on earth's like a sail-or at sea, So mer-ry are we as we're sail-ing a-long, Give a sail-or his grog and then noth-ing goes wrong.

*So merry, so merry, so merry are we,*
*No mortal on earth's like a sailor at sea,*
*So merry are we as we're sailing along,*
*Give a sailor his grog and then nothing goes wrong.*

Oh, A is the anchor and that you all know,
B is the bowsprit that's over the bow,
C is the capstan with which we heave 'round,
And D are the decks where our sailors are found.

Oh, E is the ensign our mizzen-peak flew,
F is the fo'c'sle where we muster our crew,
G are the guns, sir, by which we all stand,
And H are the halyards that oft-times are manned.

Oh, I is the iron of our stunsail boom sheet,
J is the jib that oft weathers the bleat,
K is the keelson away down below,
And L are the lanyards that give us good hold.

M is our mainmast so stout and so strong,
N is the needle that never points wrong,
O are the oars of our jollyboat's crew,
And P is the pennant of red, white, and blue.

Q is the quarterdeck where our captain oft stood,
R is the rigging that ever holds good,
S are the stilliards that weigh out our beef,
And T are the topsails we oft-times do reef.

Oh, U is the Union at which none dare laugh,
V are the vangs that steady the gaff,
W's the wheel that we all take in time,
And X is the letter for which we've no rhyme.

Oh, Y are the yards that we oft-times do brace,
Z is the letter for which we've no place,
The bo'sun pipes grog, so we'll all go below,
My song it is finished, I'm glad that it's so.

## The Loss of the New Columbia

This ballad of sea disaster from Maine is unique in that there appears to be no other collection or record of it. It comes from the extraordinary repertoire of Mrs. Carrie Grover of Gorham, Maine, who recorded over eighty traditional songs and ballads — chiefly of the sea and New England — for the Library of Congress. The ballad is factual, down to the date of sailing from Liverpool and the eyewitness account of the wreck and mangled bodies, but I have been unable to find a record of the disaster on the New England coast. It is most certainly Maine in origin and must also have been sung in the forecastle of some ship at one time or another.

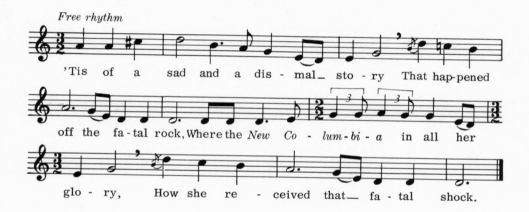

'Tis of a sad and a dis-mal sto-ry That hap-pened off the fa-tal rock, Where the *New Co-lum-bi-a* in all her glo-ry, How she re-ceived that fa-tal shock.

'Tis of a sad and a dismal story
That happened off the fatal rock,
Where the *New Columbia* in all her glory,
How she received that fatal shock.

We sailed from England in December,
From Liverpool the 18th day,
And many hardships we endured
While coming to Americay.

Two passengers from Pence came with us,
Two brothers were from Birmingham,
They took the leave of all their people
To settle in New Eng-e-land.

We anchored in four fathoms water,
Thinking all of our lives to save,
But 'twas all in vain for shortly after —
Poor souls they met a watery grave.

Our ship she dragged away her anchor
And on a rock she split in two,
And out of eighty brave young seamen,
They all were lost excepting two.

Our captain he being long afflicted,
Sick in his cabin said to his mate,
"Bring me on deck, that's my desire,
Where I may meet my unhappy fate."

He looked all 'round with eyes surrender,
He took the leave of all his crew,
He gave his papers unto his servant,
Who chanced to be one of the two.

What was most shocking early next morning
Was to see the shores all lined along
With bodies of these shipwrecked sailors,
To the *New Columbia* did belong.

Their flesh was mangled all to pieces,
Grinding upon the rocks on shore,
'Twould melt the hardest heart to pity
To see them lying in their gore.

They were all taken and decently buried,
Most melancholy to relate,
To see so many brave young seamen
All meet with such an unhappy fate.

May God protect all absent seamen,
While plowing o'er the distant main,
And keep them clear from rocks and danger,
And safe return them home again.

May God protect all absent seamen,
The mother- and the fatherless,
And send his blessing on these poor people
Who have lost their sons in such distress.

## Captain Ward and the Rainbow

Captain Ward was a real person about whom little is known except that he was a freebooter during the reign of James I of England. He preyed principally upon French and Spanish shipping, attacked three English ships during his career, and, sympathetic to the Scots, left their ships quite alone. Captain Ward admitted to being on the wrong side of the law and attempted to gain a pardon from the king through payment of sums varying from two to ten thousand pounds. The king refused to consider these offers, and Ward was ultimately captured and hanged in chains between low-water and high-water marks beside the river Thames. The traditional versions of the ballad in America omit the end of the story, closing instead with Ward's victory over the *Rainbow*. The taunt of defiance at the end was naturally popular in America, where the ballad appeared in broadside form about 1785.

"Go home, go home!" cries Captain Ward, "and tell your king from me, That if he reigns king upon the land, I will reign king at sea."

Our King built a ship, 'twas a ship of great fame,
The *Rainbow* she was called, and the *Rainbow* was her name;
He rigged her and fitted her and sent her off to sea,
With five hundred bold mariners to bear her company.

She cruised the blue waves over and sailed on many a lee;
At length a wicked pirate we chanced for to see;

He bore right down upon her, and hailed in the King's name,
We knew it was a pirate ship, a pirate of great fame.

"We've got you now, you cowardly dog, you ugly, lying thief!
What makes you rob and plunder, and keep your King in grief?"
"You lie, you lie," cries Captain Ward, "such things can never be,
I've never robbed an English ship, an English ship but three."

Our guns we trained upon her, as everyone might see,
"We'll take you back to England and hanged you shall be,
Or fill your ship with shot and shell, and sink you in the sea."

"Fire on! Fire on!" cries Captain Ward, "I value you not a pin,
If you are brass on the outside, I am good steel within."

They fought from six that morning till six o'clock at night,
And then the gallant *Rainbow* began to take her flight.
"Go home! Go home!" cries Captain Ward, "and tell your King from me,
That if he reigns king upon the land, I will reign king at sea."

# 29.

# Cow-Country Songs

These songs are representative of the cowboy and cow-country West. There are, of course, others that could be added to these to make a selection of twenty-five or fifty. But any group of fifty songs would have to include all of these, and any other strict selection of a dozen songs would have to include at least ten of them. (Another editor, for example, might have wished to substitute "Utah Carroll," "Mustang Gray," "The Strawberry Roan," "Billy Venero," or "The Zebra Dun" for "Little Joe, the Wrangler," but he would have had to wrestle with his aesthetic judgment to do so, even admitting that the others might be equal in popular folk acceptance and distribution. Some were, some were not. "Little Joe," for me, reflects more of the actual life of the cowboy than any of those others which might have been substituted. "Little Joe" also has a tighter and more readily believable dramatic story.)

A solid reading of these texts adds greatly to any knowledge one may already have of cowboy life, and, if one has none, will serve as a good introduction to it.

The songs are to be read slowly and sung slowly. No cowboy song was ever sung at a trot or gallop. They were sung at an ambling walk, slow and soothing.

## The Old Chisholm Trail

In keeping with the creak and smell of saddle leather is "The Chisholm Trail." The trail itself extended from the Washita in the Indian Territory of Oklahoma north toward Abilene and was never in Texas, but joined the long Eastern Trail of that state at the Oklahoma boundary. Popularly, but incorrectly, the whole trail, from South Texas to Kansas, has been considered the Chisholm, just as there has been confusion also between Jesse Chisholm, for whom the trail was named, and John Chisum, who owned an empire with 100,000 head of cattle in New Mexico. Jesse Chisholm was a breed trapper who probably never owned a single beef but who blazed the trail southward from Kansas when he moved a body of Indians to the Territory at the Government's request.

Originating perhaps on the Chisholm Trail, although there is no certainty of this, the song spread over the whole cattle country of the West and was sung on the Western Trail into Dodge City, the Goodnight-Loving Trail into Colorado, the Stinson Trail into New Mexico, and the lesser-known trails threading hundreds of miles into the northland of Montana, Wyoming, and Idaho.

Hundreds of thousands of head of cattle moved over the trails, north, steadily north, to railheads and greener pastures, to the Indian agencies and mountain ranches. The trail herds were on the move from Spring to Fall, long months from April to September, long miles from New Mexico to Montana. In dust and heat and storm. And the cowboy had time to make his own stanzas to "The Chisholm Trail," and to sing them to amuse himself during the slow hours of the day, or to keep the cattle quiet at night on the bed ground.

"The Chisholm Trail" is the great, single folksong — and pure folksong — of the cowboy. It has the roll and slow swing of saddle and horse. It is endless, and no one ever has collected or ever will collect its thousands of verses. Each stanza is independent, and there is no scheme or rhyme — other than the couplets — or story to follow. Into it the cowboy, like a *cosi* making stew, threw everything at hand.

The stanzas and the tune here come from Powder River Jack Lee of Montana. They might have come from any cowboy. There are no references or sources other than those you may find at a ranch here or there, in Colorado or Wyoming, Texas, or Idaho. The song is not in the books, it is on the land.

Oh, come along, boys, and listen to my tale,
I'll tell you 'bout my troubles on the old Chisholm Trail.
I rode up the trail on April twenty-third,
Oh, I rode up the trail with the Bar Ten herd.

*Cum-a ti yi yippy, yippy I, yippy ay,*
*Cum-a ti yi yippy yippy I, yippy ay,*
*Cum-a ti yi yippy yippy ay.*

I jumped on my broncho, I raked him down his flank,
Oh, he started into pitching, and I landed on the bank.
Well, I leaps to my saddle and I gives a little yell,
Oh, the leaders broke the country and the cattle went to hell.

Oh, I ride with my slicker and I ride all day,
And I packed along a bottle for to pass the time away;
With my feet in the stirrups and my hand on the horn,
I'm the best damned cowboy that ever was born.

We'll round up these cattle, boys, the weather's getting cold,
And the ornery sons of mavericks are getting hard to hold.
We'll trail 'em up to Kansas and we'll bunch 'em in the pens,
And that'll be the last of the old Bar Tens.

She's cloudy in the west and she looks like rain,
And my danged old slicker's in the wagon again;
The gale starts a-blowing and the rain begins to fall,
And it looks, by God, like we're a-going to lose 'em all.

I'm going to hang up my spurs, and my chaps and my saddle,
Never more will I ride around the longhorn cattle.
Says I, "Old boss, will you give me my roll?"
Oh, the boss had me figured ten dollars in the hole.

Oh, I know a girl who's a-going to leave her mother,
All the devils down in hell couldn't stir up such another;
She rides on a pinto and she works on the drags,
With her petticoats a-flopping like a pair of saddle bags.

Oh, I'm out night-herding by the Lone Squaw Butte,
When I run my sights on a lone coyote;
He's a hellin' and a yellin' and as he drifts by,
I snakes out my lassoo and I loops him on the fly.

No chaps, no slicker, and she pours down rain,
And I swears to my hoss I'll never ride night herd again;
Oh, I'll head back south and I'll marry me a squaw,
And live all my life on the sandy Washitaw.

Oh, the shorthorns rattle and the longhorns battle,
Never had such a ride around the locoed cattle;
I'll trade my outfit as soon as I can,
And I won't punch cows for no damned man.

It's along 'fore daylight, they start in to feed,
The steers all a-dragging, with the pointers in the lead;
They head on north where the grass grows green,
And now for the biscuits, and the bacon, and the beans.

The herd stampedes, I'm a-riding on a run,
I'm the quickest shooting cowboy that ever drew a gun;
Well we rounded them up and run 'em in the pens,
And that was the last of the old Bar Tens.

We rode into Abilene and hits her on the fly,
Oh, we bedded down the cattle on the hill close by;
A beef in the herd and the boss says, "Kill it,"
I shot him in the rump with the handle of the skillet.

Oh, Abilene City is a dang fine town,
We'll licker up and twirl those heifers all around,
Then back once more with my bridle and my hoss,
For old John Chisholm is a damned fine boss.

Old Scandalous John is the trail-herd boss,
And he yells his orders from a raw-boned hoss;
He says, "Cowboys, yo're too damned slow!"
We spool our beds and away we go.

I never hankered for to plow or hoe,
And punching steers is all I know,
With my knees in the saddle and a-hanging to the sky,
Herding dogies up in heaven in the sweet bye and bye.

## *Whoopee, Ti-Yi-O,*
## *Git Along, Little Dogies*

When Dick Devall sang a somewhat different version of this song for John A. Lomax and the Library of Congress at Dallas, Texas, in 1946, he introduced it colorfully: "This is Dick Devall, the cowboy singer from Oklahoma — Reed, Oklahoma, Route 2. I will try to sing you a little ditty. For the benefit of all those that don't know what the word 'dogie' means, I'm going to try to tell you. A dogie is just a little calf that his mammy died in a bog hole and his daddy ran away with another cow."

The present full text and tune comes from Kansas.

As I was a-walkin' one morning for pleasure,
I saw a cowpuncher a-ridin' along.
His hat was throwed back and his spurs was a-jinglin',
And as he approached he was singin' this song.

*Whoopee! Ti-yi-o, git along, little dogies,
It's your misfortune and none of my own,*

*Whoopee! Ti-yi-o, git along, little dogies,*
*For you know that Wyoming will be your new home.*

Oh, early in the springtime we round up the dogies,
Mark 'em and brand 'em and bob off their tails,
Then round up the horses, and load the chuckwagon,
And then throw the dogies out on the long trail.

Oh, some boys goes up the trail for pleasure,
But that's where they gets it most awfully wrong,
For you have no idea the trouble they give us,
While we go a-driving them all along.

Oh, your mother was raised away down in Texas,
Where the jimpson weed and the sandburs grow,
Now we'll fill you up on prickly pear and cholla,
Till you're ready for the trail to Idaho.

Oh, you will be soup for Uncle Sam's Injuns,
It's "Beef! — heap beef!" I hear them cry.
Git along, git along, git along little dogies,
You'll be beef steers bye and bye.

Oh, I ain't got no father, I ain't got no mother,
My friends they all left me when first I did roam.
I ain't got no sister, I ain't got no brother,
I'm a poor lonesome cowboy and a long ways from home.

*Whoopee! Ti-yi-o, git along, little dogies,*
*It's your misfortune and none of my own,*
*Whoopee! Ti-yi-o, git along, little dogies,*
*For you know that Wyoming will be your new home.*

## *The Night-Herding Song*

Harry Stephens, who claims authorship of "The Night-Herding Song," introduces it to John A. Lomax, who collected it from him in Dallas, Texas.

LOMAX: Harry, tell me about the famous night-herding song which you sent to me many years ago.

STEPHENS: Well, we always got night-herd years ago when they didn't have so many fences and corralls, and that was the biggest job of the cowboy. We generally have a two-hour shift, and two to four men on a shift according to the size of the herd. And when I made up this song, why, we always had so many different squawls and yells and hollers a-trying to keep the cattle quiet, I thought I might as well have a kind of song to it. . . .

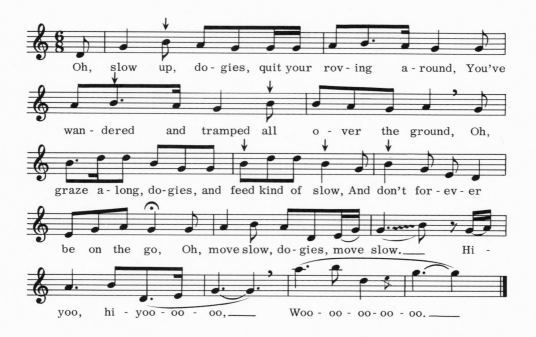

Oh, slow up, dogies, quit your roving around,
You've wandered and tramped all over the ground,
Oh, graze along, dogies, and feed kind of slow,
And don't forever be on the go —
Oh, move slow, dogies, move slow.
  *Hi-yoo, hi-yoo-oo-oo,*
  *Woo-oo-oo-oo-oo.*

I've circle-herded, trail-herded, cross-herded, too,
But to keep you together, that's what I can't do;
My horse is leg-weary, and I'm awful tired,
But if I let you get away, I'm sure to be fired —
Bunch up, little dogies, bunch up.
  *Yoo—oo-oo—oo,*
  *Hey, cattle! Whoo-oop!*

Oh, say, little dogies, when you going to lay down
And quit this forever sifting around?
My limbs are weary, my seat is sore,

Oh, lay down, dogies, like you've laid down before —
Lay down, little dogies, lay down.
> *Hay-yup, cattle! cattle!*
> *Hi-yoo, hi-yoo-oo-oo.*

Oh, lay still, dogies, since you have laid down,
Stretch away out on the big open ground;
Snore loud, little dogies, and drown the wild sound,
They'll all go away when the day rolls 'round —
Lay still, little dogies, lay still.

## *Goodbye, Old Paint*

In "Goodbye, Old Paint," we come, through Jess Morris of Dalhart, Texas, up in the Panhandle, as close to the precise origin of the song as is now possible. Morris claims to be the composer of the song, and, in terms of the folk tradition by which a song is re-created as it passes from one person to another, he quite rightly is, and no one would deny him that very pleasant honor. However, Morris himself, being an honest and forthright Texan, has written us at the Library of Congress detailing the full history of the song as he knew it. I quote verbatim from his letters: giving also some family background, since it seems of interest:

"My father, E. J. Morris, landed in Williamson County, Texas, in 1850, with a wagon train of immigrants from Springfield, Missouri. After locating a ranch on Donahugh creek, my father did farm and ranching, and for a while, around 1854 and on until the 60's, freighted from Houston, Texas, and the seaports, to Belton, Texas, and among other things, he was a circuit rider Baptist Minister. My father was in the Civil War in Texas and Louisiana, but really did not want to fight against the Government.

After the Civil War in 1865, father hired an ex-slave by the name of Charley Willis — colored — who was about 17 yrs. old, to break horses for him. Charley was born in Milam County, Texas, an adjoining County. Possibly during the work for my father on up until around 1891, when my father moved to Amarillo, Texas, Charley had gone up the trail to Wyoming — the neighborhood of Cheyenne. D. H. and J. W. Snyder of Georgetown, Texas, Williamson County, were famous cattlemen & trail drivers. Snyder brothers having driven their first herd to Wyoming in 1867, but later in 1871 the Snyders drove 10 herds, consisting of about 1,500 head in each herd, and it was with one of those herds that Charley took the trail, and on one of those trips, Charley learned to sing Ol' Paint.

I was born June 12th, 1878, in Williamson County, Texas, just one mile and a half from the line of Bell County, where Bartlett, Texas, was at the time, and is now. In 1884, and 1885, Charley was working for my father in Bell County, Texas, as father sold his interests in Williamson County and moved over in Bell County, on Indian Creek, buying a black land farm in Bell County. Charley played a jews-harp, and taught me to play it. It was on this jews-harp that I learned to play Ol' Paint, at the age of 7. In later years I learned to play the fiddle, and played Ol' Paint on the fiddle, in my own special arrangement — tuning the fiddle accordingly.

". . . at the age of 7." This would make 1885 the year in which Jess Morris learned the song from Charley.

As a footnote, Morris in one letter adds: "Many publishers swiped my song and had it published, and many old maverick 'Paints' were running wild and unbranded."

Morris's brand on "Old Paint" is clear and unmistakable: he has the oldest known version; he traces it to a point of first origin, Charley (who learned it from whom on the trail?); he made his own "special arrangement" for the fiddle; and he has, in the folk tradition, his own song.*

---

* I may note here that Jess Morris, during our correspondence, paid me the very high tribute of sending me a mounted, studio portrait of his bulldog, "Boots." I accepted the gift with genuine pleasure. I would not part with it.

Farewell, fair ladies, I'm a-leaving Cheyenne,
Farewell, fair ladies, I'm a-leaving Cheyenne,
Goodbye, my little Dony, my pony won't stand.
*Old Paint, Old Paint, I'm a-leaving Cheyenne,*
*Goodbye, Old Paint, I'm leaving Cheyenne,*
*Old Paint's a good pony, and she paces when she can.*

In the middle of the ocean there grows a green tree,
But I'll never prove false to the girl that loves me.
*Old Paint, Old Paint, I'm a-leaving Cheyenne,*
*Goodbye, Old Paint, I'm leaving Cheyenne,*
*Old Paint's a good pony, and she paces when she can.*

Oh, we spread down the blanket on the green grassy ground,
And the horses and cattle were a-grazing all 'round.

Oh, the last time I saw her, it was late in the fall,
She was riding Old Paint and a-leading Old Ball.

Old Paint had a colt down on the Rio Grande,
And the colt couldn't pace, and they named it Cheyenne,

For my feet's in my stirrups, and my bridle's in my hand,
Goodbye, my little Dony, my pony won't stand.
*Old Paint, Old Paint, I'm a-leaving Cheyenne,*
*Goodbye, Old Paint, I'm leaving Cheyenne,*
*Old Paint's a good pony, and she paces when she can.*

Farewell, fair ladies, I'm a-leaving Cheyenne,
Farewell, fair ladies, I'm a-leaving Cheyenne,
Goodbye, my little Dony, my pony won't stand.

## *The Dying Cowboy*
## (*Bury Me Not on the Lone Prairie*)

As noted earlier, "The Dying Cowboy" is a Western folk adaptation of "The Ocean Burial," a poem originally written in 1839 by the Reverend E. H. Chapin and set to music in 1850. A few stanzas from Chapin's poem nail down the relationship:

> *He had wasted and pined 'till o'er his brow,*
> *The death shade had slowly passed, and now,*
> *When the land and his fond loved home were nigh,*
> *They had gathered around to see him die.*
>
> *"O bury me not in the deep, deep sea,*
> *Where the billowy shroud will roll over me,*
> *Where no light will break through the dark, cold wave,*
> *And no sunbeams rest upon my grave.*
>
> *"O bury me not —" And his voice failed there.*
> *But they gave no heed to his dying prayer,*
> *They have lowered him slow o'er the vessel's side,*
> *And above him has closed the dark, cold tide.*

"The Dying Cowboy" today is probably the best-known of all cowboy songs. "The Ocean Burial" has been completely forgotten.

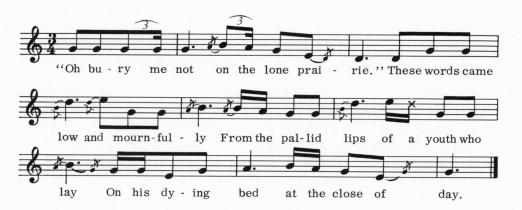

"Oh bu-ry me not on the lone prai - rie." These words came
low and mourn-ful-ly From the pal-lid lips of a youth who
lay On his dy-ing bed at the close of day.

"Oh, bury me not on the lone prairie."
These words came low and mournfully
From the pallid lips of a youth who lay
On his dying bed at the close of day.

He had wasted and pined till on his brow
Death's shadows are slowly gathering now;
He thought of his home and his loved ones nigh
As the cowboys gathered to see him die.

"Oh, bury me not on the lone prairie
Where the wild coyote will howl o'er me,
Where the wild winds sweep and the grasses wave,
And the sunbeams beat on a prairie grave.

"Then bury me not on the lone prairie
In a narrow grave just six by three,
Where the buffalo paw on the prairie free,
Oh, bury me not on the lone prairie.

"I've always wished to be lain when I die
In the little churchyard on the green hillside,
By my father's grave there let mine be,
Oh, bury me not on the lone prairie.

"Oh, let me lie where a mother's prayer
And a sister's tear might mingle there,
Where my friends can come and weep o'er me,
Oh, bury me not on the lone prairie.

"In my dreams I saw" — but his breath failed there.
They gave no heed to his dying prayer.
In a narrow grave just six by three
They buried him there on the lone prairie.

May the light-winged butterfly pause to rest
O'er him who sleeps on the prairie's crest;
May the Texas rose in the breezes wave
O'er him who sleeps in the prairie grave.

And the cowboys now as they roam the plain —
For they marked the spot where his bones have lain —
Fling a handful of roses o'er his grave
With a prayer to Him who his soul will save.

## *Little Joe, the Wrangler*

We know the author-composer of "Little Joe, the Wrangler," N. Howard ("Jack") Thorp, who created text and tune in 1898 and first published the words in his *Songs of the Cowboy*, privately printed at Estancia, New Mexico, in 1908. Thorp himself was an Easterner turned cowboy and knew the men of the West and their way of life. His collection of their songs is the earliest of all such collections, and to that first slim publication of twenty-four songs, Thorp contributed five of his own devising.

In the August 1940 issue of *The Atlantic Monthly*, Thorp recounted something of his collecting experiences in an article, "Banjo in the Cow Camps," and in it speaks of "Little Joe":

In 1898, nearly ten years after the trip I am writing about, I helped trail a herd of O cattle from Chimney Lake, New Mexico, to Higgins, Texas. There were eight of us in the crew. One night I sat by the campfire with a stub of a pencil and an old paper bag and wrote the story of little Joe, the horse wrangler, a Texas stray who had left home, he told us, and struck out for himself because his daddy had married again and his new ma beat him. The boss "sorter liked the little stray somehow," and took him on as a hand. One night in a thunderstorm everybody turned out to check a stampede. The cattle ran a ways, but were headed, and when they were milling and kind of quieted down, one of the hands was missing — our little Texas stray. He was found next morning in a wash twenty feet deep, under his horse, Rocket. . . .

I sang the song to the men who were with me on that trail trip. After our return I sang it for the first time in any man's hearing — save on that trip — in Uncle Johnny Martin's store and saloon at Weed, New Mexico. From that time on it was passed along by word of mouth. I led off my first little book with it, but didn't sign it; none of the songs in that book were signed, though five of the twenty-four were my own compositions. In the course of time "Little Joe, the Wrangler" became one of the most widely sung and best liked of cowboy songs. I have no idea how often it has been sung over the radio in the last few years. I do know that it has been put on phonograph records and more than 375,000 of them have been sold — and the author of the song not richer by a penny for having written it.

> Never a cent in our pockets,
> But what did a cowpuncher care?

Little Joe, the wrangler, he'll wrangle nevermore,
His days on [the] *remuda* they are o'er;
'Twas a year ago last summer when he rode into our camp,
Just a little Texas stray and all alone.

It was getting late one evening, when he rode into our camp,
On a little Texas pony he called Chaw;

With his brogan shoes and overalls, a tougher looking kid
You never in your life before had saw.

His saddle was a Texas kind made many years ago,
And an O K spur on one foot lightly hung;
With his "hot roll" in a cotton sack so loosely tied behind,
And his canteen from his saddle-horn was swung.

He said he had to leave his home, his pa had married twice,
And his new ma whipped him every day or two;
So he saddled up old Chaw one night and he lit a shuck this way,
And now he's trying to paddle his own canoe.

He said if we would give him work, he'd do the best he could,
Though he didn't know straight up about a cow;
So the boss he cut him out a mount and he kindly put him on,
For he sort of liked this little kid somehow.

Taught him to wrangle horses and try to know them all,
And to get them in at daybreak if he could;
And to follow the chuck-wagon and always hitch the team,
And to help old Tony rustle up the wood.

We had driven to the Pecos, the weather being fine,
We'd camped on the south side of the bend;
When a norther commenced blowing, we doubled up our guard,
For it taken all of us to hold them in.

Little Joe, the wrangler, was called out with the rest;
Though the kid had scarcely reached the herd,
When the cattle they stampeded, like a lightning streak they fled,
And we were all a-heading for the lead.

'Midst the streaks of lightning a horse we saw in the lead,
'Twas Little Joe, the wrangler, in the lead;
He was riding old Blue Rocket with a slicker o'er his head,
A-trying to check the cattle in their speed.

We finally got them milling and kind of quieted down,
And an extra guard back to the wagon went,
But there was one a-missing and I knew it at a glance,
'Twas our little Texas stray, poor wrangler Joe.

Next morning just at daybreak, we found where Rocket fell,
Down in a washout twenty feet below,
And laying flat beneath him — his spur had rung his knell —
Was our little Texas stray, poor wrangler Joe.

## The Buffalo Skinners

"The Buffalo Skinners" has an interesting history: England, Maine, Pennsylvania and Michigan, Texas. It moves also from love and the sea to lumbering, and from lumbering to buffalo and murder in the Texas Panhandle. The final product is compressed drama of the highest order, wonderfully understated: "We left old Crego's bones to bleach on the range of the buffalo. . . ."

An original English love song, "Caledonia," appeared in print some time prior to 1800 in *The Caledonia Garland*. It was used as the base upon which was built a later English sea and love song, "Canada-I-O," printed in the United States in the *Forget-me-not-Songster*, New York, 1847. The first and last stanzas are sufficient to point up its stylized text:

> *There was a gallant lady, all in her tender youth,*
> *She dearly lov'd a sailor, in truth she lov'd him much,*
> *And for to go to sea with him the way she did not know,*
> *She longed to see that pretty place called Canada-I-O.*
>
> *Come all you pretty fair maids wherever you may be,*
> *You must follow your true lovers when they are gone to sea,*
> *And if the mate prove false to you, the captain he'll prove true,*
> *You see the honour I have gained by wearing of the blue.*

The small pocket songsters of the period had wide circulation, and very probably a copy of the *Forget-me-not* fell into the hands of Ephraim Braley, a lumberjack who lived in Judson, Maine, and who had, in the spring of 1854, just returned home following a winter's lumbering in the region beyond Three Rivers, Province of Quebec. As they say in New England, Ephraim Braley probably threw a conniption fit when he read of that "pretty place called Canada-I-O." So he produced his own Maine folk original, which was to move, with changes rung on it, across the country. The first and last stanzas clearly point up how far removed his song is in spirit from any *Forget-me-not* prettiness:

*(I) Come all ye jolly lumbermen and listen to my song,*
*But do not get discouraged, the length it is not long,*
*Concerning of some lumbermen who did agree to go*
*To spend one pleasant winter up in Canada-I-O.*

*(II) But now our lumbering is over and we are returning home,*
*To greet our wives and sweethearts, and never more to roam,*
*To greet our friends and neighbors, we'll tell them not to go*
*To that forsaken G— D— place called Canada-I-O.*

The song moved with lumberjacks to Pennsylvania, where it turns up as "Colley's Run-I-O." A version of it, bearing witness to the changes of folk transmission, was recorded at the Library of Congress in 1946 from the singing of L. Parker Temple:

*Come all you jolly lumbermen and listen to my song,*
*I'll tell you all my story, and I won't detain you long,*
*Concerning some husky lumbermen who once agreed to go*
*And spend a winter recently on Colley's Run-I-O.*

*We landed in Lock Haven in the year of 'seventy-three,*
*A minister of the gospel one evening said to me:*
*"Are you the party of lumbermen that once agreed to go*
*And spend a winter pleasantly on Colley's Run-I-O?"*

*"Oh yes, we'll go to Colley's Run, to that we will agree,*
*Provided you pay good wages, our passage to and fro,*
*Then we'll agree to accompany you to Colley's Run-I-O,*
*Then we'll agree to accompany you to Colley's Run-I-O."*

*But now the spring has come again, and the ice-bound streams are free,*
*We'll float our logs to Williamsport, have friends we'll haste to see,*
*Our sweethearts they will welcome us, and bid others not to go*
*To that God-forsaken gehooley of a place called Colley's Run-I-O!*

A "minister of the gospel," by the way, is a euphemism for a hiring agent,

*The Badlands of South Dakota, 1936:*
*bleached skull on the sun-baked earth*

one who talks a good game in the matter of recruiting men for whatever work may be in hand.

Variants of the song appeared in Michigan, Canada, North Dakota, and elsewhere in lumbering country before it surfaced suddenly in the Southwest as a song related to the buffalo hunt. Its first appearance there in oral tradition was shortly after 1873. Its first appearance in print was in Jack Thorp's *Songs of the Cowboys*, 1908, two years prior to the publication of John Lomax's first collection of cowboy songs.

How it arrived in the Southwest is uncertain. Various suggestions have been made, but I like the account given to J. Frank Dobie by James B. Freeman in August 1941. Freeman was then eighty-four years old, and recorded "The Buffalo Hunt" for Dobie as he claimed to have composed it.

Austin Fife, summarizing the Dobie account in his edition of Thorp's *Songs of the Cowboys*, says that Freeman was born in Tennessee in 1857 and came to Texas in 1872. In 1877 he hired out to James Ennis, a Jacksborough buffalo hunter. Ennis was, unlike Crego (of the song), a generous and honorable man. Accompanied by a cook and two skinners, he loaded up with food, ammunition, and other supplies, and crossed Pease River, moving first northeast and then to the south. In what is now Runnels County, Texas, they saw a ten-mile stretch between the Concho and the Colorado rivers blackened by buffalos "as close together as cattle in a trail herd." Ennis killed up to ninety head in a single day. The skinners, working as a pair, got "two bits" each per carcass, averaging month in and month out five dollars per day, food and skinning knives furnished by Ennis. . . .

Freeman said he made up his song little by little while at work on the buffalo range, "not writing it down but keeping it in my head." He said that 1873 was chosen to rhyme with "me." He doubts there were buffalo hunts as early as 1873 because the Indians were too bad. But by 1877 the Comanches and the Kiowas had been rounded up, so Freeman said he put the line about their being "ready to pick us off" in memory of the old days. "In the song I made out that Ennis was trying to beat us out of our pay just as a joke on him. He was fair and square, and we all liked him. He would laugh when I sung that part of the song."

Fife, leaning towards an acceptance of this story, nevertheless says in effect, "Well and good, and fine, but. . . ." Why didn't Freeman say anything about "Canada-I-O," which he must have had to know in order to come up with "Buffalo Range" or "Buffalo Hunt"? And how did "James Ennis" get replaced by "Crego"? Unanswerables, possibly, at this point.

In 1941, John Lomax recorded his distilled variant of "The Buffalo Skinners" for the Library of Congress. He reduced its dozen or so stanzas to four in his memory-singing of it. These four tell the tale. They are succinct, tough, hard.

John Lomax: and he is well worth listening to on the record:

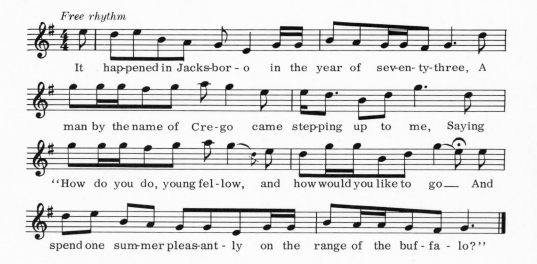

It happened in Jacksboro in the year of seventy-three,
A man by the name of Crego came stepping up to me,
Saying, "How do you do, young fellow, and how would you like to go
And spend one summer pleasantly on the range of the buffalo?"

It's me being out of employment, boys, this to Crego I did say,
"This going out on the buffalo range depends upon the pay,
But if you will pay good wages, give transportation, too,
I think that I will go with you to the range of the buffalo."

The season being over, old Crego he did say,
The crowd had been extravagant, was in debt to him that day.
We coaxed him and we begged him, and still it was no go:
We left old Crego's bones to bleach on the range of the buffalo.

Oh, it's now we've crossed Pease River, boys, and homeward we are bound,
No more in that hell-fired country shall ever we be found,
Go home to our wives and sweethearts, tell others not to go,
For God's forsaken the buffalo range and the damned old buffalo.

## The Streets of Laredo

As I have noted earlier, it must be obvious, even to those uninitiated in the folklore process of the transmission of material, that this song did not originate in Texas or the West. What cowboy, for example, was ever buried to the sound of drums and fifes? The song actually derives from a British ballad recounting the death and burial of a soldier. Here the military band is wholly appropriate:

> *Muffle your drums, play your pipes merrily,*
> *Play the dead march as you go along,*
> *And fire your guns right over my coffin,*
> *There goes an unfortunate lad to his home.*

The British ballad itself has an original Irish source, going back in time to 1790. Very noticeable changes occur in the song in order to localize it in cattle country. In the British ballad, the soldier is found "down by Lock Hospital," and not on "the streets of Laredo" or "down by Tom Sherriman's barroom." Also, his death is the result of a slow and lingering social disease, the manner of death accounting in the British ballad for the "hospital," a special one for venereal diseases located in Harrow Road, London. The soldier, "disordered" by a woman, states his case clearly:

> *Had she but told me when she disordered me,*
> *Had she but told me of it in time,*
> *I might have got salts and pills of white mercury,*
> *But now I'm cut down in the height of my prime.*

As the song moved to the Southwest, it took on a variety of local trappings — knife, six-shooter, cowboys, gamblers, spurs, rifle, saddle, and card house — all of them tending to obscure the British origin. The song has, of course, in the process of transmission, become American, and it is certainly one of the half-dozen most popular songs of the cowboy.

*506*

As I walked out in the streets of Laredo,
As I walked out in Laredo one day,
I spied a poor cowboy wrapped up in white linen,
Wrapped up in white linen as cold as the clay.

Oh, beat the drums slowly, and play the fife lowly,
Play the dead march as you carry me along,
Take me to the green valley, there lay the sod o'er me,
For I'm a young cowboy, and I know I've done wrong.

Let sixteen gamblers come handle my coffin,
Let sixteen cowboys come sing me a song,
Take me to the graveyard, and lay the sod o'er me,
For I'm a poor cowboy, and I know I've done wrong.

It was once in the saddle I used to go dashing,
It was once in the saddle I used to go gay,
First to the dram house, and then to the card house,
Got shot in the breast, and I'm dying today.

Get six jolly cowboys to carry my coffin,
Get six pretty maidens to bear up my pall,
Put bunches of roses all over my coffin,
Put roses to deaden the sods as they fall.

Oh, bury me beside my knife and my six-shooter,
My spurs on my heel, my rifle by my side,
And over my coffin put a bottle of brandy,
That's the cowboy's drink, and carry me along.

We beat the drums slowly and played the fife lowly,
And bitterly wept as we bore him along,
For we all loved our comrade, so brave, young, and handsome,
We all loved our comrade, although he'd done wrong.

## *The Texas Rangers*

Thorp in "Banjo in the Cow Camps" describes his "first hearing" of this ballad along in the 1890's in Texas:

South of Waco one night I rode in the dark. It was a night for riding! I saw a city on fire below the edge of the world, and presently the moon popped up and made the whole State of Texas so bright you could read a newspaper. A campfire flickered, and I rode in where three men were camped. They were dressed no differently than other mounted Texans — no uniforms, no brass. They invited me to get down and camp. I unpacked, unsaddled, hobbled out my horses. Seeing my banjo, they asked me to play. I did. One of the three responded with a song, a new one to me. That there was such a song I knew, but this was my first hearing of it. "The Texas Rangers" it was; and it was a ranger who sang it. These three were part of Captain Hughes's famous force, on their way to Fort McKavett, they told me, to investigate a report of trouble between sheepmen and cattlemen.

The Civil War ballad of "The Texas Rangers" was reportedly written by a fifteen-year-old soldier of the Arizona Brigade, and was first published after the war in F. D. Allan's *Lone Star Ballads* (Galveston, 1874). It moved rapidly into folk circulation, and the Yankee enemies ("I saw the Yankees coming, I heard them give a yell . . .") of the original poem were quickly replaced by Indians. The version given here is very close to the original in point of time, as well as in text. It comes from N. P. Power of Lawrence, Kansas, who, in 1938, set the song down from memory "as he heard it in 1876, while a cowboy on the John Hitson cattle ranch, eighteen miles north of Deer Trail, Colorado." Mr. Powell had never seen the song in print and had no knowledge of the author.

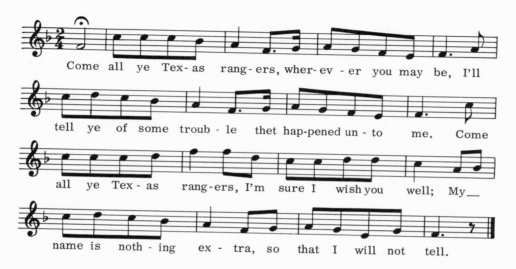

Come all ye Texas rangers, wherever you may be, I'll tell ye of some trouble thet hap-pened un-to me. Come all ye Tex-as rang-ers, I'm sure I wish you well; My name is noth-ing ex-tra, so that I will not tell.

Come all ye Texas rangers, wherever you may be,
I'll tell ye of some trouble that happened unto me.
Come all ye Texas rangers, I'm sure I wish you well,
My name is nothing extra, so that I will not tell.

When at the age of sixteen I joined the jolly band,
That marched from San Antonio down to the Rio Grande,
Our Captain he informed us, I suppose he thought it right,
"Before you reach the station, my boys, you'll have to fight."

We saw the Indians coming, we heard them give a yell;
My feelings at that moment, no human tongue can tell.
We saw the glittering lances, the arrows round me hailed;
My heart it sank within me, my courage almost failed.

We fought them nine long hours before the strife was o'er,
And the like of dead and dying I never saw before.
Twelve of the noblest rangers that ever roamed the West,
Were buried with their comrades and sank in peace to rest.

Then I thought of my dear mother, who through tears to me did say,
"These men to you are strangers; with me you'd better stay."
But I thought her old and childish, the best she did not know,
For my mind was bent on rambling and rambling I did go.

Perhaps you have a mother, perhaps a sister, too;
Likewise you have a sweetheart to weep and moan for you.
If this be your condition and you're inclined to roam,
I'll tell you by experience you'd better stay at home.

## *The Dying Ranger*

"The Dying Ranger" is a Western (and Southern) adaptation of "The Dying Soldier," a song of the Civil War period where the soldier, rather than ranger, was originally a New Englander whose traitor-enemies are clearly Confederates. Just as the North used Southern songs, so also the South (Texas here) adopted Northern ones.

Selected stanzas of "The Dying Soldier" are given for comparison with its "Dying Ranger" descendant. The relationship is obvious. It is doubtful that any palmetto ever graced the shores of the Potomac, and its presence in "The Dying Soldier" suggests either woeful Northern ignorance of semi-Southern climes or a confused borrowing back and forth between these songs.

(*1*) *The sun was setting in the West, it fell with a lingering ray*
*Through the branches of a forest where a dying soldier lay,*
*Beneath the tall palmetto, beneath the Southern sky*
*Away from his New England home we laid him down to die.*

(*4*) *"Stand up, comrades, gather 'round me, listen to the words I say,*
*There is something I would tell you, e'er my soul will pass away,*
*Far away in old New England, in that dear old Pine Tree state,*
*There's one who for my coming with a saddened heart will wait.*

(*10*) *"Stand up, comrades, closely listen to my dying prayer,*
*Who will be to her a brother, shield her with a father's care?"*
*The soldiers spoke together, like one voice it seemed to fall,*
*"She shall be to us as a sister, we'll protect her one and all."*

(*11*) *A smile of radiant brightness a halo o'er him shed,*
*One quick convulsive shudder and the soldier boy was dead,*
*On the banks of the old Potomac we laid him down to rest,*
*With his knapsack for his pillow and his musket on his breast.*

The full version of "The Dying Ranger" that follows is sad but not doleful. It has the North and the South and Texas in it, as well as old-fashioned honor and allegiance, acceptance of the fates and trust in men's words.

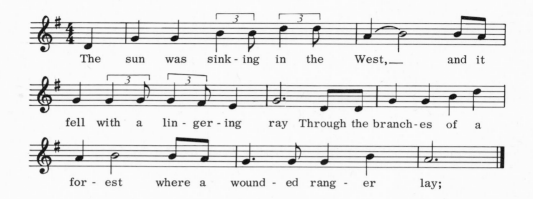

The sun was sinking in the West, and it fell with a lingering ray
Through the branches of a forest where a wounded ranger lay;
'Neath the shade of a palmetto and the sunset silver sky,
Far away from his home in Texas they laid him down to die.

A group had gathered 'round him, his comrades in the fight,
A tear rolled down each manly cheek as he bid a last good night.
One tired and true companion was kneeling by his side,
To stop the life-blood flowing, but, alas, in vain he tried.

When to stop the life-blood flowing he found 'twas all in vain,
The tears rolled down each man's cheek like light showers of rain.
Up spoke the noble ranger, "Boys, weep no more for me,
I'm crossing the deep blue waters to a country that is free.

"Draw closer to me, comrades, and listen to what I say,
I am going to tell a story while my spirit hastens away,
'Way back in northwest Texas, that good old Lone Star state,
There is one that for my coming with a weary heart will wait.

"A fair young girl, my sister, my only joy, my pride,
She was my friend from boyhood, I have no one left beside.
I have loved her as a brother, and with a father's care,
I have strove from grief and sorrow her gentle heart to spare.

"My mother she lies sleeping beneath the churchyard sod,
And many a day has passed away since her spirit fled to God.
My father he lies sleeping beneath the deep blue sea,
I have no other kindred, there are none but Nell and me.

"But our country was invaded, and they called for volunteers;
She threw her arms around me, then burst into tears,
Saying 'Go, my darling brother, drive those traitors from our shore,
My heart may need your presence, but our country needs you more.'

"It's true I love my country, for her I gave my all,
If it hadn't been for my sister, I would be content to fall.
But I'm dying, comrades, dying, she will never see me more,
But in vain she'll wait for my coming by a little cabin door.

"So, comrades, gather closer and listen to my dying prayer,
Who will be to her as a brother, and shield her with a brother's care?"
Up spoke the noble rangers, they answered one and all,
"We'll be to your sister as a brother till the last one of us do fall."

One glad smile of pleasure o'er the ranger's face was spread,
One dark, convulsive shadow, and the ranger boy was dead,
Far from his darling sister we laid him down to rest
With a saddle for a pillow and a gun across his breast.

*Quarter Circle U Ranch, near Birney, Montana, 1939:*
*branding a calf at roundup time*

## *The Trail to Mexico*

Another transfer of traditional ballad into cowboy song is apparent in "The Trail to Mexico," which stems from a seventeenth-century English broadside, "The Seaman's Complaint." "The Seaman's Complaint" passed to America in folk tradition as "Early, Early in the Spring," which has been collected fairly widely — in Tennessee, Georgia, Virginia, West Virginia, North Carolina, Mississippi. A few stanzas, as sung by a fiddler named Waters in Miller County, Missouri, in 1903, serve to establish the link between the British broadside and the cowboy ballad:

> *Early, early in the Spring,*
> *I shipped on board to serve my king;*
> *I left my dearest dear behind,*
> *Who ofttimes said her heart was mine.*
>
> *And when I clasped her in my arms,*
> *I thought she had ten thousand charms,*
> *With features fair and kisses sweet,*
> *Saying, "We'll get married next time we meet."*
>
> *So seven long years I served my king;*
> *In seven long years I returned again,*
> *Saying, "Where is the darling of my life*
> *Who's ofttimes said she'd be my wife?"*
>
> *. . . . .*
>
> *Says he, "Young man, you've come too late;*
> *My daughter has married for riches sake."*
> *So curse all gold and silver too,*
> *And curse all girls that don't prove true.*
>
> *Now that girl is married that I adore,*
> *I'll stay no more on Scotland's shore.*
> *I'll cut my way where the bullets fly*
> *And I'll sail on sea till the day I die.*

"The Trail to Mexico" I acquired from Powder River Jack Lee in Denver, Colorado, in 1941. It goes back much earlier than that and has been reported from Montana prior to 1913 (possibly where Powder River learned it) and Texas in 1922. It is a rough, snarling, bitter song, a fine "to-hell-with-you" farewell to a faithless love.

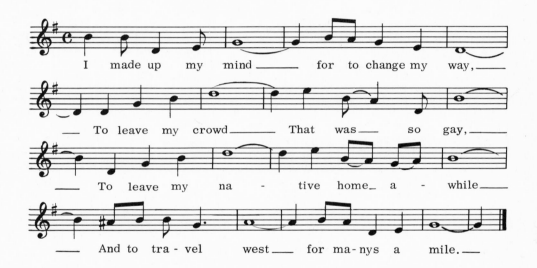

I made up my mind ____ for to change my way, ____
____ To leave my crowd ____ That was ____ so gay, ____
____ To leave my na - tive home_ a - while ____
____ And to tra - vel west ____ for ma-nys a mile. ____

I made up my mind for to change my way,
To leave my crowd that was so gay,
To leave my native home awhile
And to travel west for manys a mile.

It was early in the month of May
I started for Texas, so far away,
I left my darling girl behind,
She said her heart was only mine.

It was when I embraced her in my arms,
I thought she had a thousand charms,
Her caresses so soft, her kisses so sweet,
Saying, "We'll get married next time we meet."

It was in the year of eighty-three
That A. J. Stinson he hired me,
Saying, "Young fellow, how'd you like to go
And trail my herd into Mexico?"

Oh, it was early in that year
We started south with all them steers;
I'll tell you, boys, it was a lonesome go
As the trail herd rolled into Mexico.

When we arrived in Mexico,
I wrote the girl who had loved me so;
I wrote a letter to my dear,
But no return word did I hear.

Oh, curse your gold and your silver, too;
Oh, curse a girl who won't be true;
I'm going back to the Rio Grande
And get me out with a cowboy band.

Lord pity a girl who won't be true,
For a false-hearted love I never knew;
I'm a-going back where the bullets fly
And stay on the cow trail until I die.

# 30.

# Love Songs

### The Bugaboo

In spirit "The Bugaboo" is closely related to "The Foggy, Foggy Dew," widely known through Carl Sandburg's *American Songbag* and the singing of Burl Ives. It is, however, a little more realistic, earthy and natural, with more of the hill country speech in it than the concert stage. I like the high moral standards of the young man and the gracious understanding and forgiveness of the last two stanzas.

> *My love came to my bed side,*
> *So bitterly she did weep,*
> *At last she jumped in bed with me,*
> *She was afraid of the buggerboo.*

*All in the first part of that night,*
*Me and my love did play;*
*All in the latter part of that night,*
*She rolled in my arms till day.*

*The night being gone*
*And the day a-coming on:*
*"Wake up, wake up, my own true love,*
*For the buggerboo done gone."*

*All in the first part of that year*
*She blushed in the face,*
*All in the latter part of that year*
*Grew thicker in the waist.*

*And about nine months afterwards*
*She brought forth me a fine son,*
*And you can see as well as me*
*What the buggerboo has done.*

*In a year or two I married that girl;*
*She made me a virtuous wife;*
*I never told her of her faults*
*In all days of my life.*

*I never told her of her faults,*
*Bedog my eyes if I do!*
*But every time the baby cries,*
*I think of the buggerboo.*

## Home, Daughter, Home

This is more frequently known as "Home, Dearie, Home," and may come from British broadside tradition, although no print of it as such exists. All American college students used to know (perhaps still do) its close relatives, "Bell Bottom Trousers" and "Don't Never Let a Sailor an Inch Above Your Knee."

*It's home, daughter, home, and it's home you ought to be,*
*It's home, daughter, home, in your own countree,*
*Where the oak and the ash and the fine willow tree,*
*All a-growing green in the North Amerikee.*

*There came a jolly sailor to my house to lodge.*
*He called for a candle to light him to bed,*
*He called for a candle to light him to bed,*
*And likewise a napkin to bind up his head.*

*I lit him to bed like I ought for to do,*
*And says, "Pretty girl, won't you jump in, too?"*
*I jumped in behind him to keep myself warm,*
*Thinking a sailor wouldn't do me any harm.*

*'Long about the middle of the night he grew very bold,*
*And into my apron he threw handful of gold;*
*The gold it glistened and it shined so bright,*
*It caused me to sleep with the sailor all night.*

*But if I have a baby, what am I the worse?*
*The gold in my apron and the money in my purse,*
*The gold in my apron for to buy it milk and bread,*
*That's what I got for lighting a sailor to bed.*

*I'll buy me a nurse, and I'll pay the nurse's fee,*
*I'll buy me a nurse, and I'll pay the nurse's fee,*
*I'll buy me a nurse, and I'll pay the nurse's fee,*
*And I'll pass for some maid in a furrin countree.*

*If it's a boy, he shall fight for its king,*
*And if it's a girl, it shall wear a gold ring.*
*She shall wear a gold ring with a top-knot so blue*
*And crawl to bed with sailors like its mother used to do.*

## *Pretty Little Miss*

This is rough on the pretty little miss, but the harsh moral is there if one wishes or happens to listen to the singing of it before such a one-night seduction and betrayal. "Take warning, take a warning . . ." Rue, as evident also in "Green Willow," which follows, is the symbol of lost virginity.

*As I stepped out one bright May morning,*
*Down by yon river side,*
*There I saw a couple a-courting,*
*Which filled my heart with pride.*

*"May heaven bless you, my pretty little miss,*
*Just sing me one little song."*
*He asked her if she'd marry him,*
*She answered, "I am too young."*

*"The younger you are, my pretty little miss,*
*The better you'll be for me;*
*I will vow and I'll declare*
*I'll marry no one but thee."*

*He took her by her lily-white hand,*
*He kissed both cheek and chin,*
*He led her to some far off room*
*To talk awhile with him.*

*The night rolled on and the morning dawned,*
*The morning dawned so clear,*
*The young man arose, put on his clothes,*
*Says, "Fare you well, my dear.*

*"Now you go home to your father's house,*
*Sit down and cry your fill,*
*And when you think of what you've done,*
*Just blame your own good will.*

"There grows a little weed in your father's garden,
The people all call it rue,
The fish will all die and the swallows all fly,
But there's no young man who'll prove true."

## Green Willow, Green Willow

A reading of this is clear if it is remembered that thyme is an emblem of virginity, while rue, as H. M. Belden delicately puts it, has the opposite significance. The sad song goes back to the English "The Seeds of Love."

Come all you pretty fair maids Who flou-rish in your prime, Be
sure to keep your gar-den clean, Let no one take your thyme.

Come all you pretty fair maids
Who flourish in your prime,
Be sure to keep your garden clean,
Let no one take your thyme.

My thyme it is all gone away,
I cannot plant anew,
And in the place where my thyme stood
It's all growed up in rue.

Stand up, stand up, you pretty hope,
Stand up and do not die,
And if your lover comes to you,
Pick up your wings and fly.

The pink it is a pretty flower,
But it will bud too soon,
I have a posy of my own,
I'm sure 'twill wait till June.

In June comes in the primrose flower,
But it is not for me,
I will pull up my primrose flower
And plant a willow tree.

Green willow, green willow,
With sorrow mixed among,
To tell to all the wide world
I loved a false young man.

## *The Butcher Boy*

Stemming from eighteenth-century England, "The Butcher Boy" in its American versions appears to be an amalgamation of two English ballads, "The Cruel Father, or Deceived Maid" and "There Is an Alehouse in Yonder Town," the latter known here as the popular "There Is a Tavern in the Town." Jersey City is an American localization, where the English texts have Sheffield Park, Yorkshire Park, or London City; and the butcher boy, introduced here, was in England either "a brisk young lad," "a sailor lad," or a "postman boy." The song has been widely collected in both the United States and Canada. It is a pathetic tale of a youthful and blighted love, and a needless death: "Place . . . on my bosom a snow-white dove. . . ."

*In Jersey City where I did dwell,*
*Lived a butcher's boy that I loved full well,*
*He courted me my heart away,*
*And now with me he will not stay.*

*There is another in this here town*
*Where he goes right in and he sits right down,*
*He takes a pretty girl upon his knee,*
*And he tells to her what he won't tell me.*

*Oh, yes, oh, yes, I'll tell you why,*
*It's because she has more gold than I,*
*But her gold will melt and her silver fly,*
*And she'll see the day she's as poor as I.*

*Oh me, oh my, how can this be,*
*Shall I love a boy that don't love me?*
*Oh, no, oh, no, that'll never be*
*Till apples grow on the hickory tree.*

*I went upstairs to make my bed,*
*And nothing to my mother said,*

*But she clumb up, she follered me,*
*Says, "Daughter dear, what's a-ailing thee?"*

*And when her father he came home,*
*Says, "Daughter dear, where has she gone?"*
*He went upstairs and the door he broke,*
*And found her a-hanging by a rope.*

*He took his knife and cut her down,*
*And in her bosom these words he found:*
*"Oh, what a foolish maid am I*
*To hang myself for the butcher's boy.*

*"Oh, dig my grave both wide and deep,*
*Place a marble stone at my head and feet,*
*And on my bosom a snow-white dove*
*To show the world that I died for love."*

## Waily, Waily

In the second edition of Bishop Percy's *Reliques of Ancient English Poetry* (1767), there appeared that greatest of Scottish lyric laments for a lost love, "Waly, Waly, Gin Love be Bonny." The song is much earlier than Percy's collection of it, but almost two centuries after that date the Library of Congress was fortunate enough to record it from the singing of Eugenia (Blount) Anderson, wife of Professor Charles Anderson of Johns Hopkins University, who had acquired it orally in Georgia.

*When cockle shells turn silver bells*
*And mussels grow on every tree,*
*When blooms the rose 'neath wintry snows,*
*Then will my false love be true to me.*

*Oh, waily, waily, but love is bonny*
*A little while when it is new,*
*But when it's old, it groweth cold*
*And fades away like morning dew.*

*Oh, had I wist before I kissed*
*That love had been so ill to win,*
*I'd locked my heart in case of gold*
*And pinned it with a silver pin.*

*Oh, waily, waily, but love is bonny*
*A little while when it is new,*
*But when it's old, it groweth cold*
*And fades away like morning dew.*

## Come All You Young and Tender Ladies, or The Unconstant Lover

The chief stanza of remorse in "Waly, Waly," turns up in this Kentucky lyric, which is otherwise one of direct warning against false lovers and closely related to "Little Sparrow," which follows. The original Scotch stanza is worth noting:

> *But had I wist before I kisst*
> *That love had been sae ill to win,*
> *I had locked my heart in case of gowd,*
> *And pinned it with a siller pin.*

Eugenia Anderson's stanza in "Waily, Waily" is virtually the same as the "original," but the stanza in "Come All You Young and Tender Ladies" shows change and deterioration resulting from oral transmission on a different cultural level. The first two lines of the Kentucky stanza given here reflect the folk speech of the country, and "key" of golden is probably a mishearing for "case" or an attempt to make sense by relating the word to "locked" my heart, an example of folk etymology at work. "Come All You Young and Tender Ladies" is a good illustration also of the slippage of stanzas and lines from one love lyric to another. Note the opening stanza of this song and that of "Little Sparrow," as well as the last two lines of the second stanza of each. The next half dozen songs all have something of this slippage.

Come all you young ____ and_ ten - der_ la - dies, Be_ care-ful
how you court young men, They are like bright stars ___ on_ sum-mery
morn-ing, They'll first ap - pear and_ then they're gone. They'll tell to
you some pleas - ing sto - ry, They'll tell to you their_ love is
true And a - way they'll go and_ court an -
oth - er, Then that's the love they_ have for ___ you.

Come all you young and tender ladies,
Be careful how you court young men,
They are like bright stars on summery morning,
They'll first appear and then they're gone.

They'll tell to you some pleasing story,
They'll tell to you their love is true,
And away they'll go and court another,
Then that's the love they have for you.

I wish I'd a 'knew before I courted
That love had a' been so hard to win,
I'd have locked my heart in key of golden
And I'd a' pinned it down with a silver pin.

Don't never place your eyes on beauty,
For beauty is a thing that will decay,

For the ripest rose in yonders garden —
Oh, see now if it don't fade away.

And the ripest apples soon are rotten,
And the truest love will soon grow cold,
And a young man's words are soon forgotten —
Oh, pray, pretty miss, don't be too bold.

## *Little Sparrow*

This again is a sad cry of warning and sorrow, ending in its last lines on a helpless note of resignation. "Little Sparrow" appears widely under various titles and with textual interpolations and variations, but two elements are usually firm in it: the comparison of man's fickleness to the stars of a summer morning, and the wish of the forsaken girl to be a little sparrow so that she can fly to her love, nestle against his breast, and hear what he has to say. The present text is a composite one drawn from two versions printed by Belden, both from Missouri and both collected in 1906, the first from the manuscript ballad-book of James Ashby of Holt County in an entry dated "Aug 6th 1877," and the second from C. H. Williams of Bollinger County, who said, "I was very young when I learned this and don't remember who I heard first sing it."

*Say oh! beware, ye pretty fair maidens,*
*Say oh! beware how you love men!*
*They are like stars of a bright sunny morning,*
*They appear but soon are gone.*

*As for myself, I once had a sweetheart,*
*Indeed I thought he was my own;*
*He went straightway and loved another,*
*That showed the love he had for me!*

*He said his heart did burn like fury*
*Whenever he my face did see,*
*I told him it was a mere pretension,*
*He never intended to marry me.*

*Alas, alas! it is all over!*
*And little he thinks on what is past;*
*In Cupid's chains he was linked to another*
*For life so long as it may last.*

*I wish I were some little sparrow,*
*I quickly through this air would fly,*
*I'd fly straightway to my false-hearted lover*
*And hear his tale while I would cry.*

*And hear his tale while I would flutter*
*Upon his breast with tender tears,*
*I would ask him why he once did flatter*
*And tell so many deceitful lies.*

*But as it is, I'm no sparrow,*
*Neither wings to fly so high,*
*I'll sit me down in grief and sorrow,*
*Sing, and pass my trouble by.*

## *The Cuckoo*

In general tradition, it is the dove which is the symbol of love and constancy, while the cuckoo is usually associated with inconstancy and faithlessness. However, as in the third line of this first stanza, we have been assured as early as 1770 in English tradition that "the cuckoo brings good tidings." The mood of this — as well as texts of other versions — is closely related to "Old Smoky."

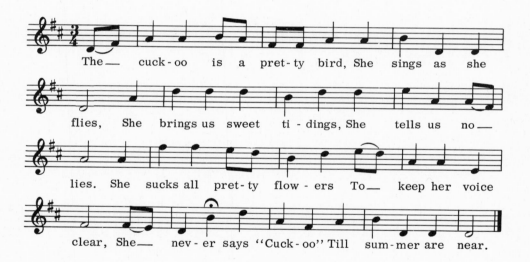

The cuckoo is a pretty bird, She sings as she flies, She brings us sweet tidings, She tells us no lies. She sucks all pretty flowers To keep her voice clear, She never says "Cuck-oo" Till summer are near.

The cuckoo is a pretty bird,
She sings as she flies,
She brings us sweet tidings,
She tells us no lies.

She sucks all pretty flowers
To keep her voice clear,
She never says "Cuckoo"
Till summer are near.

She flies the mountains over,
She flies the world around,
She flies back to the mountains
And mourns for her love.

For to meet him, for to meet him,
For to meet him I will go,
For to meet my love William,
The young man that I love.

534

## Old Smoky

This is one of the very great lyrics of love lost. The acceptance of defeat runs like a bitter thread throughout the song, but there is in it also the strength in sadness of the girl's love. The song is so personal that one wishes instinctively to put out a hand to help her, but that would not do, and the song must end on the note of despair, and she must withdraw and hide, like a wounded animal, with the wild birds and turtledoves who will understand.

On top of Old Smok-y, All cov-ered with snow, There I lost my true lov-er Through a-court-ing too slow.

On top of Old Smoky,
All covered with snow,
There I lost my true lover
Through a-courting too slow.

Courting is a pleasure,
And parting is a grief,
But a false-hearted lover
Is worse than a thief.

A thief he will rob you
And take all you have,
But a false-hearted lover
Will send you to your grave.

The grave will decay you
And turn you to dust,
Not a boy in ten thousand
A poor girl can trust.

They'll tell you they love you
To give your heart ease,
Then turn their backs on you
And court who they please.

They'll hug you and kiss you
And tell you more lies
Than the spikes in the railroad
Or stars in the skies.

As sure as the dew-drops
Fall on the green corn,
Last night he was with me,
Tonight he is gone.

I'll go back to Old Smoky,
That mountain so high.
Where the wild birds and turtle doves
Can hear my sad cry.

\* \* \*

Old Smoky, Old Smoky,
Keep watch o'er my love,
She's as true as your mountains
And as pure as the dove.

## Down in the Valley

This is another one of the great love laments out of the South. The music is slow and delicately mournful, and through it one hears the wind and sees the valley, feels the breaking heart and the loneliness of jail, and the hope of seeing love and knowing love. The loved one is present throughout in the repeated and accented "love" of the third line in each stanza, making the actual absence the more poignant. This belongs with "Old Smoky" and "Careless Love," an unhappy but beautiful trio.

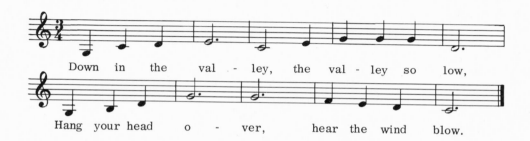

Down in the val - ley, the val - ley so low,

Hang your head o - ver, hear the wind blow.

Down in the valley, the valley so low,
Hang your head over, hear the wind blow,
Hear the wind blow, love, hear the wind blow,
Hang your head over, hear the wind blow.

If you don't love me, love whom you please,
Throw your arms round me, give my heart ease,
Give my heart ease, love, give my heart ease,
Throw your arms round me, give my heart ease.

Put your arms round me, before it's too late,
Put your arms round me, feel my heart break,
Feel my heart break, love, feel my heart break,
Throw your arms round me, feel my heart break.

Write me a letter, send it by mail,
And back* it in care of Birmingham Jail, .

* Back: an obsolete term meaning to "address" a letter.

537

Birmingham Jail, love, Birmingham Jail,
Back it in care of the Birmingham Jail.

Go build me a castle forty feet high,
So I can see her as she rides by,
As she rides by, love, as she rides by,
So I can see her as she rides by.

Roses love sunshine, the violets love dew,
Angels in heaven know I love you,
Know I love you, dear, know I love you,
Angels in heaven know I love you.

## *Careless Love*

This is the third of the great Southern three. It is a lament and specific: the girl is in a family way, the young man has left her for another, her heart is broken, there is no way out, she will complete three nights of bitter weeping, and then — resigned to the bitter, bitter fates — will "cry no more." The helpless longing of stanza four is particularly poignant. The repetition of the first three lines in each stanza, capped by the fourth, is unusual in folksong and contributes mournful and haunting suspense to the singing.

Love, oh love, oh care-less love, Love, oh love, oh care-less love, —— Love, oh love, oh care-less love, Oh, see what care-less love has done to me.

Love, oh love, oh careless love,
Love, oh love, oh careless love,
Love, oh love, oh careless love,
Oh, see what careless love has done to me.

When my apron strings would bow,
When my apron strings would bow,
When my apron strings would bow,
You'd pass my door and say hello.

But now my apron strings won't pin,
But now my apron strings won't pin,
But now my apron strings won't pin,
You pass my door, and you won't come in.

I love my mama and my papa, too,
I love my mama and my papa, too,
I love my mama and my papa, too,
But I'd leave them both and go with you.

Oh, ain't it enough to break my heart,
Oh, ain't it enough to break my heart,
Oh, ain't it enough to break my heart,
To see my love with another sweetheart.

Oh, it's done and broke this heart of mine,
Oh, it's done and broke this heart of mine,
Oh, it's done and broke this heart of mine,
And it'll break that heart of yours some time.

Oh, I cried last night and the night before,
Oh, I cried last night and the night before,
Oh, I cried last night and the night before,
I'll cry tonight and I'll cry no more.

Love, oh love, oh careless love,
Love, oh love, oh careless love,
Love, oh love, oh careless love,
Oh, see what careless love has done to me.

## *The Brazos River*

This is a rare and beautiful song celebrating the rivers of Texas. There is no other record of it. There is speculation that its origin may stem from the classroom tradition of singsong recitation of states, capitals, and rivers, just as the multiplication table was once sung to "Yankee Doodle." The love element would seem to deny this, however. But, who knows? Accept it for the greatness of the names on the land, and be thankful that we have it.

We crossed the broad Pecos, we forded the Nueces,
We swum the Guadalupe, we followed the Brazos,
Red River runs rusty, the Wichita clear,
But down by the Brazos I courted my dear.

*Then la-la-la, lee-lee-lee, give me your hand,*
*La-la-la, lee-lee-lee, give me your hand,*

*La-la-la, lee-lee-lee, give me your hand,*
*There's a-many a river that waters the land.*

The fair Angelina runs glossy and gliding,
The crooked Colorado runs weaving and winding,
And the slow San Antonio it courses the plain,
But I never will walk by the Brazos again.

*Then la-la-la, lee-lee-lee, pole the boat on,*
*La-la-la, lee-lee-lee, pole the boat on,*
*La-la-la, lee-lee-lee, pole the boat on,*
*My Brazos River sweetheart has left me and gone.*

She kissed me, she hugged me, she called me her dandy,
The Trinity's muddy, the Brazos quicksandy,
She hugged me, she kissed me, she called me her own,
But down by the Brazos she left me alone.

*Then la-la-la, lee-lee-lee, give me your hand,*
*La-la-la, lee-lee-lee, give me your hand,*
*La-la-la, lee-lee-lee, give me your hand,*
*The Trinity's muddy, but the Brazos quicksand.*

The girls of Little River they're plump and they're pretty,
The Sabine and the Sulphur have many a beauty,
On the banks of the Natchez, there's girls by the score,
And down by the Brazos I'll wander no more.

*Then la-la-la, lee-lee-lee, give me your hand,*
*La-la-la, lee-lee-lee, give me your hand,*
*La-la-la, lee-lee-lee, give me your hand,*
*There's a-many a river that waters the land.*

543

## *Last Night I Dreamed of My True Love*

This is an excellent example of the reduction of a full and lengthy ballad to a brief and moving love lyric. "Locks and Bolts," in its English ballad broadside version, is the story of a young suitor whose loved one has been locked at home by rich parents. The suitor breaks down the door, a fight ensues, and he flees with the girl, whom he eventually marries. The two stanzas here would appear to come from the opening sequence, prior to the breaking of the "locks and bolts." One can, without reservation in this instance, praise the oral transmission of song that in the folk process sloughed ballad incidentals to give us this "dazzling" lament.

*Last night I dreamed of my true love,*
*All in my arms I had her;*
*When I awoke she was not there,*
*I was left alone without her.*

*Her long yellow hair like strings of gold*
*Came dazzling o'er my pillow;*
*That pretty little girl I love so well,*
*She's gone from me forever.*

## The False True-Lover

The basic element of "The False True-Lover" is here, the young man who, in spite of true love, leaves his loved one to go ten thousand miles. Missing, however, is another element, the questions and answers:

> *"Oh, who will shoe my pretty little feet,*
> *And who will glove my hand,*
> *And who will kiss my red and rosy cheeks,*
> *While you're in the distant land?"*

> *"Your father will shoe your pretty little feet,*
> *Your mother will glove your hand,*
> *And I will kiss your red and rosy cheeks*
> *When I return from the distant land."*

Their lack, however, detracts nothing from the lyric, which becomes, in consequence, more compact and direct.

I rode out one cold winter night,
A-drinking of sweet wine,

And there I met a pretty little girl
Who stole this heart of mine.

Her cheeks are like some pretty pink rose
That blooms in the month of June,
Her voice is like some musical instrument
That has been newly put in tune.

"So fare you well, my own true love,
So fare you well for a while,
I'm going away, but I'm coming back again,
If it is ten thousand miles.

"Ten thousand miles, my own true love,
Through England, France, and Spain,
And my poor heart will never be at ease
Till I see your face again."

"Oh, don't you see that pretty turtle dove
A-sitting in yon tree?
She's mourning for her own true love,
And that's the way of me."

"The crow that is so black, my love,
Shall surely turn to white,
If ever I prove false to you,
Bright day will turn to night.

"Bright day will turn to night, my love,
The elements will mourn,
The fire will freeze and be no more,
And the raging sea will burn."

"Supposing that the sea runs dry,
And rocks would melt in the sun,
Oh stay with me, my own true love,
Till all these things are done!"

## *Once I Courted a Pretty Little Girl*

Over a period of several years, from 1933 through 1938, Asher E. Treat collected virtually the full repertoire of folksong of a Kentucky family which had migrated, because of the Depression, north into the lumber country of northern Wisconsin. This song and the two that follow are part of that collection, which he published in the *Journal of American Folklore*.

"Once I Courted a Pretty Little Girl" was sung by Mrs. M. G. Jacobs in September 1933. Mrs. Jacobs's mother before her had learned the song from a Charles Messer, ca. 1850. Asher Treat comments: "The tunes of all of the songs have been transmitted to and among the Jacobses purely by vocal tradition. No member of the family has any knowledge of musical notation. . . . So far as I know, the songs were not communicated to the children by any deliberate process of teaching. When asked where a tune has been learned, Pearl usually responds, 'Oh, I hyeard mother sing it.' "

Even though it is a sad account of fickleness, "Once I Courted a Pretty Little Girl" is a delight from beginning to end. I particularly like the restrained last stanza, while my favorite line of all, of course, is the third one in the second stanza.

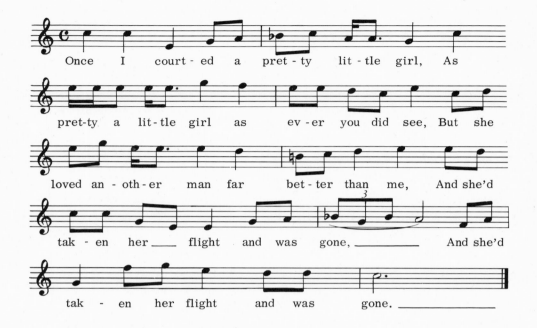

Once I courted a pretty little girl,
As pretty a little girl as ever you did see,
But she loved another man far better than me,
And she'd taken her flight and was gone,
And she'd taken her flight and was gone.

I ran up street and I ran down
In search of my bonny little girl.
I whooped and I hollered and I played on my flute,
But my bonny little girl she was gone,
But my bonny little girl she was gone.

I looked East and I looked West
As far as the eye could discern,
And there I saw my bonny little girl
Standing locked in another man's arms,
Standing locked in another man's arms.

She waved her lily-white hand at me
As if she had once been my own,
But I passed on by and I never cast an eye

Though I brought out a sigh and a moan,
Though I brought out a sigh and a moan.

Oh, now you have got my bonny little girl,
You must treat her as well as you can,
And if you don't keep her safely at home,
I will walk with her now and again,
I will walk with her now and again.

## *I Asked That Girl to Marry Me*

This is perhaps the most direct and factual account of love and courtship in all of folksong, ending with a delicate last line which turns the whole thing all upside down again. One believes in the long run that the girl must have accepted him.

I asked that girl to marry me; She said, "Oh no! I'd rather be free."

I asked that girl to marry me;
She said, "Oh, no! I'd rather be free."

I asked that girl to be my wife;
She cut at me with an old case knife.

I asked that girl to be my bride;
She sat right down and cried and cried.

And the more she cried, the worse I felt,
Till I thought to my soul my heart would melt.

*cIntosh County, Oklahoma, 1940:*
*m boy and girl playing "pleased or displeased" at a play party*

## *Oh, Love It Is a Killing Thing*

The direct simplicity of statement and question in many folksongs is incredible:

> *Oh, love it is a killing thing,*
> *Did you ever feel the pain?*

The language is pure, and the question as sharp as any arrow. Everyone has felt it, and you are brought at once into the song itself. There is no escape.

The very first time I saw my love,
I was very sick in bed,
And the only request I asked of her
Was to tie up my head.
Oh, love it is a killing thing,
Did you ever feel the pain?
Did you ever see a man so sick as I
For to get well again?

I wish my love was a rose so red
And in yon garden grew,
And if I was a gardener,
Great care I'd take of you.
There would not be a month in the year roll 'round
But what I would renew,
I'd garnish you all around and about
With sweet William, thyme, and rue.

## *Madam, I Have a Very Fine Farm*

This is a mature relative of "Paper of Pins," chiefly recognized as a children's singing game. In it the suitor offers a lady

> "*. . . a paper of pins*
> *To show you how true love begins,*
> *If you will marry me, me, me,*
> *If you will marry me.*"
>
> "*I won't accept your paper of pins*
> *To show me how true love begins,*
> *For I won't marry you . . .*"

The suitor continues to offer gifts, including variously "a coach and six, with every horse as black as pitch," "a little lapdog, that may lie in your lap when you go abroad," "a dress of red, and will stitch it with a golden thread," "a silver spoon, to feed your baby in the afternoon," all of which gifts the lady rejects out of hand. The suitor finally offers her "the key of my chest, to have all the money at your request." The lady accepts this with alacrity, whereupon the suitor reverses the role and cuts the lady off sharply:

> "*I won't give you the key to my chest,*
> *To have all the money at your request,*
> *And I won't marry you, you, you,*
> *And I won't marry you.*"

In "Madam, I Have a Very Fine Farm," comparable gift giving is proposed and rejected, but along with the proposals and rejections there is some fairly harsh dialogue, winding up at the last with a no uncertain spit right in the prissy Madam's eye!

"Mad - am, I have a ver - y fine farm And it's six - ty a - cres wide, And (a) you can (a) have it at your com - mand If (a) you will be my bride."

"Madam, I have a very fine farm
And it's sixty acres wide,
And you can have it at your command
If you will be my bride."

"Yes, sir, I know you've a very fine farm
And it's sixty acres wide,
But who would stay with me at night
When you're off playing your cards?"

"Madam, I never did do such a thing,
For I never did think it was right,
And if you will be my bride, bride, bride,
I won't stay away at night."

"Yes, sir, I know that's all just talk,
It's just to take me in,
I wonder if you think that I
Would marry a barrel of gin?"

"Madam, you are a very cruel girl
And very hard to please,
When you get old and out in the cold,
I pray to God you freeze."

"When I get old and out in the cold,
I'll have no drunkard to please, please, please,
I'll have no drunkard to please."

"Madam, I have a very fine horse
And his pace is like a kite,
And you can have him at your command
Whenever you want to ride."

"Yes, sir, I know you've a very fine horse
And he stands in yonders barn,
His master knows some very bad habits
And I'm afraid that horse would learn."

"Madam, I have a very fine mule
And he works to the buggy well,
I'll drink my wine and play my cards
And you can go to hell!"

## Sally Goodin

In spite of the dark night, it is easy to see this country boy reeling down a
Kentucky road with his mixed and happy thoughts of pie, puddin', and Sally
Goodin. I speak for myself: It would be pleasant to be that young again.

I had a piece of pie and a little piece of puddin',
I'd give it all away to hug Sally Goodin.
Night's so dark, road's so muddy
I'm so drunk I can't walk steady.

## Ibby Damsel

The relatively prosaic title of this lyric and its first stanza give way to the
beauty of the last two and to the incredibly wonderful imagery of the last
line: "Her eyebrows wove with a golden thread!" For that line alone, the
lyric belongs in any anthology of American folk poetry.

Some "old Rob - in Down" they call me, But I'm a — weav - er — by my trade, In this fair berth, in which I'm dwell - ing, And Ib - by Dam - sel my heart be - trayed.

Some "old Robin Down" they call me,
But I'm a weaver by my trade,
In this fair berth, in which I'm dwelling,
And Ibby Damsel my heart betrayed.

Her hair's as black as a raven's feather,
That do sit on yon willow tree,
Her sparkling eyes they're so enticing,
But from her chamber I can't get free.

Her heart as sweet as any posy,
Her cheeks are of the rosy red,
Her sparkling eyes are so enticing,
Her eyebrows wove with a golden thread.

## An Old Man and a Young Man

Any young girl with love in her heart will subscribe to these sentiments. Many very evidently did, for the song in one version or another has been widely reported.

An old man, an old man, An old man is gray, But a young man's heart is full of love, Go 'way, old man, go 'way.

I wouldn't marry an old man,
I'll tell you the reason why:
His face is all tobacco juice,
His chin is never dry.

*An old man, an old man,*
*An old man is gray,*
*But a young man's heart is full of love —*
*Go 'way, old man, go 'way.*

I'd rather marry a young man
With forty cows to milk,
I would not marry an old man
And dress in satin and silk.

I'd rather marry a young man
With an apple in his hand,
Than to marry an old man
With all his houses and land.

An old man comes moping in,
"I'm tired of my life,"
But a young man comes skipping in,
"Kiss me, my dear wife."

*An old man, an old man,*
*An old man is gray,*
*But a young man's heart is full of love —*
*Go 'way, old man, go 'way.*

## Cindy

"Cindy" is a fun and banjo song and a pleasant change of love-pace from the laments and sorrows. Arthur Palmer Hudson says that the "refrain comes from antebellum minstrel song," so that the core of the song goes back to the 1850's. The individual stanzas can be endless, and are tossed into the singing much as the separate stanzas are in "The Old Chisholm Trail." The song, in other words, belongs to anyone and to everyone, and there is no fixed sequence either of ideas or stanzas in its singing. For myself, I especially like the practical sentiment of the seventh stanza given here.

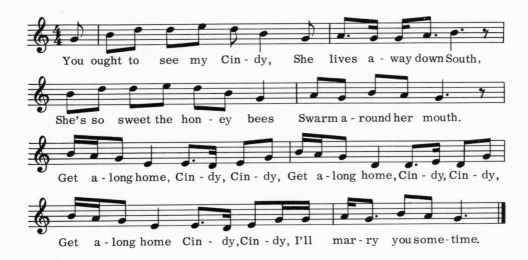

You ought to see my Cindy,
She lives away down South,
She's so sweet the honey bees
Swarm around her mouth.

*Get along home, Cindy, Cindy,*
*Get along home, Cindy, Cindy,*
*Get along home, Cindy, Cindy,*
*I'll marry you some time.*

Oh, Cindy is a pretty girl,
Oh, Cindy is a peach,
She threw her arms around me
And hung on like a leech.

She took me to the parlor,
And cooled me with her fan,
She told me I was the prettiest thing
In the shape of mortal man.

She told me that she loved me,
She called me sugar plum,
She threw her arms around me,
I thought my time had come.

I wish I was an apple
A-hanging on a tree,
And every time my Cindy passed
She'd take a bite of me.

I wish I had a needle
As fine as I could sew,
I'd sew my true love to my side,
And down the road I'd go.

I wish I had a little red box,
To put my true love in,
I'd take her out and kiss her,
And put her in again.

The higher up the cherry tree,
The riper grows the cherry,
I never saw a pretty girl
But what she wanted to marry.

*Get along home, Cindy, Cindy,*
*Get along home, Cindy, Cindy,*
*Get along home, Cindy, Cindy,*
*I'll marry you some time.*

## East Virginia

The singer's localization of this song in East Virginia and his loveless adventure in South Carolina should confuse no one about the origins of the lines and stanzas. They are a pick-me-up of verses from half a dozen lyric love songs, even though the singer may swear that they are all his or that this is the way he first fully heard it. It just can't be. It would not be a difficult task to unravel all the parts (There I spied a pretty fair maiden; And her cheeks was rosy red; I'd rather be up some dark hollow; Your papa says we cannot marry) and put them back into the songs from which they came. But why do it? This is a folksong, and the completed puzzle here has made the singer happy and is better than any academic unraveling. And for us? Having described the "pretty fair maiden's" brown and curly hair and rosy cheeks, would you really care about knowing the source of or wish to alter the wonder of the last two lines of the second stanza? And throughout, folk speech and grammar are pleasantly rampant.

My home is far in East Virginia, South Car'-
li - na did I go, There I spied a pret - ty fair
maid - en, Her name I did not know.

My home is far in East Virginia,
South Car'lina did I go,
There I spied a pretty fair maiden,
Her name I did not know.

Oh, her hair was brown and curly,
And her cheeks was rosy red,
Upon her breast she wore a lily,
Don't I wish that I was dead.

When I am asleep I am always dreaming,
When I am awake I see no rest,
Oh, them moments seem like hours,
While them pains run through my breast.

I'd rather be up some dark hollow
Where the sun don't never shine,
Than for you to be some other man's darling,
Or to think you won't be mine.

Your papa says we cannot marry,
Your mama says it'll never do,
But if you say you truly love me,
I will run away with you.

What my papa always taught me
Some day would surely come to pass:
When I left home in East Virginia,
Trouble would befall me fast.

## The Cruel War Is Raging

English texts and some American texts of this conversation between soldier and sweetheart give Lisbon as the destination of the ship on which he is to embark for the wars. The traditional song, therefore, probably relates specifically to the Peninsular Campaign of 1808. There are fully authenticated accounts in English military history of young women concealing their sex and going to the wars as soldiers or sailors in the company of their loved ones. Such devotion was grist to the mill of the balladeers and strongly appealed to the romantic concepts of the folk who have kept several of these songs alive over the centuries.

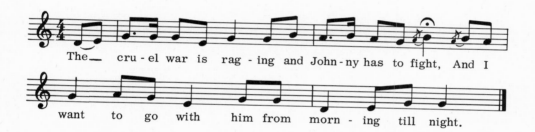

The— cru-el war is rag-ing and John-ny has to fight, And I
want to go with him from morn-ing till night.

"The cruel war is raging and Johnny has to fight,
And I want to go with him from morning till night,
And I want to go with him, and it grieves my heart so.
Won't you let me go with you?" "Oh, no, my love, no."

"Oh, tomorrow is Sunday, and Monday is the day
That his captain calls for him and he must obey,
His captain calls for him, it grieves my heart so.
Won't you let me go with you?" "Oh, no, my love, no."

"I would go to your captain, get down upon my knees,
Ten thousand gold guineas I'd give for your relieve,
Ten thousand gold guineas, it grieves my heart so.
Won't you let me go with you?" "Oh, no, my love, no."

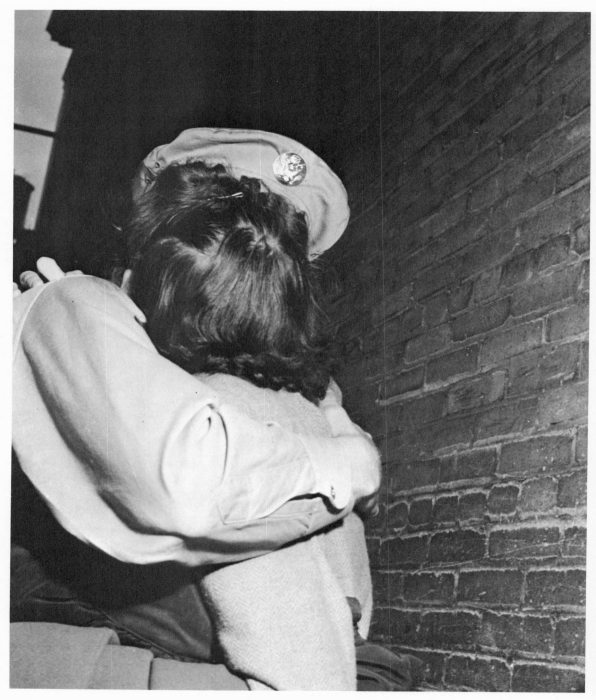

*Greyhound Bus Terminal, Chicago, Illinois, 1943:*
*Pvt. D. N. Daniels kissing his wife goodbye*

"Your fingers are too slender, your figure is too small,
Your cheeks are too rosy to face the cannon ball,
Your cheeks are too rosy . . ." "It grieves my heart so.
Won't you let me go with you?" "Oh, no, my love, no."

"Oh, Johnny, my Johnny, I think you are unkind,
For I love you much better than all other mankind.
I love you much better than tongue can express.
Won't you let me go with you?" "Oh, yes, my love, yes."

"I'll roach back my hair and men's clothes I'll put on,
And I'll pass as your comrade as we march along.
I'll pass as your comrade and none can guess.
Won't you let me go with you?" "Oh, yes, my love, yes."

## *The Broken Token*

The theme of the returned soldier or sailor who first tests the devotion of his sweetheart and then reveals himself to her by producing a ring previously broken between them is a subject immensely popular with the folk. "The Broken Token," or "A Pretty Fair Maid," has, like "The Cruel War Is Raging," survived the centuries and has been widely collected in the United States. It is romantic, sentimental, and moves with the set, stylized, and lovely precision of a crinoline ballet. True love triumphs, and the folk have happily cherished its faithful moral.

A pret-ty fair maid all in the gar-den, A gay young sol-dier came rid-ing by, He stepped up to this hon-ored la-dy, Say-ing, "O, kind miss, don't you fan-cy me?"

A pretty fair maid all in the garden,
A gay young soldier came riding by,
He stepped up to this honored lady,
Saying, "Oh, kind miss, don't you fancy me?"

"You are not a man of noble honor,
You're not the man I took you to be,
You are not a man of noble honor,
Or you wouldn't impose upon a poor girl like me.

"I have a true love in the army,
He has been gone these seven years long,
And seven more years I'll wait upon him —
No man on earth shall enjoy me."

"Perhaps he's in some watercourse drownded,
Perhaps he's on some battlefield slain,
Perhaps he's stolen some fair girl and married,
If that's the case, you'll never see him again."

"Perhaps he's in some watercourse drownded,
Perhaps he's on some battlefield slain,
Perhaps he's stolen some fair girl and married —
I'll love the girl that married him."

He took his hands all out of his pockets,
And rings and diamonds two or three,
He took a ring that was broken between them,
She saw it and fell down at his feet.

He picked her up, he did embrace her
And kisses gave her two or three,
Saying, "I am your poor single soldier,
I have just returned for to marry thee."

## The Low Lands of Holland

"The Low Lands of Holland" is a third type treating of love and the wars. Here the lovers are torn apart, the young man taken from his bride of a day and impressed into the British navy. The mother attempts to reason with the daughter, but she will have none of it, vowing instead to remain faithful to her love and to remain a virtual recluse until death. It is not accidental that the song survived and was collected on the sea lands of Maine.

Last Easter I was married, that night I went to bed,
There came a bold sea captain who stood at my bed head,
Saying, "Rise, arise, you married man, and come along with me
To the low, low lands of Holland to face your enemy."

She clasped her arms about me, imploring me to stay,
Up speaks this bold sea captain, saying, "Arise and come away!
Arise, arise, you married man, and come along with me
To the low, low lands of Holland to face your enemy."

"Oh, daughter dear, oh, daughter dear, why do you thus lament?
There are men enough in our town to make your heart content."
"There are men enough in our town, but there is not one for me,
For I never had but one true love, and he has gone from me.

"No shoes shall come upon my feet, nor comb come in my hair,
No fire bright or candlelight shine in my chamber more,
And never will I married be until the day I die,
Since cruel seas and angry winds parted my love and me."

## *Barbara Allen*

Professor Bartlett Jere Whiting of Harvard says that "probably no Child ballad has been found more often on this side of the Atlantic" than "Barbara Allen." Its origin is uncertain, but Samuel Pepys knew it and noted it in his diary in January 1666. Oliver Goldsmith was moved to tears by the singing of it. It is perhaps *the* ballad of true love, carrying over even into our day the medieval and Renaissance concept of the lover dying for love. This, together with Barbara's scorn and remorse, and the symbolism of the rose and the briar, go to make it the great ballad that it will forever be.

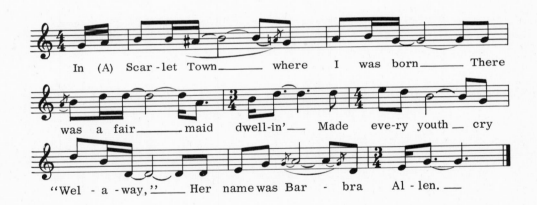

In (A) Scar-let Town\_\_\_\_ where I was born\_\_\_\_ There
was a fair\_\_\_\_ maid dwell-in'\_\_ Made eve-ry youth \_ cry
"Wel - a -way," \_\_ Her name was Bar - bra Al - len. \_\_

In Scarlet Town where I was born
There was a fair maid dwellin'
Made every youth cry "Wel-a-way,"
Her name was Barbara Allen.

'Twas in the merry month of May
When the green buds they were swellin',
Sweet William on his death bed lay
For the love of Barbara Allen.

He sent his servant to the town
To the place where she was dwellin',
Says, "My master's sick and he sends for you,
If your name be Barbara Allen."

Then slowly, slowly got she up,
And slowly came she nigh him,
But all she said when she got there,
"Young man, I think you're dyin'."

"Oh, yes, I'm sick, and I'm very sick,
And death on me is dwellin',
No better, no better I never shall be
Until I get Barbara Allen."

"Oh, don't you remember the other day
When we were at the tavern,
You drank a health to the ladies all around,
But you slighted Barbara Allen?"

"Oh, yes, I remember the other day
When we were at the tavern,
I drank to the health of the ladies all around —
But my love to Barbara Allen."

As she was walking o'er the fields
She heard the death bell knelling,
Each stroke it took it seemed to say,
"Hard-hearted Barbara Allen."

She looked to the east, she looked to the west,
She saw the pale corpse a-coming,
"Go bring the pale corpse over here to me
That I may gaze upon him."

The more she looked, the more she mourned,
Till she fell to the ground a-crying,
Saying, "Take me up and carry me home,
For I think that I'm a-dying.

"Mother, oh mother, go make my bed,
Go make it long and narrow,
Sweet William died for pure, pure love,
And I will die for sorrow.

"Father, oh father, go dig my grave,
Go dig it long and narrow,
Sweet William died for me today,
I'll die for him tomorrow."

They buried her there in the old church yard,
And buried William nigh her,
On William's grave grew a big red rose,
On Barbara's grew a green briar.

They climbed and they climbed on the old church wall
Till they couldn't climb no higher,
They tied at the top in a true loves knot,
The red rose around the green briar.

*Vicinity of Scottsboro, Alabama, 1937:*
*Mrs. Mary McLean, with fiddle*

*Natchitoches, Louisiana, 1940:*
*farmer and children on their front porch*

## The Unquiet Grave

This rare supernatural ballad from Professor Child's canon of English ballads has been found in the United States only a few times, and the variant
here given, collected by Herbert Halpert in 1937, is the second. There have
been others since, but this is the gem of all, through to the last line. In the
Child version it is the young man who weeps over the grave, but here the
positions are reversed, and it seems more natural that it be so. The Child
version also has two additional homiletic stanzas, reading:

> " 'Tis down in yonder garden green,
> Love, where we used to walk,
> The finest flower that ere was seen
> Is withered to a stalk.

> "The stalk is withered dry, my love,
> So will our hearts decay;
> So make yourself content, my love,
> Till God calls you away."

These seem to me markedly anticlimactic, and I strongly prefer as a close
the starkness and graveyard terror of the last stanza given here.

Oh, I nev - er— had but the one true— love, In the
green - woods he was slain, I'd do— as— much for
my— true love As — an - y girl— would do.

Oh, I never had but one true love,
In the green woods he was slain,
I'd do as much for my true love
As any girl would do.

I set and weeped all over his grave
Twelve months and one day;
It's when twelve months and one day was up,
Oh, this young man he arose.
Saying, "Why do you weep all over my grave,
For I cannot find no relief?"

"One kiss, one kiss from your clay, clay-cold lips,
One kiss is all that I crave,
One kiss, one kiss from your clay, clay-cold lips,
And then return to your grave."

"If I was to give you one kiss,
Oh, your days would not be long,
It's for my lips they're clay, clay-cold,
And my breath smells earthlye strong."

# 31.

# Murder Ballads

## Expert Town, or The Oxford Tragedy

This story of the girl murdered by the man who has seduced her is told in horrifying detail ("I beat her till the blood run down") and given tremendous realism with the side observation ("her hair was yellow as gold") during the brutal murdering moments. The language, as a result of folk transmission, is so earthily American that one would wager heavily against an English origin. The song, however, goes back at least to 1700 and the British broadside, "The Berkshire Tragedy, or The Wittam Miller." In it the scene of the tragedy was at Wittam, near Oxford, although some prints located it near Wexford. From "Wexford" to "Expert" was an easy transition, just as the "Oxford" title was also easily localized in this country as the "Knoxville Girl." It has even been found in Texas as "The Waco Girl." The stanzas of murder and gore culminate with the traditional death-moral while the bloodcurdling detail continues into the last lines.

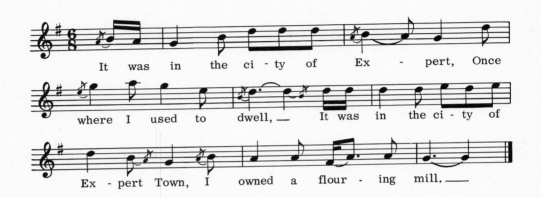

It was in the ci - ty of Ex - pert, Once where I used to dwell, — It was in the ci - ty of Ex - pert Town, I owned a flour - ing mill. —

It was in the city of Expert,
Once where I used to dwell,
It was in the city of Expert Town,
I owned a flouring mill.

I fell in love with a nice young girl,
Dark roving was her eye,
I told her that I'd marry her
If me she'd never deny.

I fell in love with another girl,
I loved her just as well,
The Devil put it in my mind
My first true lover to kill.

I called down to her sister's house
At eight o'clock one night,
But little did the poor girl think
I owed her in despite.

"We'll have a walk, we'll have a talk
Down by the meadow field,
We'll also have a private talk
And set our wedding day."

We walked along, we talked along
Till we came to the levellest ground;
I picked me up a stick of wood
And knocked the poor girl down.

She fell upon her bending knees,
Crying, "Lord have mercy on me!
Oh, Willie, oh, Willie, don't murder me now,
For I'm not prepared to die."

Little attention did I pay,
I beat her more and more;
I beat her till the blood run down, —
Her hair was yellow as gold.

I picked her up by the lifeless hair,
And swung her 'round and around,
I swung her on the water top
That flows through Expert Town.

Her sister swore my life away
Without a bitter* doubt,
She swore I was the very same man
That taken her sister out.

They took me on suspicion,
Locked me up in Expert jail,
I had no one to pay off my fine,
No one to go my bail.

And now they're going to hang me
And I'm not prepared to die,
They're going to hang me up in the air
Between the earth and the sky.

* Probably "bit of."

## Florella, or The Jealous Lover

While this is one of the most popular of the murder-love ballads and is certainly indigenous to this country, nothing is known of its origin. It goes under many titles: "Loella," "Down by the Weeping Willow," "The Death of Sweet Florilla," "Poor Lurella," and other variants, including "The Jealous Lover" above. The murder here is one of straightforward jealousy. The girl is not to be gotten rid of for love of another, or because she is with child: it is jealousy only — simple, direct, and evil. The story moves with harsh beauty within the frame of the opening stanza and the repetitive close of the last.

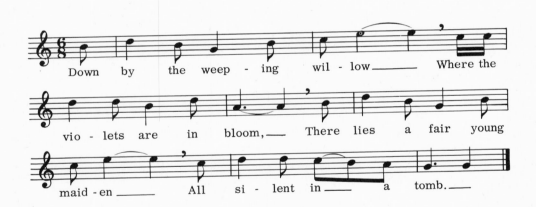

Down by the weep - ing wil - low ___ Where the vio - lets are in bloom, ___ There lies a fair young maid - en ___ All si - lent in ___ a tomb. ___

Down by the weeping willow
Where the violets are in bloom,
There lies a fair young maiden
All silent in a tomb.

She died not broken-hearted,
No sickness e'er befell,
But all in an instant parted
From the one she loved so well.

'Twas on a summer's evening,
As gently fell the dew,
Down to a lonely cottage
A jealant lover drew.

"Come, love, and let us wander
Out over the meadows gay,
Come, love, and let us ponder
All over our wedding day."

"Oh, Edward, I am weary,
And do not care to roam,
For roaming is so dreary,
I pray you take me home."

Up stepped that jealant lover
And with a silent cry,
"No mortal one shall love you,
In an instant you shall die."

Down, down she sank before him
And humbly begged for life,
But into her snow-white bosom
He plunged the fatal knife.

"Oh, Edward, I forgive you,
Though this is my last breath,
I never did deceive you,"
She closed her eyes in death.

Down by the weeping willow
Where the violets are in bloom,
There lies a fair young maiden
All silent in the tomb.

## The Lily of the West

"The Lily of the West," while thoroughly localized here in Kentucky, is actually of Irish origin and can be dated before 1839. Texts have been found in England beginning " 'Twas when I came to England. . . ." In the Middle West the locale is Michigan and the girl's name is frequently Mary rather than the more common Flora. There is often also a last stanza in which the lover, released from prison after serving sentence, travels through the country to hunt for "handsome Flora," whom he still loves. So far as I am aware "The Lily of the West" contains the only clear statement in ballad form of the use of feminine charms to influence judge and jury.

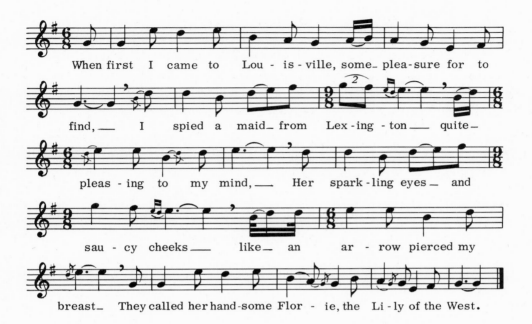

When first I came to Lou-is-ville, some pleasure for to find,— I spied a maid from Lex-ing-ton quite pleas-ing to my mind,— Her spark-ling eyes— and sau-cy cheeks— like— an ar-row pierced my breast— They called her hand-some Flor - ie, the Li-ly of the West.

When first I came to Louisville, some pleasure for to find,
I spied a maid from Lexington quite pleasing to my mind,
Her sparkling eyes and saucy cheeks like an arrow pierced my breast,
They called her handsome Florie, the Lily of the West.

Her curly locks of yellow hair in ringlets shone like gold,
They were enough to entice me then, and all men young and old;
She had a ring on every finger, so handsome was she dressed,
They called her handsome Florie, the Lily of the West.

One evening as I walked out, down by yon shady grove,
I spied a man of low degree conversing with my love.
He sung her a song of melody, which so enraged my breast,
He called her handsome Florie, the Lily of the West.

I stepped up to my rival, my dagger in my hand,
I took him by the collar and boldly bid him stand.
I was mad to desperation, I swore I'd pierce his breast,
Saying, "Go! false-hearted Florie, the Lily of the West."

In due time came my trial, I boldlye made my plea;
A flaw in the indictment they said would set me free.
But she turned both judge and jury, so handsome was she dressed,
They smiled on handsome Florie, the Lily of the West.

But now I am convicted, to prison I must go,
For five long years in Frankfort, which fills my heart with woe.
She's robbed me of my liberty, deprived me of my rest,
I never can forgive her, the Lily of the West.

## *Johnson-Jinkson*

This story of decoy-ambush and backstabbing murder is a rare find in the United States and goes back in point of time from Troy Cambron in an "Okie" camp in California to a seventeenth-century English ballad, "The Three Worthy Butchers of the North." There were, of course, variants and reductions of the text all along the line, from the original 102-line ballad to our present condensed version. Some of the language is exceptional: "three bold and struggling men," "swords keen in hand," "three shivering cries." The account is vivid, and one wishes that a Breughel could have illumined the text.

John-son he was rid-ing a-long, as fast as he could ride,——
He thought he heard a wo-man, he heard a wo-man cry.

Johnson, he was riding along, as fast as he could ride,
He thought he heard a woman, he heard a woman cry.

Johnson getting off his horse and searching, looked all around,
Until he came to a woman with her hair pinned to the ground.

"Woman, dearest woman, who has brought you here for a span?
Who has brought you here this morning, with your hair pinned to the ground?"

"It were three bold and struggling men, with swords keen in hand,
Who brought me here this morning, with my hair pinned to the ground."

Johnson being a man of his own, and being a man and bold,
He put off his overcoat to hug her from the cold.

Johnson getting on his horse, and the woman getting on behind,
Along this lonesome highway rode, their fortunes for to find.

They were riding all along, as fast as they could ride,
She drew her fingers to her ears, and gave three shivering cries.

Out sprung three bold and struggling men, with swords keen in hand,
Who did commanded Johnson, commanded him to stand.

"I'll stop then," said Johnson, "I'll stand then," said he,
"For I never worried in my life afraid of any of three."

Johnson killing two of them, not watching the woman behind,
While he was after the other one, she stabbed him from behind.

The day was free and a market day, and the people all passing by
Who saw this awful murder, and saw poor Johnson die.

## Frankie Silvers

Well-authenticated tradition has it that this song was composed in jail by Frances (Frankie) Silvers and either recited or sung by her on the scaffold before she was hanged in Morganton, North Carolina, on July 12, 1833, for the murder of her husband the preceding winter.

The murder is recounted by Arthur Palmer Hudson and H. M. Belden in *North Carolina Folklore:*

Around Christmas-time of 1831, Frances Stewart Silver, called Frankie, was living with her husband, Charles Silver, at the mouth of the South Toe River, in what was then Burke County. On the evening of December 22, having chopped a big pile of hickory wood for the holidays, Charlie lay down with his baby on a sheepskin near the fire. While he dozed, Frankie struck him a glancing but almost-decapitating blow with an axe, then, while he thrashed about the room, snatched up the child and threw herself into bed and pulled the covers over her. When he grew quiet, she arose and finished the job. She dismembered the body, burned portions of it, and hid the rest under the puncheon floor of the cabin and in a hollow sourwood tree outside. Then she "redd up" the room, scouring away some of the bloodstains, shaving away the deeper ones on the wall and mantel with the axe, and went with her children to her mother-in-law's.

After a few days the neighbors began to inquire about Charlie. Frankie explained that he had left home to buy his Christmas whiskey and suggested that he had fallen into the river, drowned, and been frozen over. The more suspicious began a search. . . . The puncheon floor and the other hiding places yielded their gruesome secret.

The cause of the murder was considered to be jealousy, although it was also reported that Silvers mistreated his wife and that she killed him in protection of herself.

The song is one which strikes terror and pity. A slow reading and rereading of it makes the flesh creep.

This dread-ful, dark and dis-mal day Has swept my glo-ries all a-way, My sun goes down, my days are past, And I must leave this world at last.

This dreadful, dark and dismal day
Has swept my glories all away,
My sun goes down, my days are past,
And I must leave this world at last.

Oh, Lord, what will become of me?
I am condemned, you all now see.
To heaven or hell my soul must fly
All in a moment when I die.

Judge Daniels has my sentence passed,
These prison walls I leave at last,
Nothing to cheer my drooping head
Until I'm numbered with the dead.

But, oh! that dreadful Judge I fear!
Shall I that awful sentence hear?
"Depart, ye cursed, down to hell
And forever there to dwell."

I know that frightful ghosts I'll see
Gnawing their flesh in misery,
And then and there attended be
For murdering in the first degree.

There shall I meet that mournful face
Whose blood I spilled upon this place,
With flaming eyes to me he'll say,
"Why did you take my life away?"

His feeble hands fell gently down,
His chattering tongue soon lost its sound;
To see his soul and body part —
It strikes with terror to my heart.

I took his blooming days away,
Left him no time to God to pray,

And if sins fall on his head,
Must I not bear them in his stead?

The jealous thought that first gave strife
To make me take my husband's life;
For months and days I spent my time
Thinking how to commit that crime.

And on a dark and doleful night
I put his body out of sight,
With flames I tried him to consume,
But Death would not admit it done.

You all see me and on me gaze;
Be careful how you spend your days;
And never commit this awful crime,
But try to serve your God in time.

My mind on solemn subjects rolls.
My little child, God bless its soul!
All you that are of Adam's race,
Let not my faults this child disgrace.

Farewell, good people, all you see
What my bad conduct's brought to me:
To die of shame and of disgrace
Before this world of human race.

Awful deed to think of death,
In perfect health to lose my breath.
Farewell, my friends, I bid adieu;
Vengeance on me must now pursue.

Great God! How shall I be forgiven?
Not fit for earth — not fit for heaven!
But little time to pray to God,
For now I try that awful road.

## *Mary Hamilton, or The Four Marys*

It is remarkable that this great and moving ballad has survived in oral tradition from the days of Queen Elizabeth and Mary Queen of Scots to be recorded in 1941 in Virginia.

Whiting summarizes the confused and conflicting stories:

The version before us [Child 173 *A*] tells a story of adultery, infanticide, and execution at the Scottish court. The principal figures are a maid of honor, Darnley, and Mary Queen of Scots, but there is no evidence that Mary had an attendant gentlewoman named Hamilton nor, despite Darnley's reputation, is he known to have been involved in any such affair as this. On the other hand, in 1563 the queen's apothecary and one of her French maids were hanged for the killing of their illegitimate child. Certainly if this event be the source of the ballad, the changes illustrate the folk's fondness for aristocratic protagonists. . . . Difficulty arises not from anything unlikely in the alteration of the story, but from the fact that a girl named Mary Hamilton, maid of honor to Peter the Great's wife, was beheaded in 1719 for the murder of at least three illegitimate children, one of whom may have been fathered by Peter. In any event, Peter insisted on the execution, attended it, kissed the lady's severed head, and "made a little discourse on the anatomy of it to the spectators." The coincidence is amazing and Mr. Child was for a time inclined to believe that the ballad . . . was late and a very conscious reworking of the Russian story. Andrew Lang, however, made so convincing a case for the traditional story that Mr. Child was persuaded, as most others have been. . . .

Word has come from the kitchen
And word has come to me
That Mary Hamilton drowned her babe
And throwed him into the sea.

Down came the old Queen,
Gold tassels around her head.
"Oh, Mary Hamilton, where's your babe
That was sleeping in your bed?

"Oh, Mary, put on your robe so black
And yet your robe so brown,
That you might go with me this day
To view fair Edinburgh town."

She didn't put on her robe so black,
Nor yet her robe so brown,
But she put on her snow-white robe
To view fair Edinburgh town.

As she passed through the Canongate,
The Canongate passed she,
The ladies looked over their casements and
They wept for this lady.

As she went up the Parliament steps,
A loud, loud laugh laughed she.
As she came down the Parliament steps,
She was condemned to dee.

"Oh, bring to me some red, red wine,
The reddest that can be,
That I might drink to the jolly bold sailors
That brought me over the sea.

"Oh, tie a napkin o'er my eyes,
And ne'er let me see to dee,
And ne'er let on to my father and mother
I died way over the sea.

"Last night I washed the old Queen's feet
And carried her to her bed,
And all the reward I received for this —
The gallows hard to tread.

"Last night there were four Marys,
Tonight there'll be but three.
There was Mary Beaton and Mary Seton
And Mary Carmichael and me."

# Folk Beliefs and Superstitions

*Folk Medicine*
*Weatherlore*
*The Folklore of Birth*
*The Folklore of Marriage*
*The Folklore of Death*

There are two delightful quotes from Tennessee:

I don't hold with none of these strange or heathenish beliefs, but some things folks call superstitions is jest as true as God's Gospel.

And the irate and wonderful:

I'd like to know what in the name of God the moon and stars are for if they're not signs and guides to go by!

The great central collection of American popular beliefs and superstitions has been (and continues to be) brought together by Professor Wayland D. Hand of the University of California at Los Angeles. By 1961, Hand had catalogued two hundred thousand popular beliefs and superstitions from *printed sources alone* in the United States: from articles in the folklore journals, from specialized book publications, from newspaper and magazine sources, and other published accounts. A whole series of definitive volumes will be the product of this great work, and some measure of what they will be can be gathered from the two volumes Hand edited on *Popular Beliefs and Superstitions* in *The Frank C. Brown Collection of North Carolina Folklore.*

In those two volumes dealing only with North Carolina, Hand probed the field and established fourteen categories to break down and control the enormous body of materials:

1. Birth, Infancy, Childhood
2. The Human Body, Folk Medicine
3. The Home, Domestic Pursuits
4. Economic, Social Relations
5. Travel, Communication
6. Love, Courtship, Marriage
7. Death and Funeral Customs
8. Witchcraft, Ghosts, Magical Practices
9. Cosmic Phenomena: Times, Numbers, Seasons
10. The Weather
11. Animals, Animal Husbandry
12. Fishing and Hunting
13. Plants, Plant Husbandry
14. Miscellaneous

The subdivisions of these run into the thousands: in the case of medicine, virtually every disease known to man; in the case of weather, every change in the clouds, winds, temperature, the fur on squirrels, and the husks on corn. In the case of witchcraft and magical practices, Harry M. Hyatt has just completed two volumes of a thousand single-spaced pages each on matter collected in the southeastern part of the United States alone; in the case of animal and plant husbandry, many farmers still go by the old traditions and the almanacs; the omens of birth, marriage, and death can be grouped by the

hundreds. This folklore is still with us. There is no need to go to the Carpathians: it is found in New York and Santa Barbara and Houston.

(A parenthetical note here is in order. Hand has by now amassed in the UCLA archives well over a quarter of a million of these popular beliefs and superstitions from printed sources. But consider those which have circulated and continue to circulate orally in the United States which have never been recorded in print! How many? Out of our population of two hundred million persons, we can roughly estimate fifty million families. Some families hold forty or fifty of these "beliefs," others twenty or thirty, some ten, and few — very few — five or less. My guess is that we can conservatively "average out" at fifteen beliefs or superstitions per family [take another look at the breadth of Hand's categories!], and we come up then with a total of seven hundred fifty million beliefs and superstitions (not all different, by any means) rocketing around the United States *today*, not counting those of our grandfathers and grandmothers and their parents before them — even though, of course, many of our "beliefs" are directly descended from them. Not all different, by any means: twenty million people may have a "superstitious" feeling about three-on-a-match, or troubles coming in three's. Not all different, but given the diversity of the heritages of our families, the diversity of our work and jobs, of our games and amusements, of our age groups, and all of the other items that set us apart or "group" us, and I am willing to go out on a limb and suggest that there must be in the United States today (and certainly within our past) fifty million *different* folk beliefs and superstitions. Without question, there are five million for medicine alone — and that is a fair starter.)

There are two ways of looking at this folklore, and the folk themselves do so. One is to take a great deal of it seriously or quasi-seriously, to believe it and follow it and pass it on in that spirit. The second is to consider it outdated and foolish, but nevertheless to continue to enjoy it in a "fun" sense (wishing on a falling star, for example), or to reject it more deeply, with astonishment at the fact that one could ever have believed in it or followed it. One, the acceptance and belief; and, two, the amused retention or flat rejection of what was once believed or half-believed by oneself or by others.

In effect, then, a belief is a belief to those who believe; to those who do not believe, it is a superstition. Both are with us.

It is not possible here to cover all the fields, so I have chosen to illustrate a few by way of example of the others: folk medicine; weatherlore; and the beliefs and omens of birth, marriage, and death.

# 32.

# *Folk Medicine*

By way of very general comment, it can be said that in terms of the history of mankind the great advancements of medical science are as new as the neon light. Home-grown medicine, on the other hand, is ageless. From the days of the Greeks and the Arabs, through the Middle Ages to the lands of our ancestors in Europe, all men everywhere have — with trial and error, with common sense and magic — fought the known and the unknown: the seen knife-cut and the unseen fever. Today, in our twentieth-century America, an enormous quantity of that home-grown medicine remains from the past, some of it brought here originally from Europe and the Mediterranean, much of it self-nurtured on the plains of Texas and Nebraska.

Folk medicine — in terms of the quantity of cures and remedies, and their importance to the individual — is the greatest of all the categories of beliefs and superstitions: it has touched (and continues to touch) millions of people from birth to death, from childhood croup and the pains of teething through to the straitened arteries and the last difficult breathing.

In 1954 I asked radio listeners to send in to me family remedies and cures for any and all diseases or afflictions. They came in from every state in the Union.

Cures for the simple wart were numerous (do children have warts today?). Dr. Francis J. Perrotta of Schenectady, New York, wrote about a young woman, a brunette, who had asked him whether the warts on her fingers could be removed without burning them, or without any operation. His answer had been a flat "no," and she had left disappointed. Some time later she returned and showed the doctor her hands. They were free of warts and bore no sign of any cicatrix or burns. She had been told by an older woman that "if a person of opposite flesh pigmentation rubs her fingers over the warts of another, they will disappear. A brunette can rub the warts of a blonde away, and a blonde those of a brunette." This had been done daily for five-minute periods, and the warts had vanished.

A recent medical theory for the effectiveness of such a cure is that both the cause and cure of warts is essentially psychogenic. This is a high-powered word which translated into the folk idiom reads: warts are caused by toads, and are cured by rainwater found in the stump of a white oak tree. In other words, virtually any cure can be effective in which one believes.

The sympathetic disappearance of warts as the result of the burial of an object which rots is a widespread and firmly held belief. Usually the object must be one which has been stolen, and all of the acts involved carried out in secrecy. The case of Andrew Ludwig of Rochester, New York, is a good example:

When I was a young man, I had a very large wart on the center knuckle of my left hand. It was rough and unsightly. I tried every kind of remedy to remove it. I tied a silk thread around it to choke it, used acid to burn it off, and tried all kinds of salves without result. One day a man told me to take a piece of raw meat, rub it on the wart, and bury it. "When the meat rots, the wart will disappear." He said I must believe what he told me, and not let anyone see me do it.

One Sunday when everybody in our family had gone to church, I went to the pantry, found some meat, cut off a small piece, and rubbed it on the wart. I didn't dare go out in the yard to bury it for fear that someone might see me, so I hid it in the cellar wall in our house. I paid no more attention to the wart. I didn't see it disappear, but about two weeks later it was gone. It was the most mysterious thing I have ever seen in my life. This is the God's honest truth.

Annie Marsh of Irvington, California, removed her childhood warts by holding her palms up towards the full moon, "taking from the moon," and then washing the warts away. "The moon is a dead planet, and warts are nothing but dead matter." Emma Miller of Slippery Rock, Pennsylvania, recommends the first quarter of a new moon: "Look up at the moon, rub your hands over each other, and say: 'What I see, increase; what I feel, decrease.' " There is, of course, magic there.

Other varied cures include one from Annie M. Wilson of Vass, North Carolina: "Draw blood from a wart, place it on a grain of corn, and feed the corn to a chicken, preferably a black one." Mrs. H. L. Fritz of Chicago counted hers and tied an equal number of knots in a piece of string: "Tie this string to the end of a down spout where the rainwater from the roof will pass over it. As the knots rot, the warts will disappear." Alice Kinney of Shelton, Connecticut, sold her warts to a sailor for a penny. Mrs. H. D. Scott of Houston, Texas, remembers a childhood friend who, on the advice of the local butcher, dropped one dried pea for each wart in a well at six o'clock in the morning. "Returning home after disposing of the last pea, she looked at her hands, and her warts were gone."

William H. Carlson of Corvallis, Oregon, wrote with evident good humor:

When I was a youngster on a Nebraska farm, it was said that if one were to let a grasshopper eat a wart, it would disappear. I tried this several times on a wart I had on my hand, but I found it difficult to get a captured and frightened grasshopper into an eating mood. Finally I did catch one who was either braver or hungrier than the rest. Once started, he proceeded voraciously until he drew blood generously, and the experiment ceased to be funny to me. The wart, however, did wither and disappear.

Mr. W. E. D. Stokes of Lenox, Massachusetts:

Many years ago I was afflicted with very bad warts on my heels. I went to several doctors who tried various methods such as electrical sparks or deep knife cuts with a knife. Nothing did any good, and the warts became large and even multiplied in number. One day I went down to Lexington, Kentucky, at a time when a State Fair was in progress. I saw a man selling little bottles of yellow oil for 25¢ from the back of a truck. He said, "What is your trouble?" I said warts on my heel were pestering me. "Just what you need," said he, "SNAKIOLA OIL." He told me to pour a little on my stocking over the warts every day and the warts would go away. Believe it or not, the warts disappeared within a space of two weeks. The stuff was wonderful. It had the appearance of turpentine and banana oil, but who knows? Label had an Indian maiden, and caption said Waneta Snakiola.

In the case of the common cold, the cures lack any "magical" qualities, and more closely resemble family recipes which have been passed on from mother to daughter. On the old theory that the bitterer the medicine, the swifter the cure, many of them smack of wormwood and smell to high heaven.

Ruby Edmonds of Louisville, Kentucky, wrote that

each Fall a large, flat whisky bottle, about a qt. I think (at least it looked that big to me, a little girl,) was filled with crushed rock candy, linseed oil and whisky. That bottle was set in a handy place, and woe to the child who coughed. We'd almost choke before we let go a cough, for sure as day, a spoon, usually what was called a dessert spoon made of brass would be produced, and against all protests the cougher would have to swallow that awful dose, and if we refused to swallow, our noses would be held and the stuff poured down our throats.

One tablespoonful of turpentine in a cup of warm melted lard, rubbed on the throat and chest and covered with warm flannel, was a childhood standby of Winnifred Schaer of Buhl, Idaho. For coughs she suggests an easily made onion syrup: sauté one large white onion, sliced thinly, in two good tablespoonfuls of butter. When the onion slices are clear and soft, add one half-cup of sugar, stirring well. "The resulting syrup is good for coughs." Wahneta Dubasky of Washington, D.C., recommends a cough syrup made of one part honey and one part lemon juice. She adds reminiscently, "We always wore a piece of flannel around our throats. That was the badge of a cold."

For tonsillitis Mrs. George E. Phillips of Ansonia, Connecticut, clearly remembered an annual winter remedy: "Slices of fat salt pork were warmed in a frying pan, and when hot and greasy, they were placed on a soft cloth and sprinkled with pepper. The cloth was then wrapped around my throat and left there until the soreness had gone. It was a gooey mess, but I honestly think it did the trick."

One of the chief folk remedies for "breaking" a fever is a poultice of boiled onions. Elizabeth Ellison of Marquette, Michigan, says that when she had pneumonia as a small child — "and when the doctor had done what he could" — the folk remedy was then used on the advice of a neighbor. "The onions were placed between flannel, and the poultice wrapped entirely around my chest and back. In half an hour the poultice was removed, the onions were shrivelled as if fried, and the temperature had broken."

For influenza, Charles Palermo of Buffalo, New York, specifically recommends the following, and I give it in his full detail:

In 1918 when the flu and pneumonia epidemic was raging, people were dying faster than grave diggers could accommodate them. During the epidemic a doctor from Rochester, New York, claims to have lost an average of only 2 patients out of 100 that were afflicted by the following method [sic!]. Peel and slice about 10 pounds of onions into a kettle (pressure cooker is best). Add two cups of water, and simmer or cook slowly until onions appear grey or transparent. Strain and make a syrup of the liquid by adding Rock Candy. — As patient is lying on back with plenty of woolen blankets close to the neck, give him about 2 ozs. of the onion syrup. Then make three equally divided poultices out of the onions. For best results make three sacks from muslin cloth. Be sure patient never as much as takes his arms from under blankets, for the more perspiration the better. — After patient has had the 2 ozs. of onion syrup, apply one poultice between the shoulders and another on the chest. Keep the third in a double boiler at a temperature that will be as hot as the patient can stand it without blistering, for the hotter the better. — After 20 minutes, take the one from the chest and replace it with the hot one from the double boiler. In another 20 minutes, change the one from the back for the one from the boiler. Repeat the process for two hours. Give patient another two ounces of syrup. — If the patient has not improved after a period of a restful 12 hours, repeat the process with the same onions and syrup. — I have tried the above treatment on three people who were dear to me. One was 78 years old. The doctor told me he doubted if he would live eight or nine days, for he had been deathly sick already for three.

The doctor laughed when I told him of the onion method. — The old gent let me go ahead with my treatment. I used the treatment twice in 24 hours, and upon the third day he got up and went home. — No doubt this might sound preposterous to anyone who has not seen the results, so why not investigate? I'll be glad to furnish proof, for I and anyone who experienced the results pray that people who have the above sickness — not alone a cold — should be acquainted with the remedy, for it sure is a godsend to the poor, let alone those who can afford a doctor's bill.

On somewhat the same order as that of Charles Palermo, Mrs. James Rumsey of Nichols, New York, says that "an old, old remedy to cure lung fever or chest colds is to bind cabbage leaves over the lungs, front and back, and change to new leaves as soon as they become transparent." Mamie Wilson of San Francisco reported that "two bars of soap tied to the bottom of the feet will draw out fever," a cure which with some variations ("tie two mackerel to the bottom of the feet") came in elsewhere from around the country.

Colonel William V. Pruett, who once practiced medicine in Mississippi, said that a local cure there for malarial chills was to boil one pint of buttermilk down to a half-teaspoonful, giving this strong and bitter concentrate to the patient one hour before the expected chill. (Malarial chills occur with a known regularity, and the timing can be anticipated.) The local dictum on this remedy: "One dose will cure."

In the realm of the near fantastic, however, come two malaria remedies from Walter M. Fickes of Badin, North Carolina, who was employed there by the Aluminum Company at the time of the opening of the Badin Lake project. To combat the existing malaria, the company employed field men to fight the mosquito menace, and also to persuade local inhabitants to use quinine. Not with immediate success, however. Mr. Fickes says that the wife of a man who ran a cable ferry confided to him: "My mammy told me how to keep from having chills. When you get up in the morning, catch you a hoppy-toad and blow your breath into its mouth, and chills and fever can't catch you." She then added: "There is some of my kinfolks that don't hold with this cure. *They* hold with plugging up a spider in a thimble and wearing it on a string around your neck. Some of them do have the chills, and I don't. Them folks say they have chills because they forgot to close the shutters at night to keep out the bad night air."

Mr. Fickes checked with the girl's kinfolks, who made fun of the hoppy-toad. Their down-to-earth comment was: "That there girl is just too plain sorry for the chills to take holt on her."

Some of these "remedies" are as wayward as Mr. Fickes's hoppy-toad and can reasonably be dismissed medically. Others cannot. Farfetched as some may seem to be, they still deserve study: a *yes*, a *no*, a *maybe so*.

Helen Steinel of Watsonville, California, wrote that many years ago when she lived in New Jersey,

my little brother was very sick with malaria. One morning a gypsy woman came along telling fortunes. She saw my brother and said that if we would follow her advice, he would get well. These were her instructions: "Go across the road into the field and pick thirteen buttercups. Take the flowers from the stems, and crush them in the palm of one hand until they make a paste. Bind that paste on the thumb of the right hand between the nail and the first joint. A running sore will come. Let it run, and he will have no more malaria." Well, we did it, and believe it or not, it worked. That sore ran for days. The child got well and never again had malaria.

Blanche Cameron of San Diego, California, vouches for an Indian whooping cough remedy which she learned in western Nebraska:

My nephew contracted whooping cough in a very severe form. Our nearest neighbors at the time were a family of Sioux Indians, who had a large cattle ranch. The mother of this family, hearing the whoops, rode over with a bunch of very dark red beets. These were scrubbed, sliced thin, covered with brown sugar, put in the oven, and the juice slowly cooked out. A tablespoonful of the juice is to be given to the patient whenever he coughs. It stops the whoop, but quick. My nephew just took two doses. I have told others, and the remedy really works.

Miss Lucille Johnston, living at the time (1954) at the Hotel Fort Pitt in Pittsburgh, Pennsylvania, had (as we say now) something else again:

When my brother and I had whooping cough, we whooped it up in great style. Then mother found the answer. (Whether it came from a neighbor or was handed down from grandma, I don't remember.) That "answer" to the whooping . . . guaranteed, you understand . . . was to put GARLIC in our shoes. The combination of hot feet and old garlic can't be beaten! For pure unadulterated

SMELL, that's it! — Strange, it sounds like something out of the Middle Ages, yet the garlic cure was actually taking place in our home around the time of World War I.

The chief and most effective folk cure for badly bleeding cuts or wounds is a bandage of cobwebs. Soot from a wood-burning fireplace or chimney may also be added to the cobwebs. (This, of course, makes good sense. As in the cases of moldy bread preceding penicillin and the psychogenic nature of wart cures, the medical profession discovered in 1882 that the principal arachnidan isolated from spider webs proved in pill form an excellent febrifuge or remedy for malarial fever and ague. A folk cure which had seemed wholly idiotic and useless prior to this medical discovery was a pill rolled from whole spider webs.)

An unusual cure for a bad cut was described by Mr. H. Carson of Chicago, who, while playing with an ax as a child of nine, cut his big left toe

into a beautiful V, right down to the joint. My mother had the remedy right at hand. After wiping — not washing — off the blood, she split open a puffball, encased the toe in this, and then bandaged the foot in clean cloths. This treatment was repeated every day or two, and the toe healed perfectly with only a seam in the middle of the nail. The puffballs she used grew in the woods like large mushrooms, and are supposed to be very poisonous. In the fall when they began to dry, my mother always picked some, and when perfectly dry, they were full of powder.

A similar one came from Mrs. David Timberlake of Tampa, Florida:

I lived in Indian country for a number of years, down south, and I remember an accident that happened in a family down there. While one of the members of the family was sawing wood, he chopped off his little toe, and his sister, not getting excited, just run to the kitchen stove and brought some soot, applied it to the open stump where the toe was hanging by a thread of flesh, and picked up the other tip of the toe and placed it on, wrapped it up with a clean piece of cloth, and today the man has a normal toe.

On the theory that the object which caused the cut should itself be "treated," Mrs. A. C. Stout of Findlay, Ohio, says that "if you run a nail in your foot, get the nail and grease it, and put it over the barn door in the dry to keep blood poison away." Mr. H. Reinhardt of Cincinnati has a similar one: "A remedy tried and worked: for severe cut, grease the knife or hatchet with fresh lard. Bury for three days. The severe cut will heal without a scar." Mrs. W. Morgan of Plymouth, Indiana, has one more reasonable: "If we had a cut or any other kind of sore, we went out to the old wagon and applied axle grease, dirt and all. But it did the work, one of the miracles of the times. These days if kids did that, they would die of blood poisoning."

Pure magic to stop the flow of blood and to ease the pain of burns has been used (and continues to be) by individuals who have very special "powers," such as those commonly attributed to the seventh son of a seventh son. Such family descent is not required, however, of the "Power" or "Powwow" practitioners in this country, although secrecy in the transmission of the "power" generally is.

Mrs. Attila Norman, writing from Winslow Bainbridge Island in Washington State, responded to my inquiry:

I have known in the Shenandoah Valley of Virginia and here and there in Appalachian America "Power" People. . . . When I was a little girl in the 1870's and 80's, old Mrs. Pfeiffer, who lived in Dayton or Bridgewater, Rockingham County (Va.) and who was a practical nurse — save the mark — said, and I am sure believed, that she had power to take the fire out of burns, measure babies for *undergrowth* (seven times from head to heel), and say words to stop bleeding. She had the usual conviction that if she told the words she would lose her power, but once when nobody but the negro cook and the little colored maid and I were near, I heard her conjur' a burn and have remembered through the years that she said three times: "Out fire, In frost, In the name of Father, Son, and Holy Ghost."

Mrs. Norman adds that "it was quite startlingly interesting to me to find this very charm set down in Mr. Pepys' *Diary* as something 'it would do no harm to try.' 'Fife' said it three times, too."

Three and multiples of three are, of course, magic numbers. Mrs. C. C. Liscomb of Alliance, Ohio, contributed a variant:

My grandmother used to powwow for burns. She would blow on the burn, and hold her breath and say (all in one breath): "Under clod, Under clay, God Almighty take the fire away." She would repeat three times while holding her breath. Then she would repeat twice more, making six times, while holding her breath three times (total). And if she told anyone, she lost her power.

Mrs. Abbie P. Mather of Miami, Florida, also remembers "powwow" within her family:

Here is an old family tradition . . . I saw my cousin's boy back up against my hot gas oven, and he turned to his mother, and she powwowed it thus: — Blow on it three times and say, "Bless this burn." Blow three times and say, "May this burn eat out and not eat in." Blow three times and say, "In the name of the Father and the Son and the Holy Ghost." Blow three times more. — I have used it so many times, and it has worked every time.

Powwowing for the stopping of blood was also reported by Mrs. Norman:

In 1921, in this far Western state, I came across another person who had "power." My husband and I were coming from Tacoma to Seattle on the old steamer that used to run between the towns. There was a pudgy apple-cheeked man who, being near us fell into conversation, as was the pleasant custom. He said he was a paper-hanger and gave details of his job of the moment. When we parted, he handed us his card, "This will surprise you," he said. It did. Beside his name, address, and phone number — lost, alas, as years went by — was the flat statement: "Knows the Scripture verse that stops blood. Call any hour."

(The Scripture verse that reputedly stops the flow of blood is Ezekiel 16:6, and I presume that I shall be drummed out of the folk establishment for revealing it.)

The next two cures come from Herb R. Wunder of Kissimmee, Florida, and both deserve a solid place in any history of American folk medicine. The first for TB, or consumption:

When I was a young man, I was told by several older men who had often witnessed the following. As I recall this occurred as late as about 1880. As a cure for "consumption" [TB] people would go to a packing house to drink fresh blood from cattle immediately after animal was killed. A particular carriage would come with the sick person, and while the coachman would stay with the horses, the footman would carry a silver goblet to the killing floor, and the patient would drink the blood (hot) within a minute or two after animal was killed.

That goes back to the deaths of bulls in Spain, and the next, fantastic as it may be to you and me, still has variants around the country:

Here's one *I saw happen* although I thought it long out of date. One afternoon when things were quiet, I was passing through the "sheep division" of a large stock yard. I saw two young men in a pen carefully going through the wool on a bunch of sheep. I went to one of the yard watchmen to get the story. He had given them permission to go into the pens. They wanted live sheep lice which they were placing in a bottle. They were going to take them home and place the *live* sheep lice in capsules and give them to grandma who had "yaller jaundice" to swallow. The capsules would dissolve and the lice would eat the "PIZEN" off grandma's liver. To date this case for you, it was about 1922.

The phrase that I like best in that account: "although I thought it long out of date." That is an incredibly wonderful "cure," and one can see the busy little sheep lice at work on grandma's innards: there is some reason and rationale behind the whole business. (Consider also the intense faith and work of the grandsons.) Balance that "reasonable" cure with one from Tennessee which seems to make no sense whatsoever, except that it falls within the same broad tradition: "For chills, take a bedbug, put it in a capsule and swallow it." Here, the bedbug is given no project to work on, no purpose. He is simply swallowed, capsuled. (Where do the folk get these capsules?) In any event, that bedbug chill "cure" came from a Clarksville High School student in 1962, and was collected by an alert teacher at the time.

Ellen Mitchell of Cleveland, Ohio, sent me twenty-five remedies including an amusing (yet seriously reported) one for the toothache: "Apply hot pancakes." Two of her cures (both effective at the time) deserve attention. I should not have liked to have been the patient in either case. However:

Years ago at Fairport Harbor Life Saving Station, a crewman had blood-poison in his foot. It spread to his knee. His home remedy failed. [Miss Mitchell does not give this "home remedy."] His doctor told him his limb must be amputated. John replied, "I'll die first. You'll never put a knife on me. You're fired!" He phoned to dear old Dr. Sherwood, a retired physician in Painesville, Ohio, now deceased. The doctor put John in a chair on the sand under trees. He dug a knee-deep hole in the sand and put John's foot in it, up to the knee. All night the doctor sat by John and trickled water on the sand encasing John's foot and leg. By daybreak the inflammation was gone, and John's leg was saved.

The second touched Miss Mitchell herself:

When I was 12, one limb was ivy poisoned. Childlike, I scratched the itching. Blood poison set in. Our fine doctor prescribed blue vitriol, the usual remedy. It failed. He prescribed "butter of alimony," the remedy for "sheep rot." No effect. Then he said, "I fear her limb will have to be amputated." — A dear old Irish lady, a neighbor, came and said to my mother, "Don't let them cut off your daughter's leg. You have soft soap in your cauldron there. Bind it on her leg. It will hurt, but it will heal." So mother did as directed. I danced and screamed, but it did the work. If no soft soap is available, make an emulsion of some strong soap and apply. Not as good, but effective.

(Butter of alimony: — folk etymology for "antimony?" Whatever it is, I like it.)

These cures cannot be lightly dismissed: some are as effective as any medicine for psychosomatic or psychological reasons; others, with some research, may well have value for the medical profession. Above all they have meaning for the folk: they mean the difference between hope and despair, often between life and death. Consider that hundreds of thousands of our people go through their entire lives without ever having seen or been visited by a doctor, let alone knowing the inside of a hospital. Many of these beliefs (and here they are solidly beliefs and not superstitions) arise, in consequence, out of poverty, fear, and ignorance. And yet with them comes faith also — faith in tradition, faith in the fact that "my grandmother told me," faith that it worked for a neighbor and can or may work for me.

Dr. G. Hobart Light, D.D.S., of Lebanon, Pennsylvania, reported an odd one:

This I got about a week ago for healing split or cracked lips, and "a sure cure." It's ax fat. Take an ax in the cellar of any home, wipe clean, place a piece of brown paper on the ax head (lying flat) and put a match to the paper. The moisture which gathers from the burning of the paper is called ax fat. Apply this to the lip, and the healing surely takes place.

The following is magic, pure and simple, but with a solid and reasonable explanation. (And I have always liked the name of the Secretary of State for Indiana.) Mr. Roland B. Craw of Oxford, Indiana, wrote:

More than 50 years ago, as a young lad, I lived in the home of a cousin in Indianapolis. In the home also for a short time was Union Banner Hunt, former Secretary of State for Indiana. Hearing me cry out in the night because of cramps in the legs, he came to the bedside and told me what a Negro pullman porter had told him: that if you turned your shoes upside down under the bed upon retiring you would not have cramps. He said it worked successfully for him — it did for me. I have not had cramps in the legs for 50 years. — I puzzled out the reason for myself: having taken a precaution against cramps my subconscious kept me relaxed, and you do not have cramps when you are relaxed.

Mrs. Anne Heald of Lake Placid, New York, sent in "old fashioned remedies which I learned from some of the old backwoods people around here": "If you cut your foot on a rusty nail, bind it with a piece of salt pork, and it will draw out the poison. . . . Yellow jaundice can be cured if you drink the juice of sheep manure steeped in boiling water. . . . A Mr. David Nye had a bad case of pneumonia, and the doctor gave him up. When his mother heard of it, she came from quite a distance to save him. Her remedy: she went to the cowshed and caught a bucket of hot, fresh manure and spread it over Dave's chest. He was cured!" (The last is not quite as far out as it sounds: the manure was an application of heat, and the astringent power of it as it dried may also have been helpful. Who knows but what the fumes may have been, also, as effective as the inhalation of some patent medicines? That hot manure cure, by the way, is not unique to Lake Placid, but comes from other parts of the country as well.)

Mrs. Mary E. Cooper of Shawnee, Oklahoma, is frequently emphatic about the efficacy of her cures:

We had sassafras tea in the Spring to thin the blood. . . . Pennyroyal tea and tansy tea for what ailed us. . . . Deadly night shade leaves bruised in sweet cream cured poison ivy. And it did. . . . A drop of turpentine on the tongue every day kept all disease away. . . . Moist tea leaves bound on the eyes at night cured sore eyes. And it did. . . . My neighbor wore a brass ring on the third finger to keep rheumatism away. And it did. Another carried an

Irish potato in his pocket for the same reason. It worked. . . . The lining of a chicken gizzard is good for stomach trouble. It is.

Mrs. George Walker recounts with some shivers:

When I lived in Punxsutawney, a town in western Pennsylvania, twenty some years ago (1934), I knew a Belgian woman who was subject to quinsey. Her cure — and she insisted it to be a cure — was this: She took a double thickness of flannel, filled it with earth worms, and pinned it around her neck. She said the worms drew the soreness out of her throat, which killed them. When the worms were dead, her quinsey was gone. — Heavens! Had I been subject to a like cure, I'm sure the worms would have outlived me!!

This transfer of a disease from an individual to an animal is quite common in folk medicine accounts.

A few years ago, a young man in Holyoke, Massachusetts (a common-sense person), had a child ill with dumb ague. By advice, he got a pup and put it in the child's cradle. The dog broke out in sores, and the child got well.

A Mexican hairless dog sleeping at the foot of one's bed cures rheumatism.

The person who keeps a guinea pig in bed with him at night never has rheumatism.

And from a recent Illinois account collected by Harry M. Hyatt:

I liked the dog and didn't see any harm letting it sleep with me. So that night I took the dog to bed with me and done just as the old man [one of the boarders in the house] said, to let the dog sleep with me and put it out of bed in the morning before sunup, and not to tell anyone. On the seventh morning I could walk to work. But when I came home that night I noticed the dog was limping. I put the dog out on the ninth morning and when I came home that night the dog didn't meet me. And on the tenth night the dog started toward me and it just screamed and screamed, it was in so much pain. The man at the house thought I had kicked the dog. "I never did a thing. I think too much of the dog." The dog was sick all night and died on the eleventh morning. Then the old man told me the dog had got my rheumatism and had died from it, and not to let anyone know what I did. And I got well. I am sixty-five now and have never had rheumatism since.

That belief goes back at least to the Middle Ages, and Sir Thomas Browne (1605–1682), in his "Notes from Commonplace Books" in Volume III of his *Works* (Chicago, 1964), takes a hearty and satirical swipe at it in a note to a credulous contemporary:

Since you are so much unsatisfied with the many rationall medicines which you say you have tried for the gout, you have leasure enough to make triall of these empericall medicines:

Wear shoes made of lyons skinne.
Trie the way of transplantation. Give pultesses from the part unto doggs, & lett a whelpe lye in the bed with you.
Eat partridge eggs.
Travel into Cappadocia wher even mules are not barren.
Make gellies of bulls and boares pizzells.

That took care of that gentleman! But the belief persists.

So many have claimed that copper has helped rheumatism that there may well be some element in the copper which does actually ease pain. The proof is in the pudding, and that is up to each individual. Some it may help, some it may not. It was of no use to the gentleman in the following Illinois account, reported by Hyatt:

I know a good cure for rheumatism — just let a cyclone hit your house, will cure you, if you have rheumatism bad. This is so, every word. When I was a girl going to school we lived back on the creek near Mendon. My father had rheumatism bad, he walked with a cane all the time, never went without one. He sit around all the time with copper wire around his legs, had mother making him poultices of ground glass to put on his joints. Well, he had it so bad that mother and us children did all the work on the place — we hated to see him hobble around and suffer, said every step he took made him suffer. Our near neighbor was about a mile across the creek. I can remember so well. There was a big old tree that had fell across the creek, and we would walk this tree across the creek to go to school or to our neighbor's house. Mother had a barrel by the kitchen door with a hen in it, setting. The old hen was about to hatch, when one day a big cyclone hit our house. Poor father was sitting by the window feeling so bad. We had all been out doing the chores, for we saw the storm coming. When it hit our house, we saw the old barrel go up in the air, hen and eggs — it was a sight. It took the roof off the house and turned it clear around. We looked for father and he was not there in the chair. We thought he too had went up in the air, for his cane was by the chair. We didn't know it then, but did in a little while. He ran over to get this neighbor that lived a mile across the creek. He even walked across the old log tree we all used. When he got to this farmer's house, the farmer said, "How did you get here? You even don't have your cane." My father said, "Hell, I left my cane back home. The cyclone scared the rheumatism out of me. I don't need a cane any more." The man came home with my father and help us. But my father never used his cane any more, and we children and mother didn't do all the work on the farm, for my father was cured of the rheumatism where nothing else help.

There are other reports of persons being scared out of their rheumatism, but it takes something pretty powerful to do it — like a cyclone, or "four big water mocassin snakes," something a little stronger, certainly, than the normal hiccup scares of "Fire!" or bursting a paper bag.

The cures are countless:

When you hear the first whippoorwill in the spring, turn a somersault three times, and you'll never have backache. Rub the hands with the first snow that falls, and you'll not have sore hands all winter. On Ash Wednesday before sunrise, dip a pail of water in a running brook (upstream), bottle it, and keep as a cure for anything. Water in which a blacksmith has cooled his iron is a cure for freckles. For chapped lips, kiss the middle rail of a five-railed fence. For a sore throat, gargle with coal oil. Skunk's oil is a cure for a cold. For earache, blow cigarette smoke into the ear and cover with a slice of hot onion. To cure a sty, heat a gold wedding ring until quite hot and then, holding it in a piece of cloth, put the hot ring as close to the sty as possible without touching it: the heat will draw the soreness out, and the sty will disappear in a day or so. For a nose bleed, wet a pine splint in the blood from each nostril, drive the splint into a crack in a tree, and as long as the splint remains in the tree, the nose will not bleed. For a bee sting, chew any three different nonpoisonous leaves (such as apple, clover, and rose), and hold the pulp on the bite. To cure colds or sore throats, wear genuine coral or amber beads for nine days. For catarrh, kiss the nostrils of a mule. Sickness among members of the household can be prevented by keeping a goat. Drop your first pulled tooth into a bird's nest, and you will never be troubled by headaches. Headaches will no longer trouble a woman, if a live toad is once bound to her forehead.

And so on into the thousands and thousands. I leave them to the M.D.'s to sort and puzzle out. And I leave them also this frightening folk belief: "Never pay the doctor's bill in full, or you will soon need him again."

# 33.

# *Weatherlore*

Weatherlore rivals medicine as the second great group of folk beliefs and superstitions. Everyone practices it, including the confirmed apartment dweller who doubts the radioed or TVed message and looks out the window to confirm his own beliefs in a reading of the skies. He *knows* that half the time the official prognostics are surely wrong, and that half the time his own are surely right. Perhaps the odds are even better in his favor. If he is a gentleman walking, let us say, from Fifty-sixth and Park down to Forty-fifth and Park, the twenty-minute weather-stroll may well be on his side (twenty minutes out of a day's forecast), but if he is a cattleman in northern Montana, a Maine fisherman off the Banks, or a farmer in Iowa, he will be thankful not only for the day's official briefing but for the long range (three or four days') and even longer-range (two to three weeks') forecast. Modern science has come to the help of these men who live and die by the weather, but it was not always so.

A sailor who could not smell the wind or read the skies was worth less than his salt, and a farmer who could not read the daily weather for the near future was likely to wind up the year with an empty barn. On farms, cattle ranches, and sailing ships, instruments for telling the weather were rarely, if ever, at hand. Men passed their knowledge on to each other, and gradually their observations became fixed in saws and proverbs. Today this knowledge is part of our folk heritage, part of the history of our land and seas.

Certain types of forecasts are based on local knowledge. Thunderstorms that break over New York City cross the Hudson from New Jersey, preceded by black clouds. In Denver the advance guards of the storm are separate, lamblike clouds followed by great white thunderheads over the Rockies. In Eastport, Maine, a steady southeast wind brings summer rain, and the gulls gather near shore and utter sharp cries presaging the storm. At Cape Hatteras a heavy ocean swell from the southeast means rain from that direction. In Cheyenne the winter wind from the north brings the heaviest blizzards. "When Lookout Mountain wears cloud caps, it will rain in six hours."

These purely local observations are drawn from long experience. They have proved out frequently enough to become local weather laws. Each community has its own.

In addition to these, there are the hand-me-down traditions. Take, for example, the long-range forecast practiced for fifty years by an Alva, Oklahoma, couple, and more recently applied by a Texan to last year's weather in the Panhandle. All the equipment needed is one large onion, twelve teaspoons of salt, a paring knife, a large piece of cardboard, and a pencil.

At 6:00 P.M. on New Year's Eve, cut the onion down the middle and remove twelve half-onion shells. Place one teaspoonful of salt in each shell. Divide the cardboard into twelve squares for the twelve months, and place a shell in each square. Then at 6:00 A.M. on New Year's Day, read the forecast for the year as follows: if the salt is moist or has collected into a small ball, moisture is indicated for that particular month; if it is dry, the month will be dry.

In terms of the science of meteorology, this type of forecast (which comes from Europe and dates back centuries) is utter nonsense. James Caskey, one-

*Gonzales, Texas, 1939:*
*longhorn weathervane with cattle brand*

time editor of the U.S. Weather Bureau's *Monthly Weather Review*, told me that those who attempt to foretell a cold winter by the heavy growth of fur on beavers, skunks, possums, and other animals are often misled: "The fact is that fur grows more heavily because it is *already* cold, not because it is going to be in future months."

Although he may be one hundred percent right, Caskey's view is not likely to sway any believer in tradition. Weather is too much with us to be taken away by the scientists. And, although the Weather Bureau may now look upon these traditional forecasts as outmoded, they were not always so considered by officialdom.

In 1881, Brigadier and Brevet Major General W. B. Hazen, Chief Signal Officer of the Army, issued from Washington City a circular to all army posts throughout the United States ordering each post to collect all "the popular weather proverbs and prognostics used throughout the country." The circular is specific in its request and lists twenty-four chief categories of proverbs and prognostics wanted, ranging from proverbs relating to the sun, to the moon, to stars and meteors, to rainbows, to mist and fog, to dew, to clouds, to frost, to snow, to rain, to thunder and lightning, and to winds; and prognostics from the actions of animals, from birds, from fish, from reptiles, from insects, from trees, and from various objects (including chairs, tables cracked before rain, coals burning brightly, corns, ditches, doors, dust, lamps, rheumatism, salt, seed, signboards, smoke, soap, sound, strings, toothache, walls); proverbs relating to days of the week, to each month of the year, to the seasons of the year, to the year itself; and, last, miscellaneous proverbs and prognostics not covered by any of the preceding.

The responses to General Hazen's request were assembled and edited by Lieutenant H. H. C. Dunwoody, a signal officer in the 4th Artillery. Dunwoody's report was published by authority of the Secretary of War for the War Department by the Government Printing Office in 1883.

Boondoggling? Not at all. The published report recognized that "the popular sayings referring to years, months, and weeks are not considered of any real value," but at the same time pointed out that many of the proverbs and omens relating to rain and storm were "based upon true meteorological conditions, and a thorough knowledge of this class of prognostics may prove of service to the observer when instruments are not at hand."

Later, in 1903, Edward B. Garriott, Professor of Meteorology, prepared a report, *Weather Folk-Lore and Local Weather Signs*, for the Weather Bureau itself, which was published by the Government Printing Office for the Department of Agriculture. It sold widely at twenty-five cents a copy. It differs from Dunwoody's report in that it is more analytical. In common, however, both reports go to the folk traditions for their materials.

The folk believed (many still do) that key or controlling days determine the weather for succeeding weeks and months. These are beliefs which Dunwoody says are of "no real value," but which he nevertheless includes in his collection. They are the stuff of which almanacs are made. There are hundreds of them, and obviously they wind up in conflict and confusion, an example of which I shall give in a moment. For the present, take your choice of these. Some of them are quite interesting, and even worth practicing, if for pastime or amusement only:

The first three days of any season rule the weather of that season. The general character of the weather during the last twenty days of March, June, September, and December will rule the following season. (Those two rules are not too bad: one can hedge through the results of prognostication, because there is quite apt to be a bit of rain, sun, snow, cold, warmth, clear, dew, and whatnot mixed up in them.) Three days of September — the 20th, 21st, and 22nd — rule the weather for October, November, and December. The first three days of January rule the coming three months. The last twelve days of January rule the weather of the whole year. But the folk believe more widely that: the twelve days commencing December 25 and ending January 5 are the keys to the weather for the year. (Make note of them this year, simply to see how the forecast turns out for your area.) If it rains on Friday, it will rain on Sunday; if it is clear on Friday, it will be clear on Sunday. There is never a Saturday without some sunshine. (That belief stems directly from the Middle Ages. In the medieval church, Saturday belonged to the Virgin, and the Council of Clermont in 1096 required all priests and monks to repeat an office in her honor on that day. It is from this relation to Mary that the day is supposed to be especially bright. The Spanish have a saying: "No Saturday without sun, no girl without love." And from Boston: "The sun shines some part of every Saturday in the year but one.") If the first Sunday in the month is rainy, every Sunday but one in the month will be rainy; if it is pleasant, the same rule applies. It often rains on the Fourth of July. (It was generally believed that this was due to the firing of cannon and rockets. The folk have carried this belief over to the present, and inclement weather today is frequently blamed on atom bomb testing.) Whatever the weather is on Friday, that will be the weather all the next week. If it rains on Sunday before church services, it will rain all week. If it rains on July 15, it will rain for forty days. (The figure forty probably derives from the biblical flood and Noah.) The first day of January determines the weather for the month of January.

Which brings me to the *reductio ad absurdum* example: If the first day of January is a fine day, then the whole month of January will be fine. The twenty-fifth day of January, which is St. Paul's day, is said to control the weather for the rest of the year — the whole year! And November 21 is supposed to control the coming winter. Now the coming winter obviously includes January of the coming year, and that month, of course, includes the first day. Therefore, if you have a fine first day in January of the first year, and if you believe in these controlling days, you will obviously have fine weather the second year, and the third, and so on, forever. Similarly, if it rains or storms on the first of January, you will be rained and stormed on forever!

That is long-range forecasting beyond the wildest dreams of the Weather Bureau. But the folk have no such qualms about forecasts as bureaucratic Washington: "If onion skins are thick, the winter will be severe." "When a cat washes behind its ears, it will storm." "There will be as many snows in winter as the moon is days old at the time of the first snow storm." "When a rooster crows at night, expect bad weather." "The date of the first snow foretells the number of snowstorms for the winter: that is, if it snows for the first time on November 17, there will be 17 snows."

The Bureau dismisses these, but there are some proverbs and omens that it does not reject out of hand, and some that it readily accepts. Take:

> *Rainbow at night,*
> *Sailor's delight;*
> *Rainbow in the morning,*
> *Sailors take warning.*

The facts are simple. You can see a rainbow only in the morning or in the late afternoon: the low position of the rising or setting sun reflecting against the clouds determines this. The Weather Bureau has proved over the years that our weather comes normally from the west. Therefore, if you see a rainbow in the late afternoon ("at night"), it means that the clouds and storm causing it are in the east, since the sun is setting in the west. It means also that the storm clouds have passed over to the east from the west. If, on the other hand, the rainbow is seen in the morning, you are seeing it in the west, since the rising sun from the east against the western clouds makes it possible. When the rainbow is in the west, then the weather — the rain and storm — will be moving eastward towards you.

The "rainbow at night" was the observed experience of sailors over centuries. It made sense, and because it did it was capsuled into the easily remembered proverb. Closely related are two other proverbs:

> *Red sky at night,*
> *Sailor's delight;*
> *Red sky in the morning,*
> *Sailors take warning.*

and

> *Evening red and morning gray,*
> *Sets the traveler on his way;*
> *Evening gray and morning red*
> *Brings down rain upon his head.*

Generally speaking, both of these proverbs are true, but the color of the red has to be qualified. A rose red or pinkish sky is due to a lack of vapor and presence of dust, usually in the evening a sign of fine weather. But an angry, lowering, violent red sky is due to excessive vapor, and presages storm.

As for the gray of the sky, in the evening it is likely to be caused by a stratiform cloud sheet, which is the sign of an approaching storm. The gray of the morning, however, appears chiefly during fine weather when the morning mist — resulting from radiation cooling at night — gives a grayness to the sunrise. Farmers and sailors undoubtedly distinguished between the shades of red, but in both proverbs the word "pink" should be substituted for "red" in the first lines to make them more scientifically accurate. Otherwise they can stand as they are and make good sense.

Farmers and countrymen believe that cobwebs on the grass are a sign of fair weather. They also believe that:

> *When the dew is on the grass,*
> *Rain will never come to pass.*

Both the belief and the proverb are true. Cobwebs can be seen on the grass only when covered with dew. And dew cannot form unless the skies are cloudless and there is no wind. A cloud sheet would prevent the radiation that causes the ground to lose its heat after sundown. A cloudless sky permits the radiation, the ground lowers its temperature and chills the air in contact with it, and the dew is formed. A windless night is also necessary: otherwise the warm air passing over the ground would not allow it to cool. Two perfect conditions — a windless and cloudless night — create the dew, and the chances are that the fine weather will continue for at least a day or more.

Two widely known proverbs have been used by seafaring men along the New England coast for generations:

> *Mackerel sky, mackerel sky,*
> *Never long wet, never long dry.*

and

> *Mackerel scales and mares' tails*
> *Make lofty ships carry low sails.*

Less known is a variant:

> *If a cloud looks as if it had been scratched by a hen,*
> *Get ready to reef your topsails then.*

Again the folk observations prove accurate. The cirrus clouds, which look like mackerel scales or herring bones, are made up of ice crystals, and travel at speeds of 100 miles an hour at altitudes between 20,000 and 30,000 feet. They are part of a lower and slower storm system, and have been caught up in the higher currents by rapidly moving eastward winds. To sailors they were always a warning, and the lofty ships bowed to the storm that followed.

Another storm warning is a ring or halo around the moon: a large ring around the moon means rain or storm close at hand, while a small ring is a sign of rain a few days away. Again the belief is true. The halo itself is simply moonlight seen through clouds. When the clouds are low and slow-moving, the halo seems larger. When the clouds are high and fast-moving, the halo appears smaller. The low clouds are a sign that the storm is virtually at hand; the high clouds are an advance warning of a storm to follow in a few days.

Certain proverbs relating to rain — all-important to farmers — are also acceptable to the Weather Bureau. "Rain before seven, Stop before eleven" is, for example, generally true, since continuous rains do not normally last more than four or five hours. "Rain long foretold, long last, Short notice, soon past" is also true, since the more slowly a depression or storm approaches, the longer the rain belt takes in passing. The short notice with which a thunderstorm comes and the relatively small area covered by it guarantee, on the other hand, that it will pass fairly quickly.

To hear train whistles or any other sound more clearly and at greater distances than usual is also an indication of rain or bad weather:

> *Sound traveling far and wide*
> *A stormy day will betide.*

The belief and the resulting proverb are accurate. Acoustical engineers and meteorologists know the reason: when the sky is cloudy and the air humid, sound — or the acoustical wave — which would be dissipated under normal conditions is bent back to earth. Rather than going upwards and outwards, the sound of the train whistle is turned back to the earth, and the distance at which it can be heard is consequently extended.

Midway between those folk beliefs which can be explained and accepted

*Lyman County, South Dakota, 1940:*
*rounding up cattle*
*during the first stages of a blizzard*

and those which are out-and-out superstition are the omens dealing with insects, birds, and animals. Farmers generally believe, for example, that "pigs can see the wind," a saying which comes from the fact that pigs — sensing weather change — run around, squeal, and are more restless before a storm than usual. (An old Negro and one-time slave, Daniel Sharper of Fairfax County, Virginia, told us at the Library of Congress that the color of the wind is red, and that this can be determined by looking through the eye of a pig at hog-killing time.) Cattle huddle together at one end of the pasture before a storm. When swallows fly high, it is a sign of good weather; when they fly low, brushing the surface of the water, it denotes bad weather — and reasonably enough, because gnats and insects fly low in the humid atmosphere. When bees stay near the hive or cluster closely about it, bad weather is on the way. ("A bee never gets wet.") If flies swarm into the kitchen or house, or bite more sharply than usual, expect a storm. When snails are numerous, due to the damp and humid air, rain is at hand. If ants are very active or travel in straight lines — the shortest distance between points — a storm is approaching. Fireflies in great numbers are a sign of fair weather. When birds wash in the dust, expect rain. If owls scream in foul weather, it will change to fair. And a nice New England picture: when grouse drum at night, there will be a deep fall of snow.

These beliefs seem reasonable enough, and might even pass inspection by a relaxed Weather Bureau official. There are, however, others which would drive a meteorologist mad. And yet thousands of Americans have believed them and still do. Many relate to the moon:

Two full moons in any calendar month will bring heavy rains or a flood. (A person taken sick in any month with two moons is apt to die.) In western Kansas it is believed that when the moon is nearly full it never storms. There is the very widespread belief that when the new moon appears with the points of the crescent turned upwards, or lying on its back so that it will hold water like a bowl, the month will be dry. When the crescent is tipped so that the water will run out, the month will be wet. This has been credited to the Indian, and the common proverb runs: "If an Indian can hang his powder horn on the crescent moon, the month will be dry; if he cannot, wet." Of longer range is the belief that "If in the Spring, a crescent moon hangs like a cradle (rests on its back), the Summer will be dry." A bright star behind a crescent moon means rain and storm, but a star in front of, or within, the crescent means fair weather. And a moon slung low in the south during February brings in thirty days of good weather.

To be your own weather prophet:

When everything is eaten at table, it indicates continued clear weather. Winter ends with the first thunder of Spring. The number of fogs in August determines the number of snows in Winter. If a rooster crows in the night, it is a sign of bad weather. In Kentucky, "It never rains at night during July." And from the same state: "There will be a frost just three months after the first katydid is heard."

From eastern Maine, but also quite general: "If you can see enough blue sky in the west to make an old woman's apron, the weather will clear." Usually this is "to make a pair of pants for a sailor" or "a pair of pants for a Dutchman." (A reasonable enough prognostic, since weather comes from the west.) From Massachusetts, a flat statement of fact: "Rain falling while the sun is shining means that the devil is beating his wife with a codfish." From eastern Massachusetts: "A load of barrels foretells wet weather." (If the barrels are filled with beer and headed for South Boston, possibly true. Otherwise, a doubtful prognostic.) From Bedford, Massachusetts: "When a great many women are seen on the street, it will rain next day." (There must be some reasonable explanation for that, but what? Shopping before rain?)

Weather is a universal topic. *Probably no day goes by without some mention of it by every adult person in the United States.* And fortunately, in spite of hell and high water, hurricanes, twisters, blizzards, floods, droughts, dust storms, and all, we can still look at it with the leavening humor that helps in its particular way to make us the people we are. Was it Mark Twain or Will Rogers who said in the nation's capital: "If you don't like the weather in Washington, just wait a few minutes"? And there is the old adage "All signs fail in dry weather," which has been rephrased with rough and wry humor to become the local "All signs fail in Oklahoma." In New England, they say there are only two seasons in the year: Winter and the Fourth of July. And in Maine perhaps not even that many:

> *Dirty days hath September,*
> *April, June, and November;*

*From January up to May,*
*The rain it raineth every day.*
*All the rest have thirty-one,*
*Without a blessed gleam of sun;*
*And if any of them had two-and-thirty,*
*They'd be just as wet and twice as dirty.*

"Everybody talks about the weather, but no one does anything about it." We are really very lucky:

If the cows come home before sundown, it is a sure sign of rain. A pigeon on the ridge of a roof means rain. If during a rainstorm a crow flies past without cawing, it is a sign that the rain will soon be over. When a dog howls at the moon in Winter, it is a sign of snow. If bears go into their dens early in the season . . .

# 34.

# The Folklore of Birth

"A woman is most beautiful just
before the birth of her first child."

Birth, marriage, death. In our lifespan these are the three great milestones around which men have woven an enormous body of folk belief, some of it gentle and humorous, some dark and tragic. The roots of these
superstitions and beliefs lie in Europe and the Mediterranean, but they
survive today in the hills of Vermont and Kentucky, the coves of the
Carolinas, the sea lands of Maine and Florida, the plains and prairies of
Texas and Oklahoma. Our cellophaned and streamlined civilization cannot
kill them. Folk memory is deep and ageless.

Of the three, the greatest is birth. It is the most mysterious, the most awe-
some. As a consequence the folk beliefs surrounding it are legion.

What, for example, are your prospects for children? How many will you
have? Will the child be a boy or a girl? Will the birth be easy or difficult?

632

What about birthmarks? Does the day or time of birth carry its omen for the child? Can you determine the child's future?

On the prospects for children there is the belief that the number of knots, lumps, or enlargements on the umbilical cord of the first baby indicates the number of future children the mother will bear. Country midwives or female relatives assisting at the first birth are careful to count these lumps and to record them for the information of the mother. In advance of the first birth, however, one can determine the number of future children simply by tying a string to one's wedding ring, lowering the ring into an empty glass, and asking, "How many children shall I have?" The ring supplies the answer by swinging to strike the sides of the glass. Each strike signifies one child. A woman may also know the number of children by counting the lesser veins branching out from the main vein in her wrist, or by counting the wrinkles in her forehead, each one standing for a child.

Other general notions on the prospect for children: twins appear in every third generation; happily married couples will produce good-looking children; the children of quarrelsome couples will be ugly; and if a married woman is the first person to see a newborn infant, she will have the next child. It is also a folk recommendation that a woman should not on her first visit to a newly born child hold it in her arms unless she herself wishes to become a mother.

The influence of the sun and the moon upon the sex of the child is not discounted. In the Ozarks it is believed that when a woman's right ovary has been removed, she can have female children only, while if the left has been removed, the children will all be male. The traditional reason for this stems from the medieval belief that the solar, or masculine, influence belongs to the right side of the body, while the lunar, or feminine, influence belongs to the left. There is, of course, no medical basis for this: male and female children have been born to women with only one ovary, left or right. Because of the power of the moon, however, it is believed that a child conceived in the light of the full moon or on the increase of the moon will be a girl. A child conceived during the waning of the moon, when the lunar influence is at its ebb, will be a boy.

During the period of gestation there are a variety of "do's" and "dont's." It is bad luck, for example, for a pregnant woman to stand in front of a mirror and observe her figure, just as it is also bad luck for a pregnant woman to have her picture taken. To attend a funeral during pregnancy will bring trouble, the nature unspecified but the juxtaposition of death and life psychologically understandable. Any preparations for the arrival of the new baby will also bring bad luck, a tempting of the fates as it were. In Europe a crib is never made by the father before the arrival of the baby, while in New England showers were never given for a baby before its birth.

For stomach trouble during pregnancy there is a nostrum from Illinois: "When you are cleaning a chicken, always save the lining of the gizzard. Cook it tender. Put it through a food chopper. Roll it with a rolling pin until a fine powder. If a woman who is pregnant has stomach trouble, give her a small portion of it three times a day and it will cure sickness of the stomach."

And from Pennsylvania, with undoubted German origins, comes the strange belief that nearness to horses during pregnancy will prolong the period of gestation. If a woman with child steps over a rope to which a horse is tied, she will carry the child to the twelfth month. "I knew a woman that was carrying a baby and she walked under her mare's head every few days to hitch her to the buggy, and she carried her baby eleven months." Still another from pre-Chrysler and Ford days: "A woman one time was carrying a baby. If was way past time, around ten months. She didn't know what was wrong, so she went to a German midwife. So the midwife said, 'Do you remember if you ever went under a horse's head or not?' And the woman thought and said she believed she did. The midwife said, 'Go home and walk back under the horse's head the other way than you walked before.' And the woman did. And just as soon as she got under that horse's head, she started with pains. And the baby came before she got into the house."

The folk belief that prenatal influences of one sort or another cause birthmarks is so universal that there seems no possibility of its dying, no matter how much the medicos may discount it or how civilized we may think we are. Birthmarks are the result either of a fright the mother-to-be has suffered or of some craving for a special food. The instances of women being frightened with the consequent result that the babies are marked are countless and implicitly believed. A child may be born with a snake across its stomach or chest if the mother was frightened by a snake; "a woman frightened by a mouse threw her hand to her forehead, and as a result the son was born with a mouse birthmark on his forehead"; another woman, cooking, burned her fingers with hot grease and touched them to her breast — on the daughter's chest there appeared the impression of the five fingers.

The inordinate craving pregnant woman may have for certain foods has no dietary meaning. Birthmarks are, however, attributed to the inability to obtain the foods: "My mother was pregnant and she wanted blackberries, and she did not get them. And when my brother was born he had a bunch of blackberries on his forehead." The very common strawberry birthmark is explained in the same way, and more unusual ones — a round brown mark for ginger cookies — are similarly accounted for.

The birthmarks can be removed either by rubbing them with a duck's foot or by wiping them with a dishrag and then placing the rag in a coffin while saying, "O Lord, take with Thee what harmeth Thee not, but harmeth me." To avoid facial birthmarks altogether, a pregnant woman should never touch her face when frightened, or should immediately cross herself and say, "In the name of the Father, Son, and Holy Ghost."

The period of confinement and birth is not overlooked: "When it's around time for your baby to be born and you get up some morning feeling real good, look out, because your baby will come inside of twenty-four hours." Mountain folk believe that if a woman eats hot biscuits, cabbage, fish, or sweet potatoes during confinement, any one of them will be the death of her. The belief is widespread also that both birth- and afterpains may be cut by placing an ax or razor beneath the bed, and country doctors will bear witness to this common practice.

Sympathetic illness on the husband's part is not infrequent. "My mother used to tell about a case of this sort which happened at Canton, Missouri. The husband not only had morning sickness and other ailments peculiar to a pregnant woman but also suffered such acute pains during his wife's delivery that he almost died. Although the wife's gestation and parturition were quite normal, she, being fearful she might kill her husband, would never have another child." In this connection it is also believed that if a pregnant woman crawls over her husband to get into bed he will have as many pains as she will at the time of birth. Deservedly so. The least he could do would be to move over!

The day and the time of birth carry their special import for the child:

> *Monday's child is fair of face,*
> *Tuesday's child is full of grace,*
> *Wednesday's child is loving and giving,*
> *Thursday's child must work for a living,*
> *Friday's child is full of woe,*
> *Saturday's child has far to go,*
> *But the child that is born on the Sabbath day*
> *Is blithe and bonny and good and gay.*

More specifically, there are these beliefs: any child born in the light of the moon is more intelligent than a child born in the dark of the moon; if a child is born on a stormy night, it will be a cross and nervous baby; if a child is born about four o'clock in the afternoon, it will be moderately rich through-out life, while if it has the jackpot luck to be born about four o'clock of a Saturday afternoon, it will be extremely wealthy.

As far as special days go, there is, from Illinois, the lucky thought that any person born on or between the twenty-first and the twenty-fourth day of any month will have good luck on the thirteenth day of any month. Why, I have no idea, any more than why a child born on the thirteenth of a month will die on that same date, or why anyone born between the twenty-first of January and the twenty-first of February will have bowel trouble. As a birth date, however, the twenty-third of June is always a lucky day, while July is fairly rough financially: "My mother told me that was why I was always poor, because I was born in July."

The physical characteristics of babies have meaning, ranging from

> *Dimple in the chin, devil within*

and

> *Ugly babies make pretty ladies,*
> *Pretty babies make ugly ladies*

to the beliefs that a child with long fingers will become a pianist, a child with a large mouth a singer, and a child with a cowlick roaringly stubborn. A nice Texas thought is the belief that a "child who is ugly in the cradle will be beautiful in the saddle." And the child who is born with a caul or a veil is lucky, and so are those who have the fortune to carry a child's caul with them. If a sailor, for example, carries a caul he will never drown at sea, nor will a soldier ever be shot in the wars. A child born with a caul will be intelligent, and if the caul is preserved, it will always bring good luck. A child born with a caul also has the power of healing, as does the seventh son of a seventh son. A seventh son in any family, by the way, always brings good luck to that family. A child born with an open hand will be generous in life, while a baby born with a closed hand will be stingy.

The folk have various nostrums to ease teething: if you hang a necklace of hog's teeth about a baby's neck, it will have no difficulty in teething; the right paw of a mole sewn in a small bag and suspended from the baby's neck will have the same effect; a necklace of Job's tears will ward off spasms during teething, while a black ribbon tied about the infant's neck will make the teething easy; in Maryland the hot brains of a wild rabbit rubbed on the child's gums will aid teething, and rubbing the gums with a silver thimble in Maine will also help. Above all, never permit anyone to place a man's hat on a baby before it begins to teethe; it will have a most difficult time.

To cure slobbering there are two efficacious remedies. The first is gentle and simple. When the mother first rises from confinement, she should fill a thimble with water and carry it to the child. The child will not slobber thereafter. The second is more complicated, with overtones of magic. From Illinois comes a mother's testimonial:

If a baby slobbers, take a live minnow and draw it back and forth three times through its mouth, then throw the minnow in running water, and the fish will swim away with the baby's slobbers. This is true because I tried it years ago. I had a baby and it slobbered all the time. One day we went fishing and I thought I would try it, for we had a bucket of minnows; so I took a large minnow and drawed it through the baby's mouth three times and threw it in the creek, and the minnow went down the stream. You may laugh at me, but my baby never slobbered after the fish went out of sight.

As for the further care of babies, there are amusing and delightful beliefs. A most practical one, fostered perhaps by country doctors, is the saying that "unless the doctor's bill is paid promptly, the baby will not grow." A baby should also see a sunrise before it sees a sunset in order to insure a long life. And in order to insure wealth and success in life, a baby should be carried upstairs before it is taken downstairs: "When Mrs. R's son was born, the grandmother carried him up a ladder into the garret of the one-storied house to make sure that he would rise in the world. I remember that the nurse who attended the mother of our prominent citizen, Mr. K., insisted on performing the same ceremony, which was in that case made easier by the existence of stairs." In our city hospitals and apartment buildings, it is possible that this "ceremony" may currently be transferred to the elevator, preferably an up-bound express. Some nurses simply place a telephone book on the floor and step up on it with the baby.

As for the looks of the child, it will have freckles if rain falls on it during the first year of its life. To insure curly hair, place the newborn infant on a curly rug before it touches any other kind of fabric, or wrap the baby in fur before dressing it for the first time, or rub the top if its head with your finger in a circular motion. On the first three Sundays of its life the baby should also be dressed in its very best clothes simply to guarantee that it will wear clothes well for the rest of its days.

In country lore there is occasionally an omen for the future based on the first louse found in a male baby's hair. In the Ozarks, if you crack on a Bible the first louse found, the baby will become a preacher. The children may, on the other hand, become excellent singers: "I have two sons, and years ago when I found the first louse in their heads, I cracked them on the bottom of a tin cup, and both boys are good singers." In our antiseptic and relatively bugless society, these fine omens tend to go by the board.

It is bad luck to select a definite name for an unborn baby. Always pick out several names and from these select one after the child is born. It is unlucky also to name a child for a dead person (the child will not live long), or to change a baby's name once the name has been selected. When a baby cries at baptism, it is a sign that the child approves of its name.

On the general behavior and care of infants, there are numerous beliefs. If a child does not, for example, fall out of bed before it is eleven months old, it will grow up to be a fool. (It is only the intelligent, curious, and healthy child that has the wit to fall out of bed.) If a baby walks before it is six months old it will be unlucky in afterlife: "My sister's boy could walk before he was six months old and he lost in everything he done. He just could not have any luck." To allow a child to see itself in a mirror before it is a year old will bring bad luck. To bring good luck to the child, however, always carry something for it to eat the first time you visit it. If by chance the first visitor to see the newborn child offers it a piece of money, the baby will be rich. And if the visitor kisses the bottom of the baby's feet, the child will have good luck.

One widely observed — as well as harmless and amusing — way of foretelling the child's future is to place several objects on the floor, each object symbolizing an occupation. The child, placed on one side of the room, crawls toward the objects. If the child, for example, selects a Bible, it will be a preacher; a hammer, a carpenter; a silver dollar, a banker; a bottle, a drunkard; a book, a lawyer or teacher; and so on with various objects that one may choose. Also, if a coin is given to a child and grasped firmly by the child, it will become wealthy, but if the coin is dropped, money will slip through its fingers.

These and a thousand more form the folklore of birth and infancy: A woman will lose a tooth for every child that is born to her. . . . Do not cut a baby's fingernails until the baby is at least a month old, or it will become a thief. . . . Measure a baby before it is a year old and it will not live to reach its second year. . . . To hand a baby through a window is unlucky. . . . Stretch out the arms of a child two years of age against the wall and measure them fingertips to fingertips. Twice this distance will be the child's height when grown. . . . It is unlucky to take a child's picture before its first birthday. . . . Placing a baby on an ironing board will cause bad luck. . . .

Which of these to believe? All of them, of course. Unless you happen to be a skeptic.

In which case? Why, then only those that your mother believed or your grandmother before her. Your own tried and true family beliefs. About which there can be no question.

You turned out rather well, didn't you?

# 35.

# *The Folklore of Marriage*

L ove and courtship precede marriage (except for some marriages of arrangement and convenience), and yet they do not form part of the
rites of passage. There is no single rite associated with love and courtship,
unless it be the culminating one of the engagement, and that more properly
belongs to marriage as the first formal step of the marriage contract. With
the engagement, one moves inexorably towards the great rite of marriage,
just as in the other milestones of life (birth and death) there is prior inex-
orable movement towards them.

(In our complex society, there are, of course, lesser milestones with their
lesser rites, but these, by and large, do not deeply — if at all — touch the
folk nor lend themselves to the creation of widely held folk beliefs and ob-
servances. They are specialized: the initiation into a fraternity, for example;
the graduation from high school or college; first apprenticeship in a union;

admission to a club; induction or appointment in the armed services; and other comparable markers in our lives. They are the honors, the hazards, and responsibilities of life which we chalk up along the way, but they are not the great milestones in the lasting sense that birth, marriage, and death are.)

The church (of whatever faith) plays its enormously important part in these rites, but its role is separate. The church's role is one of crystallized formality and fixed ritual, a confirmation and blessing through the powerful ceremonies of baptism, marriage, and funeral. The folk bow to these, yes, but around the events build their own beliefs, traditions, and customs.

Of prime interest to the folk were, and are, the proper month, day, and time for the ceremony; omens and portents preceding the marriage; the weather on the day itself; the wedding apparel of the bride; beliefs relating to the ring; events immediately following the wedding: the reception, the wedding cake, rice, old shoes, and other matters; the honeymoon, the wedding night, and the beginning of married life. They range from New Hampshire's "A white dove flying near the house foretells a marriage" to Illinois's "To stop continual quarrels in the family, sprinkle sugar on the floor, then sweep it up and burn it." In between there is the marriage.

All beliefs boiled down, I come up with the following as the very best for date and time: The month: June. The date in June: the third, fourth, or twenty-first. The day: Wednesday. The time of day: the afternoon. The hour: not particularly noticed by the folk, except that the wedding must be solemnized while the hand of the clock is rising, never falling, that is, the wedding must be between the half-hour and the hour and never between the hour and half-hour. The time of the moon: while the moon is on the increase, never on the decrease — a full moon is most propitious, a waning moon is bad. And if you live on the coast, marry also with a flowing or rising tide and never with an ebb tide. In sum, the invitation should read to the effect that the marriage will be celebrated on Wednesday, June 3 (hopefully they coincide) at half-past four o'clock, the moon and tide having been checked. If the first of the month does not agree with the moon, then one shifts to the twenty-first, where it probably will. After June, the months of October and December are the luckiest for marriage, while May constantly remains the worst. There are various rhymes and reasons bearing all these out:

> *Monday for health,*
> *Tuesday for wealth,*
> *Wednesday the best day of all,*
> *Thursday for losses,*
> *Friday for crosses,*
> *And Saturday no luck at all.*

Sunday does not appear in the days of the marriage rhymes, since any ceremony might conflict with those of the normal services. Friday and Saturday in all rhymes are days of bad omen (Friday presumably the day of the Crucifixion), while the auguries for Monday, Tuesday, and Thursday are always variable, from bad to fair to good. Wednesday remains firm: "the best day of all." I do not know why, any more than why the third, fourth, and twenty-first of June are good days.

June itself as the best month goes back to the days of Rome and the worship of Juno, the wife of Jupiter, who was patroness of the young and goddess of marriage; while May is named for Maia, goddess of growth and patroness of the old, and is the month that honors the unhappy dead. Not, obviously, a good month for youth and the early joys of wedlock.

The rising hand of the clock, the growing or full moon, and the flowing or incoming tide all presage rising fortunes, while the falling hand, the waning moon, and the ebb tide suggest falling fortunes and failure.

The afternoon? This goes back to the English clergy of the seventeenth century, who refused marriages in the morning because the bridegroom was apt to appear "unshaven and with dirty and negligent attire" as the result either of early morning work in the country or a last round of all-night bachelor parties in the city. Evening marriages were also prohibited because the clergy noted with horror that the "wedding party frequently took the bridal couple off by sheer force to the ale-house." The traditions of month and time of day persist in the United States — and certainly with no knowledge or remembrance of Juno or Maia or seventeenth-century English clergy.

Quite as interesting:

> *Happy the bride*
> *The sun shines on,*

*Woe to the bride*
*The rain rains on.*

which has numerous variants, including:

*Happy is the bride the sun shines on,*
*Tears for the bride the rain falls on.*

and the very specific: "A rainy wedding day means that the bride will shed a tear for each raindrop." And why all that belief? Do you remember the Wife of Bath in Chaucer's *Canterbury Tales* who, introducing herself, frankly says: "Housbondes at chirche-dore I have had fyve . . ." ? Five husbands *at the church door*. Not *in* church. It was not until the reign of Edward VI (1537–1553) that church door weddings were discountenanced, although even not then firmly abolished. In Chaucer's time (1340–1400), weddings were still held outside the church on the "church porch" and were not permitted in the holy body of the church itself. Naturally then, when there was a pleasant, sunshiny English day, the bride and the whole wedding party were happy. But when it rained — at a time when umbrellas had not been invented, when the "church porch" so-called had no roof over it — then the bride and the entire party might well become, under English rain, as bedraggled and unhappy a lot as seen anywhere. So, this rhyme and tradition, existing widely in the United States, stems from at least fifteenth-century England, with the fact that it does and the reason for it known to very few using or believing it here and now.

Americans have added a few wedding weather items of their own. From Maryland: "If it snows on your wedding day, you will get a dollar for every flake that falls on you." Illinois: "If it snows on the wedding day, the husband will be good to his wife." Massachusetts: "Thunder during a wedding is a sign of unhappiness all one's married life." But I like Alabama, and the simple phrasing: "If you marry on a pretty day, you will live happy."

As for the wedding dress, be careful: "If a drop of blood falls on your wedding dress while it is being made, your husband will kill you." Other than that, the traditional omens and rhymes are:

*Married in blue, love ever true,*
*Married in white, you've chosen right,*
*Married in red, you'll wish yourself dead,*
*Married in black, you'll wish yourself back,*
*Married in gray, you'll go far away,*
*Married in brown, you'll live out of town,*
*Married in green, ashamed to be seen,*
*Married in pink, of you only he'll think,*
*Married in pearl, you'll live in a whirl,*
*Married in yellow, jealous of your fellow,*
*Married in lavender, you'll always be savage.*

More briefly and more Ozark folk:

*Blue is true,*
*Yaller's jealous,*
*Green's forsaken,*
*Red is brazen,*
*White is love,*
*And black is death.*

And:

*If when you marry, your dress is red,*
*You'll wish to God that you was dead;*
*If when you marry, your dress is white,*
*Everything will be all right.*

Red and black are symbolic of deviltry and witchcraft, but any other colors may be worn in an informal wedding. A widow may wear black at her wedding "if she puts a rose in her hair, but if the flower falls out, she will lose her second husband." White is the accepted color for all formal weddings, but it was not always so. Prior to eighteenth-century England — and certainly in Elizabethan England — wedding gowns were of gold and green and purple, of velvet and taffeta and silk, incredibly rich and weighty, and made to be worn on subsequent great occasions. In the late eighteenth century, white began to be fashionable, and the fashion was confirmed in Victorian times. White is, of course, a symbol of purity and innocence, a symbol that returns to the days of the Greeks.

Apart from the gown, the bride should, of course, wear:

*Something old,*
*Something new,*
*Something borrowed,*
*Something blue,*
*And a new dime in the shoe.*

Or:

*New and blue,*
*Old and gold.*

The "old" must be something that has belonged to a happily married woman. The wedding veil of one's grandmother (if it still exists) is singularly blessed. The wearing of such an item insures the transfer of happiness to a bride. The "new" is the wedding gown itself, the shoes, or other clothes of the bride. The "borrowed" must be some object of gold to guarantee wealth and fortune, a brooch or pin worn under the dress if gold does not fit the costume. The "blue" is symbolic of the heavens and of true love, and tradition here leans to fancy blue garters. (One conservative bride eschewed such frippery, and carried instead a blue PTA card borrowed from a friend.) The coin (in England it is a sixpence) should be worn in the heel of the left shoe.

Pearls are the symbol of tears and should not be worn: for each one that the bride wears, her husband will give her cause for weeping. The bridegroom should carry a horseshoe in his pocket for good luck (Illinois), and a bride will be happy if she wears or carries a bit of salt (in glove, shoe, or pocket) when she goes to be married. Salt has two exceptional virtues: it is abhorred by witches and devils and, as a preservative, it has symbolized lasting friendship and loyalty since the days of the Greeks. The bride will have good luck if she carries her mother's prayer book; and if she wears — hidden in her hair — a small laurel leaf, it will be reminiscent of the Roman crown of victory: *Amor vincit omnia!*

## The Ring

"It is best to purchase a wedding ring from a mail-order house, because the ordinary 'store bought' ring may have absorbed bad luck from someone who tried it on in the store."

The reasons for placing the ring on the fourth finger of the left hand are three:

The first, the most practical is from the Romans, who believed that the fourth finger of the left hand best protected the valuable ring. The left hand is used less than the right, and of the fingers on the left hand, the fourth is the only one that cannot be extended except in the company of another. (Try it.) Therefore protection: the ring is as safe as it can be.

As for the second, the Egyptians believed that a vein ran from the fourth finger of the left hand directly to the heart. Since they believed that the heart controlled both life and love, this finger was the most honored. It deserved the ring, the pledge of love.

The last reason stems from the Christian church, which, to impress the seriousness of the ceremony upon bride and groom, lectured that the thumb and first two fingers of the hand stood respectively for the Father, the Son, and the Holy Ghost, and that the fourth stood for the earthly love of man for woman, their marriage together, and the hope of Heaven to follow.

William Jones in his *Finger Ring Lore* (London, 1898) suggests:

The reason why a ring was pitched upon for the pledge, rather than anything else, was because anciently the ring was a seal by which all orders were signed and things of value secured, and therefore the delivery of it was a sign that the person to whom it was given was admitted into the highest friendship and trust. For which reason it was adopted as a ceremony in marriage to denote that the wife, in consideration of being espoused to the man, was admitted as a sharer in her husband's counsels, and a joint partner in his honour and estate, and therefore we find that not only the *ring*, but the *keys*, were, in former times delivered to her at marriage.

Some look upon the ring as a "toy fetter" symbolical of "the restraint in which wives are held"; others hold that it is "a symbol of purchase"; but most feel that the "bridal hoop — a circle without end — symbolizes the endlessness and perpetuity of matrimonial love, and the groom's devotion to, and perfect trust in, the bride." Let us accept, with Robert Herrick, that last:

> *And as this round*
> *Is no where found*
> *To flaw, or else to sever:*
> *So let our love*
> *As endless prove:*
> *And pure as Gold for ever.*

At the ceremony itself, the bride must remember to put her right foot first always: as she steps over the sill on entering the church; at the altar itself (her right foot should be just a bit in front of her left, and ahead of her husband's); on turning to leave the altar; and stepping over the sill as she leaves the church. The right foot first will bring luck and happiness: "If a man and woman get married and the wife steps out of the church with her left foot first, her marriage will be very unsuccessful and will end up in court." And from England and carried over to this country: "If the bride be prudent, she will take care when at the altar to put her right foot before that of the bridegroom, for then she will get the better of her husband during her married life." Tsk, tsk!

And at the altar the bride and groom must take care to stand parallel to the planks or cracks of the floor, and not at right angles to them. "If they stand crossways, they'll have a cross life."

There are a million and one things about weddings, but space to touch only a few.

## Orange Blossoms

Orange blossoms have been traditional since the Middle Ages, when they were worn or used for decoration only by the noble and wealthy. And why orange blossoms rather than, say, white roses? The orange blossom stands for innocence, purity, love, and fertility, all in one: Because the tree is an evergreen, it symbolizes the lasting nature of love. Because it bears both blossoms and fruit at one and the same time, it symbolizes, in the delicate blossoms, the innocence and purity of young love, and, in the fruit, the proved promise of fertility and motherhood. On her wedding night, Juno was presented with that rarest of gifts, "golden apples."

## Tears

A bride should, of course, weep: "A bride crying on her wedding day is a lucky sign, for it shows that she has wept all her tears away."

## Rice

"Rice should be thrown over a bride so that some of it falls in her bosom." Rice was not always, however, the happy fertility symbol: it came into being rather late. In Roman days, wheat was used, and much later in England whole kernels of corn and wheat were tossed on the bride's head. The use of rice in England — and subsequently America — begins precisely with the year 1872. Mr. John Jeaffreson reports: "My friend, Mr. Moncure Conway, tells me that not long since he was present at a wedding in London, when rice was poured over the head of the bride. The bride and groom of this wedding were English people, moving in the middle rank of prosperous Londoners." I like Jeaffreson's precise definition of the people involved, and at the same time appreciate his reporting of rice and 1872: he was sufficiently astonished to make note. Such dates are quite as important as Trafalgar, Waterloo, and 1849. Rice in 1872.

## The Shoe

Hurling a shoe (or, exuberantly, shoes) after a bridal couple is a custom going back at least to the Anglo-Saxons. From earliest times, the symbol of domestic authority has always been the shoe. The father — in Anglo-Saxon times — demonstrated the transfer of his authority over the bride to the groom by giving the groom a shoe, with which the groom lightly tapped the bride on the head to show his newly won power over her. So, when the shoe is thrown after the bridal couple, it is a symbol of that transfer of authority. The shoe should, therefore, properly be thrown by the father of the bride.

The word *bridal*, by the way, comes from *bride-ale*, the special permission given in England to a family to sell ale in the house or yard where the celebration was held following the wedding ceremony, the money raised helping to defray the cost of the festivities. And *honeymoon* comes from the Anglo-Saxon custom of drinking mead or honey-wine for one moon, or for "the first sweet month of matrimony," after the marriage.

There are conflicting beliefs about the wedding day and the days after: some believe that the wedding day is the bride's day, and that the day following is the groom's day, and that the weather on either of these days is symbolic of the wedded life to follow for each of the participants. Others believe that the symbolism of the weather begins on the day after the wedding, and not on the wedding day itself. You have your choice. There is, however, one tradition which has been reported in Maine, Kentucky, and Illinois, and it would be interesting to know of it elsewhere. That is the *infair*, or *infare*, dinner. Gordon Wilson of Western Kentucky University (a great teacher who left us recently) recalled it in his State: "Old people tell, with real joy, of the *infair* (or *infare*), the big dinner at the bridegroom's parents' house the next day after the wedding. The couple nearly always spent their first night at the home of the bride's parents; the next day they and their attendants (usually two couples) came in their buggies to the big dinner. In my youth I remember having attended, as a younger brother, two such celebrations: in 1896 and 1903." In Maine, the infair was also called "the second-day wedding." A pleasant custom in country America.

For the wedding night itself, there are a variety of interesting beliefs: "My mother said the first one to blow the lamp out that night when people get married would be the first one to die. Some people would let the lamp burn all night." "The person turning over first in bed on the wedding night will be the first to die." "I had always heard this and on my wedding night I got out of bed forgetting the old saying — it is very bad luck for a bride to put her feet on the bare floor on her wedding night — and put my feet on the bare floor, and I had nothing but bad luck and hell all through my married life." "The night of your wedding always sleep with heads to the east and feet to the west for luck." (Some say heads to the north.) "If on their wedding night the bride and bridegroom sleep with backs together, they will have a quarrelsome life; if with faces together, a peaceful life." And this incredible item from Adams County, Illinois: "A pound of limburger cheese spread between two towels and laid under the pillows of a bridal couple on their first night together will give them good luck and many children."

A bride should be carried over the threshold of her new home, a tradition going back to the Romans, who believed that she was most vulnerable to witchcraft and the evil eye at this transitionary moment in her life. Also, "If a bride and bridegroom pour boiling water over the doorstep just before they walk into their new home, they will have good luck and happiness." Salt scattered across the threshold is also helpful against witches.

Married life has its ups and downs: "I went to see my niece after she was married several years and she had everything so nice. I said, 'You have everything you want.' Then she said, 'We took a package of rice in our house first, that is why. Mother said if you do this, you will always have plenty, and we did.' " "The first white lie told by a bride will bring her money." "Another thing — if a man asks you to marry him, you ask him who is going to carry the pocketbook, the groom or the bride; for it is bad luck for the groom to carry it the first year." "A wife can hold her husband's love by blackening her shoes every Sunday morning." "Men who sit on rocking chairs all the time love their wives." "Always choose your second mate at the grave of the first one and your second marriage will be successful." "The thirteenth year of your married life is always the luckiest."

And simply by way of reminder (I never know myself where to look for them), these anniversaries:

| | | | |
|---|---|---|---|
| First: | cotton | Seventh: | woolen |
| Second: | paper | Eighth: | rubber |
| Third: | leather | Ninth: | willow |
| Fourth: | fruit and flowers | Tenth: | tin |
| Fifth: | wooden | Eleventh: | steel |
| Sixth: | sugar | Twelfth: | silk and fine linen |

| | | | |
|---|---|---|---|
| Thirteenth: | lace | Twenty-fifth: | silver |
| Fourteenth: | ivory | Thirtieth: | pearl |
| Fifteenth: | crystal | Fortieth: | ruby |
| Twentieth: | china | Fiftieth: | golden |

Seventy-fifth: diamond

# 36.

# *The Folklore of Death*

"Death takes place at ebb tide."
*New England*

Death is the last and greatest and final passage. We have done with all the others — big and little — and move out of this world which has been permitted us so briefly. Nothing will ever touch us again.

Death creeps on us little by little: as children, it means nothing to us — even the word is alien; as sophomores in college or thereabouts in age, we look upon it romantically, with weeping willows and Keats; in middle age, we sense it a bit, a bit fearful; and as we come down the last stretch —in the late years — we look to it with no fear. It is our lot. We follow our fathers.

There are skirmishes with it along the way, yes: the wars, crossing a street, a bad accident at home. Those are the sudden moments, but they are not part of the long ordered progression from birth to grave.

The folk believe deeply in the omens and portents of death, and I think none of us are immune to these beliefs. We wish, perversely, to know the unknowable.

The two most prevalent and firmly believed warnings are the howling of a dog (three times) and a bird flying into and out of a house or death-room, the dog credited with extrasensory powers to feel death, and the bird the symbol of the departure of the soul.

I believe when a dog howls that awful pitiful howl, someone will die. The truth is they always do. We had a dog about two years ago, and one night it started that mournful howling, that makes the cold chills run all over you, out in the yard. I made my husband get up and go out and stop the dog. He no sooner got back in bed until the dog started again. I said, "Get up and put the dog in the kitchen, maybe it's cold." I didn't want to think it was a warning. He put the dog on some old carpets, then went back to bed. About three o'clock that dog started again that mournful howl, getting us all out of bed. That was the third time that night. And it was no time until we got word my brother was killed about three o'clock that morning just when the dog gave its last howling. So the dog was giving us the warning.*

And another shivering omen:

One night we heard a dog give three keen howls about eight o'clock. Mother said, "We will hear of a death before this time tomorrow night: if you hear a dog give three keen howls at night, it's a sign of death before twenty-four hours." And my mother died the next morning at eight o'clock.

(How often, by the way, do you hear that particular use of "keen"?)

Dogs are not only generally aware of the approach of death, but have specific knowledge of it as well and to whom it applies. Look between a dog's ears, for example:

I knew a man, his dog was howling, and he went out to look between his ears to see what the dog was seeing, and he saw his own picture. And the man died in three days.

\* \* \*

If a dog howls while looking up, the person about to die will go to heaven; if while looking down, to hell.

* Unless otherwise noted, all quoted items here are from Harry M. Hyatt's great Illinois collection cited in the Notes.

\*   \*   \*

One day our dog got on the bed, holding his head up in the air with his ears up, looking across the river. Whenever a dog gets on the bed, holding his head up in the air with his ears up, looking in one direction, he is scenting a death in the family and one is sure to happen. We were living on Third Street [Quincy, Illinois], and the dog just kept getting on the bed and looking across the river. He was scenting a death. And it was no time until my aunt across the river died.

\*   \*   \*

My grandma was sitting in the room one day, just as well as anyone, and our family dog went over to her and holler real pitiful three times, looking up at her. She patted its head and said, "What is wrong, Dick?" My mother was out in the kitchen and said, "I don't like that." And in three days my grandma was dead.

Birds are perhaps an even greater omen of death than dogs, and not only flying into the house but perched on the roof of the house, sitting on the windowsill, pecking at the window, circling over a person's head, crying at night, and otherwise bringing their ill news.

A dove sitting on the top of a house and cooing three times is a sign of death in the family.

Just before before my husband died, a turtledove came and sit on my clothesline, giving that mourning sound. The bird came back for three mornings straight. I said to my husband, "I don't like that." It made me just sick, for I knew something would happen. In six weeks my husband was dead.

\*   \*   \*

My mother was very sick in bed and we pulled the bed up by the window, and two white doves came and sat on the windowsill until my mother died; and just as she was dead, they disappeared and we did not see them again.

\*   \*   \*

My daughter was not feeling well. I was sitting at the window and a white dove came and picked on the window. And I said, "My God! that's bad luck to the house." The next day the dove came again and picked on the same window. Then I knew sure it was an omen. And my daughter died that week.

\*   \*   \*

About fifty-five years ago we were living across the street from some people and the woman was sick. I went over to the house and when I got to the gate, two white doves flew over the gate, went to the front door and flutter around

*neca, Illinois, 1937: a recent death in the family*

the door several times, then flew off to the cemetery. I said to her son that was in the yard, "I don't like that, for that is a token of death." And his mother died that day.

The soul takes its flight even more immediately: "I had a man boarding with me two years ago, and we were all sitting here in this room, and a big white bird came to the window. It looked as large as an eagle. We all got up and went on the porch. We could see the bird flying away. And the man that was boarding with me drop dead while we were watching that bird fly away." "When my grandmother died, a big white bird flew through the house one night, and she died the next morning." "One day a bird flew in our house. It came in at the front door and flew out the back door, which is bad luck. That night my grandson, that was well as could be, took a spasm and died before morning."

I had always thought that the call of the whippoorwill was a delightful sound, but not to some: "If the call of a whippoorwill on your farm is loud, it forebodes a death; if soft, sickness." "My mother always told me if a whippoorwill sings near your house, you will have a death in the family. One night a whippoorwill came and sit on the corner of our house and hollered. I went out and run it away. The next morning it came back again. I run it away again. But inside an hour we got word my sister was dead." "He had a very sick aunt. They were all there to visit her, and about dark a whippoorwill flew in and sat on the head of the bed and hollered 'whip-poor-will' three times, and the folks said, 'Aunt Mary will die in three days.' And the whippoorwill flew away hollering 'whip-poor-will' three times. And in three days at the same time Aunt Mary died."

Roosters and crowing hens (always bad luck) bring their portents, as testified to in the folk idiom:

It's an old saying to kill a hen the minute she crows. We had a white bantam hen that we thought of a lot, and one day she came and stood on the doorstep, and crowed and flop her wings three times. We didn't want to kill her because she was a pet. And in three days our little baby girl took sick and died. A few years after than an old Plymouth Rock hen came to the door at noon while we were eating and started to crowing. My son jump up from the table and said, "I am going to kill that hen, we don't want another death in the family." He kill her and we didn't have any death from that hen crowing. If we had of let her live, someone in the family would of died.

*   *   *

We had a rooster that did not belong to us to come and crow in our front door (with his head sticking in), and my mother died.

*   *   *

Just last week my neighbor up the road had a hen to fly in the kitchen through the window, and her grandfather died that week.

*   *   *

My brother was sick. We didn't think he was sick, but we were sitting up with him because he didn't want to be alone. One night just at twelve o'clock our old hen that was setting out in the yard on some eggs came off her nest and came right into the house. It was summertime and those days we didn't have screens like now. Well, this old hen went right to the fireplace and started to scratching in the ashes in the fireplace. It was an omen, for my brother died before morning.

There are countless others: To carry a peacock feather into the house is a sign of death. Three strange cats in a yard at the same time means a death in the family. A sound in one's ear like the ringing of a bell, sometimes called the *death bell*, signifies a death. A person laughing in his sleep will soon die, and sneezing in bed or at the breakfast table is a bad omen. "My baby sneezed one Monday morning at the breakfast table. My grandfather died before the week was over." Clothes falling from a hook are a portent of death. (In the change-rooms of the mines in the West, when a miner's clothes fall from the hook, he frequently refuses to go down in the mine, but instead takes the day off.) A brick often tumbles off a chimney preceding a death in the house. An umbrella opened in a room where there is a bed means that someone will die in that bed before the year is ended. To carry a shovel, hoe, ax, or rake into or through the house brings death: "Just two months ago, this is April sixteenth, the man that lived downstairs went out to the woodshed, got the ax and took it all through the house to the front door, and gave it to a man that wanted to borrow it. In three weeks he was a corpse. It's an old saying, the one that carries an ax through the house will die soon." To fall out of bed denotes a death in the family. "My brother would never let anyone move a broom, to keep a death out of the family. One day in some way his wife forgot or didn't want to leave the new broom be-

657

*Vicinity of Jackson, Kentucky, 1940:*
*mountain people carrying a homemade coffin*
*up a creek bed to the family plot on the hillside*

hind, so put it on the wagon when they moved. Her husband was sure mad about it, for in three weeks his mother took sick and died. He never forgave his wife. They parted over her putting the broom in the wagon." To have a candle flicker three times and then go out presages death. "I believe in tokens. We had a clock that didn't run for years. One day it struck three times and never struck again. And we had three deaths that year." (A clock striking for no apparent reason always means death.)

Notice again and again the recurrence of the number three: striking three times, crowing three times, three weeks, three deaths, three cats, dead in three days. It is the magic number above all others, sometimes for good, often for evil. Seven is also important: "If you go to a beauty parlor and find six women ahead of you so that you are the seventh waiting, return home at once; unless you do, you will die before the end of the year."

Restless deathbed actions are reminiscent of Falstaff's passing: "My husband was sick. I knew he was going to die because he would pick at the curtains all the time, just keep picking at them. That is a sure sign of death. All at once he rose up and got hold of the curtain and almost pulled it down, and said, 'Sally, let us go.' I said, 'Not now.' And he died in a few minutes." "The week before my husband died he kept pulling and pulling all the time at the sheets. We could not keep them on the bed."

Difficult deaths are sometimes attributed to featherbeds: "My brother-in-law was sick for weeks and the doctor told us he could not die on chicken feathers. As soon as we moved the featherbed from under him, he passed away." "A dying person cannot die while lying on pigeon or dove feathers; they must be taken from under him." Prolonged death pangs may also be eased by placing an open Bible under the dying person's head or, according to a tradition from the Indians, "placing a pinch of wood ashes on the dying person's lips."

An old Scottish tradition that survives in Illinois in somewhat debased "luck" terms also helps to ease the passing: "My mother always did this: forty years ago when my brother was dying, she opened the window for his soul to pass on to heaven. If you leave the window down and the soul stays in, you will have very bad luck."

It is an ill omen, presaging another death, when rain falls into an open and empty grave, but a good omen when rain falls after the death: "Blessed are the dead that the rain falls on." And a hard rain while someone is dying shows that the person will die happy. At the burial itself, the beliefs about rain are conflicting — some say a good omen, some say bad. A peal of thunder following the burial, however, is a sign that the soul has gone to heaven. A shooting star that night is a sign of the same.

Various rites must be performed within the house after the death, and some of these I observed in my youth in New England with the deaths of distant relatives or of neighbors. They are still practiced and are fairly common around the country. In New England days the corpse was placed in an open coffin in the parlor, and relatives and neighbors came to view the body. Some of the dead were pleasant and even amusing to look upon: a lady, who in her lifetime would never have dreamed of being seen in such a thing, wearing a pink peignoir, and her normal steel-rimmed glasses.

First, the clocks in the house must be stopped as soon as the death occurs. This belief is universal. The valid "reasons" for it are: (a) "if a clock strikes while there is a corpse in the house, it is striking another member out of the family," and (b) the time cycle — culminating in the death of one person — must be broken, so that continuing deaths do not occur. One starts over, and time must wait: time cannot continue its destruction.

Mirrors must be covered or turned to the wall: looking into a mirror while the corpse still lies in the house will bring another death within the year and "at the same time and on the same day" that the looking occurred. Also, anyone looking into a mirror while the corpse is in the house will be the next to die, and usually before the end of the year. Or: "We were burying our boy and just before they started out with the coffin someone uncovered the mirror, and I saw the coffin in the mirror. I almost fainted because I knew we would have another death, and before the year was out we lost our other boy." I have seen mirrors covered, but never knew any reason for the act, and doubt that anyone in the house was acting on anything but folk tradition.

All the pictures in a death-room should be covered, turned to the wall, or put away. Unless this is done, another member of the family will die within the year. And separate from that is the belief that as soon as a person dies, his picture begins to fade.

There is the very old Scottish-Irish-English (and before that Continental) tradition that the bees must be told of any death in the family. Otherwise the

*New Roads, Louisiana, 1938:*
*family praying at the grave of a relative*
*on All Saints' Day*

bees will leave or die. "I lost my little girl and I was so worried that I forgot to go and tell the bees. You must go to each beehive and tell them who died so they will not leave or die. I had two hives and lost them both." And another: "When my grandfather died fifty-five years ago, we had an orchard full of beehives, and we went out and covered every hive, and told the queen that he was dead, to keep the bees from leaving."

As for coins (and the use of them on the eyes of the dead goes back to the Greeks): "If you can get a coin that was used on the eyes of a corpse and keep it, you will always have good luck." "Another thing my mother did if anyone died, she always put some money under their pillow so they would have money to travel on. She did this to my brother forty years ago, put two silver dollars under the pillow in his coffin so he would have money on his way." "The family should always spend at once the coins used on the eyes of the dead."

Jewelry should not be left on or placed on a corpse, since not only will it bring bad luck to the family, but the dead person will also never go to heaven. This comes from early New England, as does also the continuing belief that flowers should never be placed in the coffin with the corpse. Pamela McArthur Cole reported in the *Journal of American Folklore* in 1894:

I have been told by a friend that in 1855 she was assisting in some preparations for the funeral of a young girl who had died, after a short illness, away from home. As she stood beside the coffin, she felt she could not endure its cold, bare look, void of all beauty, and she said, "I cannot bear the thought of laying her away without a flower; can't we get some flowers." It was in the very earliest days of Spring, and having no flowers accessible, she asked if some one would go to the woods near by, and bring a handful of the tender young sprays of leaves just budding — something to suggest a thought of the freshness of hope and of life —, but her proposition was received with such a stare of surprise and an air of disapproval that she said no more.

Today flowers are welcomed, but they should never be brought back from a funeral: there will be another death in the family.

As family and visitors viewed the corpse in its coffin — either at the house or funeral service — it was customary to touch the forehead of the dead person, a superstitious precaution taken to avoid dreaming of the dead or seeing them, a sort of "be on your peaceful way, and leave us alone in peace."

In the matter of the funeral procession itself, there are omens and forebodings, of which these two from Illinois are representative.

A mile right up the road here an old woman was not able to go to the church to see her daughter that they had brought here, so on the way to the cemetery they stopped in front of her house, took the coffin in the house and open it to let her see her daughter that she had not seen for some time. It's an old saying and it's so: if the horses nicker in front of a house while a corpse is in that house, another will follow that year. The mother died in three months. Of course they were looking for her to go, for she was very poorly; but they were not looking for her other daughter to die that she was living with. But she did before the year was out. It never fails, if the horses nicker in front of a house when there is a corpse in it.

And the colorful second:

About sixteen years ago there was a funeral in the neighborhood around Monroe Street. While they were all in the house and were just about ready to start to the cemetery, a big red rooster got up on the hearse and crowed three times looking in the house. That is a sure sign of three more deaths. We lived across the street and my husband said, "Look at that son-of-a-bitch, he is calling three more deaths in the neighborhood." And they did have another death in that house. In three weeks my husband was the next to go. In about two months after that the third one died in that neighborhood before the three months was up.

There are a variety of other advices and warnings: never let your shadow fall on a passing hearse — you will be the next to ride in it; never continue walking towards a funeral procession — turn around as soon as you see it, and walk in the same direction with it, to avoid death; if a car in a funeral procession stops three times on the way to the cemetery, there will be another death in the family within three months (cars in a procession actually do now move, with lights burning, with considerable unbroken rapidity); never count the cars in a funeral procession — the numbers of cars counted are the number of years before your own death; if the hearse gets stuck in a mudhole on the way to the cemetery, there will be another death before the year is out; a funeral procession should never cross a river, and the corpse must not pass twice over any part of the same road; never walk through a funeral procession, either between the carriages or the files of mourners on foot; and always say a prayer for luck when you see a funeral procession.

The matter of the grave itself has its symbolism. The headstone should be to the west with the feet of the corpse to the east, so that on the terrible Day of Judgment, the body may rise and face the rising sun. That is New England tradition, and it is also harsh New England tradition that suicides (euphemistically, those who died "suddenly") and other comparable derelicts were buried to the north of the church, separate from honest folk who lay buried to the sheltered south of it. The north side was the Devil's side, and in New England the bitter winds came from that direction.

Let us hope that when the time comes the most of us lie to the comforting south.

# Sources and Notes

# *Folklore Journals*

As of possible use to the general reader, student, teacher, and librarian, I append a list of the leading journals and the addresses where subscriptions may be placed, the frequency of issue, the annual subscription rate, and the initial year of publication. Subscription usually carries with it membership in the given society as well.

AS     *American Speech*, Columbia University Press, New York City. Quarterly. $6. (1925)

CFQ     *California Folklore Quarterly*, 1941–1946 (changed to *Western Folklore* in 1947, *q.v.*)

FF     *The Folklore Forum:* The Folklore Institute, Indiana University, 714 East 8th Street, Bloomington, Indiana 47401. Six issues of the *Forum* annually plus two issues in its Bibliographic and Special Series. $4. (1968)

FSGW     Folklore Society of Greater Washington, P.O. Box 19303, 20th Street Station, Washington, D.C. 20036. Ten "Newsletters" annually plus three issues of the society's *Journal*. $5. (1968)

HFB     *The Hoosier Folklore Bulletin*, 1941–1945 (changed to *Hoosier Folklore*)

HF     *Hoosier Folklore*, 1946–1950 (changed to *Midwest Folklore*)

IF     *Indiana Folklore:* Secretary-Treasurer, Hoosier Folklore Society, 714 East 8th Street, Bloomington, Indiana 47401. Twice a year. Individual membership $4, student membership $2, institutional membership $6. (1968)

JAF    *Journal of American Folklore:* American Folklore Society, University of Texas Press, Austin, Texas 78712. Quarterly. Individual $10, student $5, institutional $12. (1888) [All past as well as present book publications of the society are now distributed by the University of Texas Press.]

JPC    *Journal of Popular Culture:* University Hall, Bowling Green University, Bowling Green, Ohio 43402. Quarterly. $4. Three-year subscription $10. (1967)

JFI    *Journal of the Folklore Institute:* 714 East 8th Street, Indiana University, Bloomington, Indiana 47401; or directly to the printer-publisher: Mouton & Co., P.O. Box 1132, The Hague, Holland. Three times a year. $4. (1964)

KFR    *Kentucky Folklore Record:* Charles S. Guthrie, Kentucky Folklore Society, Western Kentucky University, Box 169, Bowling Green, Kentucky 42101. Quarterly. $3. (1955)

KFQ    *Keystone Folklore Quarterly:* Dr. Robert Byington, The Pennsylvania Folklore Society, Point Park College, Pittsburgh, Pennsylvania 15222. Quarterly. $4 (1956)

LFM    *Louisiana Folklore Miscellany:* Lee Morgan, Louisiana Folklore Society, Centenary College of Louisiana, Shreveport, Louisiana 71104. Irregular. $3 per volume. (1958)

MF    *Midwest Folklore*, 1951–1964 (discontinued: the national and international materials were channeled into *Journal of the Folklore Institute*, 1964 –, while the local and regional materials appear in *Indiana Folklore* 1968 –)

MFR    *Mississippi Folklore Register:* Ovid S. Vickers, Mississippi Folklore Society, Department of English, Box 697, East Central Junior College, Decatur, Mississippi 39327. Quarterly. $3. (1967)

NAMES    *Names:* The American Name Society, Mrs. Ann Sampson, Secretary, State University College, Pottsdam, New York, 13676. Quarterly. $8. (1953)

NCF    *North Carolina Folklore:* North Carolina Folklore Society, North Carolina State University, Box 5308, Raleigh, North Carolina 27607. Twice a year, May and November. $2 (1948)

NEF    *Northeast Folklore:* "B" South Stevens Hall, University of Maine, Orono, Maine 04473. Originally a quarterly, now an annual. With curious Maine logic: $2 for member, $3 for nonmember. (1958)

NMFR    *New Mexico Folklore Record:* Mrs. E. W. Baughman, New Mexico Folklore Society, 606 Vassar Drive, Albuquerque, New Mexico 87106. Irregular. (1946)

NYFQ    *New York Folklore Quarterly:* New York Folklore Society, The Farmers' Museum, Cooperstown, New York 13326. Quarterly. $5. (1945)

NWF    *Northwest Folklore:* Department of English, University of Oregon, Eugene, Oregon 97403. Irregular.

PTFS    *Publications of the Texas Folklore Society:* Texas Folklore Society, English Department, University of Texas, Austin, Texas 78712. Hardbound annual volumes, each with different title, as *Texas Folk and Folklore, The Sunny Slopes of Long Ago.* $5. (1916)

SFQ    *Southern Folklore Quarterly:* Southern Folklore Society, 108 Anderson Hall, University of Florida, Gainesville, Florida 32601. Quarterly. $8. (1937)

TFSB    *Tennessee Folklore Society Bulletin:* Ralph W. Hyde, Middle Tennessee State University, Murfreesboro, Tennessee 37130. Quarterly. Individual $3, student $2, institutional $4. (1935)

WF    *Western Folklore:* California Folklore Society, University of California Press, Berkeley, California 94720. Quarterly. Individual $8, institutional $10. (Formerly *California Folklore Quarterly*, 1941–1946) (1947)

WVF    *West Virginia Folklore*, 1951–1966 (discontinued)

# The Library of Congress
# Recordings of Folk Music

The Library of Congress records issued for public sale have two distinct advantages: (1) they are authentic (the majority are field recordings); they come with transcriptions of the texts of the songs; and the notes are prepared by folklore scholars and experts; and (2) they are always "in print." There is never the problem of referring to a record only to find that it can no longer be purchased or easily found. The Library of Congress folksong records have been continuously available for more than twenty-five years, and they will be fifty years hence.

As of this writing, the Library has issued 62 long-playing records, which include approximately 1000 titles of folksongs, ballads, dances, instrumental pieces, and folktales from the Anglo-American, Negro, and Indian traditions in the United States, as well as some Latin American material. A 100-page *Folk Music Catalog* describing the LP's may be ordered from the Superintendent of Documents, Government Printing Office, Washington, D.C. 20402 at a cost of forty cents. (A mimeographed listing of the LP's, giving the titles alone, may be had free of charge from the Recording Laboratory, Music Division, the Library of Congress, Washington, D.C. 20540.) Each LP is priced at $4.95, mailing and tax included.

In the text and notes I have identified these LP's with the letter "L." The "L" (L26, for example, "American Sea Songs and Shanties") distinguishes the records issued for general sale from the original tape and acetate holdings of the Archive of Folksong, which number 20,000 different pieces (cylinders, discs, tapes) with more than 100,000 separate titles. These Archive holdings are noted as AFS with a following much higher number (as, AFS 2527B, Maitland's singing of "Roll, *Alabama*, Roll"). Duplicates of these original records (all have been tape dubbed for preservation) can be specially made on order by the laboratory for the seriously interested.

# General Words

A number of books are useful to further understanding the field of American folklore as a whole: Jan Harold Brunvand, *The Study of American Folklore: An Introduction*, New York, 1968; Kenneth and Mary Clarke, *Introducing Folklore*, New York, 1963; Richard Dorson, *American Folklore*, Chicago, 1959; Tristram P. Coffin (ed.), *Our Living Traditions: An Introduction to American Folklore*, New York, 1968. These four books, with their textual references and bibliographies, will carry the reader well on his way. Coffin's work includes essays on individual topics from twenty-five of the leading folklorists in the United States;

# SOURCES AND NOTES

Brunvand's and the Clarkes' works discuss the types, sources, and "fields of folklore"; and Dorson, with a lifetime of folklore scholarship under his belt, perceptively analyzes the main and contributory streams of American folklore.

## GENERAL WORKS ON REGIONAL AMERICAN FOLKLORE

Within the framework of their separate fields (folksong, place names, superstitions) these works, in book and article form, are legion. I give here only a few representative works that cover — umbrellalike — many aspects of the folklore of a region: Harold W. Thompson, *Body, Boots, and Britches* (New York State), reprint edition, New York, Dover Publications, 1964; Horace P. Beck, *The Folklore of Maine*, Philadelphia and New York, 1957; Richard Dorson, *Buying the Wind: Regional American Folklore*, Chicago, 1964; Newman Ivey White and Paul F. Baun (general editors), *The Frank C. Brown Collection of North Carolina Folklore*, 7 vols., Durham, 1952–1964 (a monumental collection edited with exacting scholarship by nine associate editors, specialists in their fields: Henry M. Belden, Paul G. Brewster, Wayland D. Hand, Arthur Palmer Hudson, Jan Philip Schinhan, Archer Taylor, Stith Thompson, Bartlett Jere Whiting, and George P. Wilson). The three following collectors deserve special mention also for the coverage they have given their states and regions: Vance Randolph for Missouri, Arkansas, and the Ozarks (Randolph is without question the greatest field collector America has known: four volumes of folksongs, six volumes of tales, the authoritative work on the folk speech of the region, the authoritative volume on superstitions found in the Ozarks, not counting innumerable articles — and all from direct personal field collecting!); J. Frank Dobie for Texas and the Southwest (for his many books on the people and folklore of his state and region, and for his driving force shaping the Texas Folklore Society); and George Korson for Pennsylvania and, more specifically, for the folklore of the mines and miners of Pennsylvania.

## GENERAL BIBLIOGRAPHIES

A most useful and handy bibliography is that of Robert Wildhaber, "A Bibliographic Introduction to American Folklife," NYFQ, 21 (1965) 259–302. It is sold as an offprint (85 cents) by the New York Folklore Society, Farmers' Museum, Cooperstown, New York 13326. Tristram P. Coffin's *An Analytical Index to the Journal of American Folklore* (Publications of the American Folklore Society, Bibliographical and Special Series, vol. 7), 1958, is essential for locating material in the *Journal*, continuously published since 1888. Ralph S. Boggs's annual bibliographies in the *Southern Folklore Quarterly* are equally important for the entire field, and are not limited to material in SFQ. The largest work, valuable in spite of being uneven in some respects, is Charles Haywood's *A Bibliography of North American Folklore and Folksong* (rev. ed., 2 vols.), New York, Dover Publications, 1962.

## DICTIONARY (ENCYCLOPEDIA)

Maria Leach (ed.), *The Standard Dictionary of Folklore, Mythology, and Legend*, 2 vols., New York, Funk & Wagnalls, 1949–50. This is most uneven in quality, but there are superb articles throughout that make it a must.

# Chapter References

## 1. AMERICAN FOLKLORE

The opening segment appeared as part of an article by me in *Holiday*, July 1955. Marius Barbeau's definition is from *The Standard Dictionary of Folklore*, vol. I, p. 398. He states strongly — and perhaps I should have placed the sentence in the main text to bolster my own sentiments — that folklore "is the born opponent of the serial number, the stamped product, and the patented standard." (There are twenty-one "definitions" of folklore under that heading in the *Dictionary*, most of them narrow and with which American folklorists are not now in agreement. We were a long time catching up to the European approach of Van Gennep, Pitré, Cocchiarra, Wildhaber, O'Sullivan, and the rest.) Dobie's comments come from an honoring article after his death, "J. Frank Dobie on Folklore" (passages collected by William D. Wittliff) in *The Sunny Slopes of Long Ago*, PTFS, 33 (1966) 89–99. Wittliff says: "In folklore and storytelling, as in everything he did, he never ran with the herd." Dobie could be happily caustic: "You're not going to get tales that linger in the imagination except from people who have time to linger, time to stare at cows or anything else that comes along. In my experience, the best tale-tellers did not spend hours a day scrubbing themselves."

## 2. SOME GUIDEPOSTS

The source for Phillips Barry's views is in his article on communal re-creation in *The Bulletin of the Folk-Song Society of the Northeast*, 5 (1933) 4–6. The strong comment from Mr. Berry Sutterfield is reported by John Quincy Wolf in his "Folksingers and the Re-Creation of Folksong," WF, 26 (1967) 101–111, an excellent article dealing with transmission of song. The Kittredge article appeared in JAF, 30 (1917) 351. On "The Bastardization of Folklore," it is most instructive to read L. Zemljanova, "The Struggle between the Reactionary and the Progressive Forces in Contemporary American Folkloristics," in *Sovetskaja Etnografija*, 4 (1962) 191–197. It appears in "The Articles in Translation" section of the *Journal of the Folklore Institute*, edited by the Fellows of the Folklore Institute, Indiana University, vol. I, no. 1/2. It is nonsense and a sterling example of monolithic, hewing-to-the-party-line, Soviet "scholarship." It is a pathetic effort. Bear with Zemljanova for a moment only:

the progressive folklorists [Zemljanova names those of whom she approves] of the United States wage an uncompromising struggle with the reactionary forces. The forms of struggle against the reactionary forces in folkloristics are varied — from reviews of works of reactionary folklorists to song parodies ridiculing Freudianism and other reactionary tendencies. Such flexibility guarantees the effectiveness of the struggle, helps attract to it large numbers of participants, and strengthens the ties of the folklorists with the masses. . . . Contemporary progressive folkloristics in the United States is developing in difficult conditions. It is not easy to overcome the ossified traditions of bourgeois scholarship, the influence of bourgeois ideology, the obstacles of censorship. But on the side of progressive folkloristics are the creators and performers of folklore creations themselves, and the people; and this is the best guarantee of the successful development of a science of folk creation."

"Science of folk creation?" Am I reading right? Who's "ossified," Zemljanova? Anyhow, bosh. Vance Randolph, would you like to take Zemljanova on a walking tour through the Ozarks? The Fellows of the Folklore Institute head the translated article with a note: "The editors do not necessarily endorse the views expressed in these articles, and may indeed strongly disagree with them." The editors have done us a great service by translating the article and permitting us to take a look at folklore "scholarship" in the USSR.

### 3. FOLK LANGUAGE AND GRAMMAR

The two journals chiefly dealing with this subject are *American Speech* (1926 — ) and *Publications of the Dialect Society* (1943 — ). H. L. Mencken's *The American Language* (rev. 4th ed.), New York, 1936, remains the classic in its field, while Vance Randolph and George P. Wilson's *Down in the Holler: A Gallery of Ozark Folk Speech*, Norman, Okla., 1953, is a lively, highly readable, and most informative work on both speech and grammar in that region of America. (Strongly recommended, even for bedtime reading.) Added valuable works are C. C. Fries, *American English Grammar*, New York, 1940; George P. Krapp, *The English Language in America*, New York, 1925; and W. Nelson Francis, *The Structure of American English*, New York, 1958. To the last Raven I. McDavid contributes a thorough chapter on "The Dialects of American English." Ramon F. Adams's *Cowboy Lingo*, Boston, 1936, and *Western Words*, Norman, Okla., 1968, and Joanna Colcord's *Sea Language Comes Ashore*, New York, 1945, are valuable and readable for the speech of both industry (cattle and seafaring) and region (the West and the New England coast).

### 4. A MANUSCRIPT OF THE FOLK LANGUAGE: SAMUEL M. VAN SWEARENGEN

I first reported this manuscript, with more extended excerpts, in WF, 11 (1952) 266–283.

### 5. PROVERBS AND PROVERBIAL SPEECH

The chief work is Archer Taylor's *The Proverb*, Cambridge (Harvard) 1931, reissued Hatboro, 1962. The standard proverb dictionary is Archer Taylor and Bartlett Jere Whiting's *A Dictionary of American Proverbs and Proverbial Phrases, 1820–1880*, Cambridge (Harvard) 1958. Both are basic to any library, as are also the following four extensive collections: Bartlett Jere Whiting (ed.), "Proverbs and Proverbial Sayings" in *The Frank C. Brown Collection of North Carolina Folklore*, vol. I, Durham, 1952; Archer Taylor, *Proverbial Comparisons and Similes from California*, University of California Folklore Studies, No. 3, Berkeley, 1954; Jan Harold Brunvand's *Proverbs and Proverbial Phrases from Indiana Books Published before 1890*, Indiana University Folklore Series, No. 15, Bloomington, 1961; Frances M. Barbour, *Proverbs and Proverbial Phrases of Illinois*, Carbondale, 1965. Full bibliographies in these works are helpful in locating the many articles on proverbs and the collectanea appearing in all the folklore journals. Brunvand's bibliographic notes in his *The Study of American Folklore* (pp. 46–47) and his chapter on the subject are equally useful.

Valuable collections of English Proverbs are G. L. Apperson, *English Proverbs and Proverbial Phrases, An Historical Dictionary*, London, 1929; W. G. Smith and Janet E. Heseltine, *The Oxford Dictionary of English Proverbs*, Oxford, 1935; and 2nd rev. ed. by Sir Paul Harvey, 1948; Bartlett Jere Whiting, *Proverbs, Sentences, and Proverbial Phrases from English Writings Mainly before 1500*, Cambridge (Harvard), 1968. The best collection of international proverbs is Selwyn G. Champion, *Racial Proverbs*, London, 1938, 2nd ed., New York, 1950.

Sources for proverbs and proverbial speech are cited in the order of their appearance within the chapter and by states: George Monteiro, "Proverbs in the Remaking," WF, 27 (1968) 128; Ruth B. Tolman, "Proverbs and Sayings in Eighteenth Century Almanacs," WF, 21 (1962) 35–42.

*Maine:*   The WPA files in the Library of Congress.
*Tennessee:*   Herbert Halpert, "Proverbial Comparisons from West Tennessee," TFSB, 17 (September 1951) 49–61.
*Texas:*   George D. Hendricks, "Texas Folk Similes," WF, 19 (1960) 245–262, and "Texas Folk Proverbs," WF, 21 (1962) 92; Mary Jourdan Atkinson, "Familiar Sayings of Old-Time Texas," in *Texas Folk and Folklore*, PTFS 26, Dallas, 1954; and A. W. Eddins, "Grandma's Sayings," in *Texas Folk and Folklore*, PTFS 26, Dallas, 1954.
*New York State:*   From Harold Thompson's *Body, Boots, and Britches*, New York, 1939 (Dover reprint, 1962).
*New Mexico:*   T. M. Pearce, "The English Proverb in New Mexico," CFQ, 5 (1946) 334–338, and "Rhymes and Sayings," NMFR, 6 (1951–52).
*Mississippi:*   Ernest Cox, "Rustic Imagery in Mississippi Proverbs," SFQ, 11 (1947) 263–267.
*Nebraska:*   Ruth Odell, "Nebraska Smart Sayings," SFQ, 12 (1948) 185–195.
*North Carolina:*   Anon., "Proverbs," NCF, 1 (June 1948) 26–27; Joseph D. Clark, "Proverbs and Sayings from North Carolina," SFQ, 26 (1962) 145–173; George P. Wilson, "Some Folk Sayings from North Carolina," NCF, 6 (December 1958) 7; and Leonidas Betts, "Folk Speech from Kipling, North Carolina," NCF, 14 (1966) 37–40.
*Massachusetts:*   Anon., "Proverbs and Phrases," JAF, 5 (1892) 60; Helen M. Thurston, "Sayings and Proverbs from Massachusetts," JAF, 19 (1906) 122.
*The Ozarks:*   From Vance Randolph and George P. Wilson, *Down in the Holler: A Gallery of Ozark Folk Speech*, Norman, Okla., 1953.
*Oregon:*   Helen M. Pearce, "Folk Sayings in a Pioneer Family of Western Oregon," CFQ, 5 (1946) 229.
*Kentucky:*   Gordon Wilson, "Some Mammoth Cave Sayings," KFR, 15 (1969) 12–21, and "Studying Folklore in a Small Region," TFSB, 31 (December 1965); George Boswell, "Folk Wisdom in Northeastern Kentucky," TFSB, 33 (March 1967); anon., "Proverbial Material from the Western Kentucky Folklore Archive," KFR, 6 (1960) 47; and Herbert Halpert, "A Pattern of Proverbial Exaggeration from West Kentucky," MF 1 (April 1951) 41. From eastern Kentucky: Leonard Roberts, "Additional Exaggerations from Eastern Kentucky," MF, 2 (1952) 1963.
*Louisiana:*   Duncan Emrich from Congressman T. A. Thompson, *ca.* 1950.
*Illinois:*   from Frances M. Barbour, *Proverbs and Proverbial Phrases of Illinois*, Carbondale, 1965.
*California:*   Owen S. Adams, "Traditional Proverbs and Sayings from California," WF, 6 (1947) 59–64, and "More California Proverbs," WF, 7 (1948) 136–144.
*Idaho:*   Herbert Halpert, "Proverbial Comparisons from Idaho," WF, 6 (1947) 379–380.
*Pennsylvania:*   Mac E. Barrick, "Proverbs and Sayings from Cumberland Country," KFQ, 8 (1963) 139–203, and "Popular Comparisons and Similes," KFQ, 10 (1965) 3–34.

# American Names

*Names* is the excellent quarterly in this field, covering all types of names and all aspects of naming. (Subscriptions: *Names*, The American Name Society, The State University College, Potsdam, New York, 13677.) Ernst Pulgram's "Theory of Names" is basic to any study. It was first published as a monograph in *Beiträge zur Namenforschung* (vol. V, no. 2) and was reprinted (1954) by the American Name Society.

## 6. PLACE NAMES

George R. Stewart's *Names on the Land*, New York, 1945 (reprinted 1967), is a highly readable and solid introduction. His more recent book, *American Place-Names*, New York, 1970, is a dictionary listing, with description and accounts of the naming of the more important and interesting geographic features and populated places. Notable state collections include: William C. Barnes, *Arizona Place Names*, Tucson, 1935 (revised and enlarged by Byrd H. Granger, 1960); A. R. Dunlap, *Dutch and Swedish Place Names in Delaware*, Newark, 1956, and A. R. Dunlap and C. A. Weslager, *Indian Place-Names in Delaware*, Wilmington, 1950; Edwin G. Gudde, *California Place Names*, Berkeley, 1949 (reprinted 1969); Hamill Kenny, *The Origin and Meaning of the Indian Place-Names of Maryland*, Baltimore, 1961; Hamill Kenny, *West Virginia Place Names*, Piedmont, W. Va., 1945; Lewis A. McArthur, *Oregon Geographic Names*, Portland, 1928 (revised 1952); George Davis McJimsey, *Topographic Terms in Virginia*, New York, 1940; Edwin Wallace McMullen, Jr., *English Topographical Terms in Florida*, Gainesville, University of Florida Press, 1953; Donald J. Orth, *Dictionary of Alaska Place Names*, Washington, D.C. (Government Printing Office), 1967; T. M. Pearce, *New Mexico Place Names*, Albuquerque, 1965; Warren Upham, *Minnesota Geographic Names*, St. Paul, 1920; Virgil J. Vogel, *Indian Place Names in Illinois*, Springfield, 1963. The basic bibliography to the large literature is Richard B. Sealock and Pauline A. Seely, *Bibliography of Place-Name Literature, United States and Canada*, Chicago, 1948 (reprinted 1957), with a "Supplement" in *Names*, vol. 16, 1968. For a survey of the field and suggested directions for study and control, see Francis Lee Utley, "A Survey of American Place Names," in *Proceedings of the Ninth International Congress of Onomastic Sciences* (University College, London, July 3–8, 1966), International Centre of Onomastics, Blijde-Inkomstraat 5, Louvain, n.d.

## 7. NAMES OF WESTERN MINING CAMPS AND MINES

One runs across the names of mines casually and incidentally in virtually any book dealing with the mining West and in the various (WPA) State Guides of the Western States, and while they are an incredibly rich field there have been no particular studies of them. An exception is Helen Carson's "Mine Names on the Nevada Comstock Lode," WF, 15 (1956) 49–57.

## 8. CATTLE BRANDS

The best general book on the subject of cattle brands is Oren Arnold and John P. Hale, *Hot Irons, Heraldry of the Range*, New York, 1940. It covers the field and is well illustrated. The growth of brands within a county is well described by Orlan L. Sawey, "Origins of Uvalde County Cattle Brands," in *Folk Travelers*, PTFS, 25, Dallas, 1953.

## 9. QUILT NAMES

The following books contain names, descriptions and illustrations of patterns, and something of the history and origin of the quilts. One can spend a very pleasant hour with any of these and be the better informed about our past: The Art Institute, *American Quilts*, Chicago, 1966; Lillian Baker Carlisle, *Pieced Work and Appliqué Quilts at Shelburne Museum*, Shelburne, Vt., 1957; Averil Colby, *Patchwork Quilts*, New York, 1966; *Denver Art Museum Quilt Collection*, Denver, 1963; Ruth E. Finley, *Old Patchwork Quilts and the Women Who Made Them*, Philadelphia, 1929; Carrie A. Hall and Rose G. Kretsinger, *The Romance of the Patchwork Quilt in America*, Caldwell, Id., 1947; Marguerite Ickis, *The Standard Book of Quilt Making and Collecting*, New York, 1949; Ruby Short McKim, *One Hundred and One Patchwork Patterns*, Independence, Mo., 1931; Florence Peto, *American Quilts and Coverlets*, New York, 1949; Elizabeth Wells Robertson, *American Quilts*, New York, 1948; Margaret E. White, *Quilts and Counterpanes in the Newark Museum*, Newark, 1948; also Paul Brewster, "Names of Indiana Quilt Patterns," CFQ, 3 (1944) 61.

## 10. NAMES OF OZARK FIDDLE TUNES

Vance Randolph, "Ozark Fiddle Tunes," MF, 4 (1954) 81–86. See also: Samuel P. Bayard, *Hill Country Tunes*, Philadelphia (American Folklore Society), 1944, 24–25; Carl Carmer, *Stars Fell on Alabama*, New York, 1961 (reprint), 275–277; Joan Moser, "Instrumental Music of the Southern Appalachians: Traditional Fiddle Tunes," NCF, 12–2 (1964) 1–8; Howard W. Odum, *An American Epoch: Southern Portraiture in the National Picture*, New York, 1930, 201–207.

## 11. NAMES OF RACEHORSES

Louise M. Ackerman, "Naming the Nags," *Names*, 1 (1953) 262–265. It is quite probable that the vast majority of readers of this book have not up to this moment made it anything of a regular habit to turn to the sports pages of the papers to read the postings and track results for the day. I suggest, as an added window on America, that this become at least a once-a-week habit. There is, after all, more permanence in the name of a racehorse than there is in the headlines.

## 12. HOUND DOG NAMES

To the best of my knowledge the subject of the naming of hound dogs has not been treated other than in this paper by Lynn Mann.

## 13. NICKNAMES

Some of the Western nicknames are drawn from Jerome J. Quinlan, "As I Remember Them," Carson City (?), n.d., a six-page poem honoring the old-timers on the Comstock Lode. For the very special collection of names of the ladies of the line, I am indebted to Fred and Jo Mazzulla of Denver, Colorado, whose *Brass Checks and Red Lights*, Denver, 1966, affectionately preserves this aspect of the early West. The Mazzullas — as dedicated pack rats as Vance Randolph and Harry M. Hyatt in their fields — have collected now "over ¼-million photographs and negatives," in addition to sketches, drawings, and prints, and over five hundred hours of wire and tape recordings of the early Western scene. (The *Brass Checks* booklet, privately printed, may be had from Mazfoto, 1930 East 8th Avenue, Denver, Colorado 80206, at $3 and, in my opinion, quite worth it.)

# Children's Folklore

## 14. RIDDLES

Archer Taylor's *English Riddles from Oral Tradition*, Berkeley, 1951, is the great single study of the true riddle, with complete bibliography to date of publication. The puzzle or problem riddle has not been the subject of study or general collection per se. The conundrum has been collected, but not studied in depth. See: C. Grant Loomis, "Traditional

American Wordplay: The Conundrum," WF, 8 (1948) 235–247; Archer Taylor, "Biblical Conundrums in *The Golden Era*," CFQ, 5 (1946) 273–276; Archer Taylor, "The Riddle," CFQ, 2 (1943) 129–148.

### 15. NONSENSE SPELLING

No intensive collection of these has been made. Paul G. Brewster, " 'Spelling Riddles' from the Ozarks," SFQ, 8 (1944) 301–303; Clifton Johnson, "Spelling" in *What They Say in New England*, Boston, 1896; reprinted (Carl Withers, ed.) New York, 1963; Nellie M. Coates, "Children's Rhymes," HF, 6 (1947) 73–74; and Josiah H. Combs, "Spellin' 'Em Down in the Highlands," KFR, 3 (1957) 69–73.

### 16. GAME RHYMES

Paul G. Brewster, "Children's Games and Rhymes," in *The Frank C. Brown Collection of North Carolina Folklore*, vol. I, Durham, 1952; Roger D. Abrahams, *Jump-Rope Rhymes: A Dictionary*, published for the American Folklore Society by the University of Texas Press, Austin, 1969; Duncan Emrich, *The Nonsense Book*, New York, 1969. Each of these works contains extensive bibliographies on the game rhymes of American children, with references both to books and articles. They lead to all other sources. Abrahams' work is the standard in its field. Emrich's bibliography lists virtually all folklore journal articles from the inception of the various journals to 1969. See also Charles Francis Potter in *The Standard Dictionary of Folklore*: "Skip-Rope Rimes," "Counting-Out Rimes," "Eeny Meeny Miny Mo." The repetitive ubiquitousness (ha!) of the children's rhymes makes attempts to assign specific rhymes to a specific child and place relatively senseless. Other than an occasional reference in the text, no attempt is made to do so here. The rhymes are everywhere, and for their distribution in time and space, and for their repetition, see the bibliographies in the works cited above. The source of any fresh body of rhymes should be noted, of course, in terms both of group and place, as I have done with the jump-rope rhymes here.

### 17. AUTOGRAPH ALBUM RHYMES

These are found in current tradition and are being studied. Alan Dundes, "Some Examples of Infrequently Reported Autograph Verse," SFQ, 26 (1962) 127–130, and Duncan Emrich, *The Nonsense Book*, New York, 1970, have bibliographies. Charles Francis Potter's "Autograph Album Rimes" in *The Standard Dictionary of Folklore* is a good introductory study. W. K. McNeil's "The Autograph Album Inscription of Nineteenth Century Upstate New York," unpublished dissertation, Cooperstown Graduate Program of Oneonta State College, New York, 1967, is a thorough area study with suggested classifications.

### 18. BOOK OWNERSHIP RHYMES

Clifton Johnson, "Flyleaf Scribblings," from *What They Say in New England*, Boston, 1896 (ed. Carl Withers, New York, 1963), and from current tradition.

## Street Cries and Epitaphs

### 19. STREET CRIES

There is no book or extended article that brings together American street cries, and one should be undertaken before all record is lost. Even a solid bibliography is lacking. See the following from which many of the cries in the text are drawn: Samuel Wood, *The Cries of New York*, New York, 1808; reprinted, The Harbor Press, New York, 1931; anon., *The New-York Cries in Rhyme*, Printed & Sold by Mahlon Day, at the New Juvenile Bookstore, No. 376 Pearl Street, (New York, n.d.); Richardson Wright, *Hawkers and Walkers in Early America*, Philadelphia, 1927 (full chapters on New York and Philadelphia cries); Edward Pinkowski, "Philadelphia Street Cries," KFQ, 5 (1960) 10–12; Henry F. Albrecht, "Troy Street Cries," NYFQ, 1 (1945) 238; George Phillips, "Street Cries of American Chimney Sweepers," NYFQ, 8 (1952) 191–198; Lyle Saxon, *Gumbo Ya-Ya*, Cambridge, 1954 (WPA Writers' Project, full chapter on New Orleans cries); Elizabeth Hurley, "Come Buy, Come Buy," in *Folk Travelers*, PTFS 25, Dallas, 1953 (Texas cries, chiefly San Antonio); Annie Weston Whitney and Caroline Canfield Bullock, *Folklore from Maryland*, Memoirs of the American Folklore Society, vol. 18, New York, 1925 (Baltimore cries, entries 2423–2440); Harriette Kershaw Leiding, "Street Cries of An Old Southern City," Charleston, S.C. (privately printed), 1910 (with some music), a nostalgic and affectionate look at this aspect of her city's life.

## 20. EPITAPHS

The best general book is that by the Rev. Charles W. Wallis, *Stories on Stone: A Book of American Epitaphs*, New York, 1954. It is an excellent introduction and will stimulate the student-collector. It is regrettably out of print, but hopefully this notice may nudge it into reappearance in useful paperback. Other works include Thomas C. Mann and Janet Greene, *Over Their Dead Bodies: Yankee Epitaphs and History*, Brattleboro, Vt., 1962; Robert E. Pike, *Granite Laughter and Marble Tears: Epitaphs of Old New England*, New York, 1938; Timothy Alden, *A Collection of American Epitaphs*, 5 vols., New York, 1814 (a very solid collection but hard to come by); W. H. Beable, *Epitaphs, Graveyard Humor & Eulogy*, London, 1925 (chiefly British epitaphs, but some American); Walter H. Howe, *Here Lies, Being a Collection of Ancient and Modern Humorous and Queer Inscriptions from Tombstones*, New York, 1901; J. R. Kippax, *Churchyard Literature*, Chicago, 1877; Harriette M. Forbes, *Gravestones of Early New England and the Men Who Made Them, 1653–1800*, Boston, 1927 (graveyard art and stonecutters, but some epitaphs); and Allan I. Ludwig, *Graven Images: New England Stonecarving and Its Symbols, 1650–1815*, Wesleyan University Press, Middletown, Conn., 1966 (excellent study, profusely illustrated, with basic bibliography; little on epitaphs, but most valuable as part of the total picture). The Appendix to James Truslow Adams, *Memorials of Old Bridgehampton* printed at the Press of the *Bridgehampton News*, Long Island, New York, 1916, gives a fine group of cemetery inscriptions, while the entire work is an excellent example of research in local history and folklore, each complementing the other.

# Legends and Tales

Stith Thompson's *The Folktale*, New York, 1946, is the authoritative survey, and Ernest W. Baughman's *Type and Motif-Index of the Folktales of England and North America*, The Hague, Mouton & Co., 1966, is a valuable working tool for the student. Good collections of American tales and legends include: J. Frank Dobie, *Legends of Texas*, PTFS, no. 3, 1924, reprinted 1964; Richard M. Dorson, *Bloodstoppers and Bearwalkers: Folk Traditions of the Upper Peninsula*, Cambridge, Harvard, 1952, and *Jonathan Draws the Long Bow: New England Popular Tales and Legends*, Cambridge, Harvard, 1946; Ruth Ann Musick, *The Telltale Lilac Bush and Other West Virginia Ghost Tales*, Lexington, Ky., 1965; all of Vance Randolph's Ozark collections of tales, including *We Always Lie to*

*Strangers: Tall Tales from the Ozarks*, New York, 1951; *Who Blowed Up the Church House? And Other Ozark Folk Tales*, New York, 1952; *The Devil's Pretty Daughter and Other Ozark Folk Tales*, New York, 1957; *Sticks in the Knapsack and Other Ozark Folk Tales*, New York, 1958 (each with notes by Herbert Halpert or Ernest W. Baughman); Leonard W. Roberts, *South from Hell-fer-Sartin*, Lexington, Ky., 1955, and reissued in paperback, Berea, Ky., 1964, and *Up Cutshin and Down Greasy*, Lexington, Ky., 1959 (excellent field collections meticulously reported). Daniel G. Hoffman's *Paul Bunyan, Last of the Frontier Demigods*, Philadelphia, 1952, is the definitive work on the real place of the Bunyan legend in American folklore.

21. LEGENDS

*Santa Claus:* George H. McKnight, *St. Nicholas*, New York, 1917 (as patron saint, the legends, the cult); James H. Barnett, *The American Christmas: A Study in National Culture*, New York, 1954 (the social role and celebration of Christmas in the United States; good bibliography). For Santa Claus's New York origins, the authoritative studies are found in *The New-York Historical Society Quarterly:* R. W. G. Vail, "Santa Claus Visits the Hudson," NYHSQ, 35 (1951) 337–343, and "Encore for Santa Claus," NYHSQ, 37 (1935) 327–330; Charles W. Jones, "Knickerbocker Santa Claus," NYHSQ, 38 (1954) 357–383. Clement Moore's poem first appeared in book form in *The New-York Book of Poetry*, New York, 1837, pp. 217–219. *Thomas Nast's Christmas Drawings for the Human Race*, New York, 1890, includes 32 of Santa Claus, which served to fix the nation's concept of Santa Claus's dress and appearance.

*The Cowboy:* The best single portrait of the cowboy is Ramon F. Adams's *The Old-Time Cowhand*, New York, 1961, with illustrations by Nick Eggenhofer. (All quotations, beginning with the item on "Courage," are from this book.) Anything by Ramon Adams on the cowboy is recommended. *Come an' Get It: The Story of the Old Cowboy Cook*, Norman, 1952, is a delight in its special field, and *The Rampaging Herd: A Bibliography of Books and Pamphlets on Men and Events in the Cattle Industry*, Norman, 1959, introduces one to all the literature. A special (selected!) bibliography citing novels, "Westerns," short stories, representative films, art works, and other items contributing to the American legend of the cowboy is wanted, as are also studies of the folk adoption of the legend, i.e., children's cowboy games, the use of cowboy lingo, cowboy dress, and other spill-offs.

*Jesse James:* Recorded by Artus M. Moser from the singing of Bascom Lamar Lunsford at Swannanoa, North Carolina, 1946. Library of Congress record L20. For accounts of the ballad and its growth and spread: Randolph, *Ozark Folksongs*, II, 17; Belden, *Ballads and Songs*, 401–404; H. M. Belden and Arthur Palmer Hudson, *North Carolina Folklore*, II, 557–562; Laws, *Native American Balladry*, 176. For Jesse James in fact and legend: Homer Croy, *Jesse James Was My Neighbor*, New York, 1949 (Dorson points out that when Croy says, "I am not putting in this book any legends or folktales," he fails to recognize that "these word-of-mouth narratives bear the unmistakable imprint of folklore"); Richard M. Dorson, *American Folklore*, Chicago, 1959, 236–243; Haldeen Braddy, "Jesse James' Chivalry," JAF, 69 (1957) 62; Kent L. Stickmesser, "Robin Hood and the American Outlaw," JAF, 79 (1966) 348–355.

*Sam Bass:* Recorded by Sam Eskin from the singing of Lannis Sutton at Palo Alto, California, 1949. Library of Congress record L30. For accounts of the ballad: Austin E. and Alta S. Fife (eds.), N. Howard ("Jack") Thorp, *Songs of the Cowboys*, New York, 1966, 112–120; Laws, *Native American Balladry*, 177. For Sam Bass in fact and legend: Walter Prescott Webb, "The Legend of Sam Bass," in *Texas Folk and Folk-Lore*, PTFS, 16 (1954) 112–116; Wayne Gard, *Sam Bass*, Boston, 1936; J. Frank Dobie, "The Robinhooding of Sam Bass," in *Tales of Old-Time Texas*, Boston, 1928.

*Custer's Last Charge:* Recorded by Sidney Robertson Cowell from Warde H. Ford at Central Valley, California, 1938. Record L30. A perceptive book (with a good bibliography) on the Little Big Horn fight is by Western authority Mari Sandoz, *The Battle of the Little Big Horn*, New York, 1966.

*Frankie and Johnny:* Collected during the Depression period by field workers of the Writers' Unit of the Works Progress Administration (WPA), manuscript number W 7348 of that collection in the Library of Congress. For the ballad: Laws, *Native American Balladry*, 247–248; Belden, *Ballads and Songs*, 330–333. Laws comments: "Many conflicting reports concerning the age and factual basis of the piece have been circulated, but so far research has failed to settle its origin."

*George Lyman Kittredge.* From personal notes, as indicated in the text.

### 22. URBAN BELIEF TALES

*The Rape Trial:* Bill Gold, "The District Line," *The Washington Post*, March 30, 1970. Used by special permission of the *Post*.

*The Second Blue Book:* Lew Girdler (San Jose State College), "The Legend of the Second Blue Book," WF, 29 (1970) 111–113.

*The Runaway Grandmother:* Linda Dégh, "The Runaway Grandmother," IF, I-1 (1968) 68–69.

*The Hook* and *The Boyfriend's Death:* Linda Dégh, "The Hook" and "The Boyfriend's Death," IF, I-1 (1969), 92–106.

*The Roommate's Death, The Decapitated Victim, The Furry Collar:* Linda Dégh, "The Roommate's Death and Related Dormitory Stories in Formation," IF, II-2 (1969) 55–74.

*The Ghostly Hitchhiker:* Richard K. Beardsley and Rosalie Hankey, "The Vanishing Hitchhiker," CFQ, 1 (1942) 303–335 and "A History of the Vanishing Hitchhiker," CFQ, 2 (1943) 13–26; Louis C. Jones, "Hitchhiking Ghosts of New York," CFQ, 4 (1945) 284–292, and *Things That Go Bump in the Night*, New York, 1959. The last is an excellent collection of New York State ghost tales and legends.

### 23. THE JACK TALES

Recorded by Duncan Emrich from the telling by Mrs. Maud Long of Hot Springs, North Carolina, at the Library of Congress, 1947. Records L47 and L48. See also Richard Chase, *The Jack Tales*, Boston, 1943, with notes by Herbert Halpert. Chase's collection is from another branch of the Harmon family.

### 24. TALES TOLD IN THE GULLAH DIALECT

Recorded by Duncan Emrich from the telling by Albert H. Stoddard of Savannah, Georgia, at the Library of Congress, 1949. Records L44, L45, L46. Certain of the Buh Rabbit tales told by Mr. Stoddard are found in Joel Chandler Harris's Uncle Remus stories, although the versions quite naturally differ. On the Gullah, see Guy B. Johnson, *Folk Culture of St. Helena Island*, Hatboro, S.C., reprint, 1968; for Buh Rabbit, see Stella Brewer Brooke, *Joel Chandler Harris, Folklorist*, University of Georgia Press, Columbia, Ga., 1950. On the Gullah, see Guy B. Johnson, *Folk Culture on St. Helena Island, South Carolina*, University of North Carolina Press, 1930 (Hathboro, Pa., reprint, 1968); for Brer Rabbit, see Stella Brewer Brooke, *Joel Chandler Harris, Folklorist*, University of Georgia Press, 1950.

*graphical Sketch of James Bridger, Mountaineer, Trapper, and Guide*, New York, 1905 (contains the account of the "Two Oceans Pass").

26. THE CANTE-FABLE

Leonard Roberts, "The Cante Fable in Eastern Kentucky," MF, 6 (1956) 69–88; Edward D. Ives, "Larry Gorman and the Cante Fable," *The New England Quarterly*, 23 (1959) 226–237; and Herbert Halpert, "The Cante Fable in Decay," SFQ, 5 (1941) 191–200.

*Little Dickie Whigburn:* Recorded by Herbert Halpert from Samuel Harmon of Cade's Cove, Blount County, Tennessee, 1939. AFS 2798B and 2799A. Earlier collected (in summary form only) from the same informant by Mellinger E. Henry and reported in "Still More Ballads and Folksongs from the Southern Highlands," JAF, 45 (1932) 34–35. See also Isabel Gordon Carter, "Mountain White Folklore: Tales from the Southern Blue Ridge," JAF, 38 (1925) 366–8, in which she reports the collection of "Little Dickie Whigburn" from Mrs. Jane Gentry of Hot Springs, North Carolina. In this version the "passenger" (not a "parson"!) is hung, and Dickie's wife burnt. In still another version the parson is gelded and the wife spayed.

*The Irresistible Captain:* Collected by Herbert Halpert from Charles Grant at New Egypt, New Jersey, and reported in "The Cante Fable in New Jersey," JAF, 55 (1942) 133–143. In this same article Halpert reports "No Use Knockin' on the Blind" and "The Parson Tricked by Boy's Song."

*Mr. Garfield:* Recorded by Duncan Emrich from Bascom Lamar Lunsford of South Turkey Creek, North Carolina, at the Library of Congress, 1949. Record L29. Previously recorded from the same informant by Artus M. Moser at Swannanoa, North Carolina, in 1946. AFS #7960B.

# *Folksongs and Ballads*

FOLKSONGS

There are four basic collections that include (with extensive notes) ballad and lyric song: H. M. Belden, *Ballads and Songs Collected by the Missouri Folk Song Society*, Columbia (University of Missouri Studies, vol. 15, no. 1) 1940, and reprinted 1960; Cecil J. Sharp, *English Folk Songs from the Southern Appalachians*, 2 vols., 1932, and reprinted (2 vols. in one), New York, 1960; Vance Randolph, *Ozark Folksongs*, 4 vols., Columbia (State Historical Society of Missouri), 1946–1950; and *The Frank C. Brown Collection of North Carolina Folklore* (Newman Ivey White, General Editor): vol. 2, *Folk Ballads* and vol. 3, *Folk Songs*, both 1952, edited by H. M. Belden and Arthur Palmer Hudson, and vol. 4, *The Music of the Ballads*, 1957 and vol. 5 *The Music of the Songs*, 1962, edited by Jan P. Shinhan, Durham, Duke University Press. General collections include John A. and Alan Lomax, *Our Singing Country*, New York, 1941, and Carl Sandburg, *An American Songbag*, New York, 1927. There are numerous excellent regional and state collections in the bibliographies in Belden's *Ballads and Songs* and in the *North Carolina Folklore* volumes. The Library of Congress also distributes gratis a 12-page mimeographed "Brief List of Material Relating to American Folk Music," giving the chief works in the field of folksong, ballad, and music. It may be obtained by addressing the Archive of Folksong, Library of Congress, Washington, D.C. 20540.

BALLADS

I have not in the text separated the ballad from lyric and work song, but have, rather, grouped the matter by subject, mixing lyric and ballad together — which is probably the way they were sung in any case. There are a goodly number of ballads here for the student: "Expert Town," "Barbara Allen," "The Unquiet Grave," "The Loss of the *New Columbia*," "The Streets of Laredo," "Frankie Silvers," "The Buffalo Skinners," "The Texas Rangers," "Sam Bass," "Jesse James," "The *Cumberland*'s Crew," "The Dying Ranger," "Frankie and Johnny," "The Butcher Boy." — In addition to *North Carolina Folklore*, noted above, and the works of Belden, Randolph, and Sharp, all of which contain both traditional British and American ballads, these studies may be cited: Tristram P. Coffin, *The British Traditional Ballad in North America*, Philadelphia (Publications of the American Folklore Society), 1963; G. Malcolm Laws, Jr., *American Balladry from British Broadsides*, Philadelphia (Publications of the American Folklore Society), 1957; G. Malcolm Laws, Jr., *Native American Balladry: A Descriptive Study and Bibliographic Syllabus*, (rev. ed.) Philadelphia (Publications of the American Folklore Society), 1964; and Evelyn K. Wells, *The Ballad Tree*, New York, 1950. The definitive work on the music of the Child canon of English ballads is Bertrand H. Bronson, *The Traditional Tunes of the Child Ballads*, Princeton (4 vols. in process with 3 published) 1959 —. Exceptional ballad collections are: Phillips Barry, Fannie Hardy Eckstorm, and Mary Winslow Smyth, *British Ballads from Maine*, New Haven, Yale, 1929; Arthur Kyle Davis, Jr., *Traditional Ballads of Virginia, Collected under the Auspices of the Virginia Folk-Lore Society*, Cambridge, Harvard, 1929, and *More Traditional Ballads of Virginia*, Chapel Hill, University of North Carolina Press, 1960; and Helen Hartness Flanders, *Ancient Ballads Traditionally Sung in New England*, Philadelphia, University of Pennsylvania Press, vols. 1–4, 1960–1965. Except for Laws's bibliographic study (*Native American Balladry*), the American ballad has not received the separate book treatment accorded the British ballad surviving in America.

27. HISTORICAL SONGS

*Free America:* As noted in the text, from Carl Sandburg; tune: "The British Grenadiers."
*Washington the Great:* Recorded by John A. Lomax from Mrs. Minta Morgan at Bells, Texas, 1937. Record L29.
*Hunters of Kentucky:* Recorded by Duncan Emrich from Sam Hinton of La Jolla, California, at the Library of Congress, 1947. AFS record 8932A6.
*The Southern Soldier:* Recorded by John A. Lomax from Mrs. Minta Morgan at Bells, Texas, 1937. Record L29.
*The Bonny Blue Flag:* Text from H. M. Belden, *Ballads and Songs*, p. 357. Traditional tune from Alan Jabbour of the Library of Congress.
*The Homespun Dress:* Text from H. M. Belden, *Ballads and Songs*, p. 360. Tune the same as for "The Bonny Blue Flag."
*Good Old Rebel:* Recorded by Duncan Emrich from Eugenia and Charles Anderson of Ruxton, Maryland, at the Library of Congress, 1947. AFS record 8934A1. The variant recorded by Vance Randolph from Booth Campbell of Caneville, Arkansas, 1942, appears on record L20.
*Phil Sheridan:* Recorded by Alan Lomax from Judge Learned W. Hand at the Library of Congress, 1942. Record L29.
*The Iron Merrimac:* Recorded by Alan Lomax from Judge Learned W. Hand at the Library of Congress, 1942. Record L29.
*The Cumberland's Crew:* Recorded by Alan and Elizabeth Lomax from Captain Pearl R. Nye at Akron, Ohio, 1937. Record L29.

## SOURCES AND NOTES

*We Are Coming, Father Abraham:* Words by James Sloan Gibbons, music by Stephen Foster. Text with music published by S. T. Gordon, New York, 1862.

*Father Abraham's Reply to the Six Hundred Thousand:* Words by George F. Root; music adapted and partly composed by George F. Root. Published by Root & Cady, Chicago, 1862.

*Mademoiselle from Armentières:* Text and tune from traditional and current usage.

### 28. SEA SHANTIES

There are four excellent collections of sea shanties: Joanna C. Colcord, *Songs of American Sailormen*, New York (reprint) 1964; William Main Doerflinger, *Shanteymen and Shanteyboys*, New York, 1951; Frederick Pease Harlowe, *Chanteying Aboard American Ships*, Barre, Mass., 1962; and Stan Hugill, *Shanties from the Seven Seas*, New York, 1961. Doerflinger and Hugill are complete, with full references to variants, and with full bibliographies. Both contain all of the shanties given here. Ten of these fifteen songs also appear on Library of Congress records L26 and L27, "American Sea Songs and Shanties," and one on record L21, "Anglo-American Songs and Ballads."

*A-Roving, or The Amsterdam Maid:* Recorded by Alan Lomax from Richard Maitland, Sailors' Snug Harbor, Staten Island, New York, 1939. Record L26.

*Shenandoah:* Text and tune from David W. Bone, *Capstan Bars*, Edinburgh, 1931, p. 104.

*Rio Grande:* Recorded by Sidney Robertson Cowell from Captain Leighton Robinson, as shantyman, and Alex Barr, Arthur Brodeur, and Leighton McKenzie at Belvedere, California, 1939. Record L27.

*Rolling Home:* Recorded by Sidney Robertson Cowell from the singing of Captain Leighton Robinson and others, as cited. Record L27.

*Homeward Bound, or Goodbye, Fare You Well:* Recorded by Sidney Robertson Cowell from the singing of Captain Leighton Robinson and others, as cited. Record L27.

*The Dead Horse:* Recorded by Sam Eskin from the singing (solo) of Captain Leighton Robinson at Mill Valley, California, 1951. Record L26.

*Blow, Boys, Blow:* Recorded by Helene Stratman-Thomas and Aubrey Snyder from Noble B. Brown at Woodman, Wisconsin, 1946, on a joint field collecting project for the University of Wisconsin and the Library of Congress. Record L26.

*Roll,* Alabama, *Roll!:* Recorded by Alan Lomax from Richard Maitland at Sailors' Snug Harbor, Staten Island, New York, 1939. AFS records 2527B, 2528A. The historical matter in the headnote is drawn from Robert Selph Henry, *The Story of the Confederacy*, Indianapolis, 1936, and is used with the kind permission of Mrs. Henry.

*Hanging Johnny:* Recorded by Sidney Robertson Cowell from Captain Leighton Robinson and others, as cited. AFS record 4231A1.

*Paddy Doyle:* Recorded by Alan Lomax from Richard Maitland at Sailors' Snug Harbor, Staten Island, New York, 1939. Record L26.

*Haul the Bowline:* Recorded by Alan Lomax from Richard Maitland, Sailors' Snug Harbor, Staten Island, New York, 1939. Record L26.

*The Drunken Sailor:* Recorded by Alan Lomax from Richard Maitland, Sailors' Snug Harbor, Staten Island, New York, 1939. Record L26.

*The Sailor's Alphabet:* Recorded by Sam Eskin from Captain Leighton Robinson, Mill Valley, California, 1951. Record L26.

*The Loss of the* New Columbia: Recorded by Alan Lomax from Mrs. Carrie Grover, Gorham, Maine, 1941. Record L21.

*Captain Ward and the* Rainbow: Text and tune from Phillips Barry, Fannie Hardy Eckstorm, Mary Winslow Smyth, *British Ballads from Maine*, New Haven, 1929, p. 348.

29. COW-COUNTRY SONGS

Austin E. and Alta S. Fife's edition of N. Howard ("Jack") Thorp's, *Songs of the Cowboys*, New York, 1966, is a model of scholarship, restoring Thorp to his rightful position as the first collector of American cowboy songs. A facsimile of the first privately printed edition (News Print Shop, Estancia, N. M., 1908) is included; the commentary and notes on each song are exhaustive, the variants numerous, and the bibliography thorough. (Four of the songs in this present book are treated in the Fifes' edition of Thorp: "Little Joe, the Wrangler"; "The Cowboy's Lament (The Streets of Laredo)"; "The Buffalo Range (The Buffalo Skinners)"; and "Sam Bass." — The Fifes' more recent work, *Cowboy and Western Songs: A Comprehensive Anthology*, New York, 1969, and Richard E. Lingenfelter, Richard A. Dwyer, and David Cohen's *Songs of the American West*, Berkeley, 1968, more broadly cover the field (with excellent bibliographies) and deserve place in any library of Americana. — The classic in the cowboy field (apart from Thorp) is John Lomax, *Cowboy Songs and Other Frontier Ballads*, first published in 1910 and subsequently reprinted in enlarged and revised editions, the most recent of which is that of 1966 (New York). Cowboy songs will be found also in Western and Southwestern regional collections: Louise Pound, *American Ballads and Songs*, New York, 1922; Ethel and Chauncey O. Moore, *Ballads and Folksongs of the Southwest*, Norman, Okla., 1964; and William A. Owens, *Texas Folksongs*, Austin, 1950 (PTFS, no. 23).

*The Old Chisholm Trail:* Collected by Duncan Emrich from Powder River Jack Lee at Denver, Colorado, 1941.
*Whoopee, Ti-Yi-O, Git Along, Little Dogies:* Dick Devall's version, recorded by John A. Lomax at Dallas, Texas, 1946, is found on Library of Congress record L20. The full Kansas text with tune, given here, is from Myra E. Hull, "Cowboy Ballads," *The Kansas Historical Quarterly*, 8 (1939) 41.
*The Night-Herding Song:* Recorded by John A. Lomax from Harry Stephens (of Denison, Texas) at Dallas, Texas, 1942 and 1946. Record L28.
*Goodbye, Old Paint:* Recorded by John A. Lomax from the singing (with fiddle accompaniment) of Jess Morris at Dalhart, Texas, 1942. Record L28.
*The Dying Cowboy,* or *Bury Me Not on the Lone Prairie:* Composite text from H. M. Belden, *Ballads and Songs Collected by the Missouri Folk-Lore Society*, Columbia, 1940, (version C), p. 390, and the recording by John A. Lomax from the singing of Sloan Matthews at Pecos, Texas, 1942. Record L28.
*Little Joe, the Wrangler:* Recorded by Charles Todd and Robert Sonkin from Mrs. Mary Sullivan, at Shafter, California, 1940. AFS record 4116B. N. Howard ("Jack") Thorp, "Banjo in the Cow Camps." *The Atlantic Monthly*, August 1940.
*The Buffalo Skinners:* "Colley's Run-I-O," recorded by Rae Korson from the singing (with guitar) of L. Parker Temple at Washington, D.C., 1946. "The Buffalo Skinners," recorded at the Library of Congress from the singing of John A. Lomax, 1941. Record L28.
*The Streets of Laredo:* Recorded by John A. Lomax from Johnny Prude at Fort Davis, Texas, 1942. Record L28.
*The Texas Rangers:* Text and tune from Myra E. Hull, "Cowboy Ballads," *The Kansas Historical Quarterly*, 8 (1939). AFS record 5266A. A shorter variant is on L28, recorded by John A. Lomax from the singing of Sloan Matthews of Alpine, Texas, 1942.
*The Dying Ranger:* Recorded by John A. Lomax from Johnny Prude at Fort Davis, Texas, 1942. Record L28.
*The Trail to Mexico:* Collected by Duncan Emrich from Powder River Jack Lee at Denver, Colorado, 1941.

30. LOVE SONGS

*The Bugaboo:* Mellinger E. Henry, "Still More Ballads and Folksongs from the Southern Highlands," JAF, 45 (1932) 47–48. Obtained from Mrs. Samuel Harmon, Cade's Cove, Blount County, Tennessee, 1930.

*Home, Daughter, Home:* Mellinger E. Henry, "Still More Ballads and Folksongs from the Southern Highlands," JAF, 45 (1932) 41–43. Obtained from Mrs. Samuel Harmon, Cade's Cove, Blount County, Tennessee, 1930.

*Pretty Little Miss:* Recorded by Margot Mayo from Mrs. Fannie Jarrell, Prestonburg, Kentucky, 1946. AFS record 8484B1.

*Green Willow, Green Willow:* Recorded by Vance Randolph from Mrs. May Kennedy McCord, Springfield, Missouri, 1938.

*The Butcher Boy:* Recorded by Vance Randolph from Mrs. Lillian Short, Galena, Missouri, 1941. AFS record 5262B2.

*Waily, Waily:* Recorded at the Library of Congress by Duncan Emrich from Eugenia Anderson of Ruxton, Maryland, 1947. AFS record 8934A2.

*Come All You Young and Tender Ladies,* or *The Unconstant Lover:* Recorded by Herbert Halpert from Finley Adams, Dunham, Kentucky, 1939. AFS record 2774A2.

*Little Sparrow:* Text: Belden, *Ballads and Songs,* pp. 477–478. Music: to be found in the Works Progress Administration (WPA) manuscript volume, "Kentucky Folksongs," in the Archive of Folksong, Library of Congress.

*The Cuckoo:* Cecil J. Sharp, *English Folksongs from the Southern Appalachians* (1932), II, 177. Obtained from Mrs. Mollie Broughton, Barbourville, Kentucky, 1917.

*Old Smoky:* Composite text: Herbert Halpert from Mrs. Goldie Hamilton, Hamiltontown, Virginia, 1939, AFS record 2834A2; and Duncan Emrich from I. J. Greer, Thomasville, North Carolina, 1945, record L14. Music: I. J. Greer.

*Down in the Valley:* Composite text from current usage. Music from Alan Jabbour, Library of Congress.

*Careless Love:* Composite text from current usage. For the tune see Carl Sandburg, *The American Songbag,* New York, 1927; also AFS record 8934B1 from the singing of Eugenia and Charles Anderson of Ruxton, Maryland, 1947.

*The Brazos River:* Recorded by Vance Randolph from Mrs. Irene Carlisle, Farmington, Arkansas, 1942. Record L30. Mrs. Carlisle learned the song some twenty years earlier, in 1921, from a hired hand from Texas.

*Last Night I Dreamed of My True Love:* Belden, *Ballads and Songs,* 168. "Reported in 1909 by Hunter Jones of the West Plains High School [Missouri] as 'sung by his mother's hired girl.'"

*The False True-Lover:* Recorded by Herbert Halpert from Mrs. Hettie Swindel, Freeling, Virginia, 1939. AFS record 2814B1.

*Once I Courted a Pretty Little Girl:* Asher E. Treat, "Kentucky Folksong in Northern Wisconsin," JAF, 52 (1939) 33. Obtained from Mrs. M. G. Jacobs, Bryant, Wisconsin, 1933.

*I Asked That Girl to Marry Me:* Asher E. Treat, as above, p. 17. Obtained from Pearl Jacobs Borusky, Bryant, Wisconsin, 1938.

*Oh, Love It Is a Killing Thing:* Asher E. Treat, as above, p. 38. First stanza obtained from Mrs. M. G. Jacobs, and the second from her daughter, Pearl Jacobs Borusky, Bryant, Wisconsin, 1933.

*Madam, I Have a Very Fine Farm:* Recorded by Charles Todd and Robert Sonkin from Vernon Allen, Shafter, California, 1940. AFS record 4114B2.

*Sally Goodin:* From the Works Progress Administration (WPA) manuscript volume of "Kentucky Folksongs" in the Archive of Folksong of the Library of Congress.

*Ibby Damsel:* Cecil J. Sharp, *English Folksongs from the Southern Appalachians,* II, 137. From Mrs. Rosie Hensley, Carmen, North Carolina, 1916.

*An Old Man and a Young Man:* Emelyn E. Gardner and Geraldine J. Chickering, *Ballads and Songs of Southern Michigan,* Ann Arbor, 1939, 420. Obtained from Mr. and Mrs. Mirchler, Kalkaska, Michigan, 1934.

*Cindy:* Composite text from traditional sources. Music from Alan Jabbour, Library of Congress.

*East Virginia:* From the Works Progress Administration (WPA) manuscript volume of "Kentucky Folksongs" in the Archive of Folksong of the Library of Congress.

*The Cruel War Is Raging:* Recorded by Vance Randolph from Charles Ingenthron, Walnut Shade, Missouri, 1941. Record L20.

*The Broken Token:* Recorded by Duncan Emrich from Mrs. Maud Long of Hot Springs, North Carolina, at the Library of Congress, 1947. Record L21.

*The Low Lands of Holland:* Recorded by Alan Lomax from Mrs. Carrie Grover of Gorham, Maine, at the Library of Congress, 1941. Record L21.

*Barbara Allen:* Recorded by Artus M. Moser from Bill Nicholson, accompanied by Zane Shrader on the guitar, both of New Albany, Indiana, at Renfro Valley, Kentucky, 1946. Record L14. (Stanzas 7 and 11 interpolated to round out a full text). See also record L54, edited by Charles Seeger, which gives 30 variants of "Barbara Allen" from the Archive of Folksong collections, 9 of these with complete text and the remaining 21 with partial texts.

*The Unquiet Grave:* Collected by Herbert Halpert from Allen Clevenger (aged 82), near Magnolia, New Jersey, 1937, and reported by him in JAF, 52 (1939) 53.

### 31. MURDER BALLADS

*Expert Town,* or *The Oxford Tragedy:* Recorded by Vance Randolph from Mrs. Mildred Tuttle, Farmington, Arkansas, 1942. Record L12.

*Florella,* or *The Jealous Lover:* Recorded by Vance Randolph from Callista O'Neill, Day, Missouri, 1941. AFS record 5243B1. Stanza 3 is interpolated from Belden (p. 329) with the reading of *jealant* for *jealous* to agree with Randolph's text.

*The Lily of the West:* Recorded by Vance Randolph from Charles Ingenthron, Walnut Shade, Missouri, 1941. AFS record 5245B1.

*Johnson-Jinkson:* Recorded by Charles Todd and Robert Sonkin from Troy Cambron at Arvin, California, 1940. AFS record 4138B1.

*Frankie Silvers:* Recorded by George W. Hibbitt and William Cabell Greet from Bascom Lamar Lunsford of South Turkey Creek, North Carolina, at Columbia University, 1935. AFS record 1817A and B1. For a full account of the murder and hanging, see Belden and Hudson, *North Carolina Folklore,* II, 699.

*Mary Hamilton,* or *The Four Marys:* Recorded by Alan Lomax from Mrs. Texas Gladden, Salem, Virginia, 1941. Record L7. The headnote matter comes from Professor B. J. Whiting's *Traditional British Ballads* (Crofts Classics), New York, 1955.

# Folk Beliefs and Superstitions

Vance Randolph's *Ozark Superstitions,* New York, 1947 (reprinted by Dover and retitled *Ozark Magic and Folklore,* 1964) is the most readily available and readable book on the subject. (The descriptive "Ozark" should not be considered limiting: many of the beliefs are found elsewhere.) Harry M. Hyatt's *Folklore from Adams County, Illinois* (Memoirs of the Alma Egan Hyatt Foundation), New York, 1935, 2nd ed., enlarged and revised, 1965, is a monumental collection (16,537 entries) of beliefs and superstitions from one county in heartland America. Both editions are now out of print, but available in college and university libraries. Ray B. Browne's *Popular Beliefs and Practices from Alabama* (University of California Folklore Studies, 9), Berkeley, 1958, gives good coverage for one state (4340 entries), and Wayland D. Hand's (ed.) *Popular Beliefs and Superstitions from North Carolina*, vols. 6 and 7 of *The Frank C. Brown Collection of North Carolina Folklore*, Durham, 1961–1964 (8569 entries), is a standard of and for scholarship in the field. All of these works contain extensive entries on each of the divisions considered below.

### 32. FOLK MEDICINE

The folk and family cures were contributed to me by mail by listeners to the 1954 NBC radio programs on folklore. (There is as yet no single work that covers the field of folk medicine in depth. Hand has indicated that the first publication of material from his vast UCLA collection will be two volumes on folk medicine.)

### 33. WEATHER LORE

H. H. C. Dunwoody, *Weather Proverbs*, Signal Service Notes, No. 9, War Department, Washington, D.C., Government Printing Office, 1883; Edward B. Garriott, *Weather Folk-Lore and Local Weather Signs*, U.S. Department of Agriculture Bulletin No. 33, Weather Bureau No. 294, Washington, D.C., Government Printing Office, 1903; Richard Inwards, *Weather Lore*, *A Collection of Proverbs*, *Sayings & Rules Concerning the Weather*, London, 1898, (Dover reprint, New York, 1968); Eric Sloane, *Folklore of American Weather*, New York, 1963. Inwards's collection is a general one with some American entries. For technical weather advice, I am indebted to James Caskey and Jerome Namias of the Weather Bureau.

### 34–36. THE FOLKLORE OF BIRTH, MARRIAGE, AND DEATH

I am particularly indebted here to Harry M. Hyatt and Vance Randolph, who generously gave me permission to draw on their works to illustrate these fields of folklore. The quotations in the "Folklore of Death" section are, for example, entirely from Hyatt's second, revised edition of *The Folklore of Adams County, Illinois*. With Frank C. Brown, Hyatt and Randolph are the most dedicated and greatest field collectors of American folklore that this country has known. The thoroughness of their collecting and the extent of their collections will remain landmarks forever in studies of American folklore. The following books may be cited as well: Fanny D. Bergen, *Current Superstitions* (Memoirs of the American Folklore Society, 4), Boston, 1896, and *Animal and Plant Lore* (MAFS, 7) Boston, 1899; Annie Weston Whitney and Caroline Canfield Bullock, *Folklore from Maryland* (MAFS, 18), New York, 1925; Daniel Lindsey Thomas and Lucy Blayney Thomas, *Kentucky Superstitions*, Princeton, 1920. British works of general interest, chiefly by antiquarians of the last century, include: John Brand, *Observations on Popular Antiquities*, London, 1877; Robert Chambers, *Book of Days*, 2 vols, London, 1879; William Hone, *The Every-Day Book and Table Book*, 3 vols., London, 1827, and *The Year Book*, London, 1832; John Cordy Jeaffreson, *Brides and Bridals* 2 vols., London, 1872.

# Acknowledgments

Acknowledgment is made to the following publishers, editors of journals, and individuals for permission to reprint selected materials as noted:

The editors and secretary-treasurers of *Midwest Folklore, Indiana Folklore, Journal of the Folklore Institute, Kentucky Folklore Record, Keystone Folklore Quarterly, New York Folklore Quarterly, Names* (American Name Society), *New Mexico Folklore Record, North Carolina Folklore, Tennessee Folklore Society Bulletin, Publications of the Texas Folklore Society, Southern Folklore Quarterly,* and *Western Folklore* for all items from their publications noted both in the text and in the bibliographical notes.

*The Washington Post* for "The Rape Trial" from Bill Gold's column, "The District Line," March 30, 1970. Copyright © 1970 by *The Washington Post.*

Harry M. Hyatt for selections from *Folklore from Adams County, Illinois,* (2nd and revised edition, privately printed). Copyright © 1965 by Harry M. Hyatt.

Fred and Jo Mazzulla for the nicknames of Western ladies-of-the-line and madams in their *Brass Checks and Red Lights.* Copyright © 1966 by Fred and Jo Mazzulla.

The Macmillan Company for passages from Ramon F. Adams, *The Old-Time Cowhand.* Copyright © 1961 by Ramon F. Adams.

# ACKNOWLEDGMENTS

Duke University Press for the account of Frankie Silvers' murder of her husband from *The Frank C. Brown Collection of North Carolina Folklore*, vol. II, 1952. Copyright 1952 by Duke University Press.

Houghton Mifflin Company for lines from Archibald MacLeish's "Oil Painting of the Artist as the Artist," *The Collected Poems of Archibald MacLeish*, Sentry Edition. Copyright © 1962 by Archibald MacLeish; and for selected street cries from Lyle Saxon, *Gumbo Ya-Ya*, Copyright 1945 by The Louisiana Library Commission.

*The Saturday Review of Literature* for excerpts from Duncan Emrich, "The Poet and the General," March 20, 1948. Copyright 1948 by The Saturday Review Associates, Inc.

Southern Illinois University Press for selections from Frances M. Barbour, *Proverbs and Proverbial Phrases of Illinois*, Copyright © 1965 by Southern Illinois University Press.

Four Winds Press for selections from Duncan Emrich, *The Nonsense Book*. Copyright © 1970 by Duncan Emrich.

Vanguard Press for passages from Duncan Emrich, *It's an Old Wild West Custom*. Copyright 1949 by Duncan Emrich.

Columbia University Press for selections from Vance Randolph, *Ozark Superstitions*. Copyright 1947 by Columbia University Press.

Funk & Wagnalls Company for Marius Barbeau's definition of folklore in *The Standard Dictionary of Folklore, Mythology, Legend* (ed. Maria Leach). Copyright 1949 by Funk & Wagnalls Company.

Yale University Press for "Captain Ward and the *Rainbow*" from Phillips Barry, Fannie Hardy Eckstorm, and Mary Winslow Smyth, *British Ballads from Maine*. Copyright 1929 by Yale University Press.

University of Oklahoma Press for selected matter from Vance Randolph and George P. Wilson, *Down in the Holler: A Gallery of Ozark Folk Speech*, Norman. Copyright 1953 by University of Oklahoma Press.

*Holiday* for excerpts from Duncan Emrich, "America's Folkways," July 1955. Copyright © 1955 by Curtis Publishing Company.

American Heritage Press for selections from Duncan Emrich, *The Folklore of Weddings and Marriage*. Copyright © 1970 by Duncan Emrich. And for selections from articles by Duncan Emrich appearing in *American Heritage*: "A Certain Nicholas of Patara" (December 1960); "Riddle Me, Riddle Me, What Is That?" (December 1955); "Odd Remedies from Folk Medicine" (April 1955). Copyright © 1955, 1960 by Duncan Emrich.

*Journal of Lifetime Living* for selections from Duncan Emrich, "Weatherlore." Copyright © 1957 Lifetime Living, Inc.

J. B. Lippincott and Company for selections from Harold W. Thompson, *Body, Boots, and Britches*, Philadelphia. Copyright 1939 by Harold W. Thompson; © renewed 1966 by Marion Thompson. And for selections from Horace P. Beck, *The Folklore of Maine*. Copyright 1957 by Horace P. Beck.

The *Atlantic* for paragraphs from Willard Thorp, "Banjo in the Cow Camps," the *Atlantic*, August 1940. Copyright 1940, © 1968 by The Atlantic Monthly Company, Boston, Mass. Reprinted with permission.

Harcourt Brace Jovanovich, Inc., for permission to reproduce the text and music for the sea-shanty "Shenandoah" from *Capstan Bars* by David W. Bone.

Appleton-Century-Crofts for headnote material for the ballad "Mary Hamilton," from B. J. Whiting, *Traditional British Ballads* (Crofts Classics). Copyright © 1955 by Appleton-Century-Crofts, Inc. Reprinted by permission of Appleton-Century-Crofts, a Division of Meredith Publishing Company.

Barnes & Noble Publishers, New York, New York, for selected proverbs relating to women adapted from Selwyn G. Champion's *Racial Proverbs*, 2nd edition, 1950.

# Indexes

# General Index

# Index of Song Titles
# and First Lines